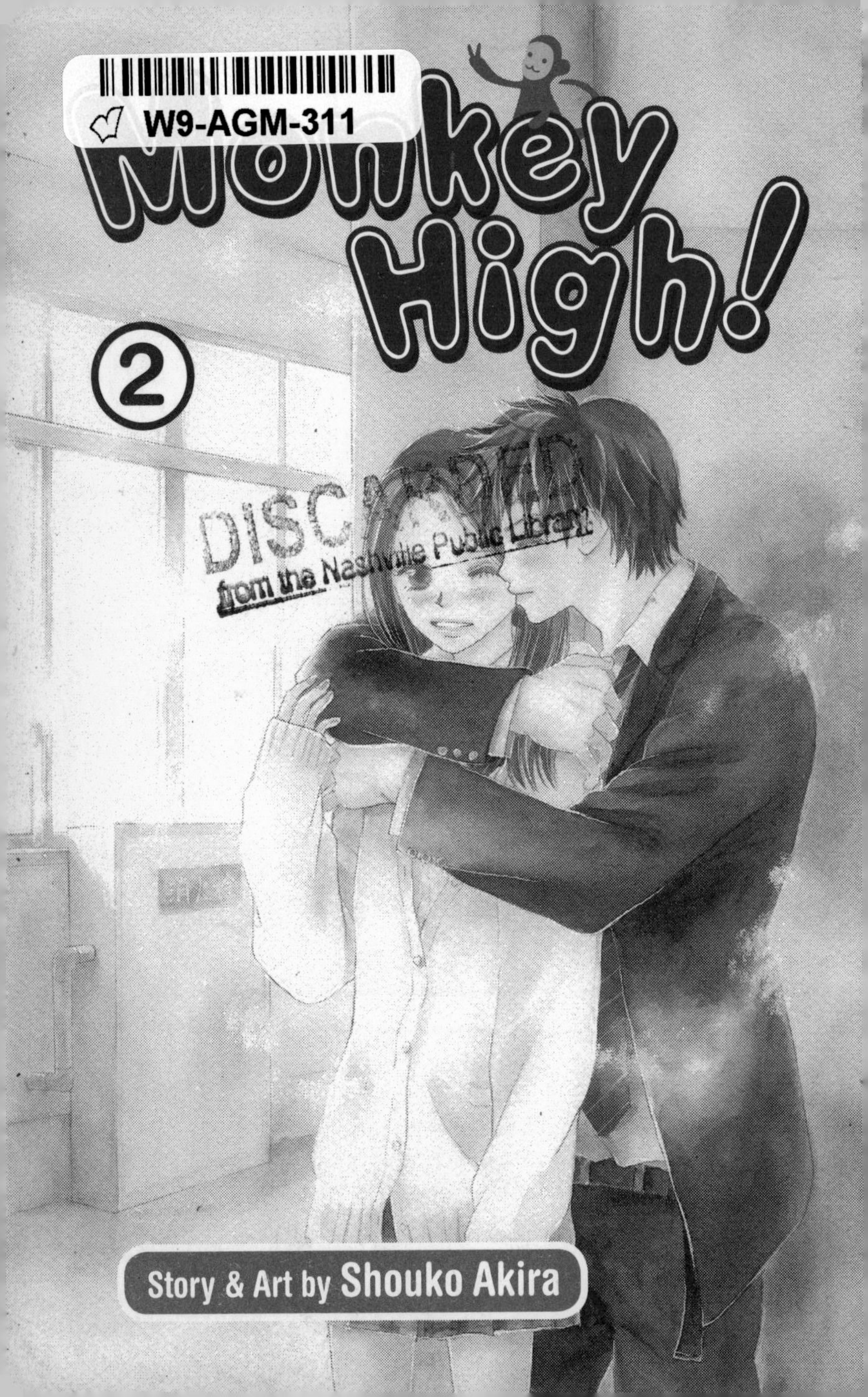
Monkey High!
2
Story & Art by Shouko Akira

Monkey High!

2

CONTENTS

Story Thus Far

Masaru Yamashita
(Nickname: Macharu)

Haruna was forced to transfer to a new school because of her father's involvement in a corruption scandal. She compares her crazy new classmates to a troop of monkeys but finds herself drawn to one of them—Macharu. They establish that they are both attracted to each other and decide to start dating, but...?!

Haruna Aizawa

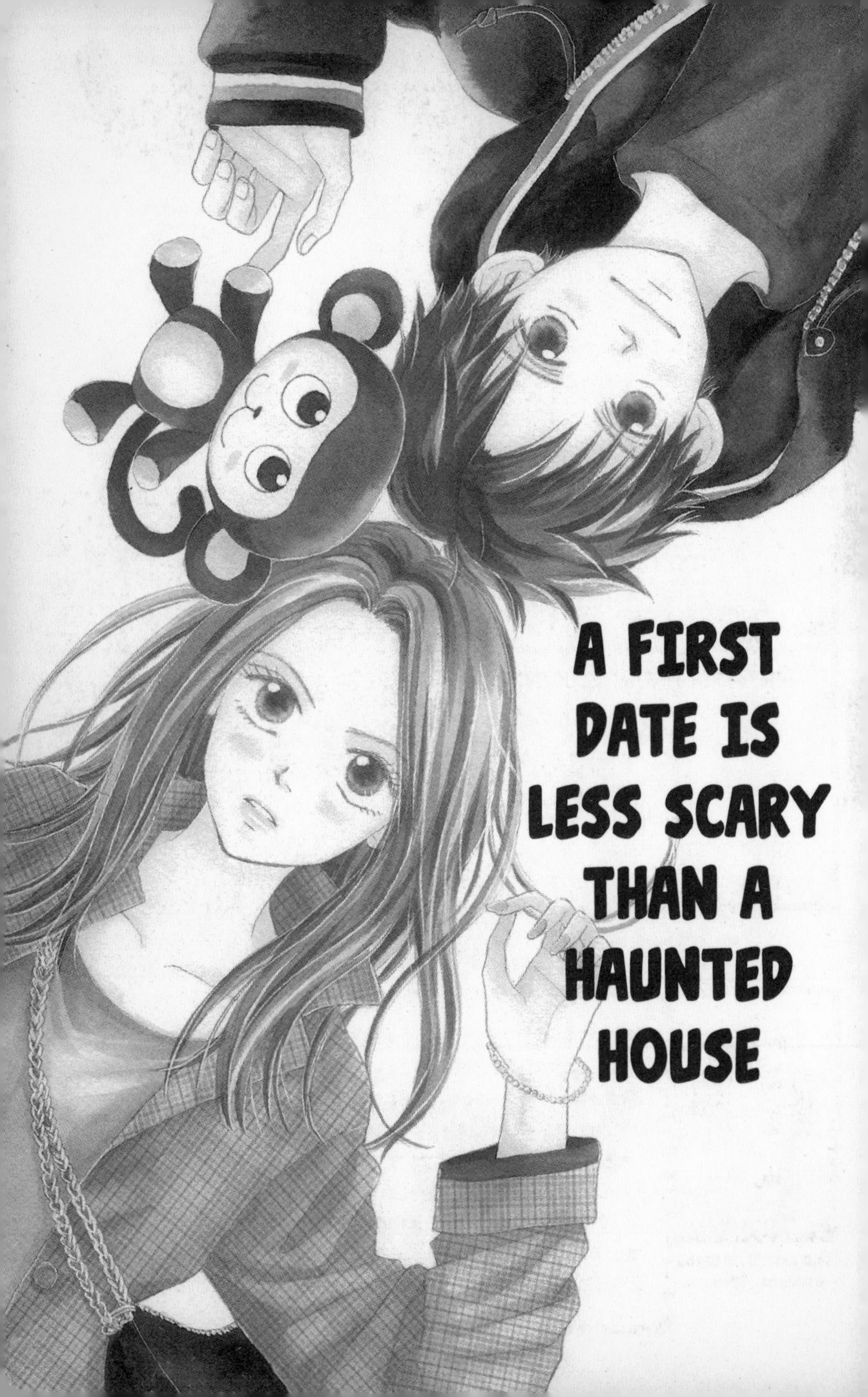

A FIRST DATE IS LESS SCARY THAN A HAUNTED HOUSE

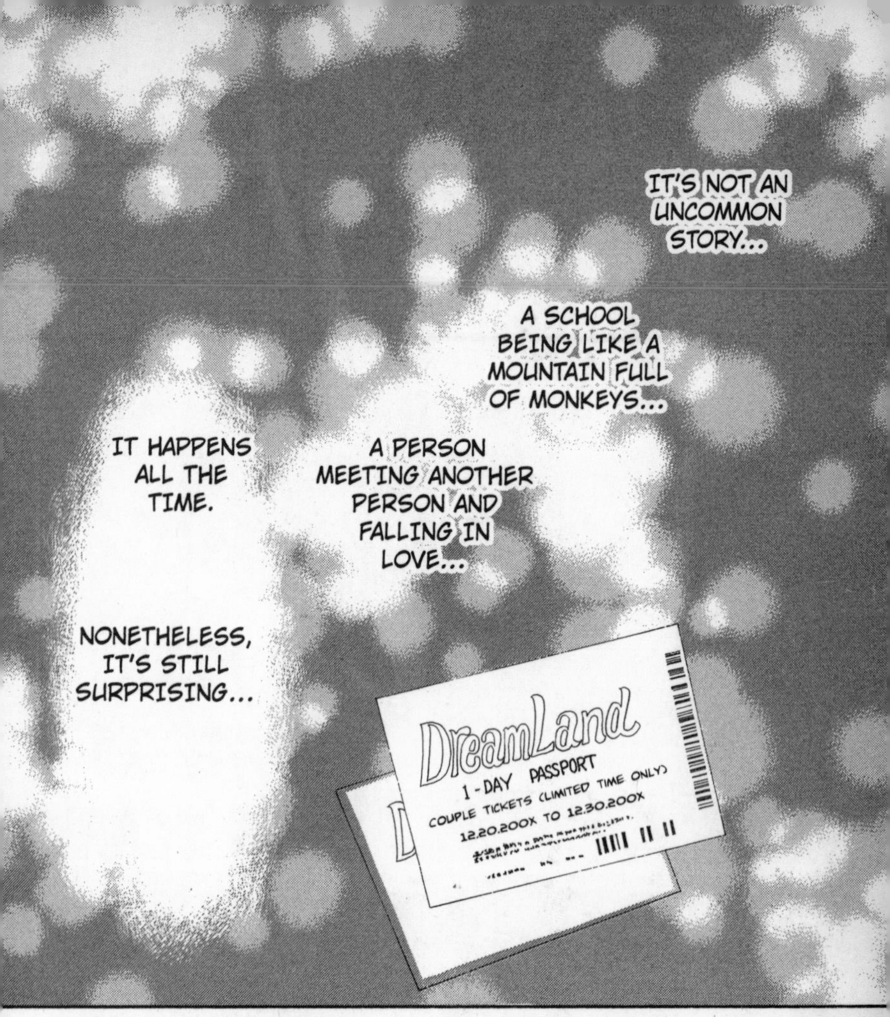
IT'S NOT AN UNCOMMON STORY...
A SCHOOL BEING LIKE A MOUNTAIN FULL OF MONKEYS...
A PERSON MEETING ANOTHER PERSON AND FALLING IN LOVE...
IT HAPPENS ALL THE TIME.
NONETHELESS, IT'S STILL SURPRISING...
DreamLand
1-DAY PASSPORT
COUPLE TICKETS (LIMITED TIME ONLY)
12.20.200X TO 12.30.200X

Monkey High!

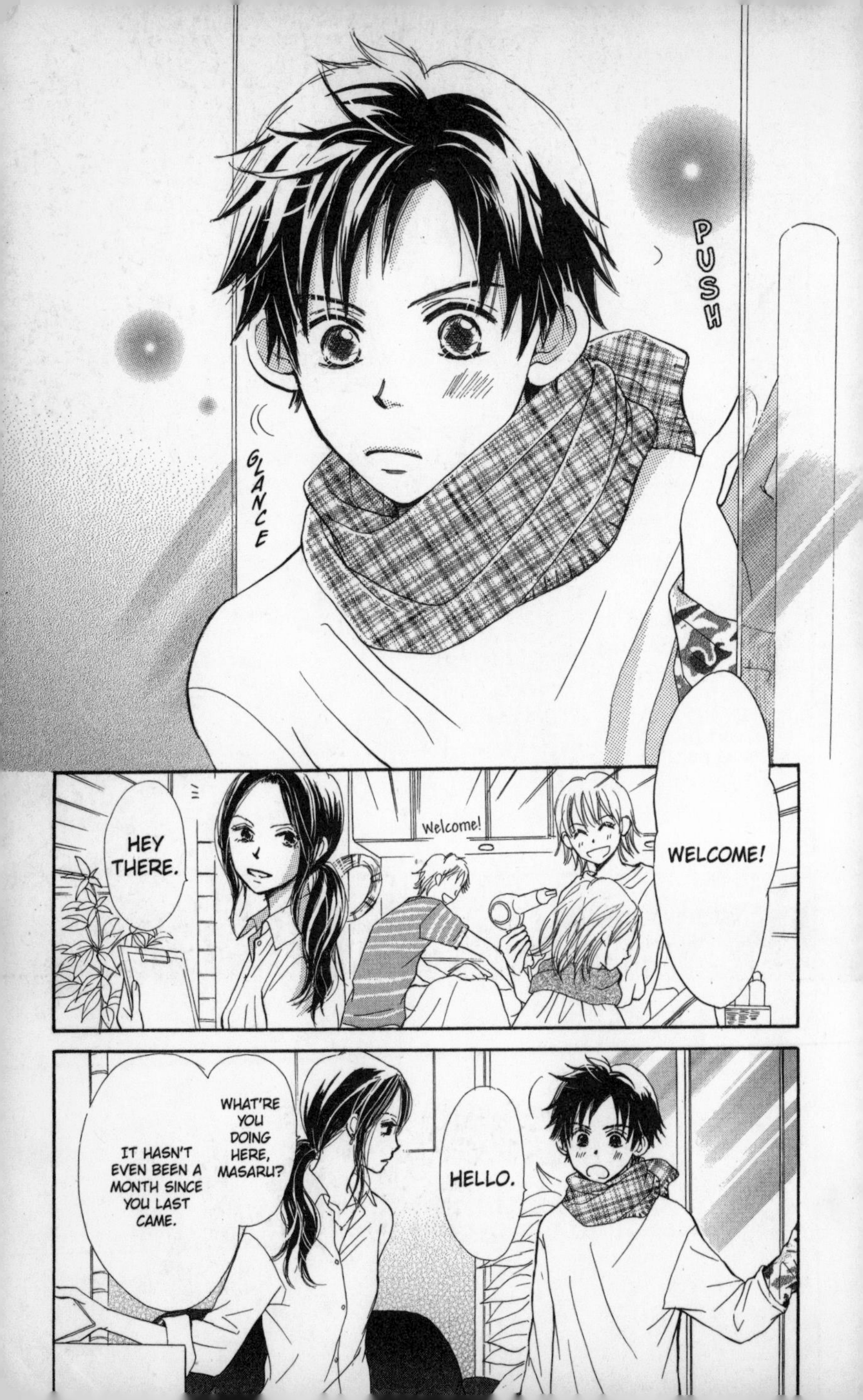
PUSH
GLANCE
WELCOME!
Welcome!
HEY THERE.
HELLO.
WHAT'RE YOU DOING HERE, MASARU?
IT HASN'T EVEN BEEN A MONTH SINCE YOU LAST CAME.

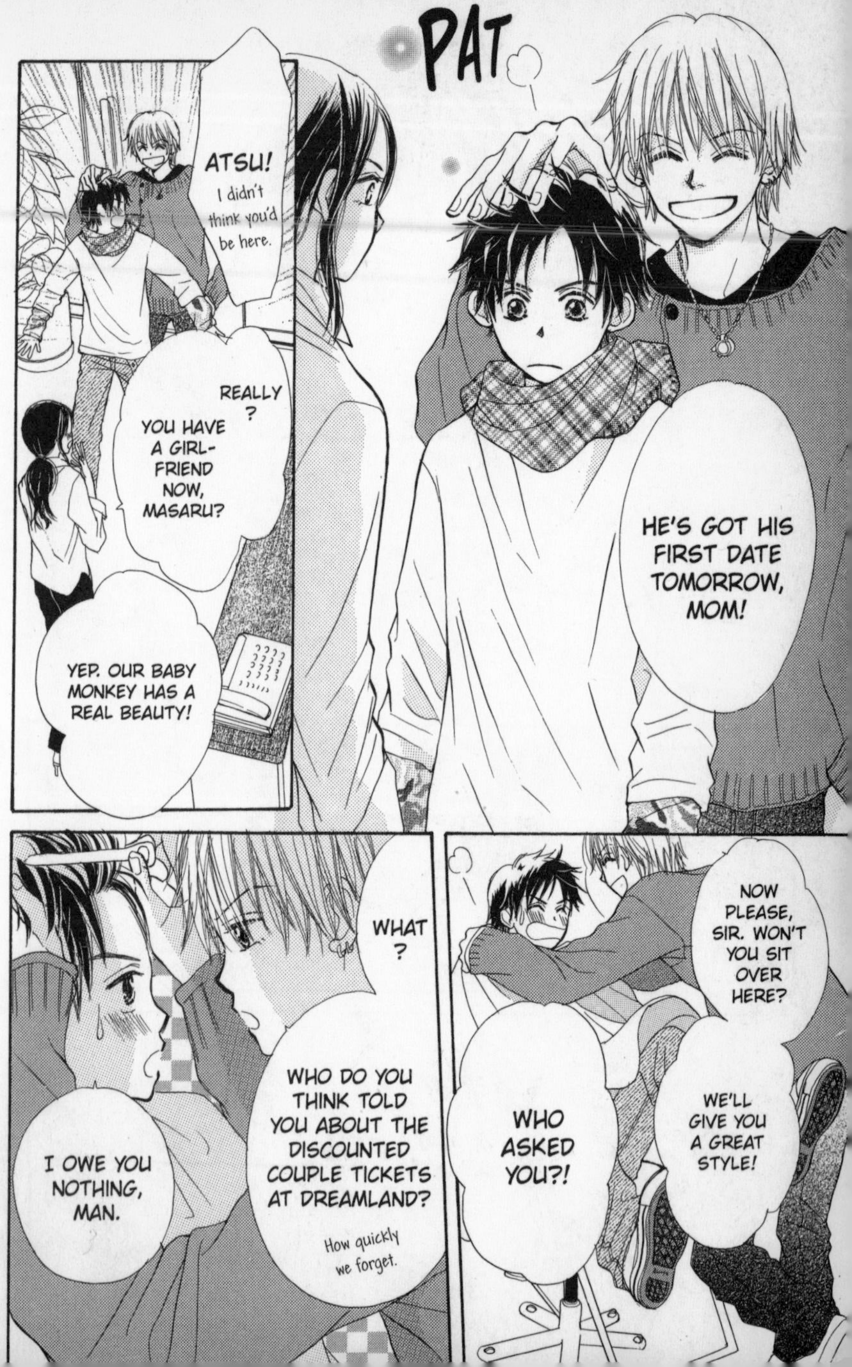
PAT
HE'S GOT HIS FIRST DATE TOMORROW, MOM!
ATSU! I didn't think you'd be here.
REALLY?
YOU HAVE A GIRLFRIEND NOW, MASARU?
YEP. OUR BABY MONKEY HAS A REAL BEAUTY!
NOW PLEASE, SIR. WON'T YOU SIT OVER HERE?
WE'LL GIVE YOU A GREAT STYLE!
WHO ASKED YOU?!
WHAT?
WHO DO YOU THINK TOLD YOU ABOUT THE DISCOUNTED COUPLE TICKETS AT DREAMLAND?
How quickly we forget.
I OWE YOU NOTHING, MAN.

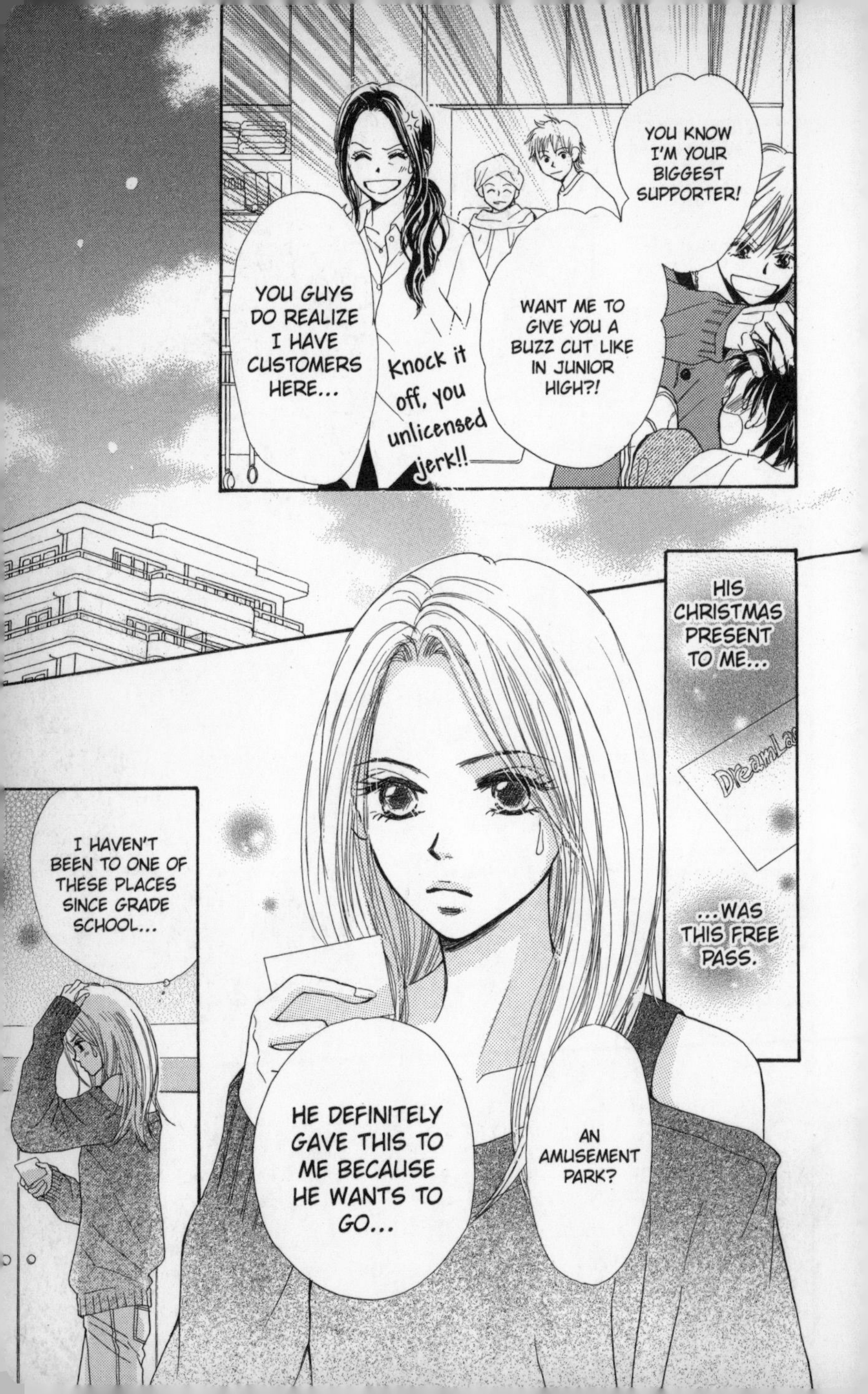
YOU KNOW I'M YOUR BIGGEST SUPPORTER!
WANT ME TO GIVE YOU A BUZZ CUT LIKE IN JUNIOR HIGH?!
Knock it off, you unlicensed jerk!!
YOU GUYS DO REALIZE I HAVE CUSTOMERS HERE...
HIS CHRISTMAS PRESENT TO ME...
...WAS THIS FREE PASS.
AN AMUSEMENT PARK?
HE DEFINITELY GAVE THIS TO ME BECAUSE HE WANTS TO GO...
I HAVEN'T BEEN TO ONE OF THESE PLACES SINCE GRADE SCHOOL...

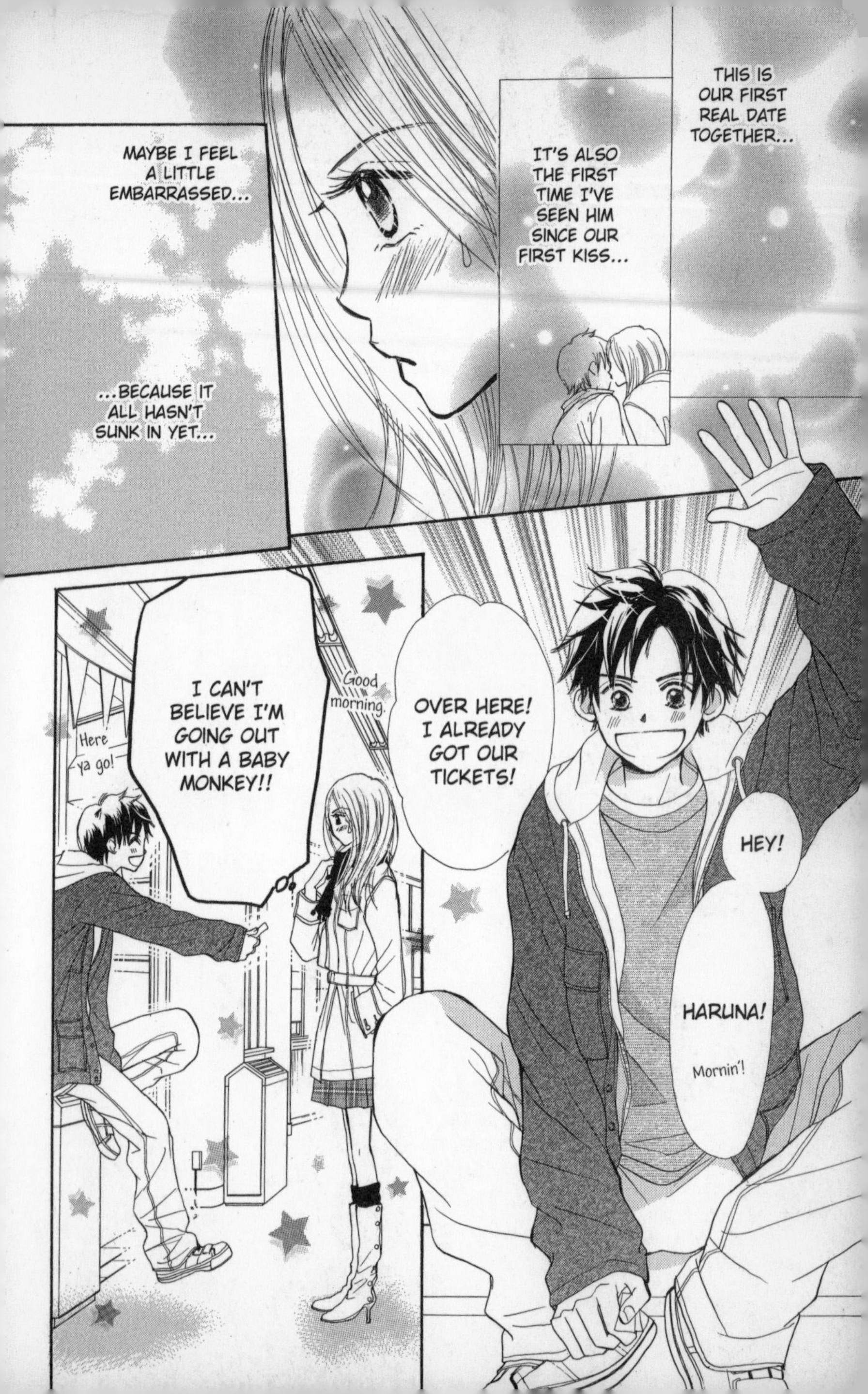
THIS IS OUR FIRST REAL DATE TOGETHER...
IT'S ALSO THE FIRST TIME I'VE SEEN HIM SINCE OUR FIRST KISS...
MAYBE I FEEL A LITTLE EMBARRASSED...
...BECAUSE IT ALL HASN'T SUNK IN YET...
HEY!
HARUNA!
Mornin'!
OVER HERE! I ALREADY GOT OUR TICKETS!
Good morning.
I CAN'T BELIEVE I'M GOING OUT WITH A BABY MONKEY!!
Here ya go!

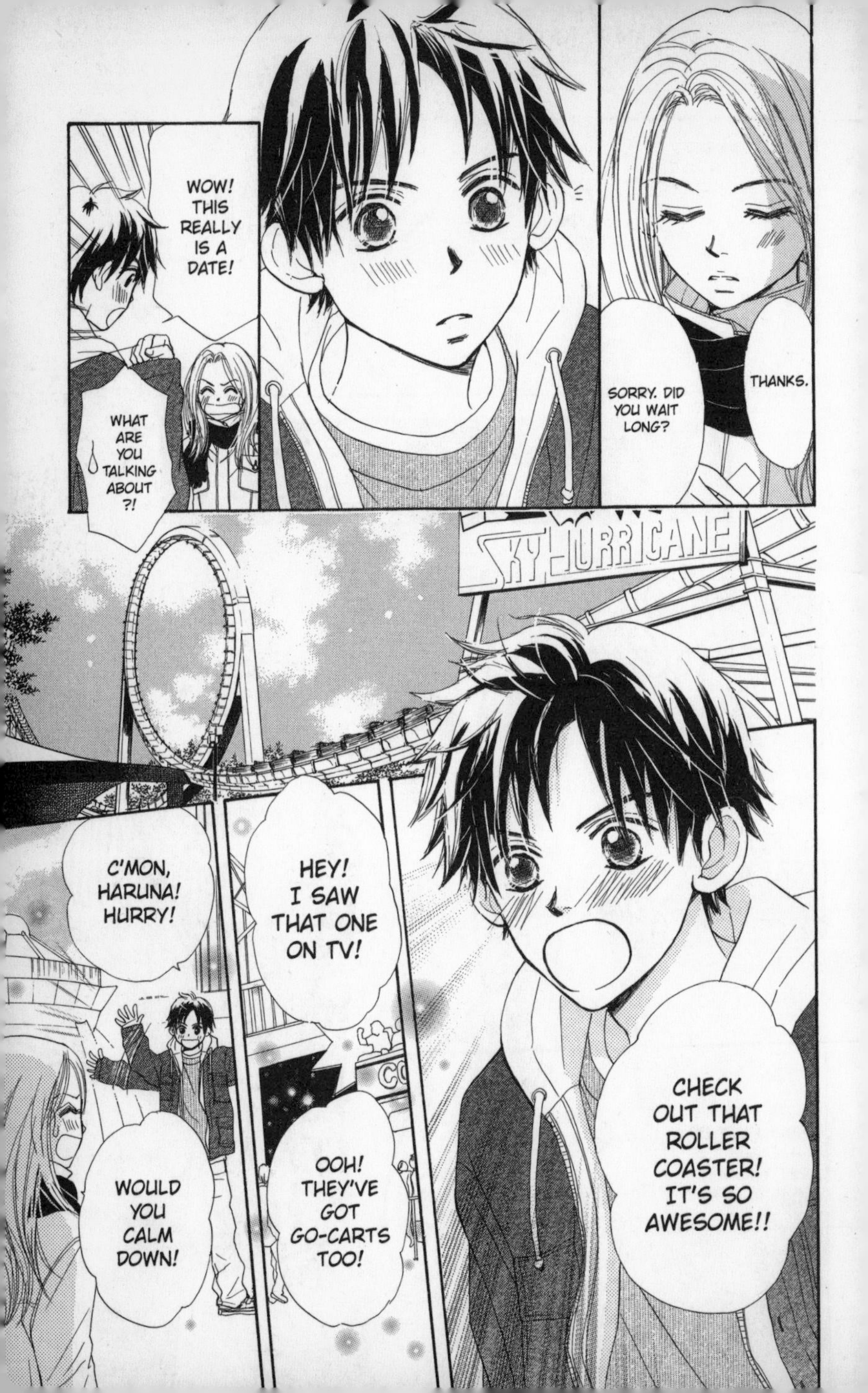
THANKS.
SORRY. DID YOU WAIT LONG?
WOW! THIS REALLY IS A DATE!
WHAT ARE YOU TALKING ABOUT?!
SKY HURRICANE
CHECK OUT THAT ROLLER COASTER! IT'S SO AWESOME!!
HEY! I SAW THAT ONE ON TV!
OOH! THEY'VE GOT GO-CARTS TOO!
C'MON, HARUNA! HURRY!
WOULD YOU CALM DOWN!

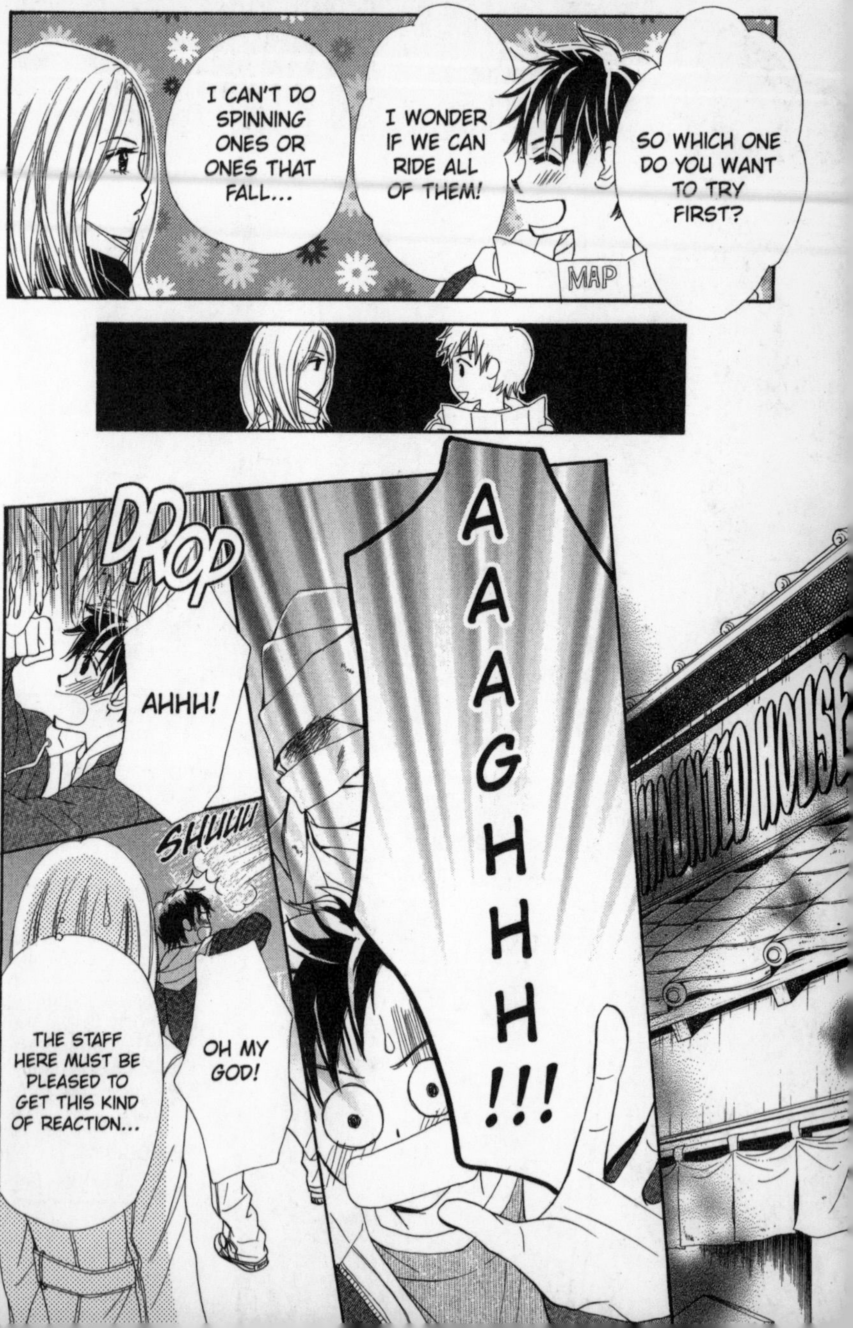
SO WHICH ONE DO YOU WANT TO TRY FIRST?
MAP
I WONDER IF WE CAN RIDE ALL OF THEM!
I CAN'T DO SPINNING ONES OR ONES THAT FALL...
HAUNTED HOUSE
AAAGHHH!!!
DROP
AHHH!
SHUUU
OH MY GOD!
THE STAFF HERE MUST BE PLEASED TO GET THIS KIND OF REACTION...

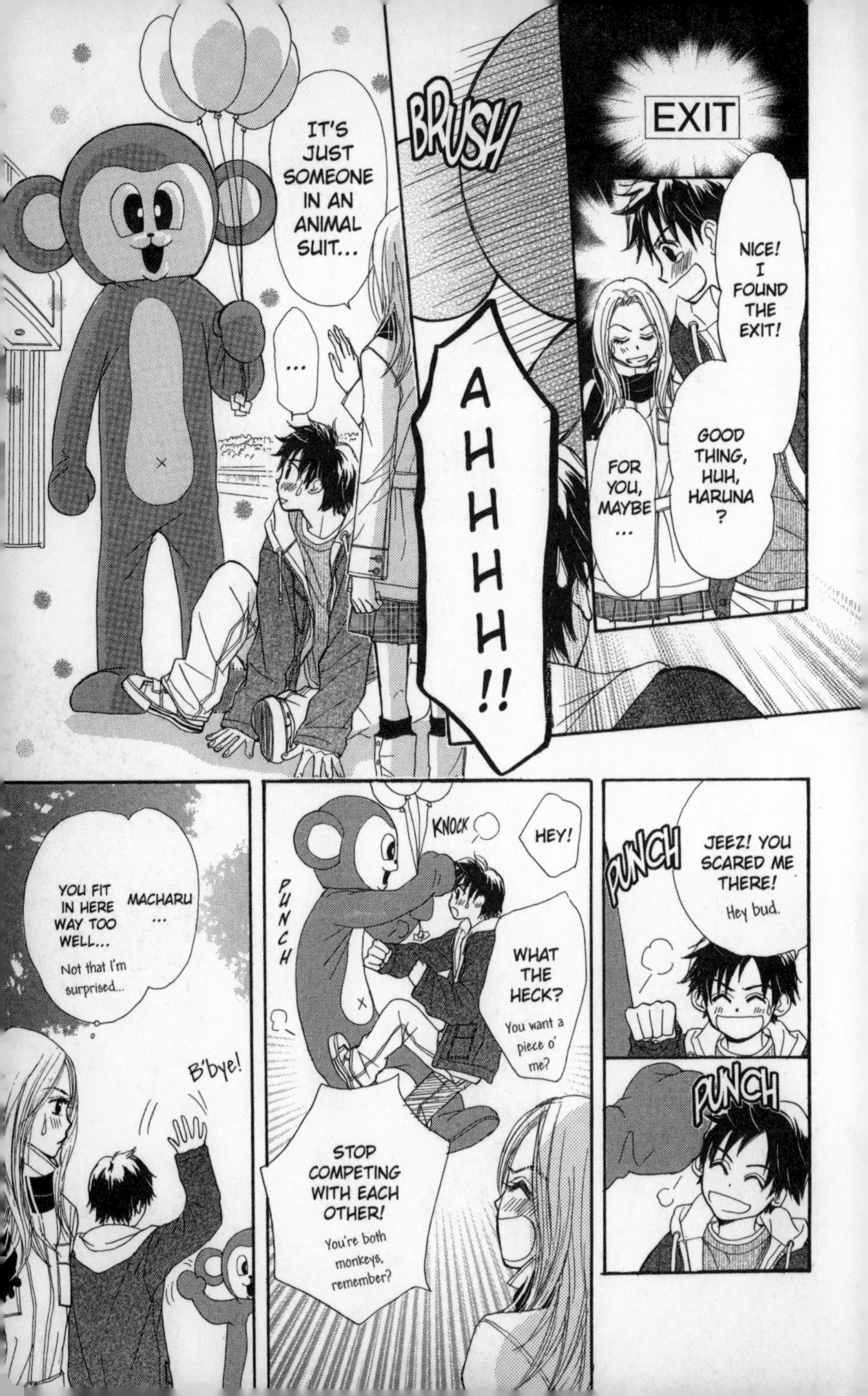
EXIT
NICE! I FOUND THE EXIT!
GOOD THING, HUH, HARUNA?
FOR YOU, MAYBE...
BRUSH
AHHHH!!
IT'S JUST SOMEONE IN AN ANIMAL SUIT...
...
PUNCH
JEEZ! YOU SCARED ME THERE!
Hey bud.
PUNCH
HEY!
KNOCK
PUNCH
WHAT THE HECK?
You want a piece o' me?
STOP COMPETING WITH EACH OTHER!
You're both monkeys, remember?
MACHARU...
YOU FIT IN HERE WAY TOO WELL...
Not that I'm surprised...
B'bye!

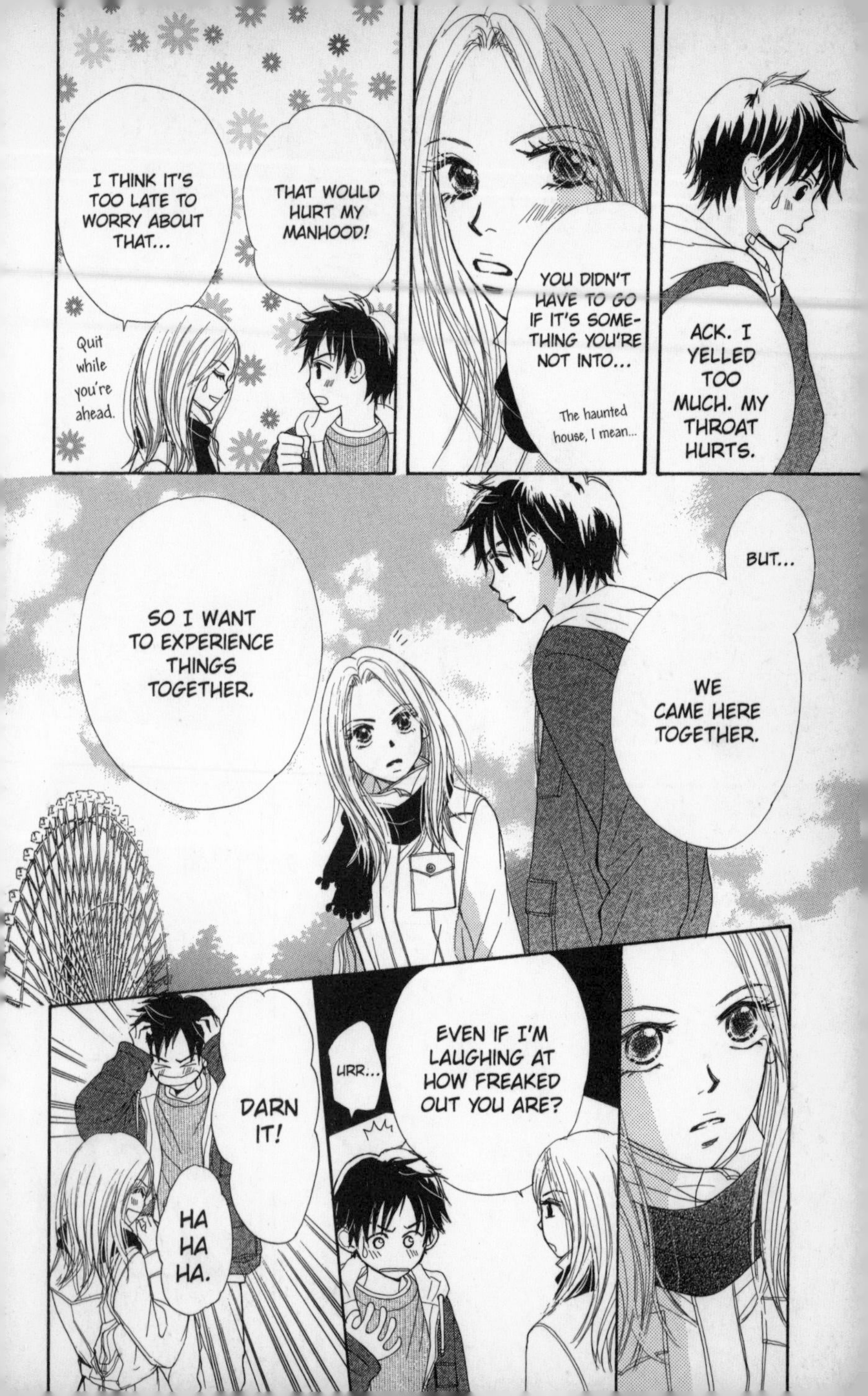
ACK. I YELLED TOO MUCH. MY THROAT HURTS.
YOU DIDN'T HAVE TO GO IF IT'S SOME-THING YOU'RE NOT INTO...
The haunted house, I mean...
THAT WOULD HURT MY MANHOOD!
I THINK IT'S TOO LATE TO WORRY ABOUT THAT...
Quit while you're ahead.
BUT...
WE CAME HERE TOGETHER.
SO I WANT TO EXPERIENCE THINGS TOGETHER.
EVEN IF I'M LAUGHING AT HOW FREAKED OUT YOU ARE?
URR...
DARN IT!
HA HA HA.

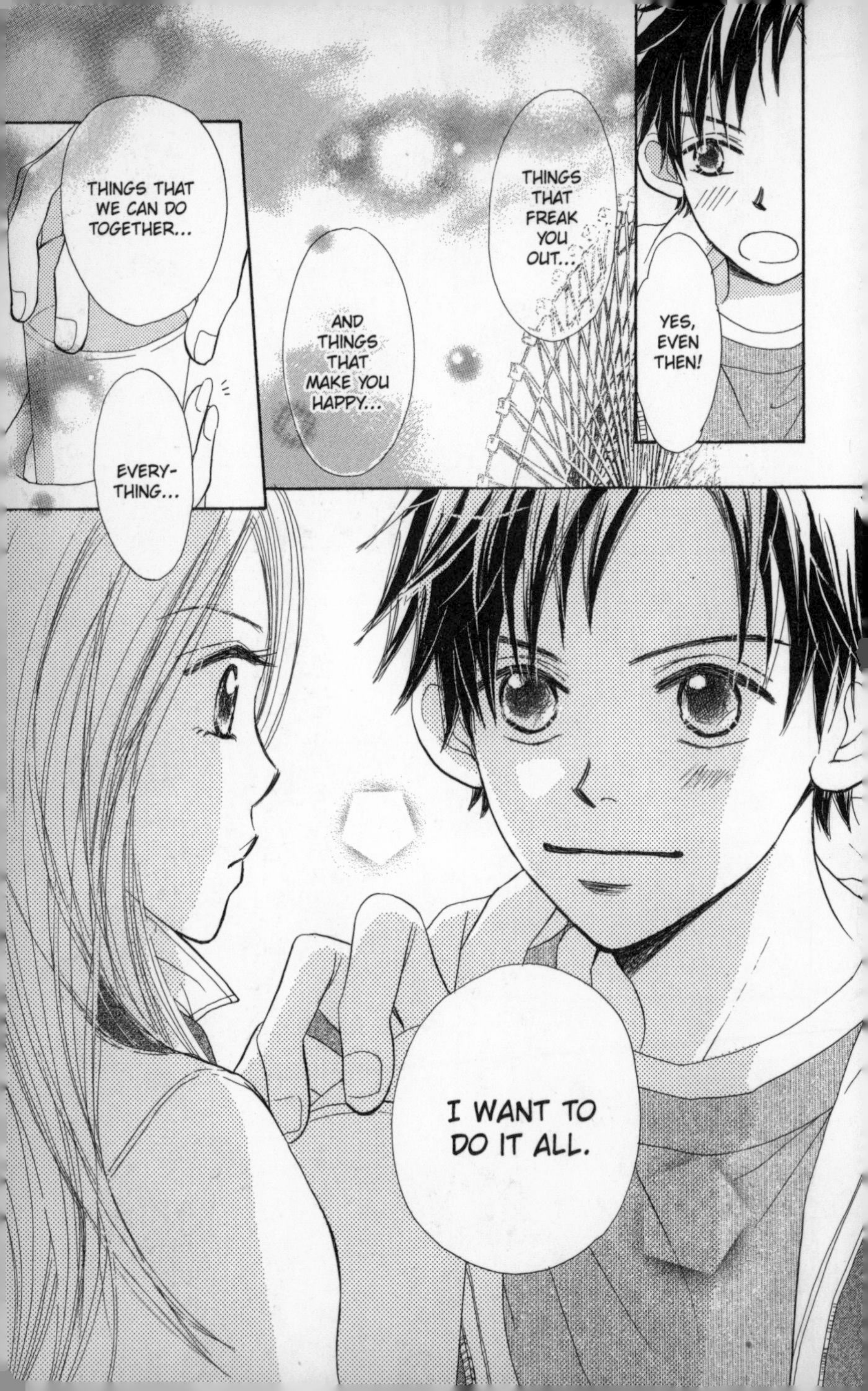
THINGS THAT FREAK YOU OUT...
YES, EVEN THEN!
AND THINGS THAT MAKE YOU HAPPY...
THINGS THAT WE CAN DO TOGETHER...
EVERY-THING...
I WANT TO DO IT ALL.

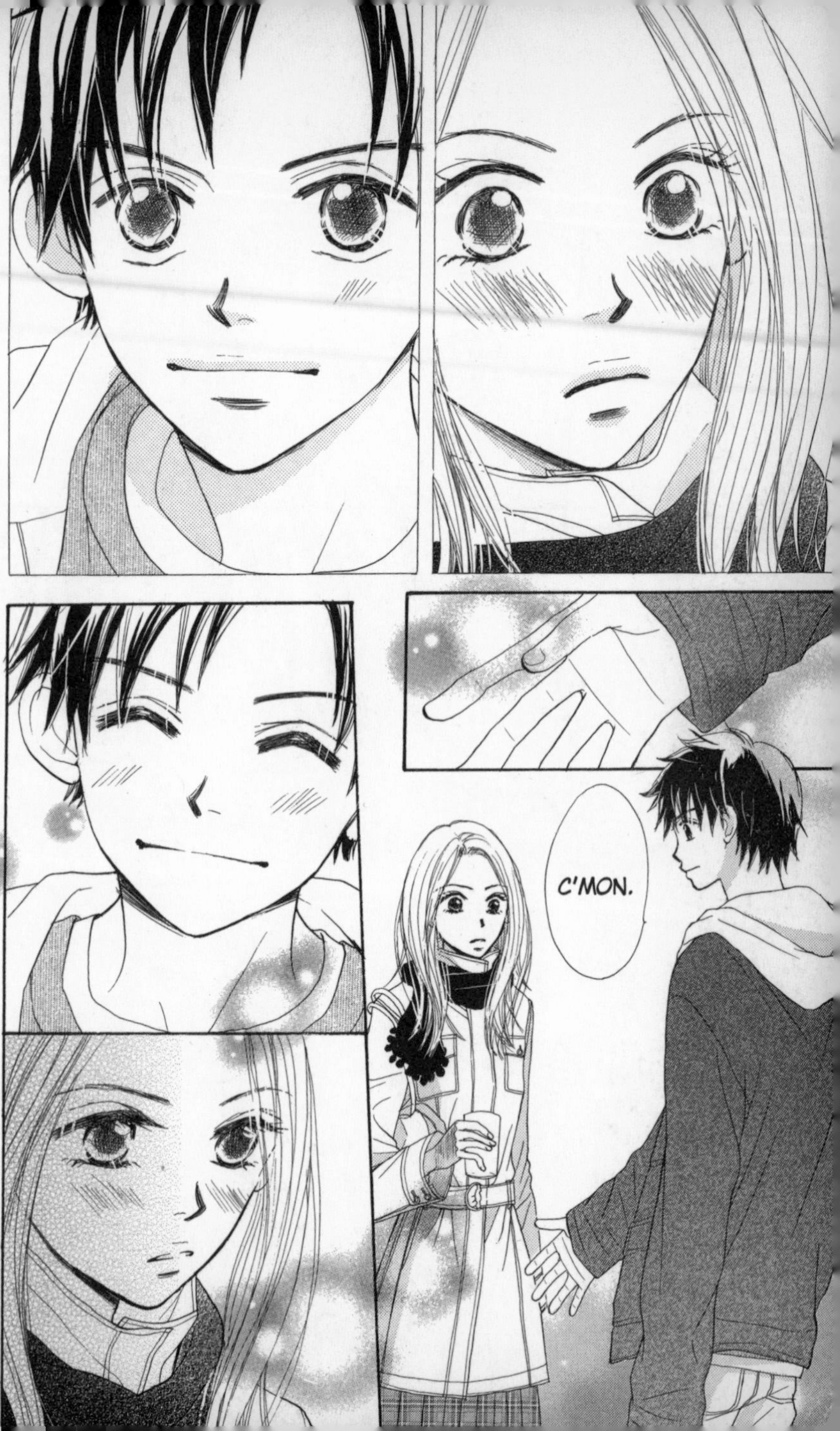
C'MON.

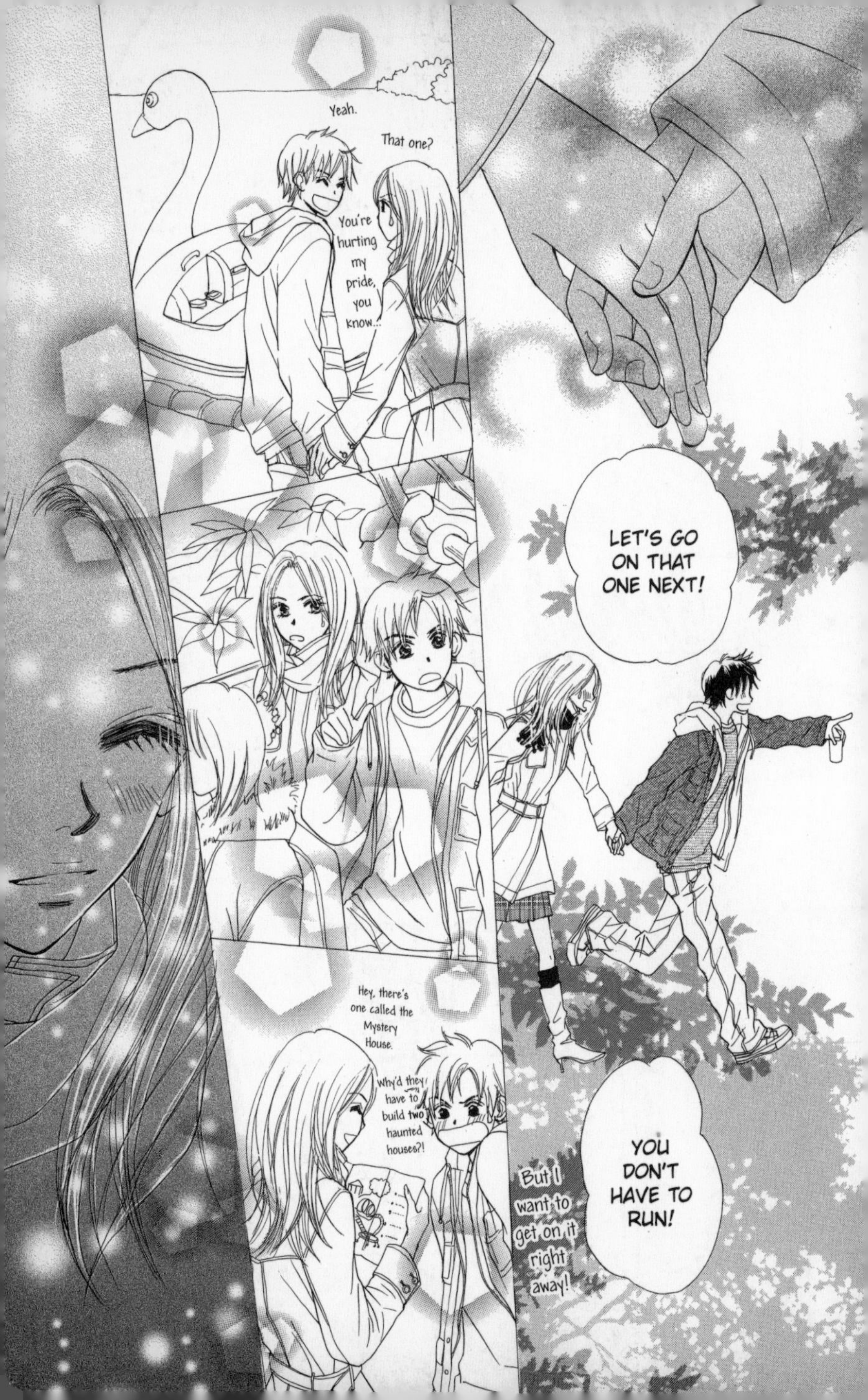
LET'S GO ON THAT ONE NEXT!
YOU DON'T HAVE TO RUN!
But I want to get on it right away!
That one?
Yeah.
You're hurting my pride, you know...
Hey, there's one called the Mystery House.
Why'd they have to build two haunted houses?!

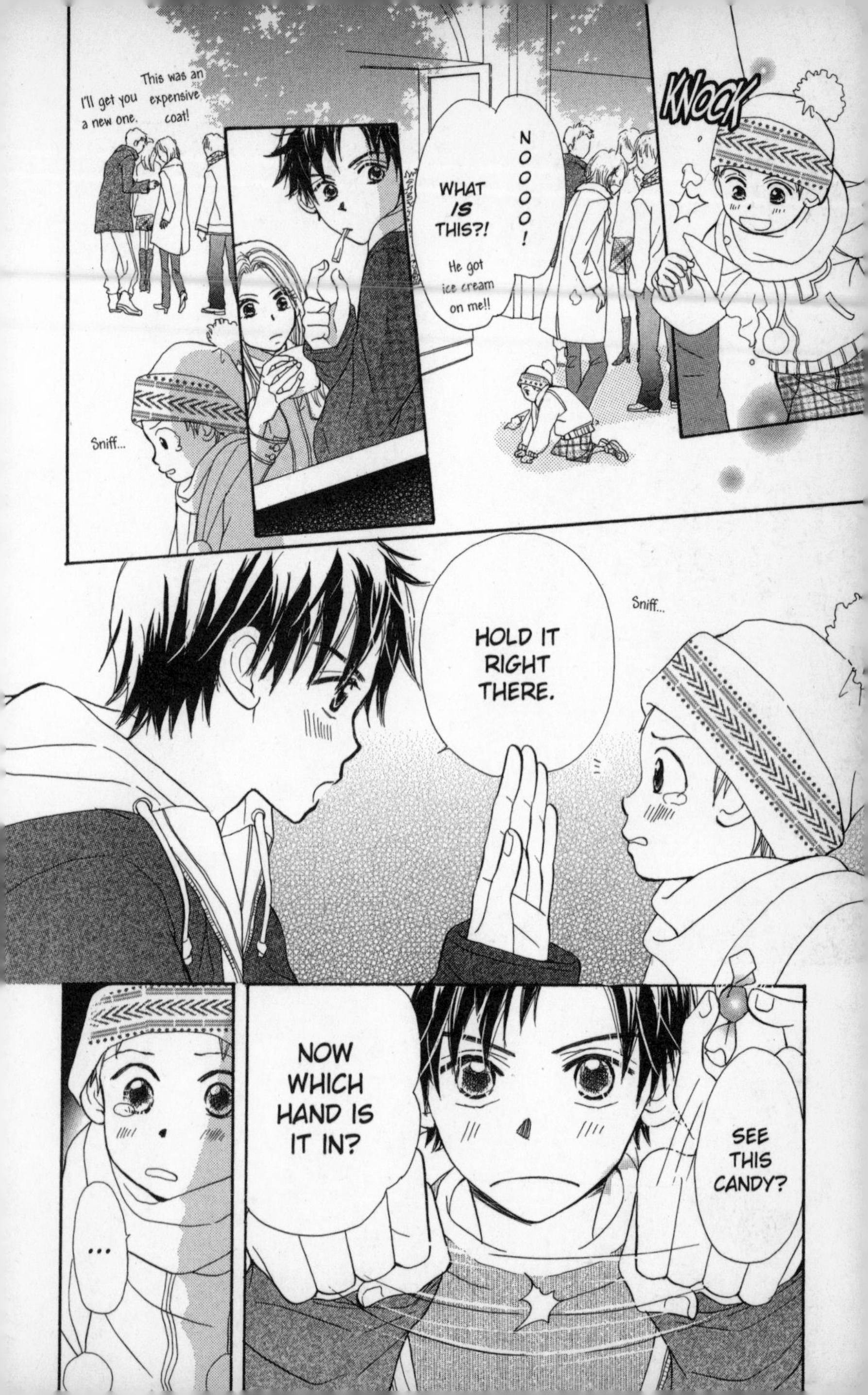
KNOCK
NOOOOO!
WHAT IS THIS?!
He got ice cream on me!!
This was an expensive coat!
I'll get you a new one.
Sniff...
Sniff...
HOLD IT RIGHT THERE.
SEE THIS CANDY?
NOW WHICH HAND IS IT IN?
...

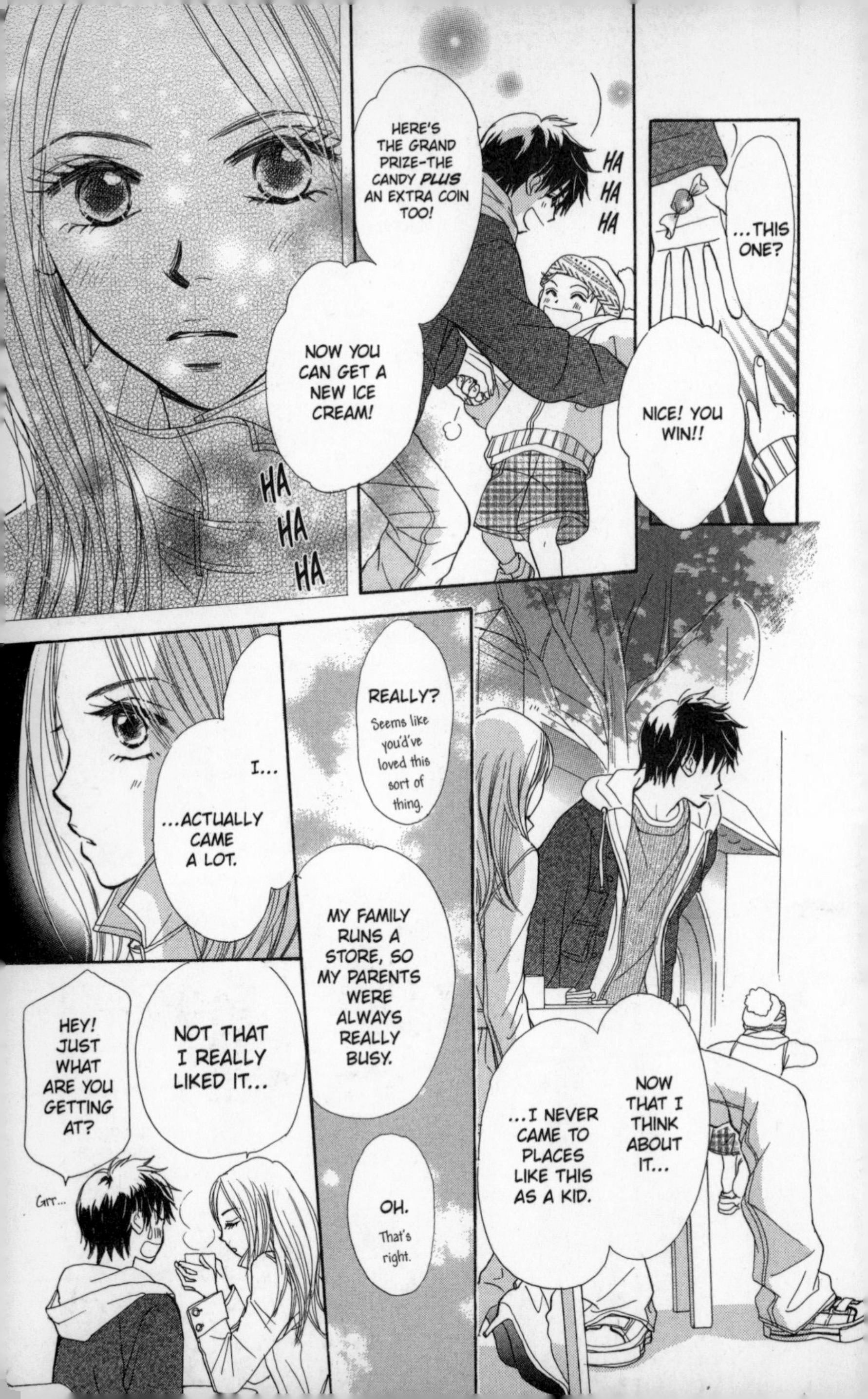
...THIS ONE?
NICE! YOU WIN!!
HERE'S THE GRAND PRIZE–THE CANDY PLUS AN EXTRA COIN TOO!
HA HA HA
NOW YOU CAN GET A NEW ICE CREAM!
HA HA HA
NOW THAT I THINK ABOUT IT...
...I NEVER CAME TO PLACES LIKE THIS AS A KID.
REALLY? Seems like you'd've loved this sort of thing.
I...
...ACTUALLY CAME A LOT.
MY FAMILY RUNS A STORE, SO MY PARENTS WERE ALWAYS REALLY BUSY.
OH. That's right.
NOT THAT I REALLY LIKED IT...
HEY! JUST WHAT ARE YOU GETTING AT?
Grr...

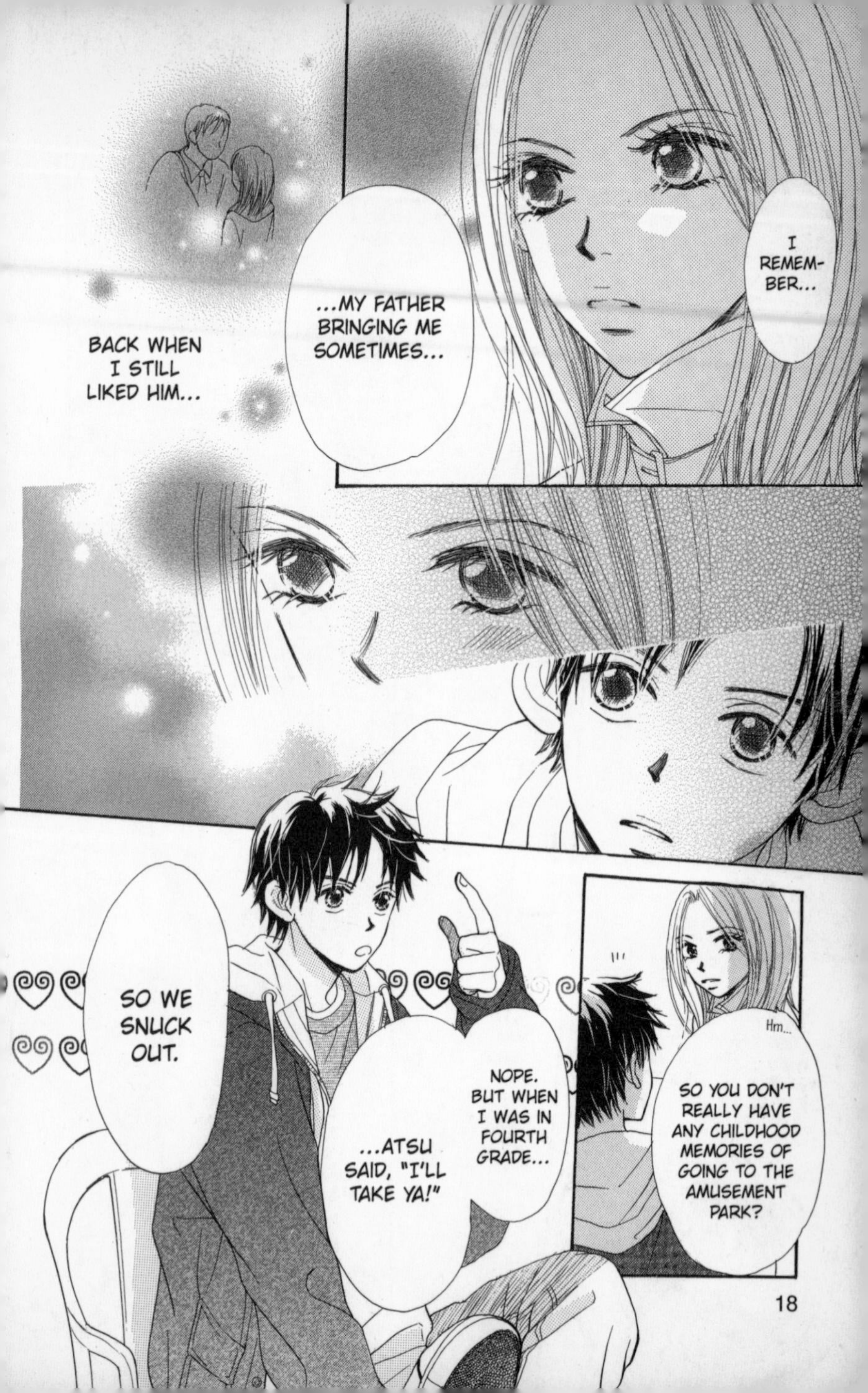
I REMEMBER...
...MY FATHER BRINGING ME SOMETIMES...
BACK WHEN I STILL LIKED HIM...
Hm...
SO YOU DON'T REALLY HAVE ANY CHILDHOOD MEMORIES OF GOING TO THE AMUSEMENT PARK?
NOPE. BUT WHEN I WAS IN FOURTH GRADE...
...ATSU SAID, "I'LL TAKE YA!"
SO WE SNUCK OUT.

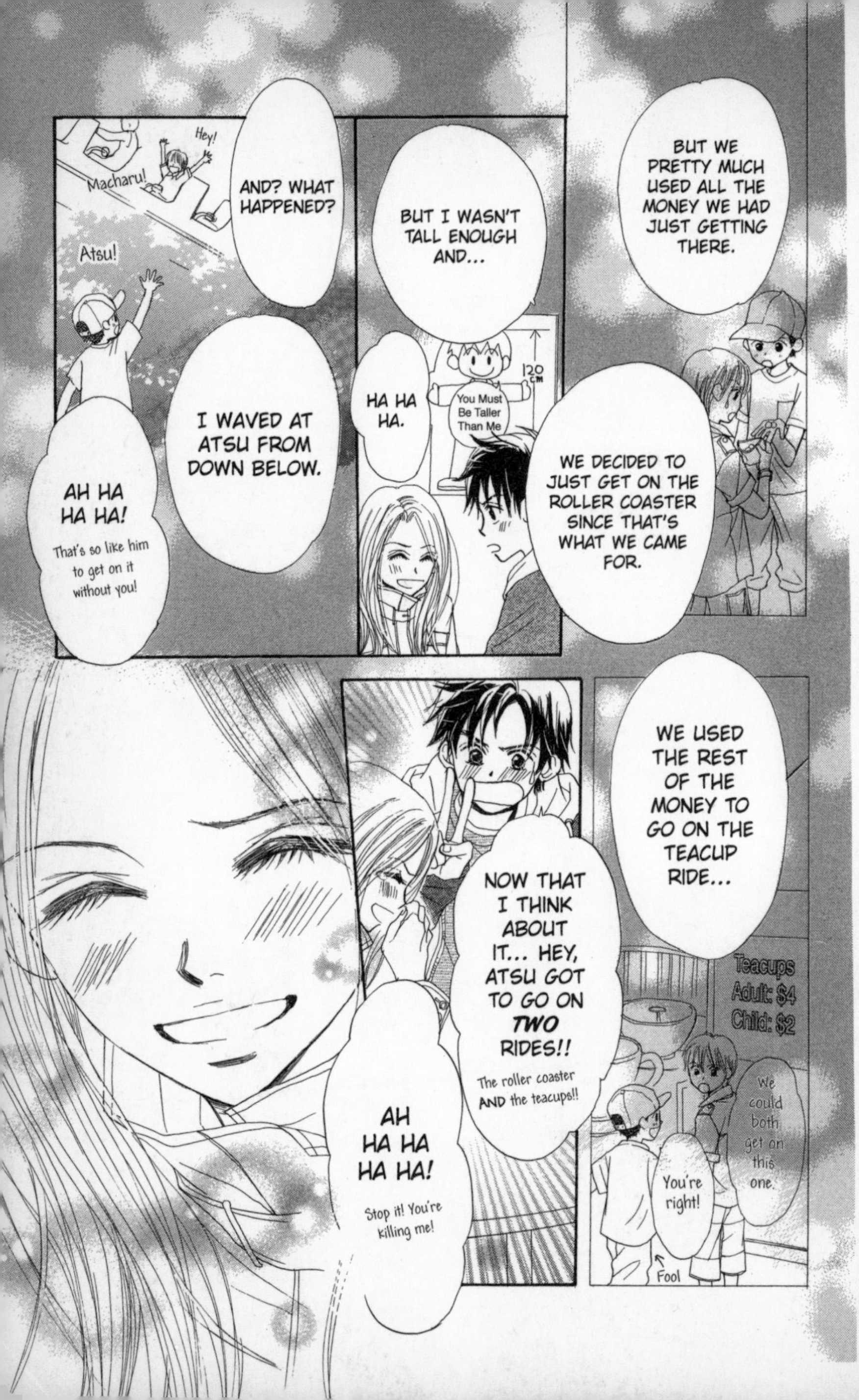
BUT WE PRETTY MUCH USED ALL THE MONEY WE HAD JUST GETTING THERE.
WE DECIDED TO JUST GET ON THE ROLLER COASTER SINCE THAT'S WHAT WE CAME FOR.
AND? WHAT HAPPENED?
BUT I WASN'T TALL ENOUGH AND...
120 cm
You Must Be Taller Than Me
HA HA HA.
Hey!
Macharu!
Atsu!
I WAVED AT ATSU FROM DOWN BELOW.
AH HA HA HA!
That's so like him to get on it without you!
WE USED THE REST OF THE MONEY TO GO ON THE TEACUP RIDE...
Teacups
Adult: $4
Child: $2
We could both get on this one.
You're right!
Fool
NOW THAT I THINK ABOUT IT... HEY, ATSU GOT TO GO ON TWO RIDES!!
The roller coaster AND the teacups!!
AH HA HA HA HA!
Stop it! You're killing me!

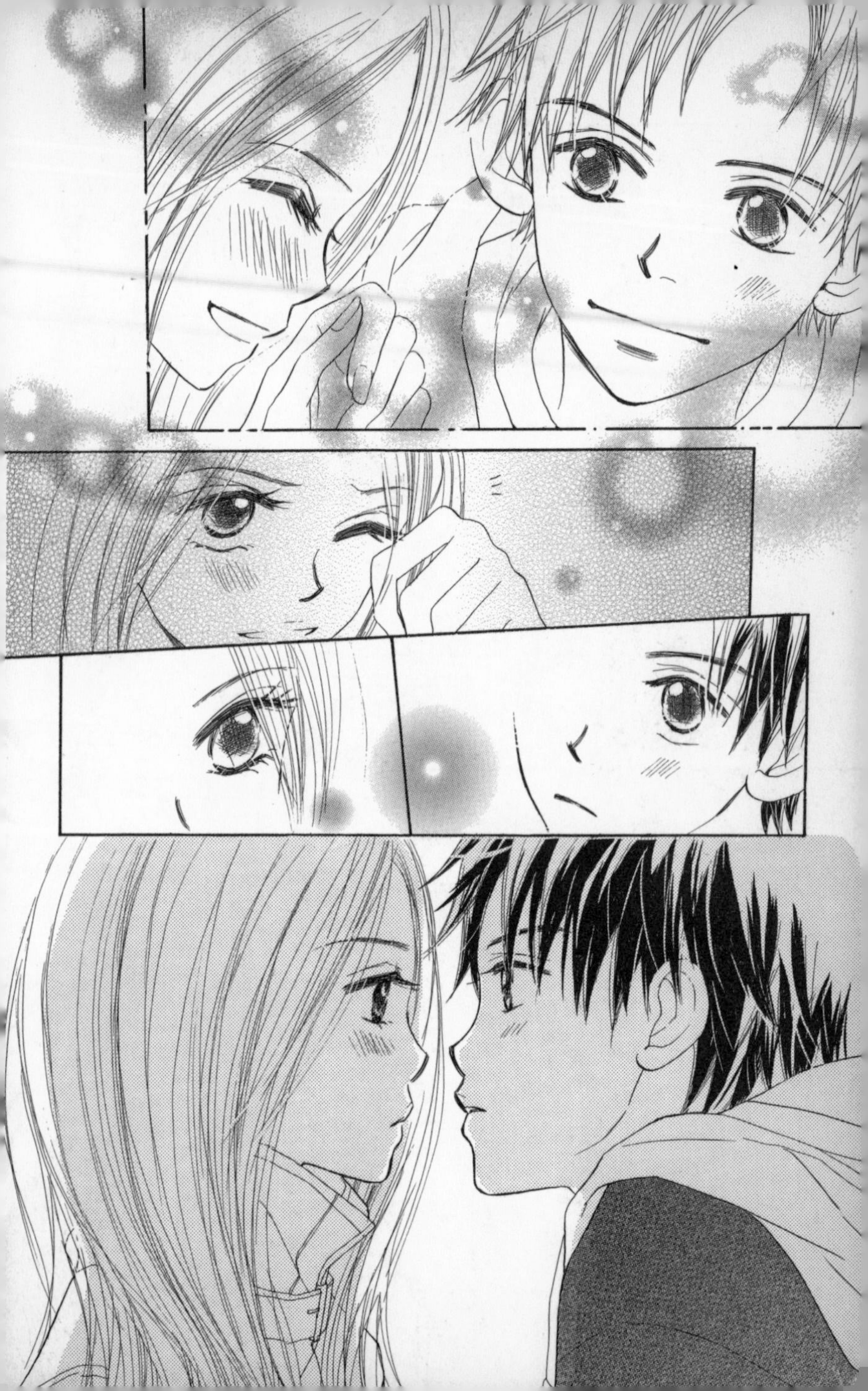

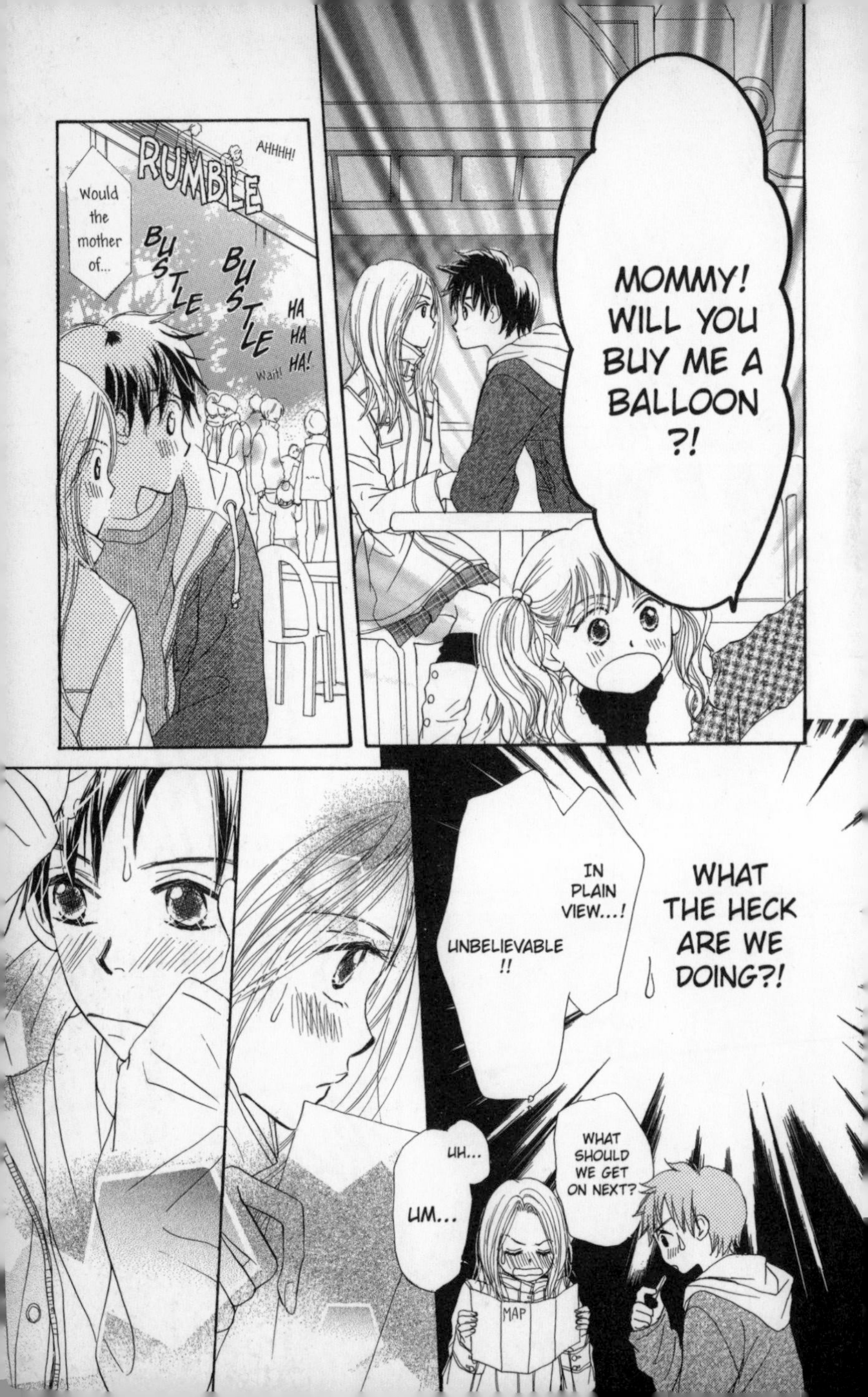
MOMMY! WILL YOU BUY ME A BALLOON ?!
Would the mother of...
RUMBLE
AHHHH!
BUSTLE
BUSTLE
HA HA HA!
Wait!
WHAT THE HECK ARE WE DOING?!
IN PLAIN VIEW...!
UNBELIEVABLE !!
WHAT SHOULD WE GET ON NEXT?
UH...
UM...
MAP

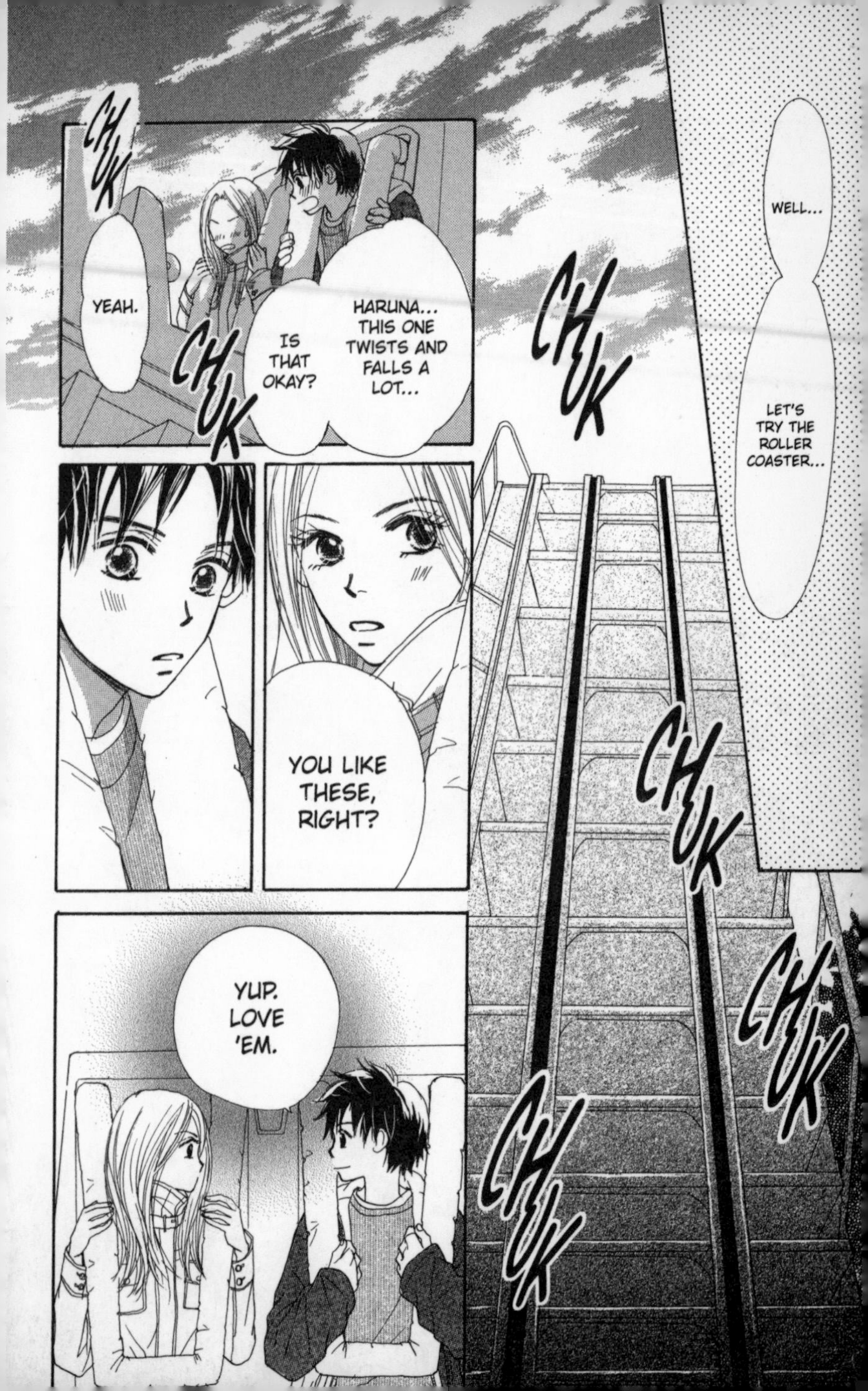
WELL...
LET'S TRY THE ROLLER COASTER...
CHUK
CHUK
CHUK
CHUK
HARUNA... THIS ONE TWISTS AND FALLS A LOT...
IS THAT OKAY?
CHUK
YEAH.
CHUK
YOU LIKE THESE, RIGHT?
YUP. LOVE 'EM.

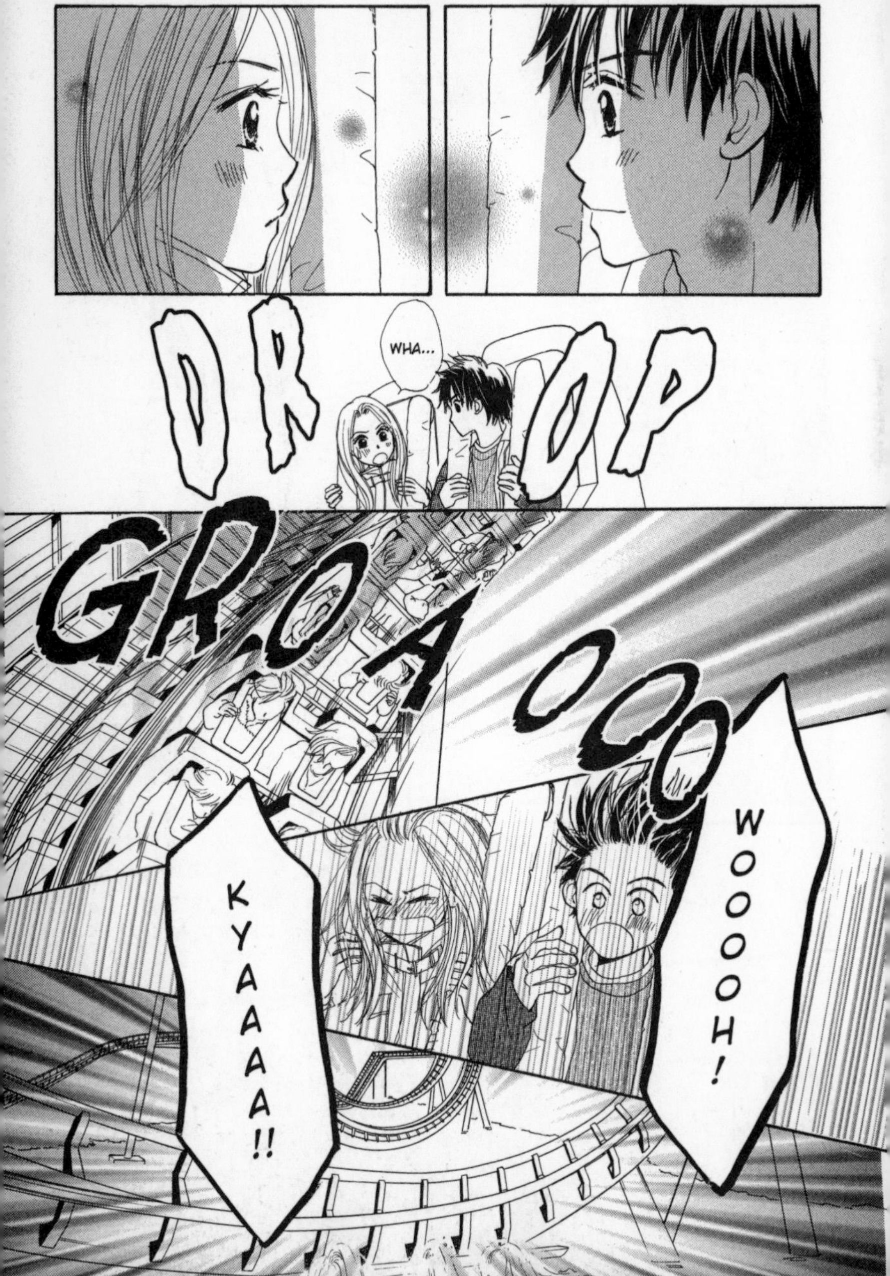
DROP
WHA...
GROAOOO
WOOOOOH!
KYAAAA!!

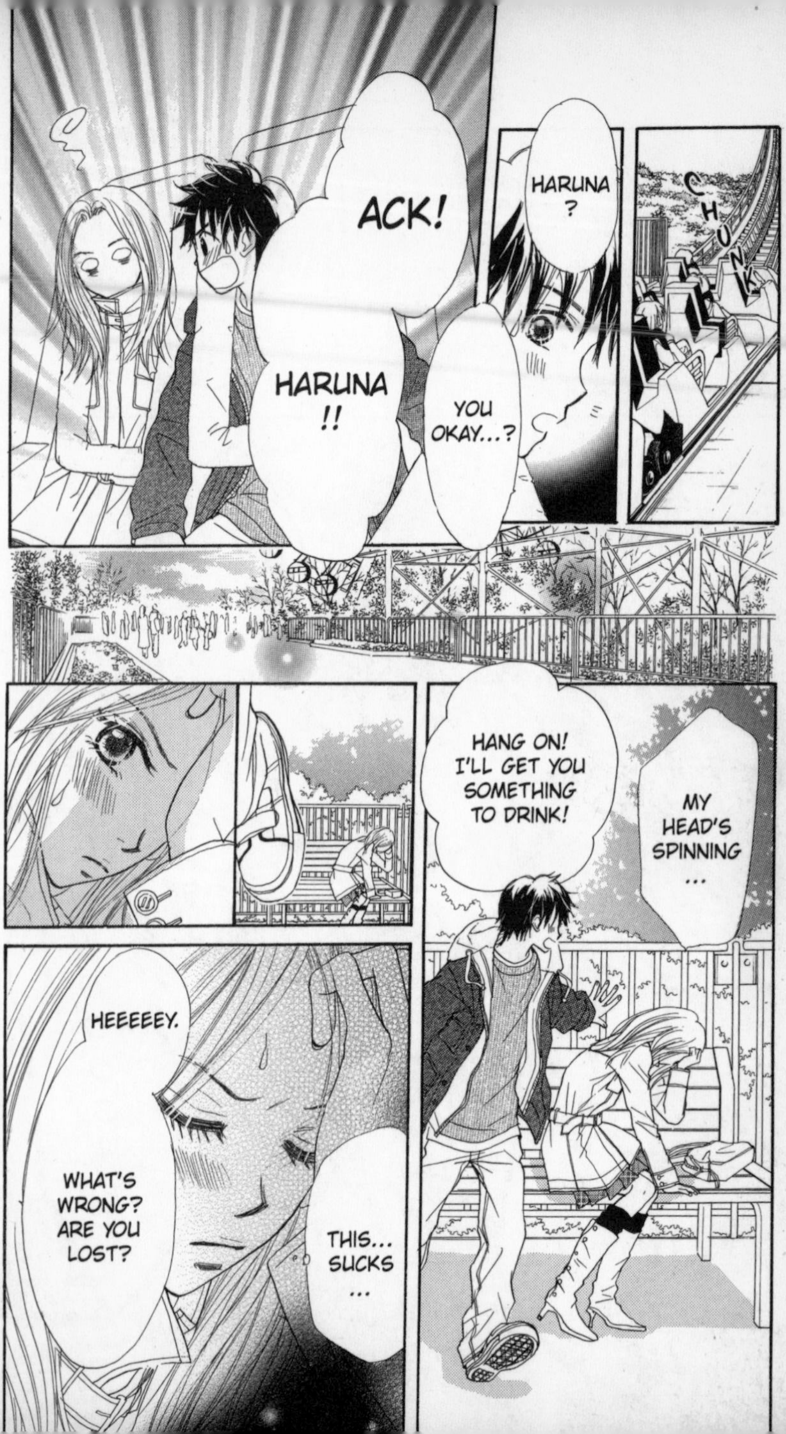
CHUNK
HARUNA ?
YOU OKAY...?
ACK!
HARUNA !!
MY HEAD'S SPINNING ...
HANG ON! I'LL GET YOU SOMETHING TO DRINK!
THIS... SUCKS ...
HEEEEEY.
WHAT'S WRONG? ARE YOU LOST?

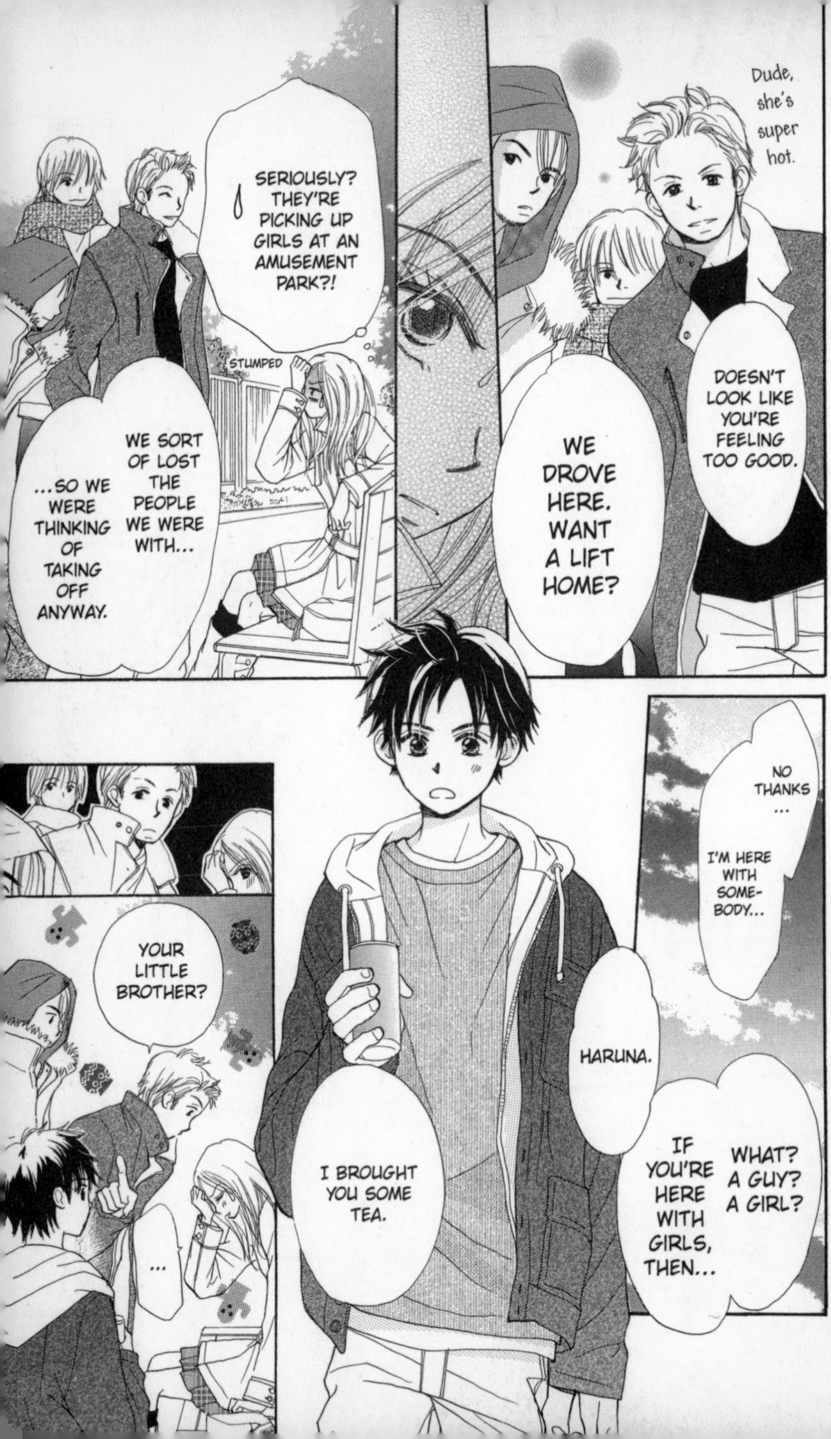
Dude, she's super hot.
DOESN'T LOOK LIKE YOU'RE FEELING TOO GOOD.
WE DROVE HERE. WANT A LIFT HOME?
SERIOUSLY? THEY'RE PICKING UP GIRLS AT AN AMUSEMENT PARK?!
STUMPED
WE SORT OF LOST THE PEOPLE WE WERE WITH...
...SO WE WERE THINKING OF TAKING OFF ANYWAY.
NO THANKS... I'M HERE WITH SOME-BODY...
WHAT? A GUY? A GIRL?
IF YOU'RE HERE WITH GIRLS, THEN...
HARUNA.
I BROUGHT YOU SOME TEA.
YOUR LITTLE BROTHER?
...

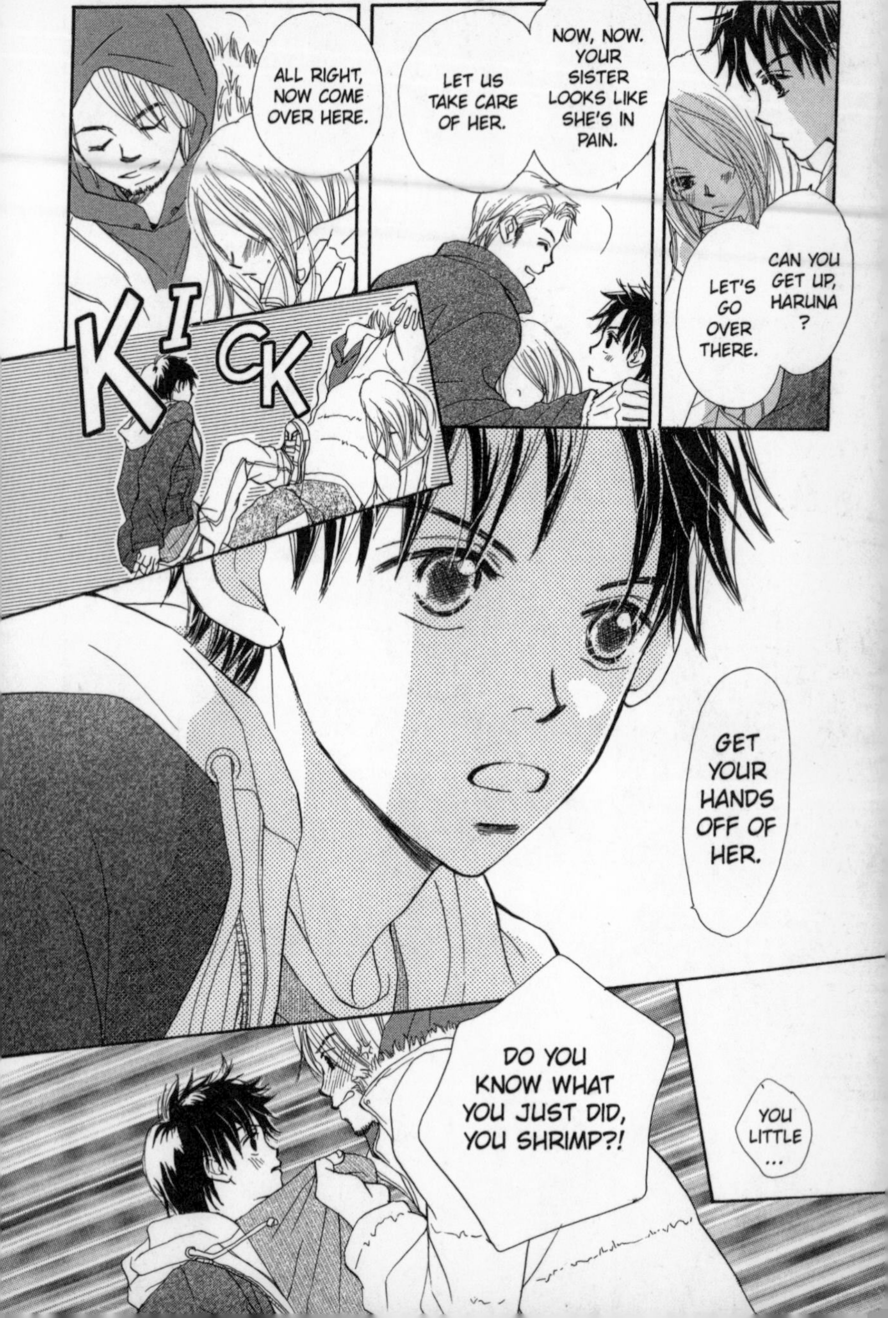
CAN YOU GET UP, HARUNA?
LET'S GO OVER THERE.
NOW, NOW. YOUR SISTER LOOKS LIKE SHE'S IN PAIN.
LET US TAKE CARE OF HER.
ALL RIGHT, NOW COME OVER HERE.
KICK
GET YOUR HANDS OFF OF HER.
YOU LITTLE...
DO YOU KNOW WHAT YOU JUST DID, YOU SHRIMP?!

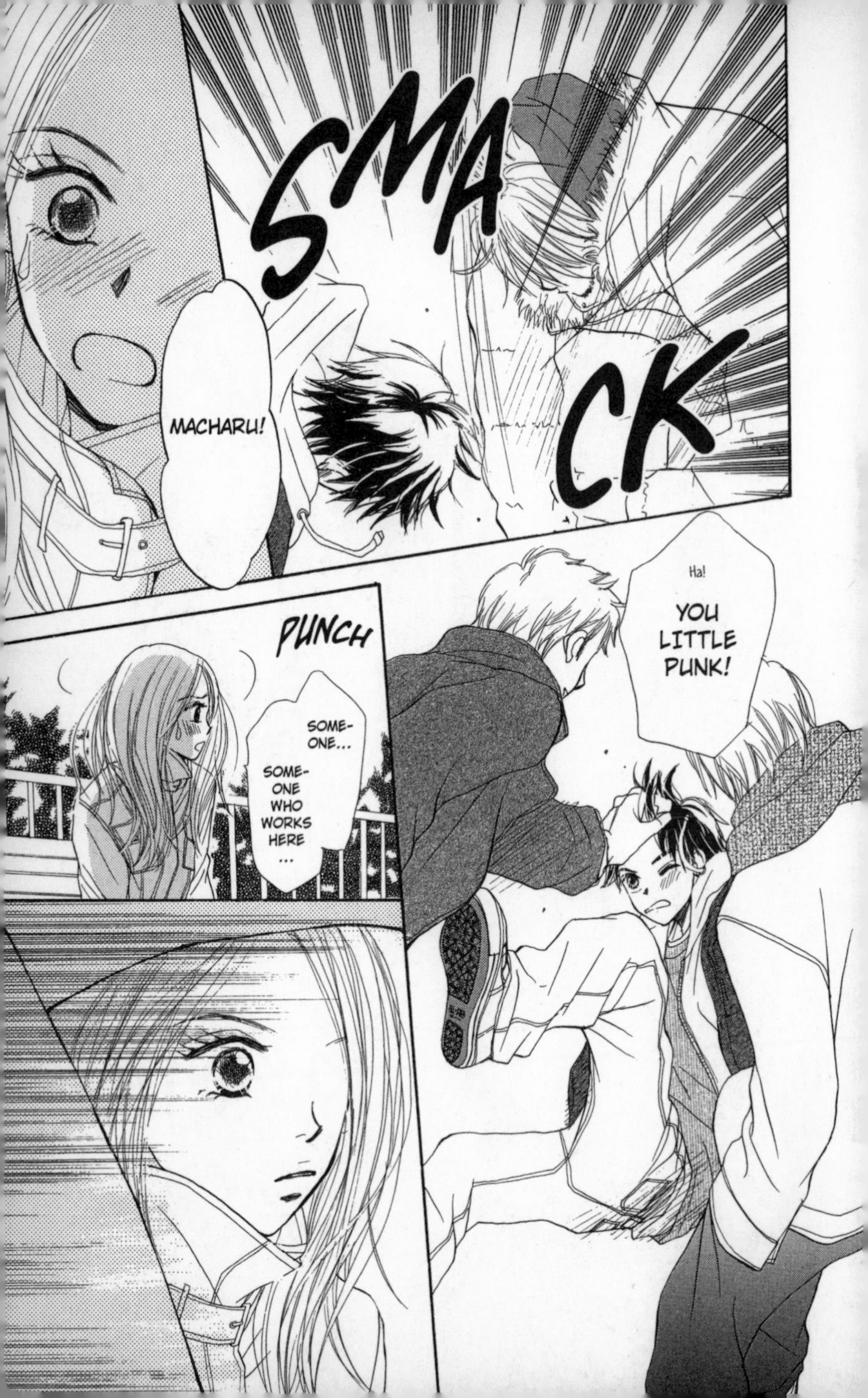
SMACK
MACHARU!
Ha!
YOU LITTLE PUNK!
PUNCH
SOME-ONE...
SOME-ONE WHO WORKS HERE ...

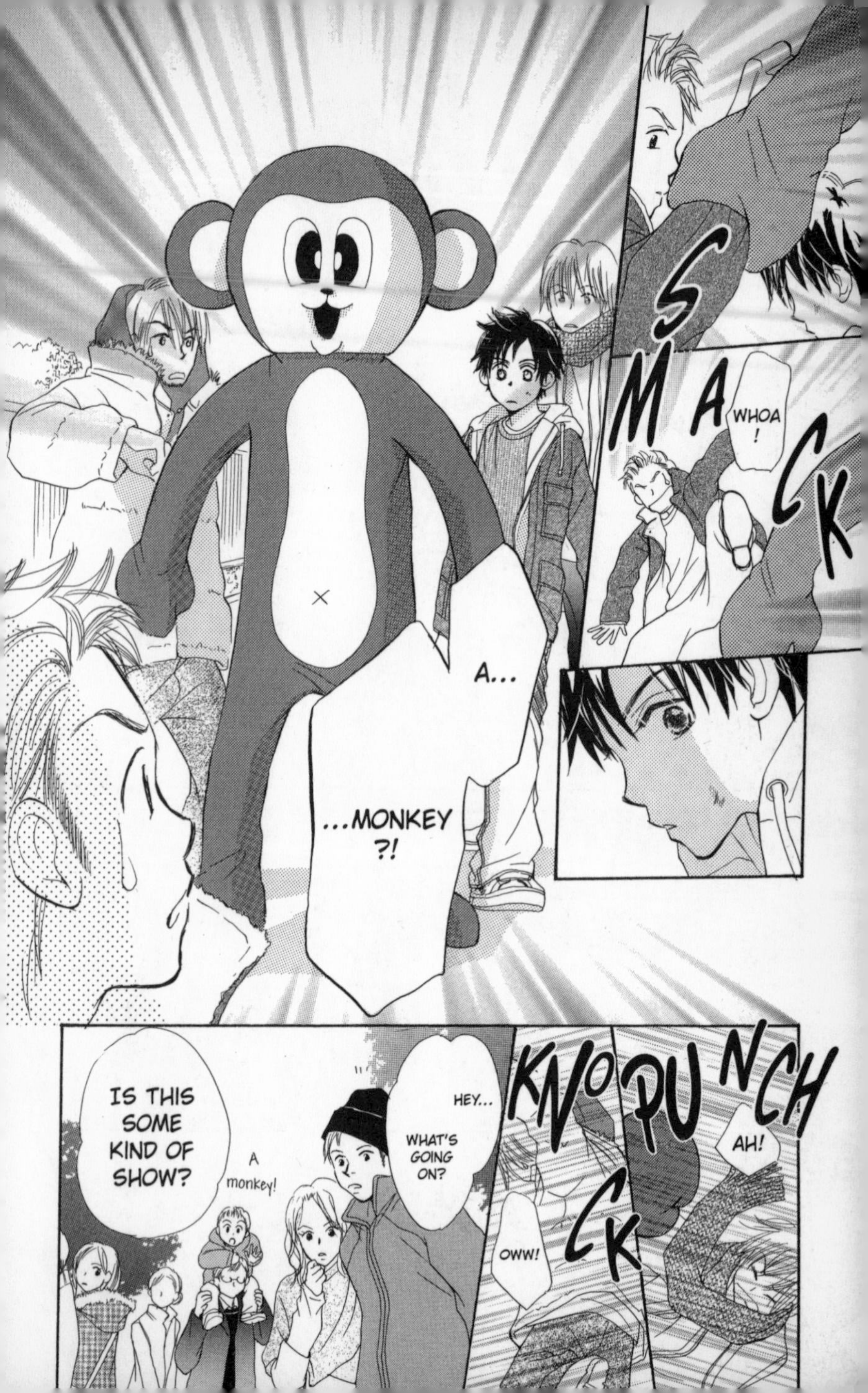
SMACK
WHOA!
A...
...MONKEY ?!
PUNCH
KNOCK
AH!
OWW!
HEY... WHAT'S GOING ON?
A monkey!
IS THIS SOME KIND OF SHOW?

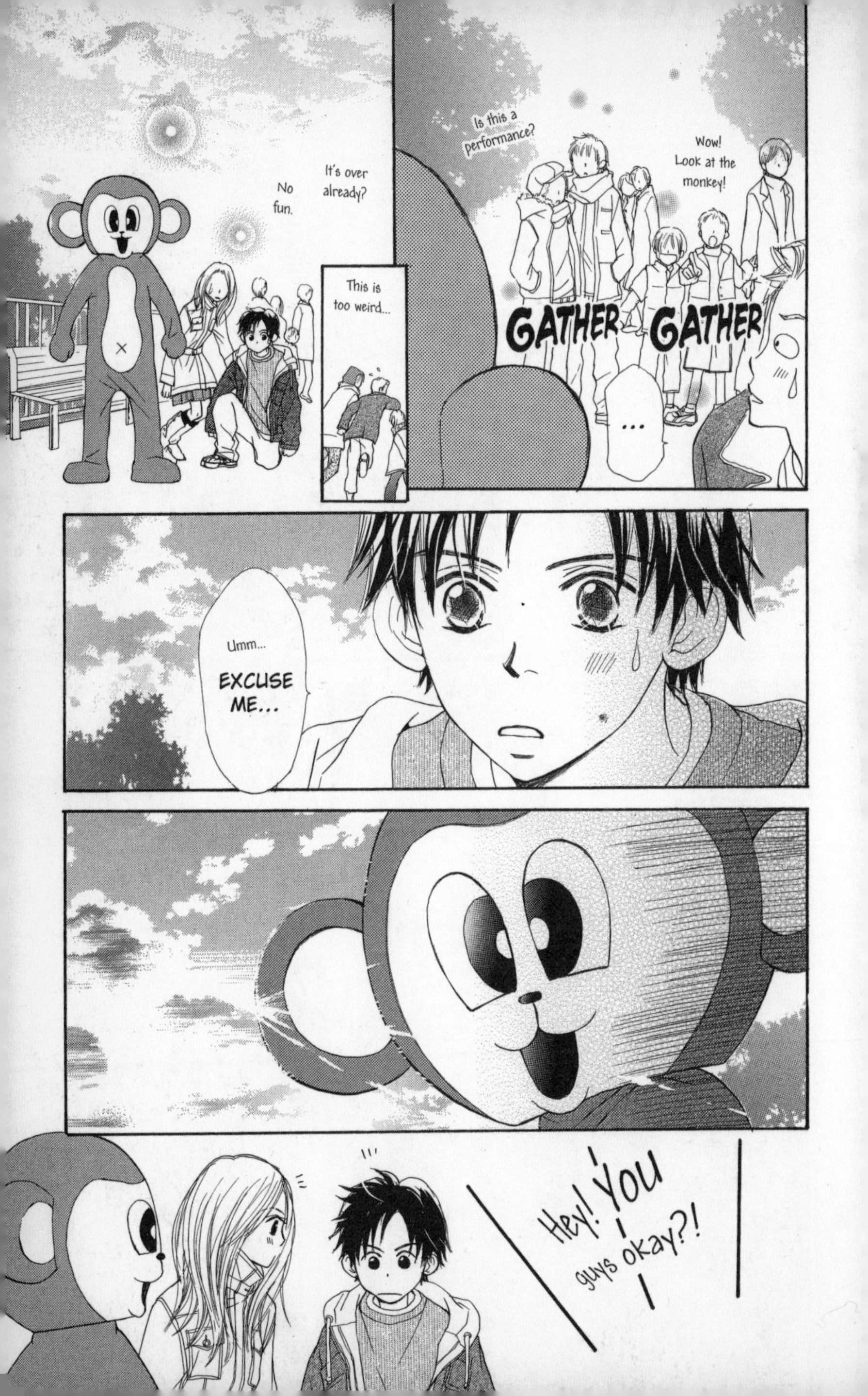
Wow! Look at the monkey!
Is this a performance?
GATHER GATHER
...
This is too weird...
It's over already?
No fun.
Umm... EXCUSE ME...
Hey! You guys okay?!

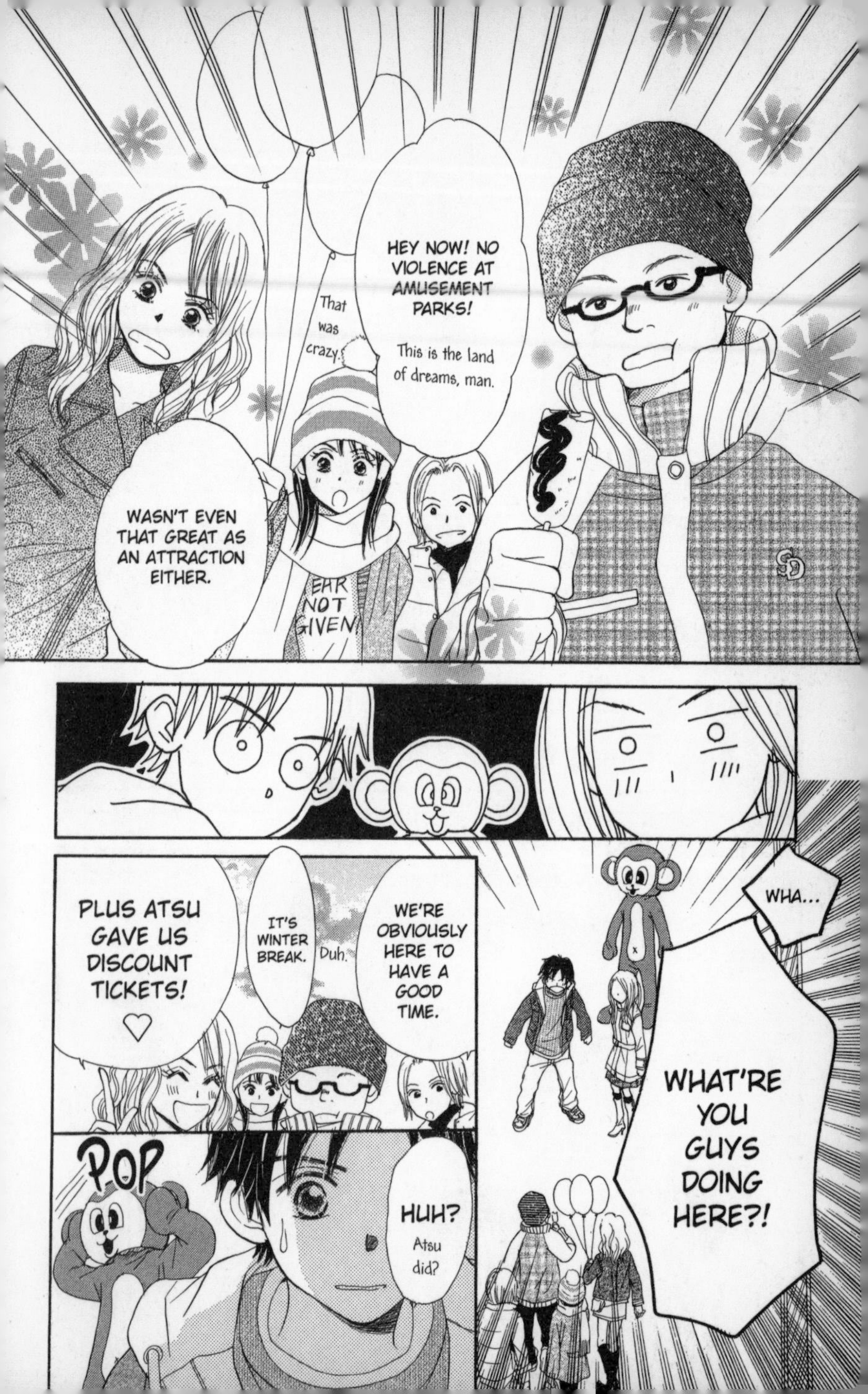
HEY NOW! NO VIOLENCE AT AMUSEMENT PARKS!
This is the land of dreams, man.
That was crazy.
WASN'T EVEN THAT GREAT AS AN ATTRACTION EITHER.
WHA...
WHAT'RE YOU GUYS DOING HERE?!
WE'RE OBVIOUSLY HERE TO HAVE A GOOD TIME.
IT'S WINTER BREAK.
Duh.
PLUS ATSU GAVE US DISCOUNT TICKETS! ♡
HUH?
Atsu did?
POP

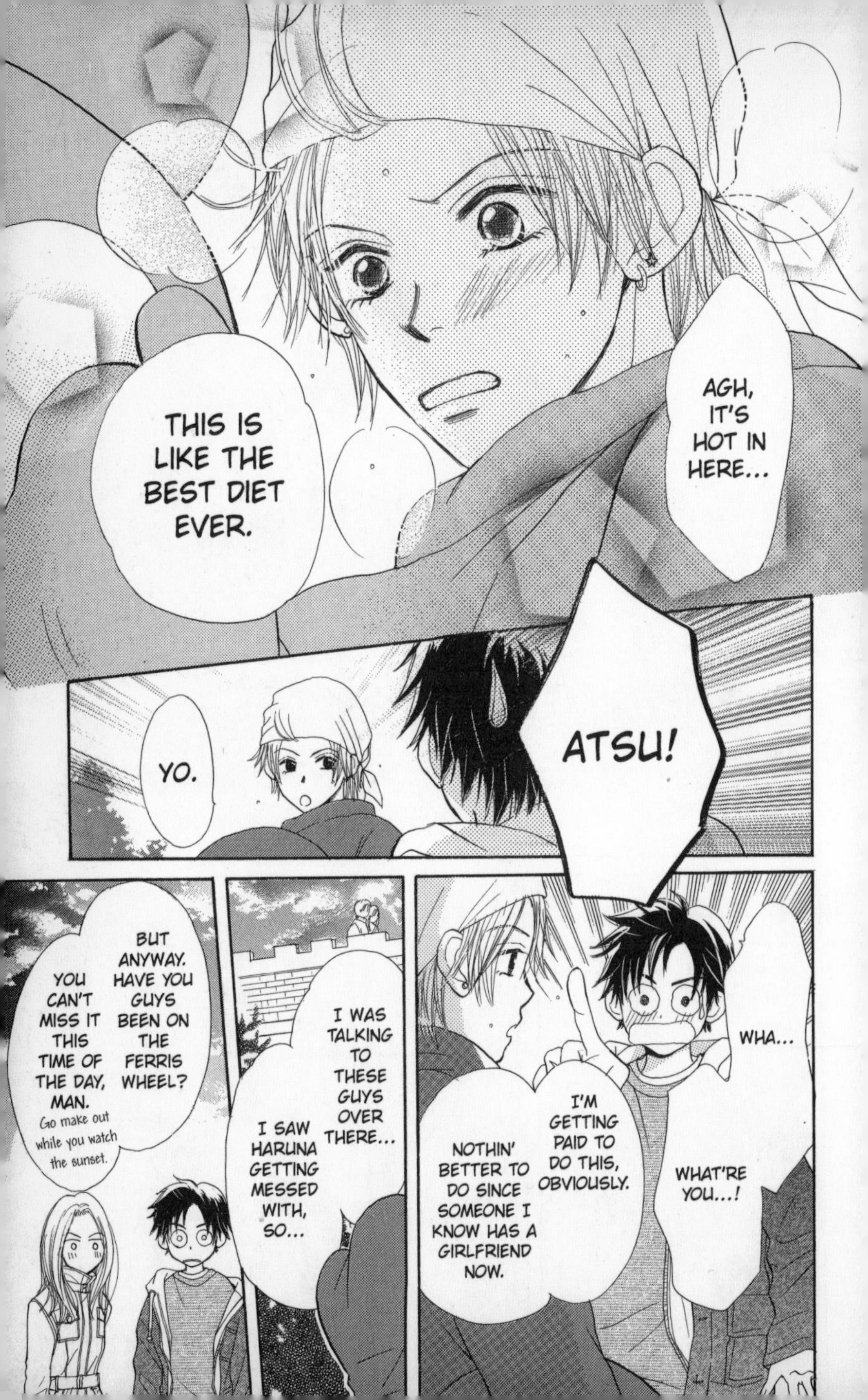
AGH, IT'S HOT IN HERE...
THIS IS LIKE THE BEST DIET EVER.
ATSU!
YO.
WHA...
WHAT'RE YOU...!
I'M GETTING PAID TO DO THIS, OBVIOUSLY.
NOTHIN' BETTER TO DO SINCE SOMEONE I KNOW HAS A GIRLFRIEND NOW.
I WAS TALKING TO THESE GUYS OVER THERE...
I SAW HARUNA GETTING MESSED WITH, SO...
BUT ANYWAY. HAVE YOU GUYS BEEN ON THE FERRIS WHEEL?
YOU CAN'T MISS IT THIS TIME OF THE DAY, MAN.
Go make out while you watch the sunset.

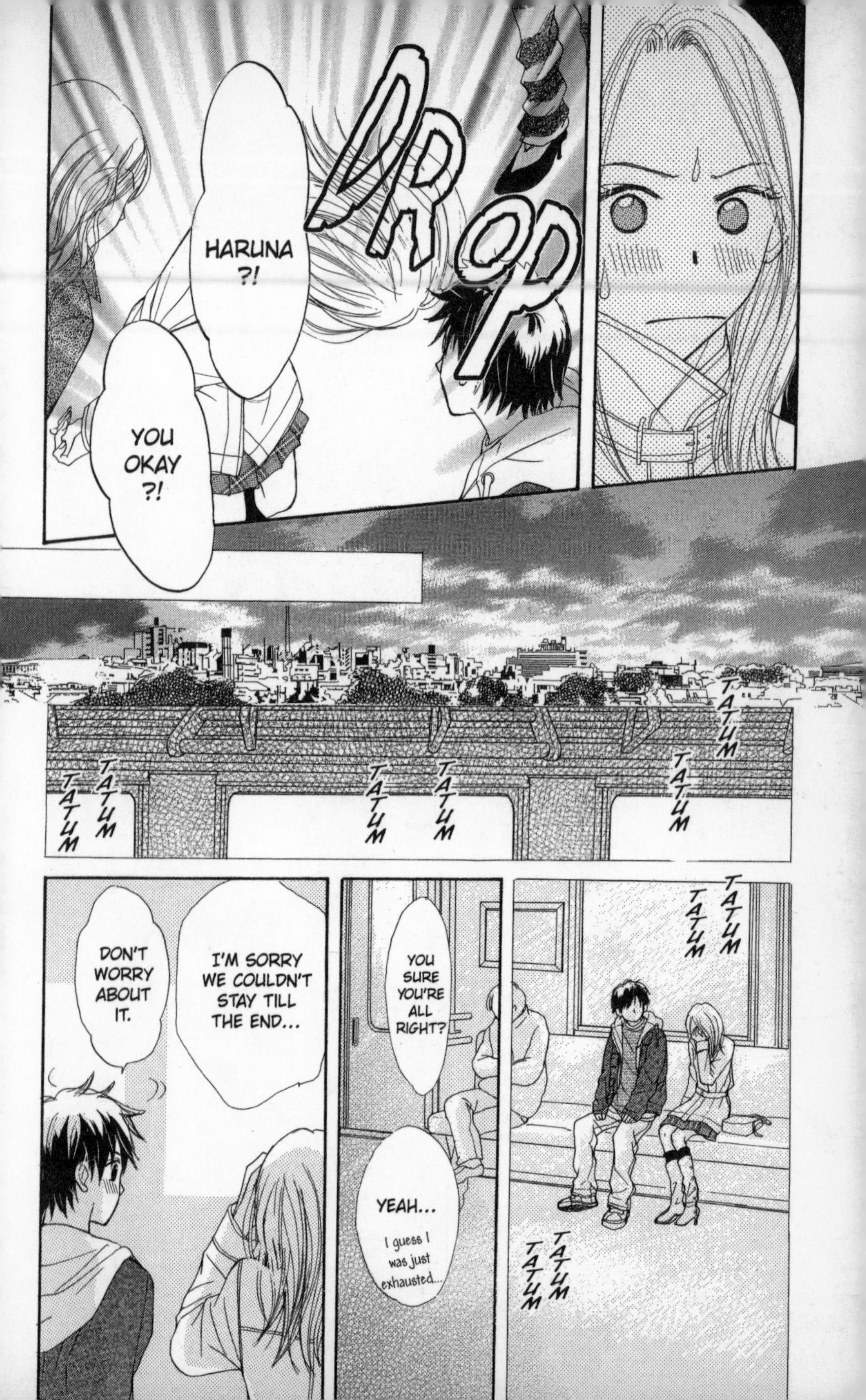
DROP
HARUNA ?!
YOU OKAY ?!
TATUM
TATUM
TATUM
TATUM
TATUM
TATUM
TATUM
TATUM
TATUM
TATUM
YOU SURE YOU'RE ALL RIGHT?
YEAH...
I guess I was just exhausted...
I'M SORRY WE COULDN'T STAY TILL THE END...
DON'T WORRY ABOUT IT.

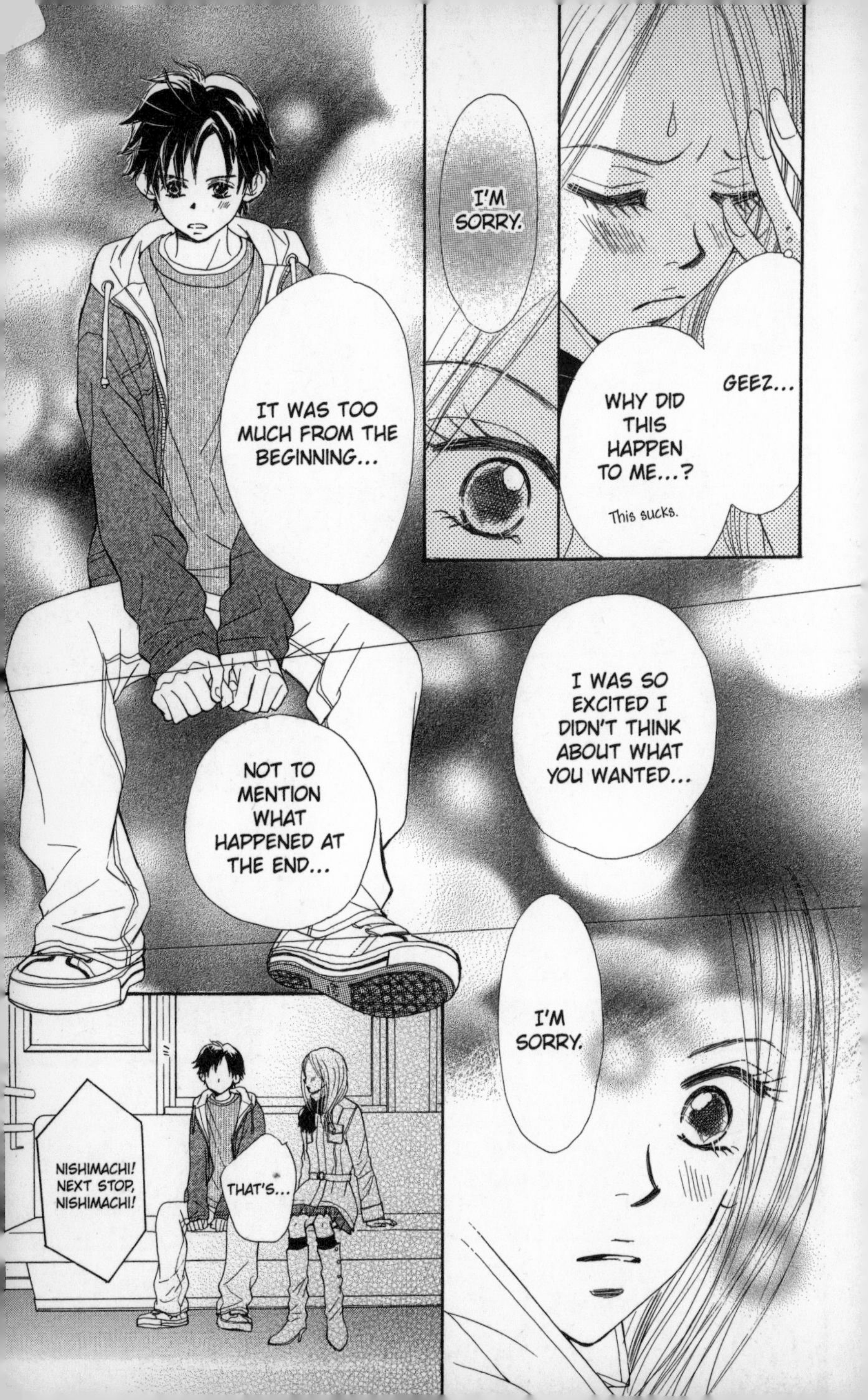
GEEZ...
WHY DID THIS HAPPEN TO ME...?
This sucks.
I'M SORRY.
IT WAS TOO MUCH FROM THE BEGINNING...
I WAS SO EXCITED I DIDN'T THINK ABOUT WHAT YOU WANTED...
NOT TO MENTION WHAT HAPPENED AT THE END...
I'M SORRY.
NISHIMACHI! NEXT STOP, NISHIMACHI!
THAT'S...

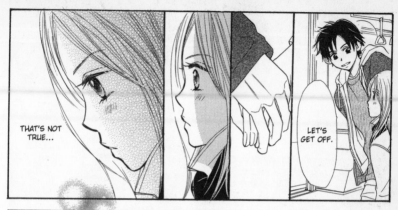

THAT'S NOT TRUE...

LET'S GET OFF.

I WAS TOO...

YOU WEREN'T THE ONLY ONE EXCITED...

THIS IS FINE. THANKS.

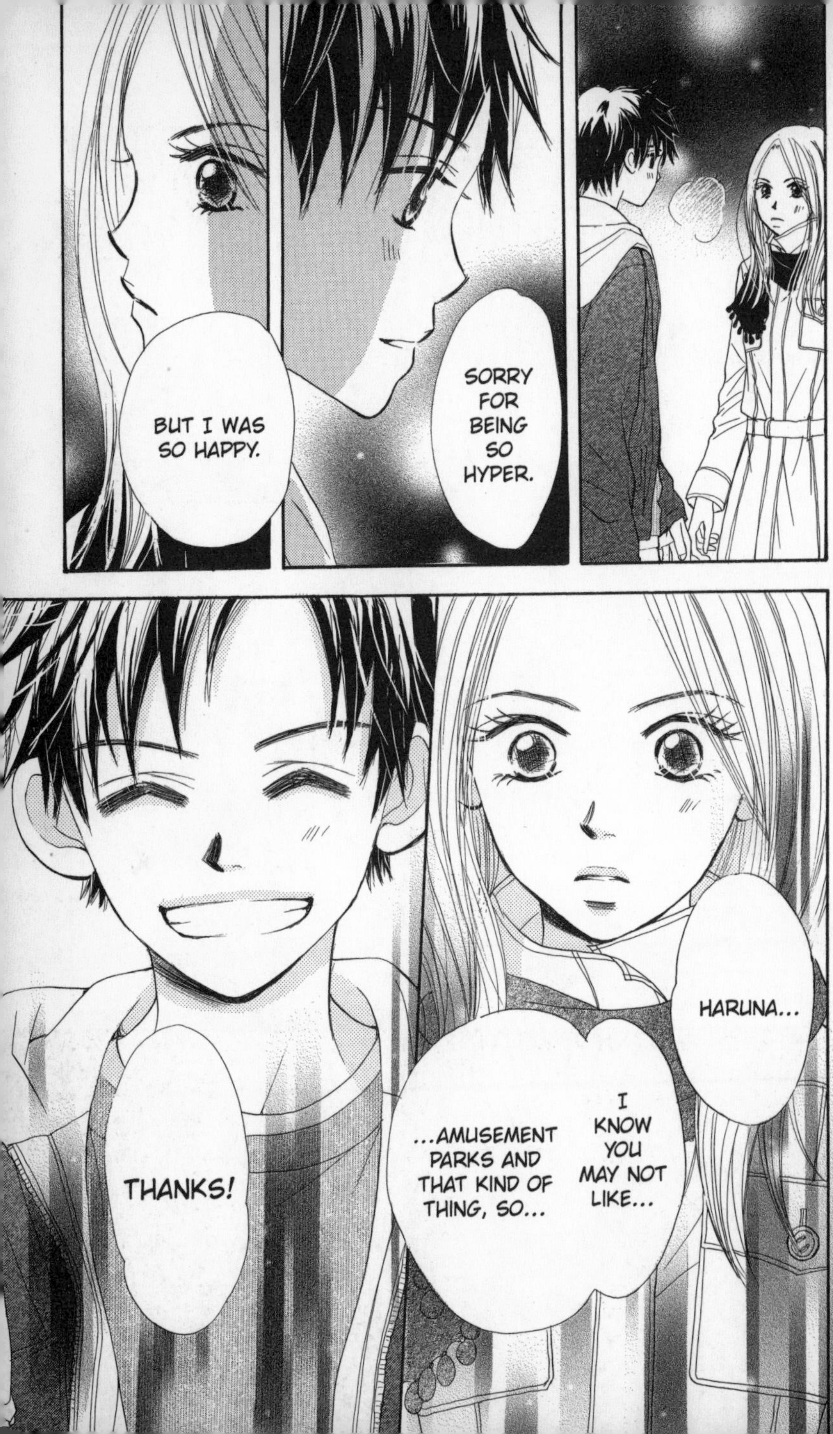
SORRY FOR BEING SO HYPER.
BUT I WAS SO HAPPY.
HARUNA...
I KNOW YOU MAY NOT LIKE...
...AMUSEMENT PARKS AND THAT KIND OF THING, SO...
THANKS!

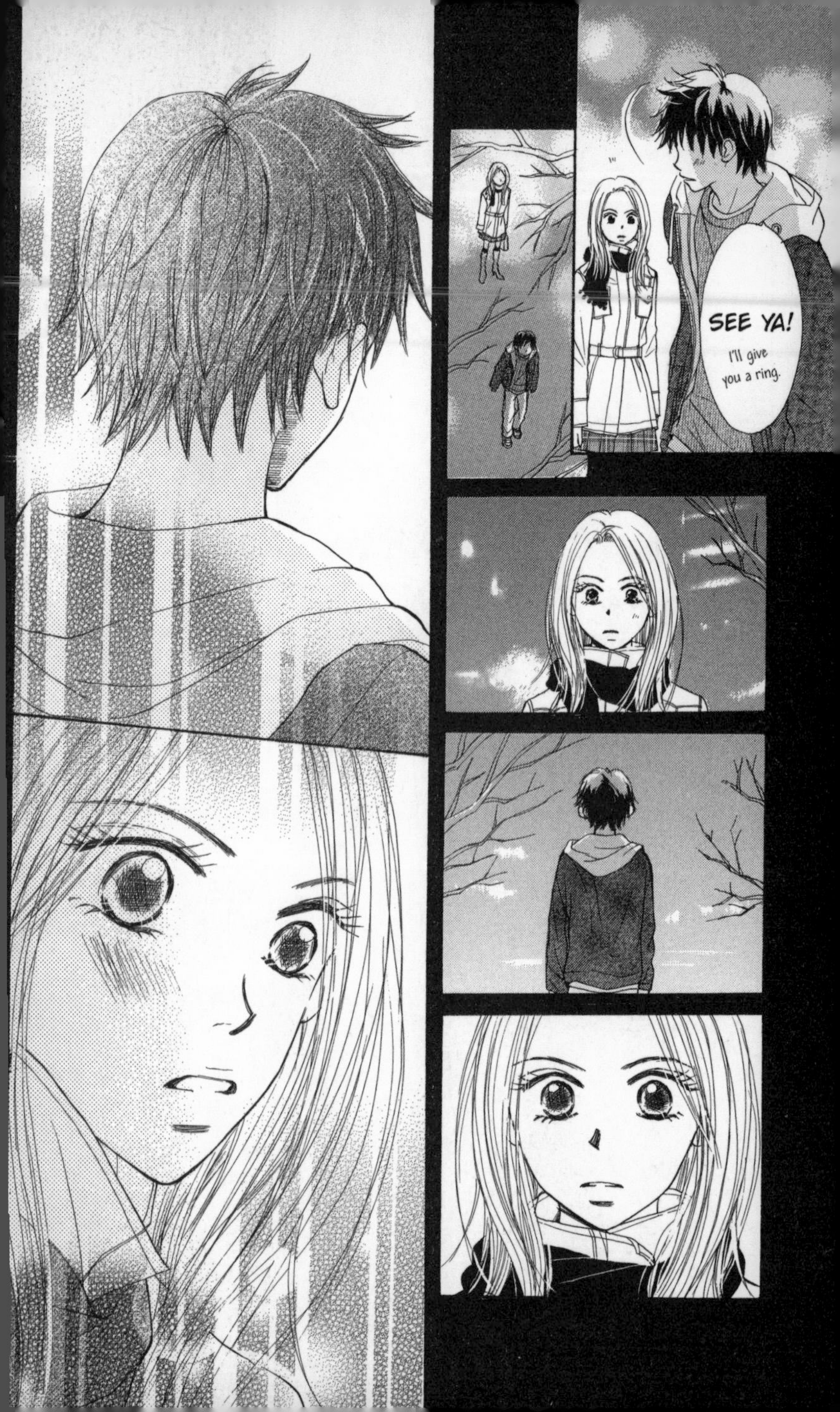
SEE YA!
I'll give you a ring.

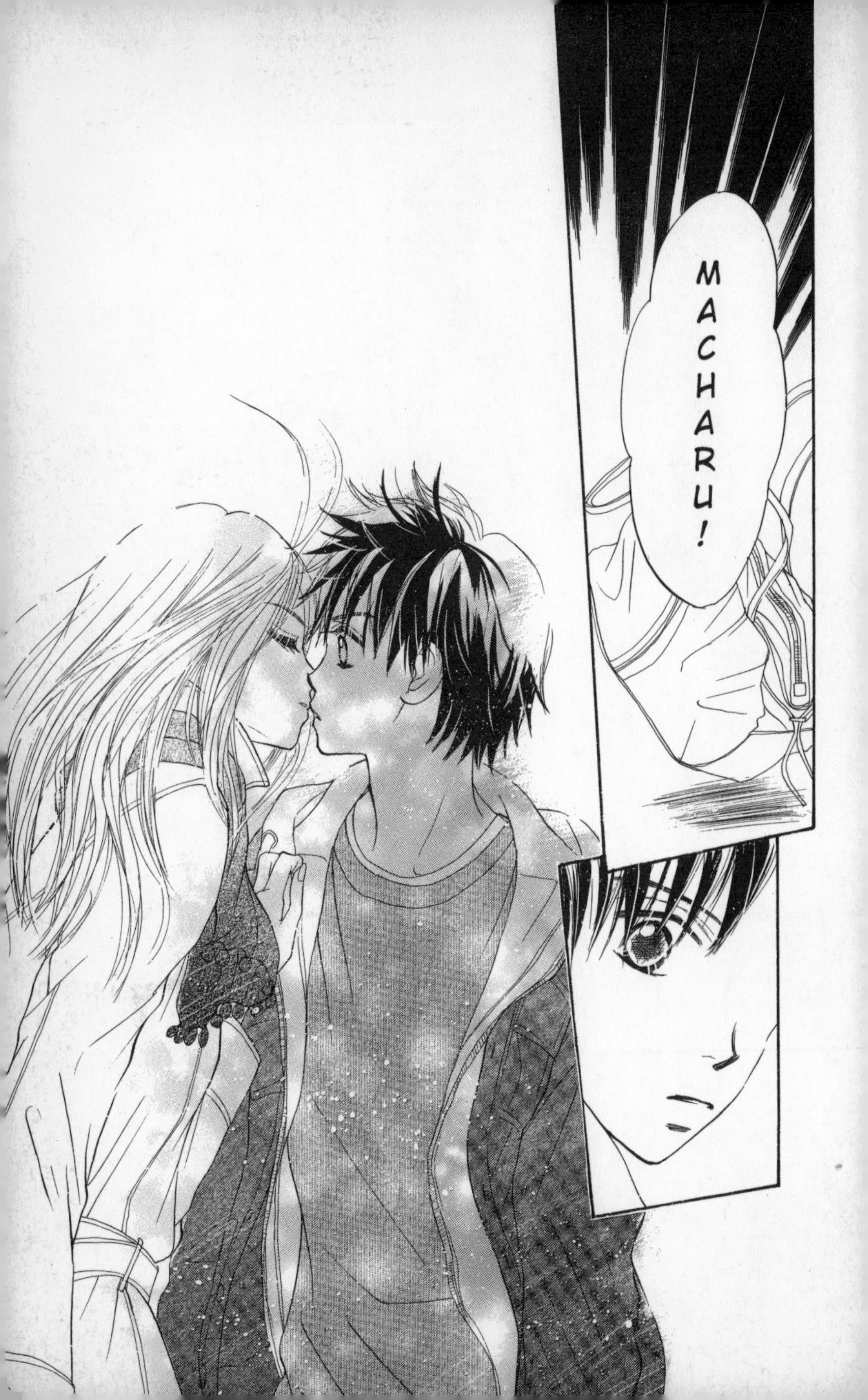
MACHARU!

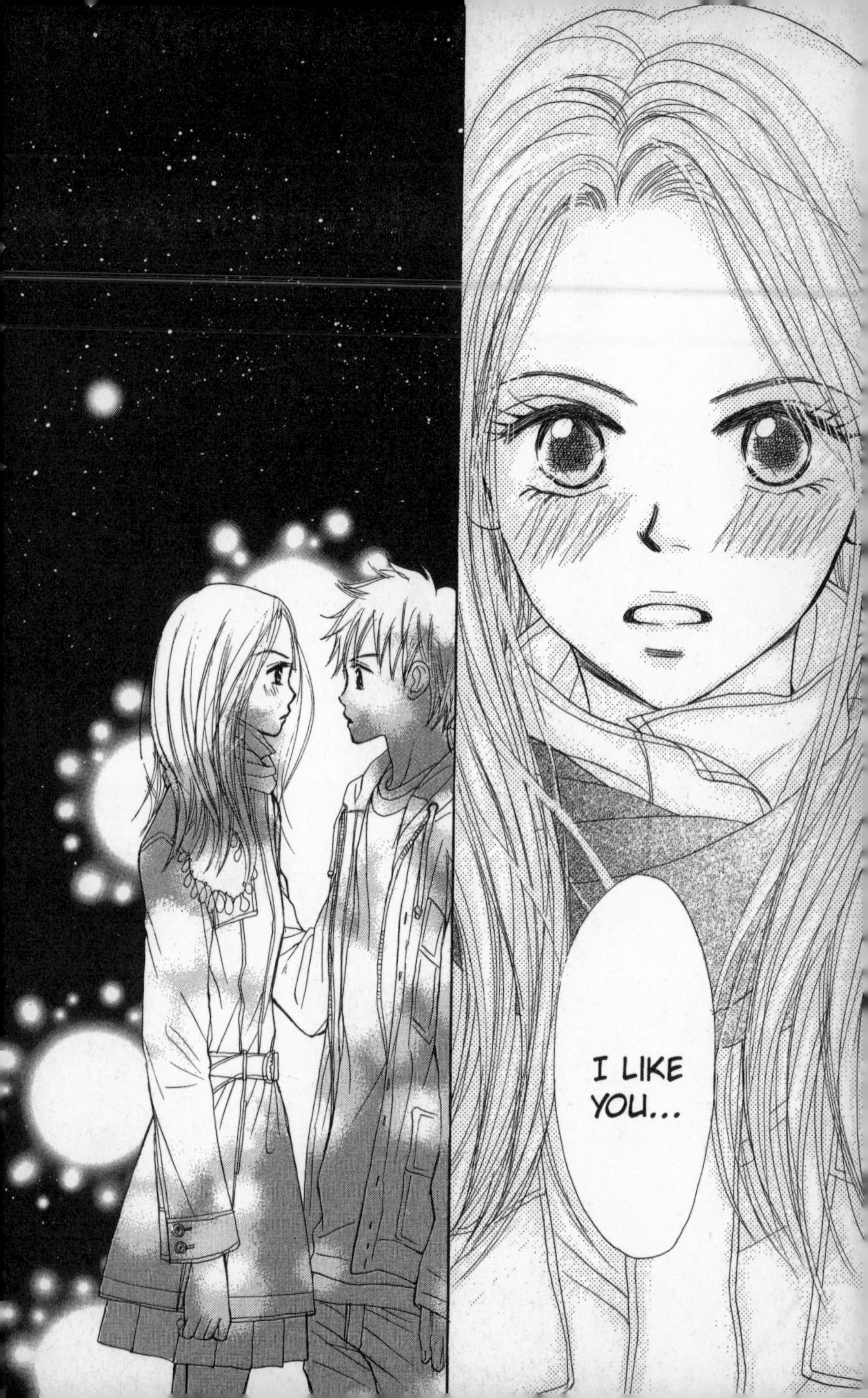
I LIKE YOU...

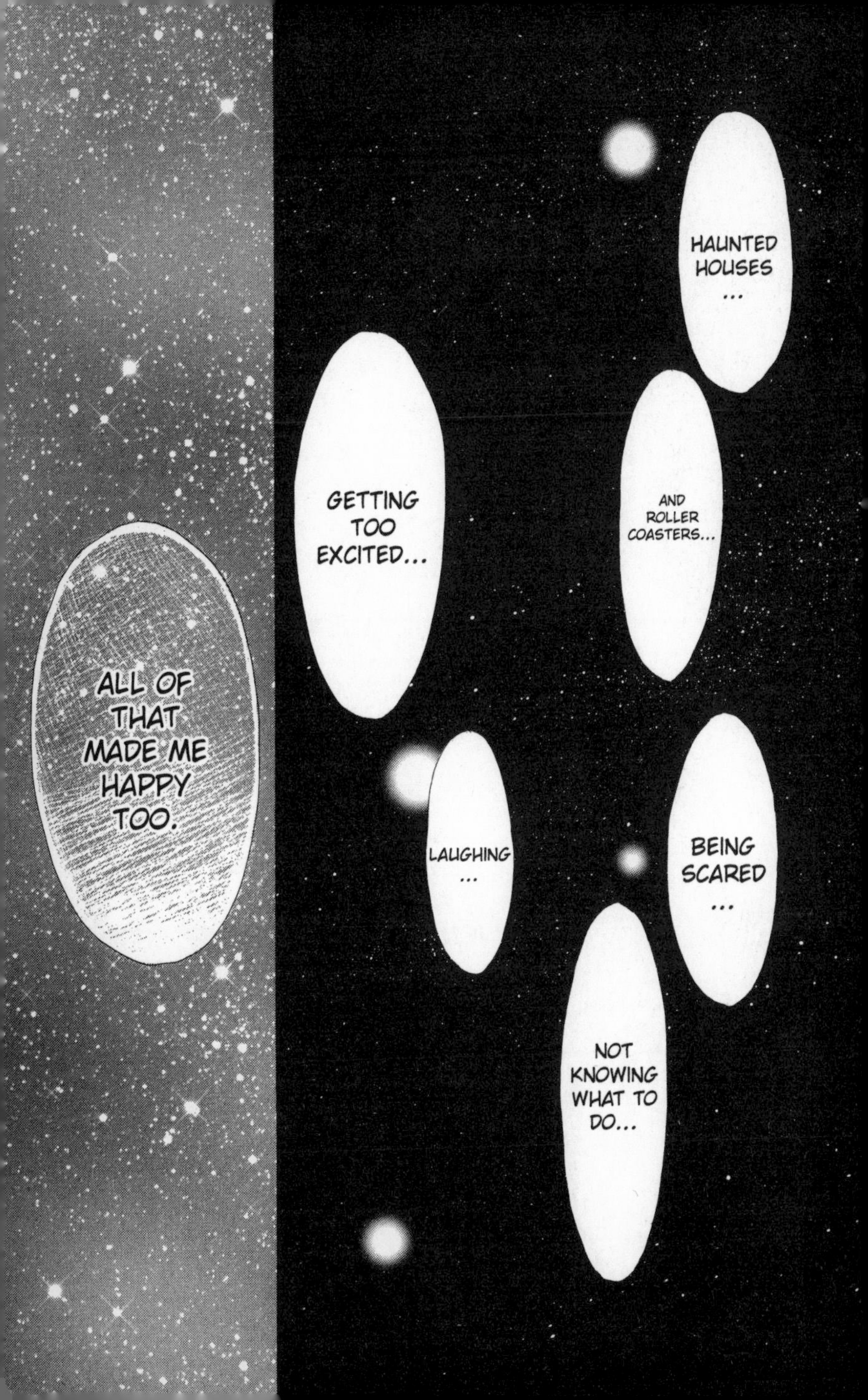
HAUNTED HOUSES...
AND ROLLER COASTERS...
GETTING TOO EXCITED...
BEING SCARED...
LAUGHING...
NOT KNOWING WHAT TO DO...
ALL OF THAT MADE ME HAPPY TOO.

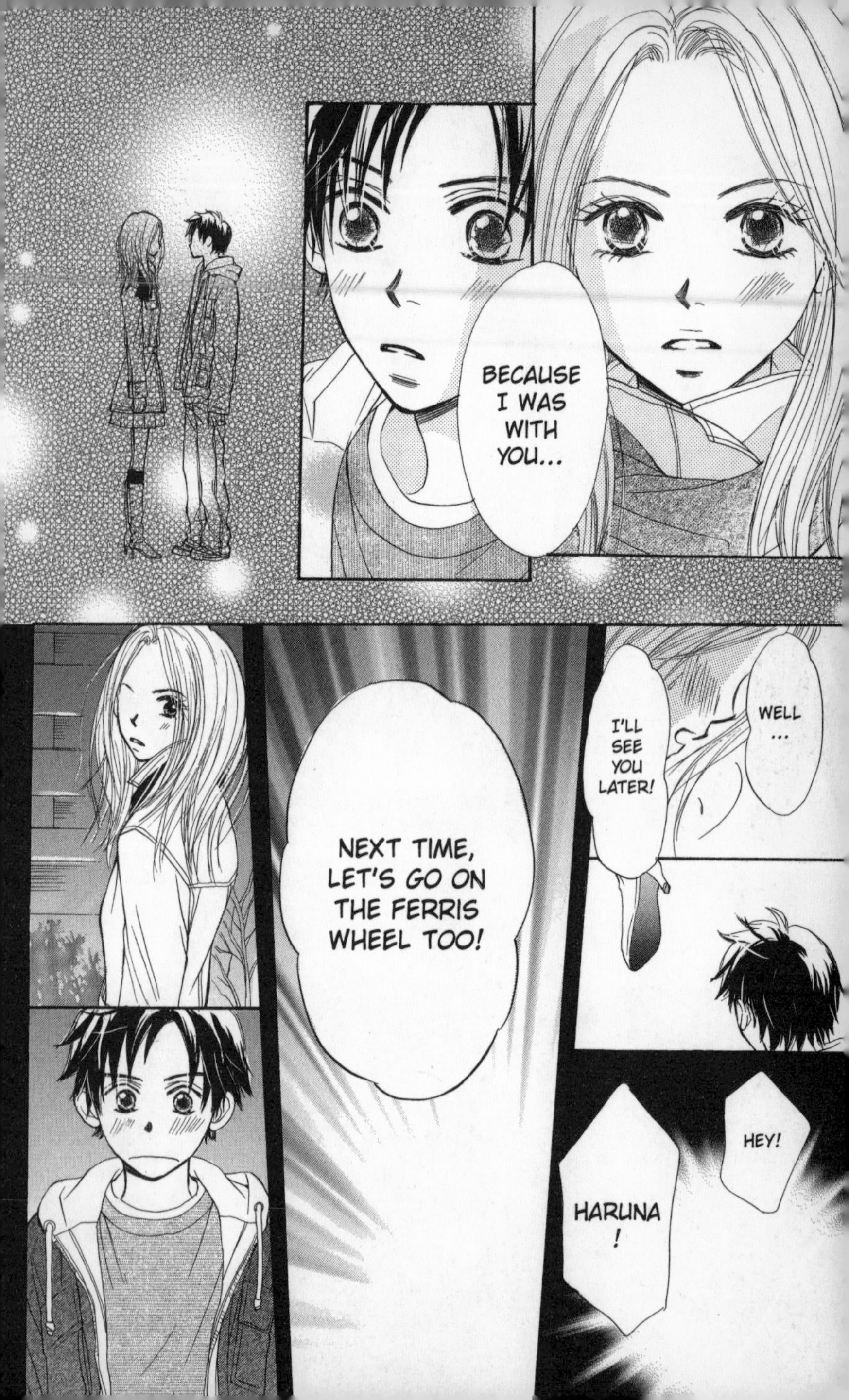
BECAUSE I WAS WITH YOU...
WELL...
I'LL SEE YOU LATER!
HEY!
HARUNA!
NEXT TIME, LET'S GO ON THE FERRIS WHEEL TOO!

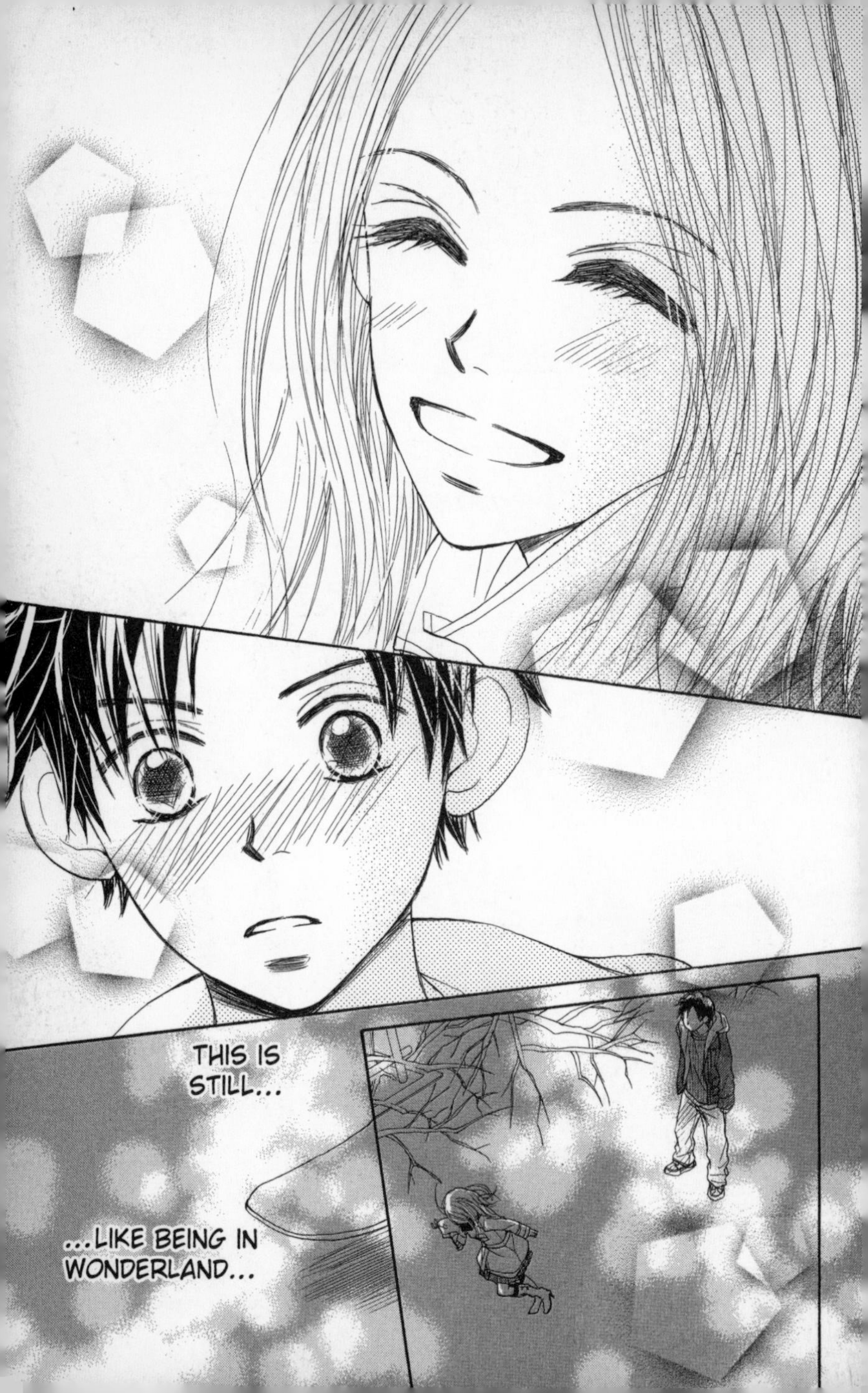
THIS IS STILL...
...LIKE BEING IN WONDERLAND...

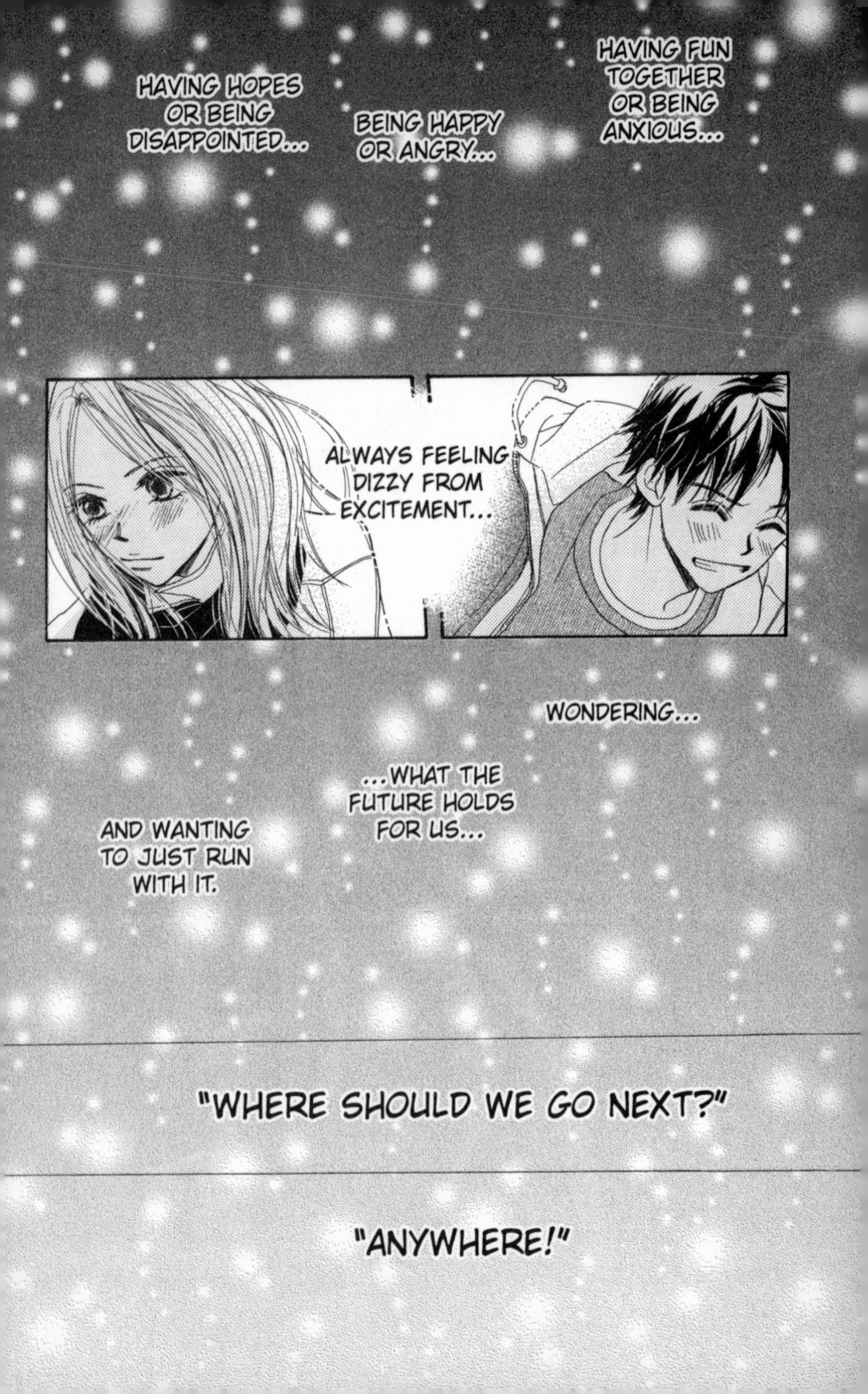
HAVING FUN TOGETHER OR BEING ANXIOUS...
BEING HAPPY OR ANGRY...
HAVING HOPES OR BEING DISAPPOINTED...
ALWAYS FEELING DIZZY FROM EXCITEMENT...
WONDERING...
...WHAT THE FUTURE HOLDS FOR US...
AND WANTING TO JUST RUN WITH IT.
"WHERE SHOULD WE GO NEXT?"
"ANYWHERE!"

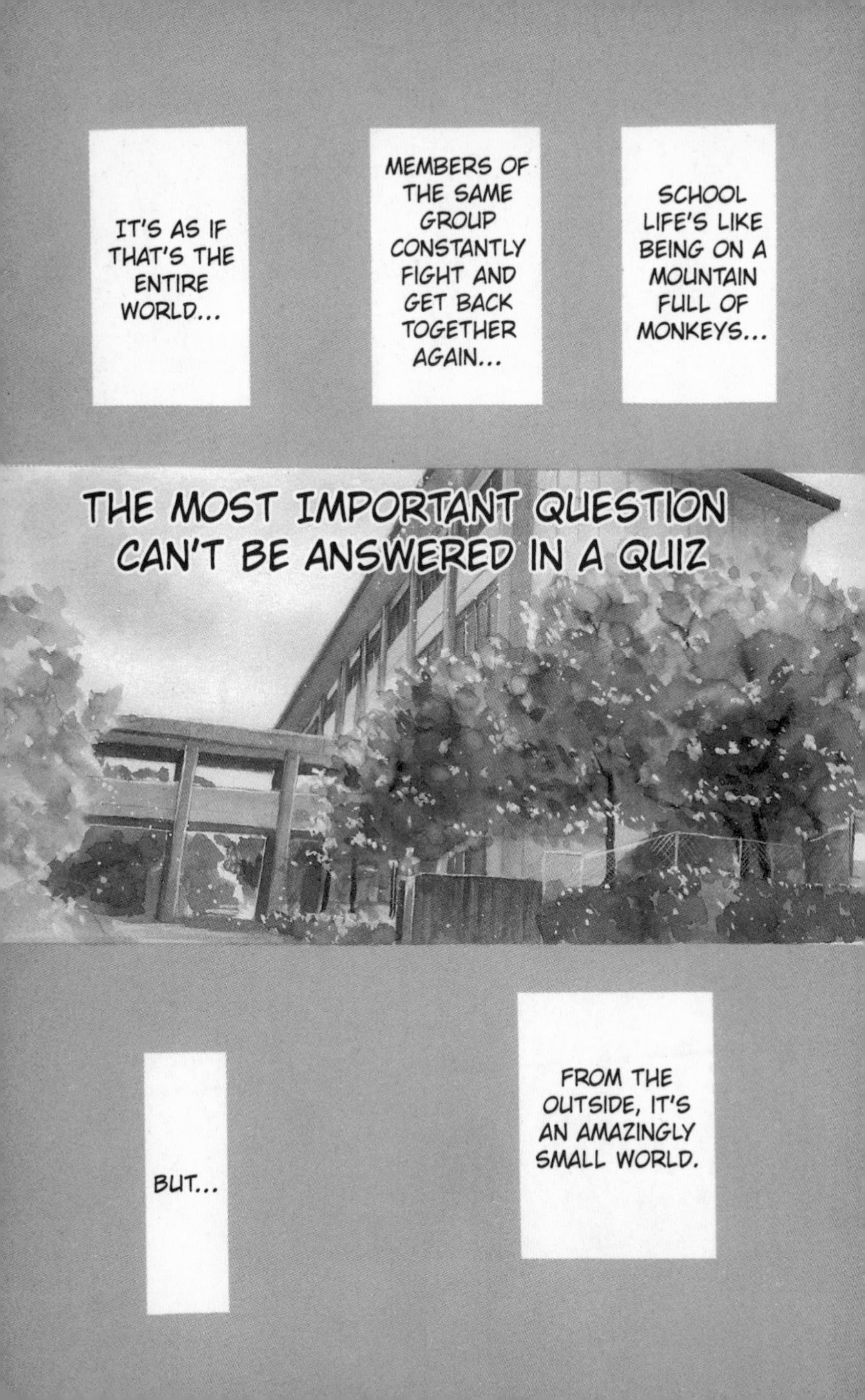
SCHOOL LIFE'S LIKE BEING ON A MOUNTAIN FULL OF MONKEYS...
MEMBERS OF THE SAME GROUP CONSTANTLY FIGHT AND GET BACK TOGETHER AGAIN...
IT'S AS IF THAT'S THE ENTIRE WORLD...
THE MOST IMPORTANT QUESTION CAN'T BE ANSWERED IN A QUIZ
FROM THE OUTSIDE, IT'S AN AMAZINGLY SMALL WORLD.
BUT...

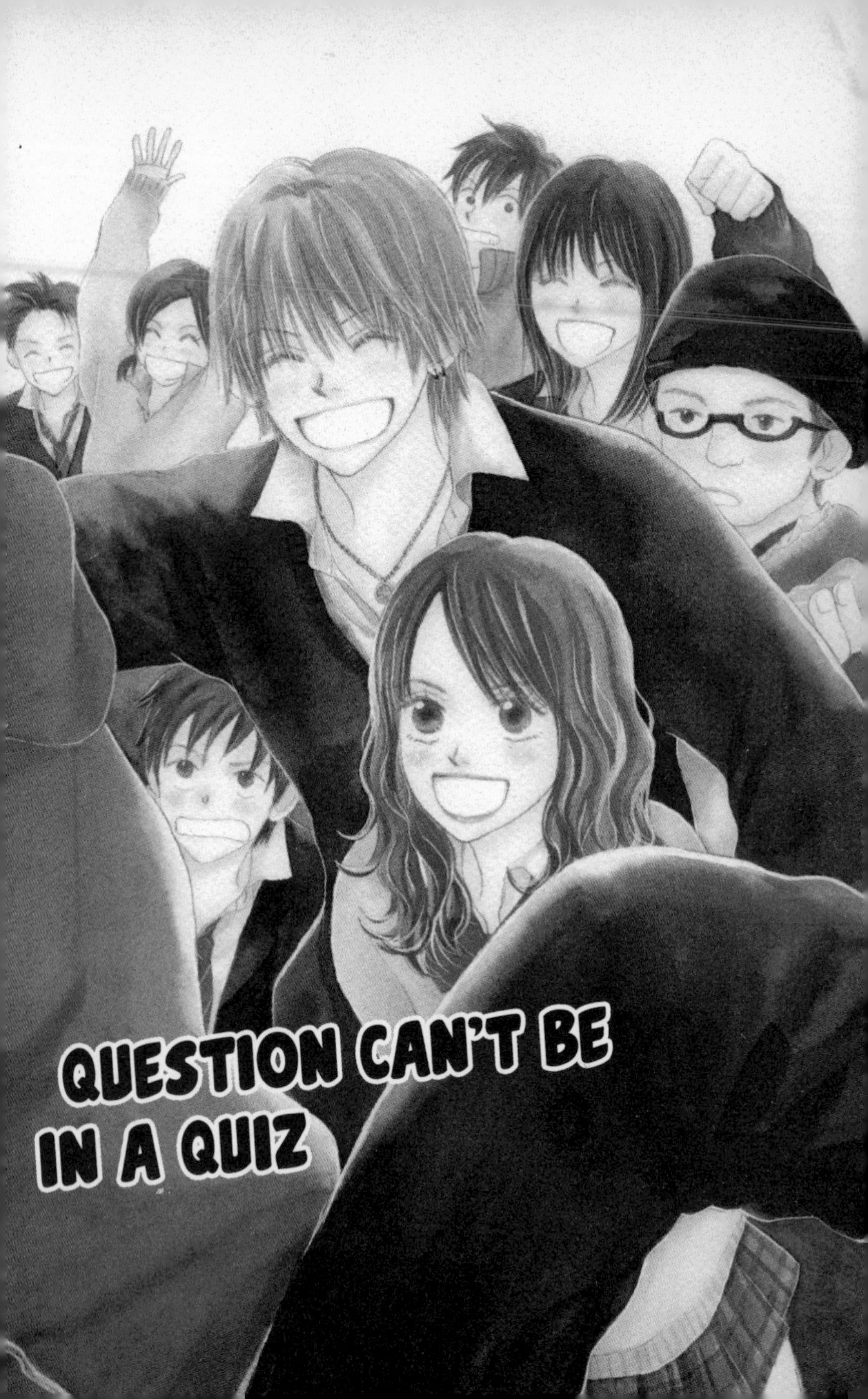
QUESTION CAN'T BE
IN A QUIZ

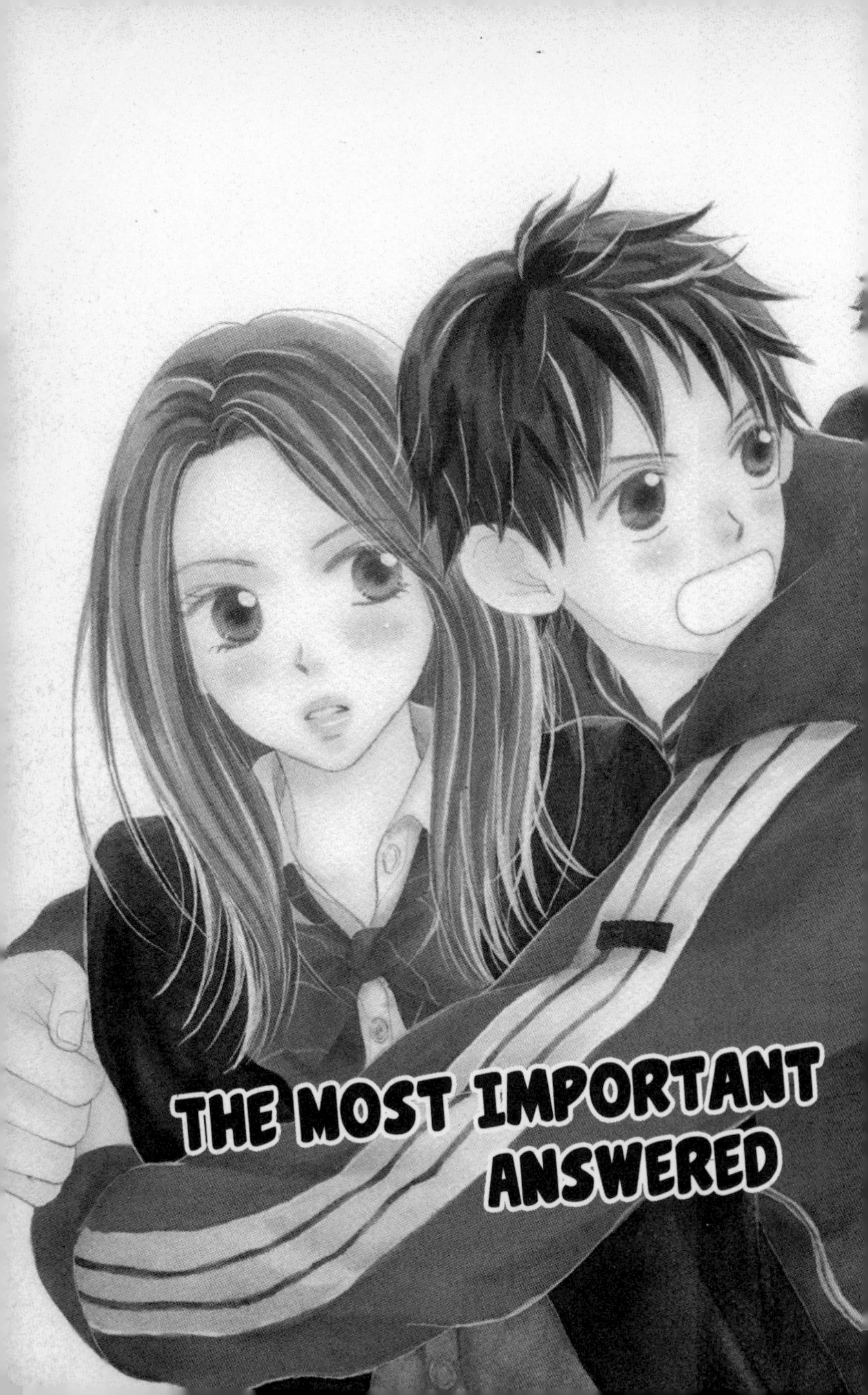
THE MOST IMPORTANT
ANSWERED

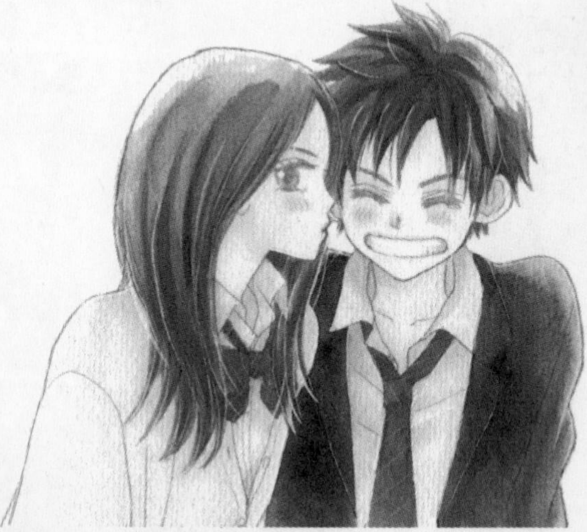

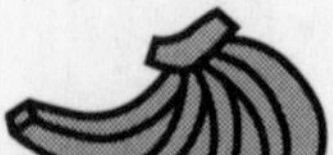

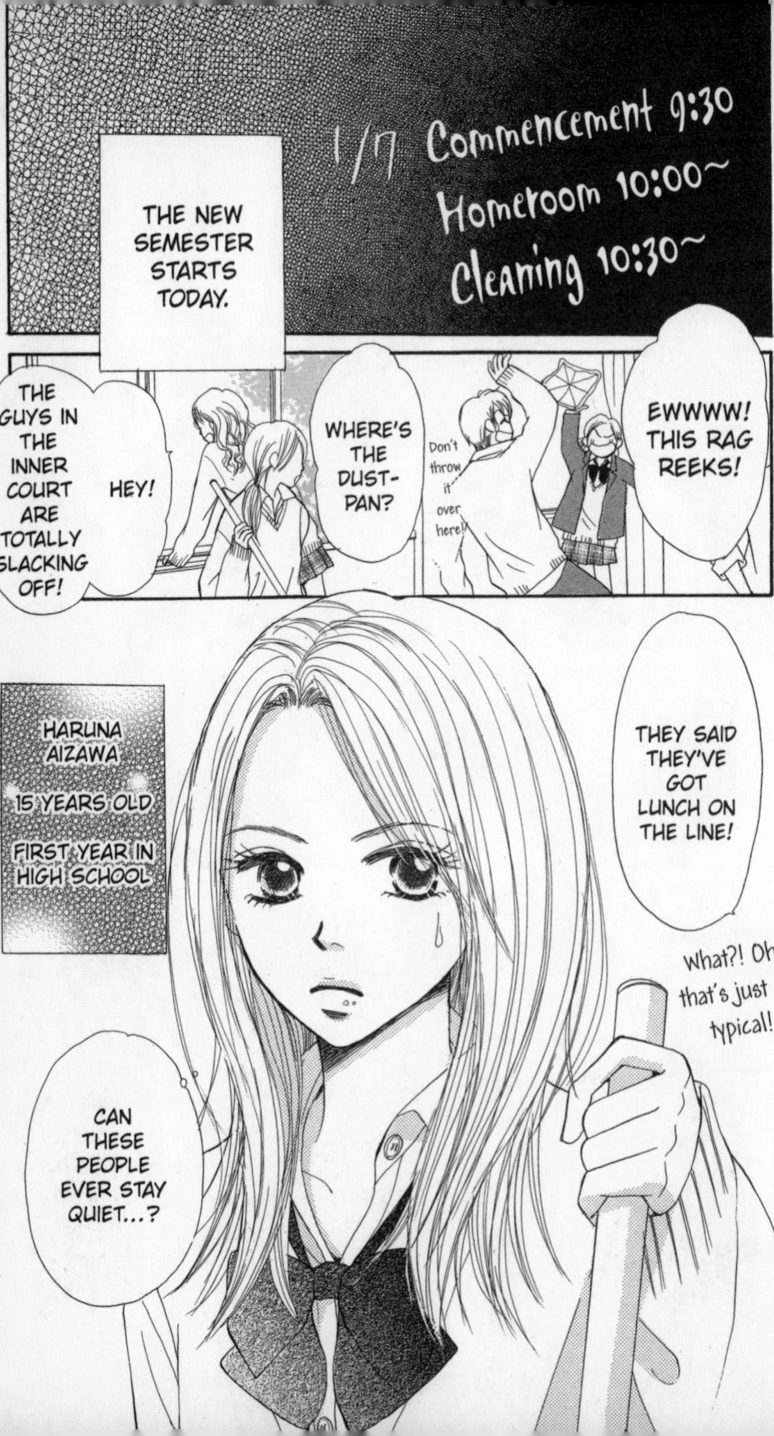
1/17 Commencement 9:30
Homeroom 10:00~
Cleaning 10:30~
THE NEW SEMESTER STARTS TODAY.
EWWWW! THIS RAG REEKS!
Don't throw it over here!
WHERE'S THE DUST-PAN?
HEY!
THE GUYS IN THE INNER COURT ARE TOTALLY SLACKING OFF!
THEY SAID THEY'VE GOT LUNCH ON THE LINE!
What?! Oh, that's just so typical!
HARUNA AIZAWA
15 YEARS OLD
FIRST YEAR IN HIGH SCHOOL
CAN THESE PEOPLE EVER STAY QUIET...?

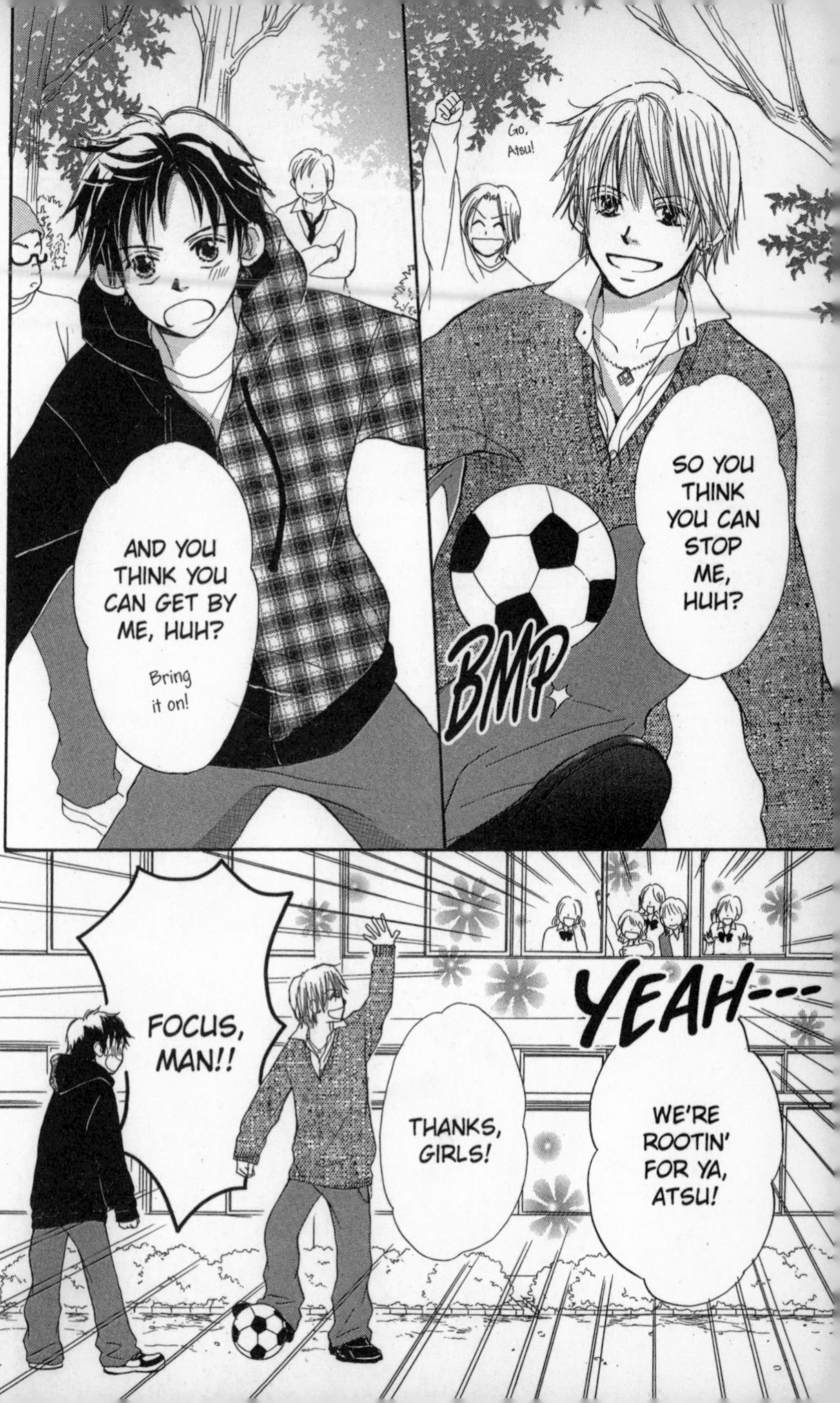
Go, Atsu!
SO YOU THINK YOU CAN STOP ME, HUH?
BMP
AND YOU THINK YOU CAN GET BY ME, HUH?
Bring it on!
YEAH---
WE'RE ROOTIN' FOR YA, ATSU!
THANKS, GIRLS!
FOCUS, MAN!!

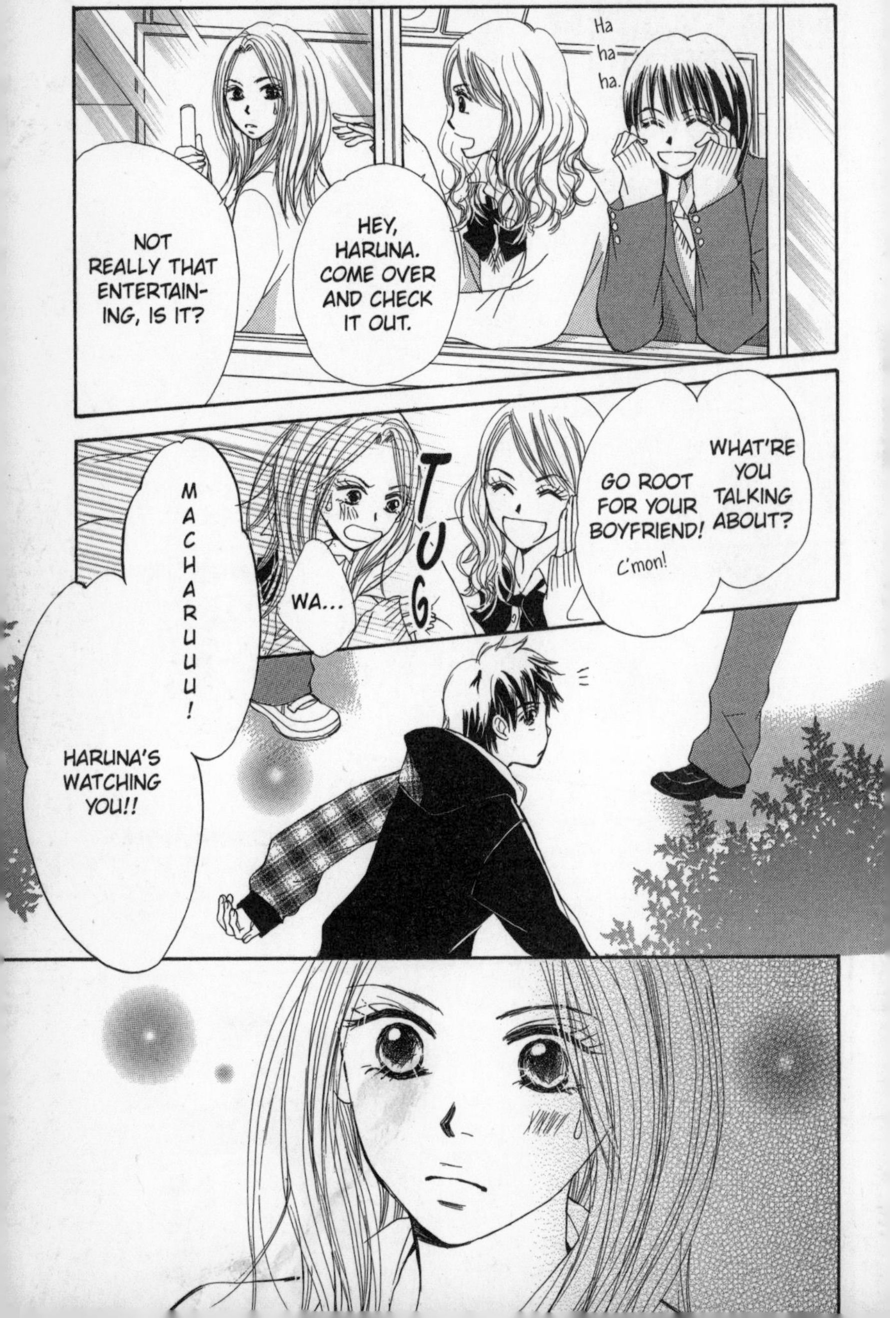
Ha ha ha.
HEY, HARUNA. COME OVER AND CHECK IT OUT.
NOT REALLY THAT ENTERTAIN-ING, IS IT?
WHAT'RE YOU TALKING ABOUT?
GO ROOT FOR YOUR BOYFRIEND!
C'mon!
TUG
WA...
MACHARUUUU!
HARUNA'S WATCHING YOU!!

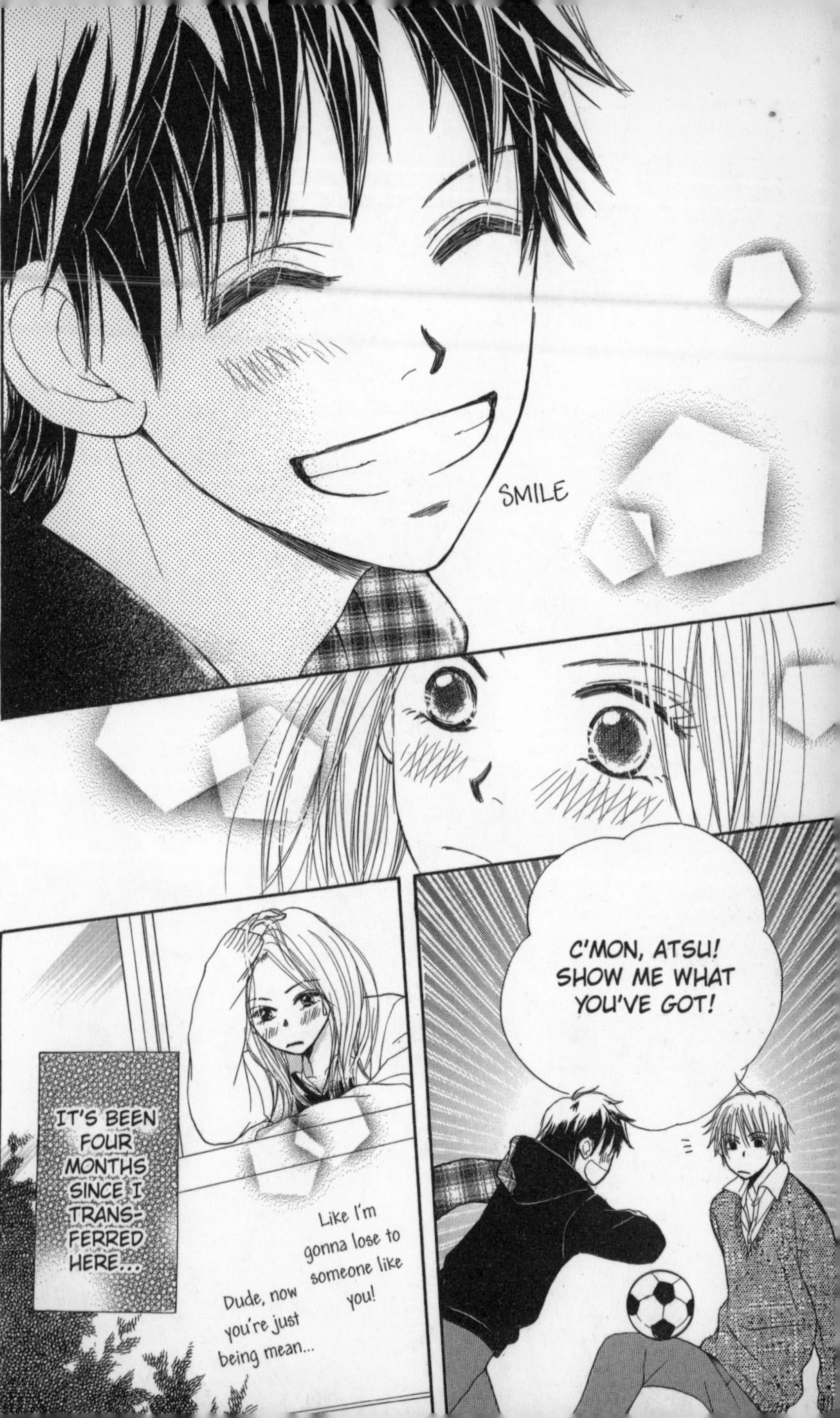
SMILE
C'MON, ATSU! SHOW ME WHAT YOU'VE GOT!
Like I'm gonna lose to someone like you!
Dude, now you're just being mean...
IT'S BEEN FOUR MONTHS SINCE I TRANSFERRED HERE...

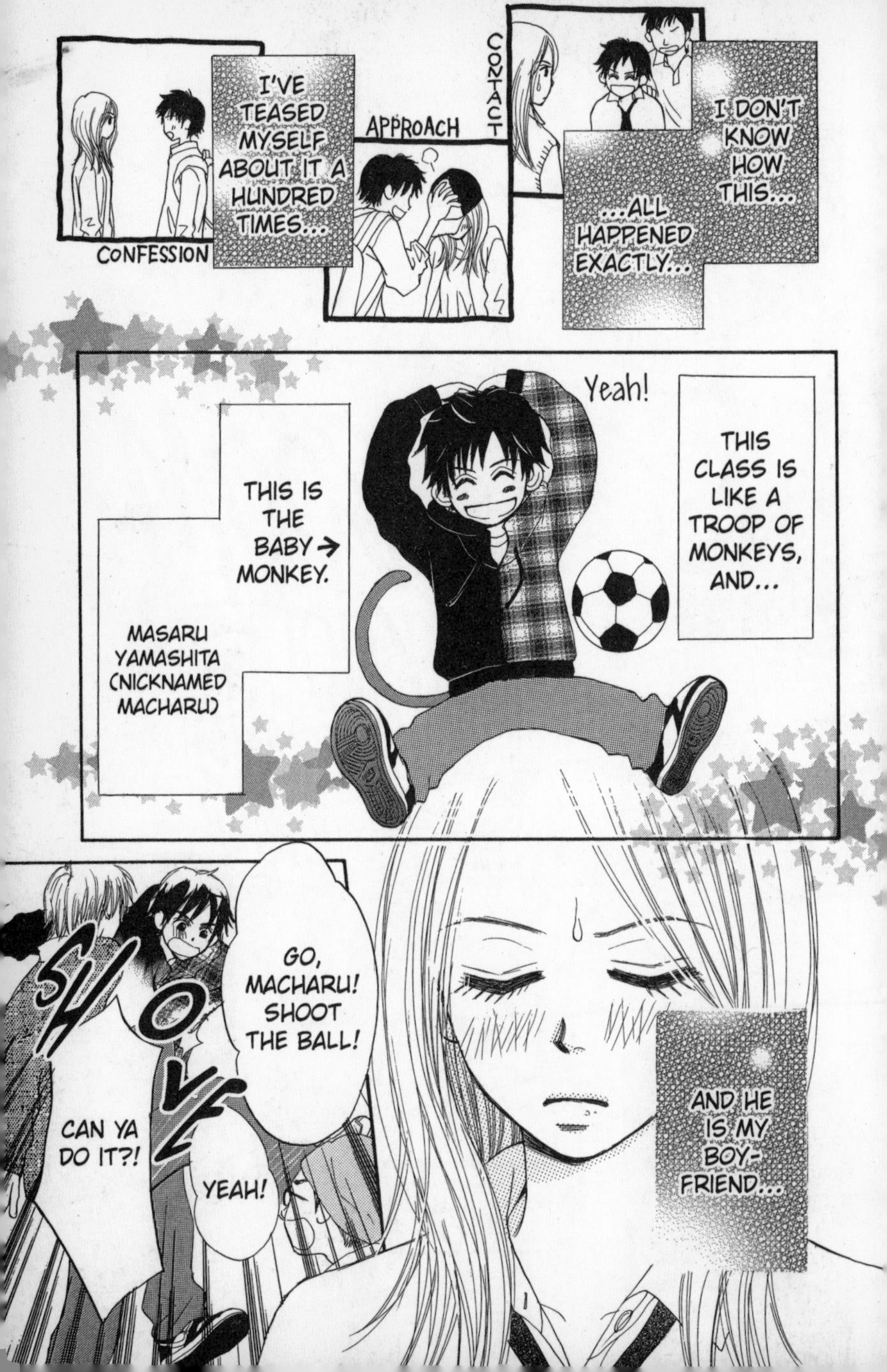
CONTACT
I DON'T KNOW HOW THIS...
...ALL HAPPENED EXACTLY...
APPROACH
I'VE TEASED MYSELF ABOUT IT A HUNDRED TIMES...
CONFESSION
Yeah!
THIS CLASS IS LIKE A TROOP OF MONKEYS, AND...
THIS IS THE BABY → MONKEY.
MASARU YAMASHITA (NICKNAMED MACHARU)
AND HE IS MY BOY-FRIEND...
GO, MACHARU! SHOOT THE BALL!
SHOVE
CAN YA DO IT?!
YEAH!

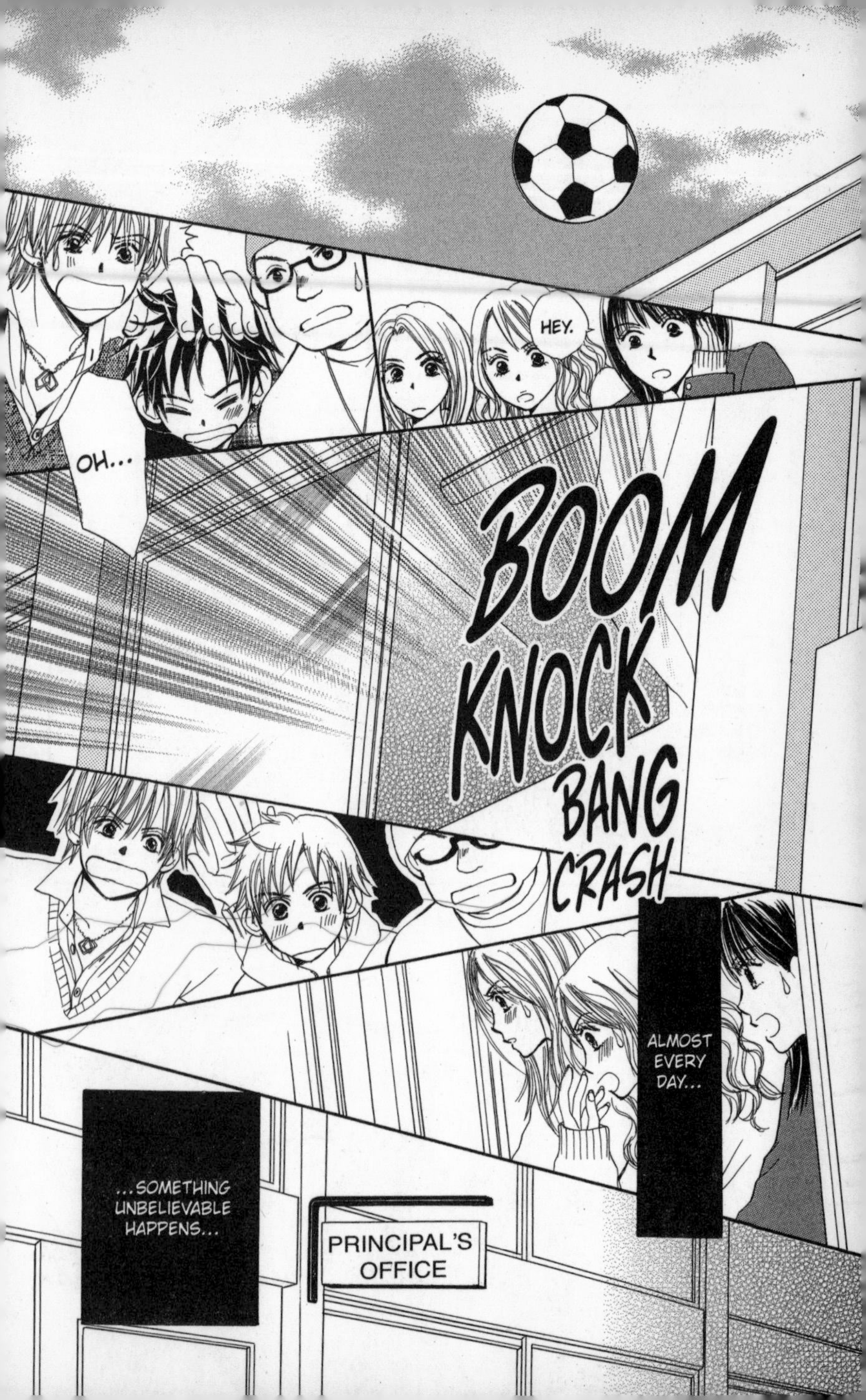
HEY.
OH...
BOOM
KNOCK
BANG
CRASH
ALMOST EVERY DAY...
...SOMETHING UNBELIEVABLE HAPPENS...
PRINCIPAL'S OFFICE

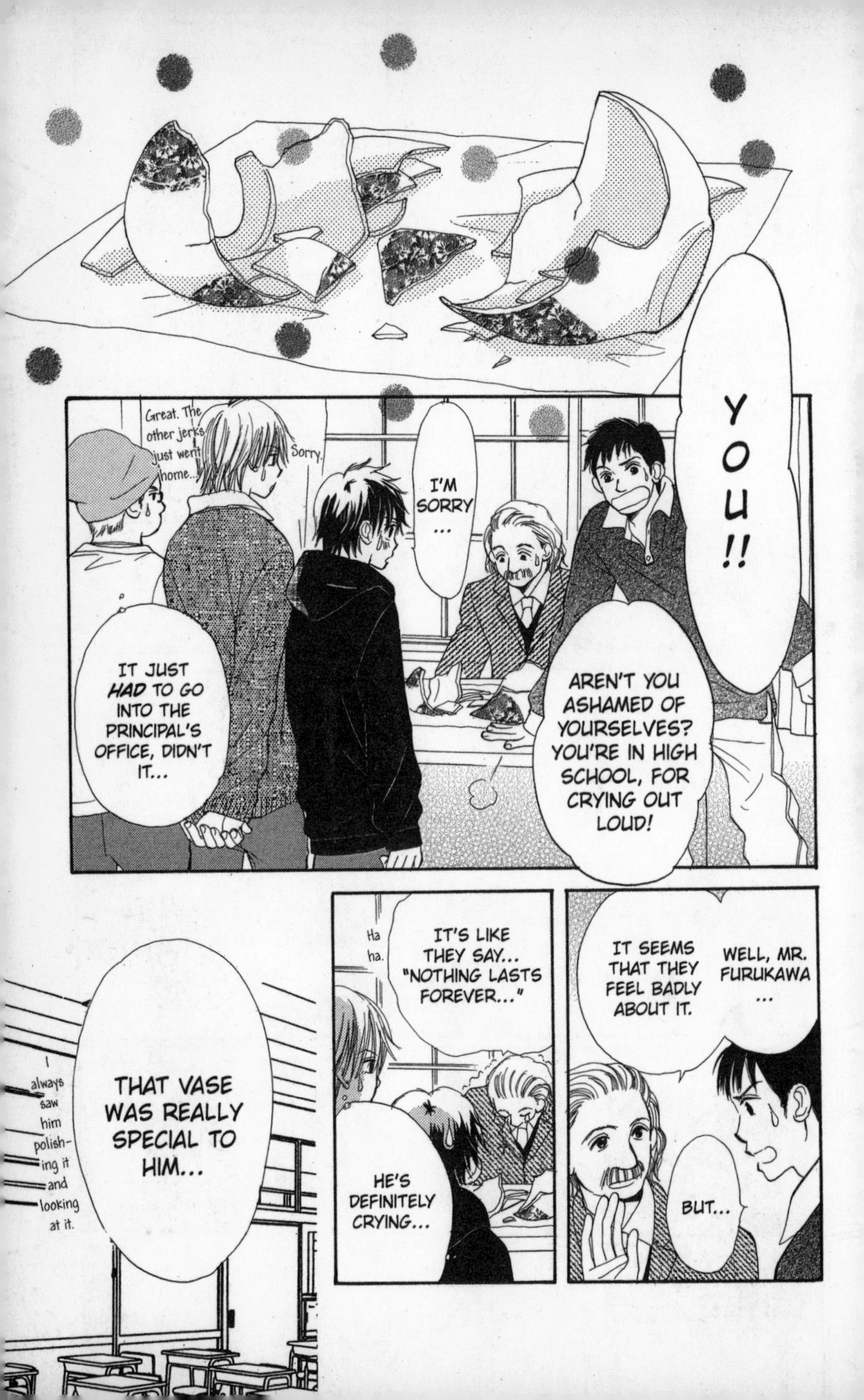
YOU!!
AREN'T YOU ASHAMED OF YOURSELVES? YOU'RE IN HIGH SCHOOL, FOR CRYING OUT LOUD!
I'M SORRY...
Sorry.
Great. The other jerks just went home...
IT JUST HAD TO GO INTO THE PRINCIPAL'S OFFICE, DIDN'T IT...
WELL, MR. FURUKAWA...
IT SEEMS THAT THEY FEEL BADLY ABOUT IT.
BUT...
IT'S LIKE THEY SAY... "NOTHING LASTS FOREVER..."
Ha ha.
HE'S DEFINITELY CRYING...
THAT VASE WAS REALLY SPECIAL TO HIM...
I always saw him polish-ing it and looking at it.

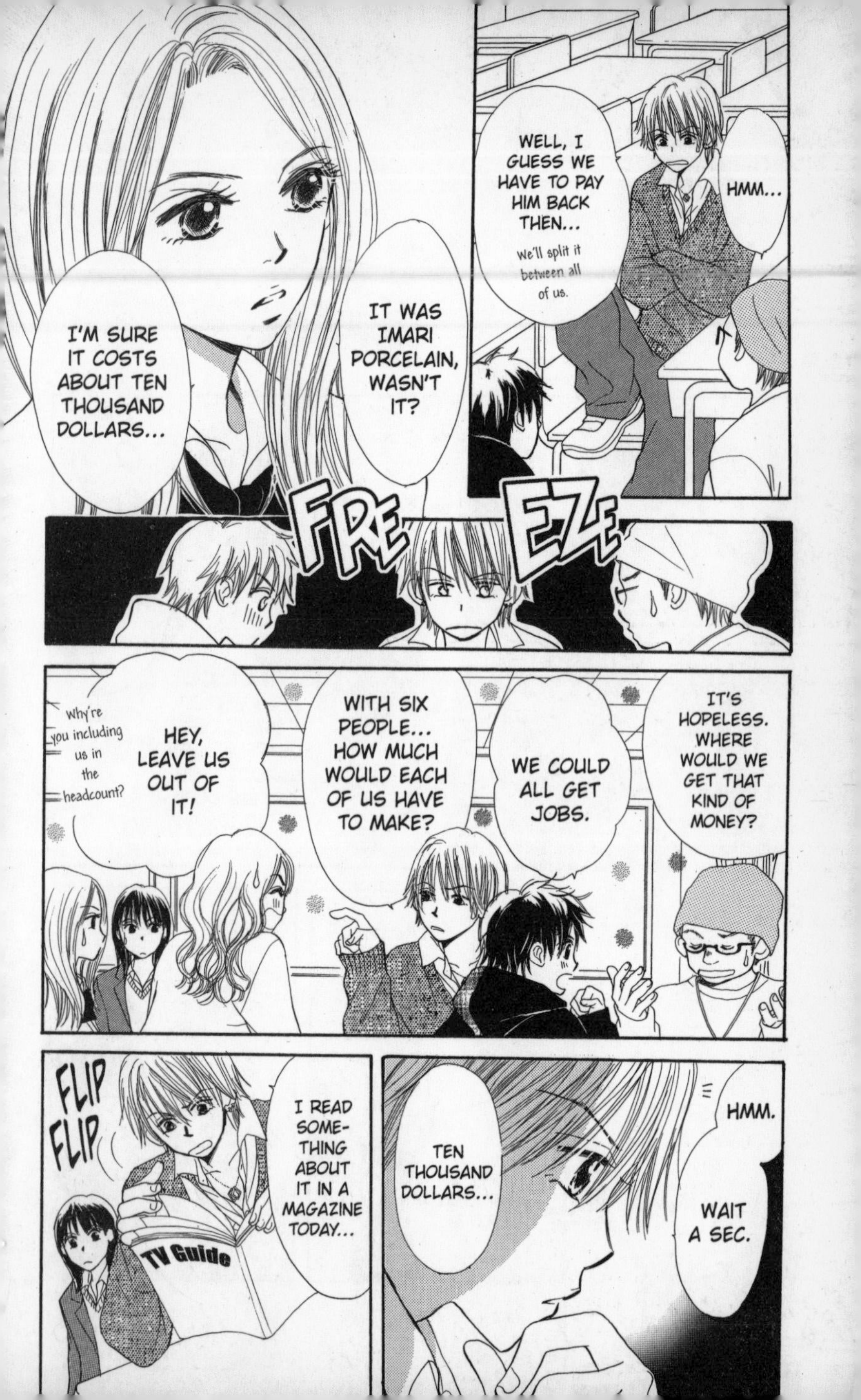
HMM...
WELL, I GUESS WE HAVE TO PAY HIM BACK THEN...
We'll split it between all of us.
IT WAS IMARI PORCELAIN, WASN'T IT?
I'M SURE IT COSTS ABOUT TEN THOUSAND DOLLARS...
FREEZE
IT'S HOPELESS. WHERE WOULD WE GET THAT KIND OF MONEY?
WE COULD ALL GET JOBS.
WITH SIX PEOPLE... HOW MUCH WOULD EACH OF US HAVE TO MAKE?
HEY, LEAVE US OUT OF IT!
Why're you including us in the headcount?
HMM.
WAIT A SEC.
TEN THOUSAND DOLLARS...
I READ SOME-THING ABOUT IT IN A MAGAZINE TODAY...
FLIP FLIP
TV Guide

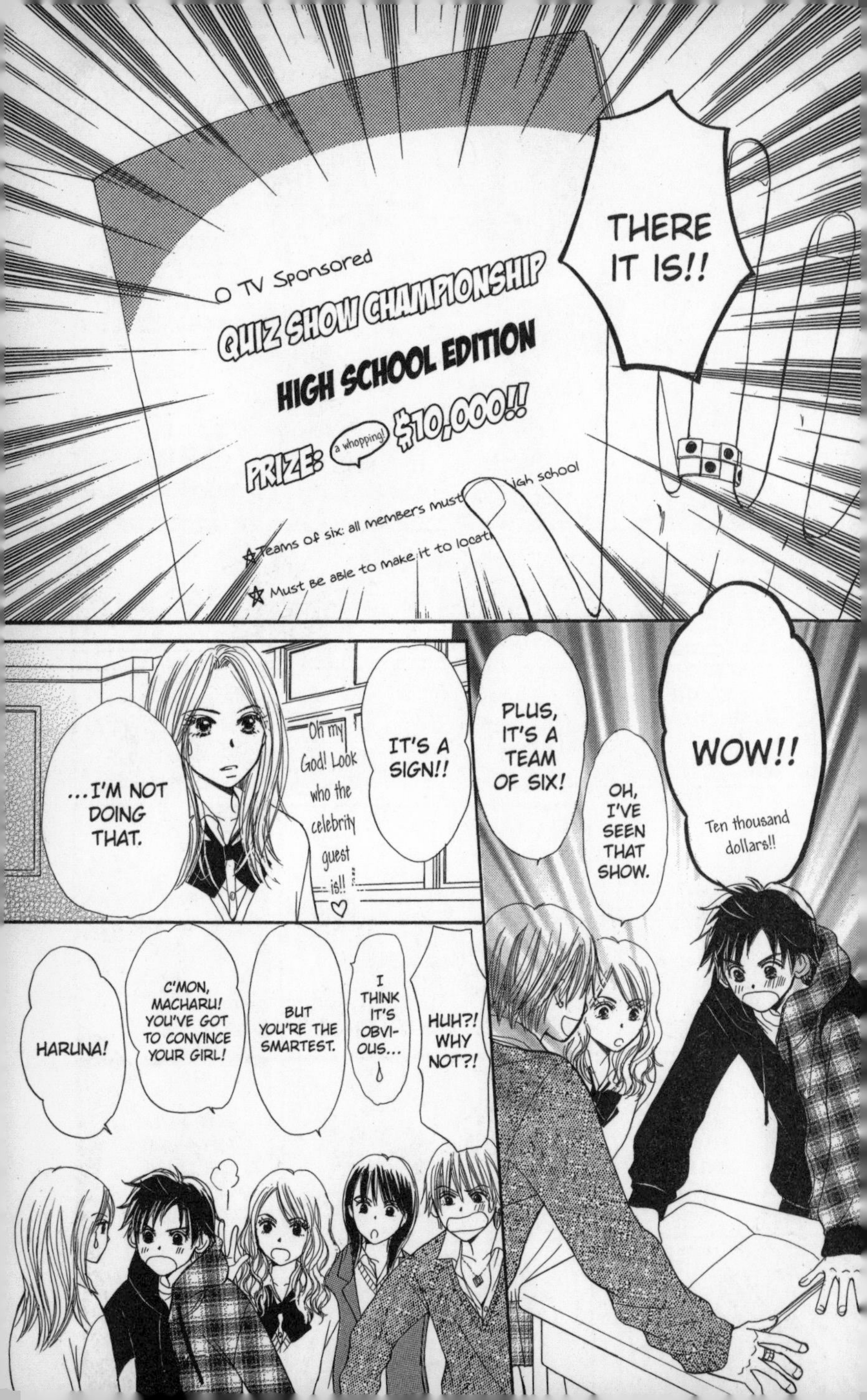

O TV Sponsored
QUIZ SHOW CHAMPIONSHIP
HIGH SCHOOL EDITION
PRIZE: a whopping! $10,000!!
☆Teams of six: all members must igh school
☆ Must be able to make it to locat
THERE IT IS!!
WOW!!
Ten thousand dollars!!
PLUS, IT'S A TEAM OF SIX!
OH, I'VE SEEN THAT SHOW.
IT'S A SIGN!!
Oh my God! Look who the celebrity guest is!! ♡
...I'M NOT DOING THAT.
HUH?! WHY NOT?!
I THINK IT'S OBVI-OUS...
BUT YOU'RE THE SMARTEST.
C'MON, MACHARU! YOU'VE GOT TO CONVINCE YOUR GIRL!
HARUNA!

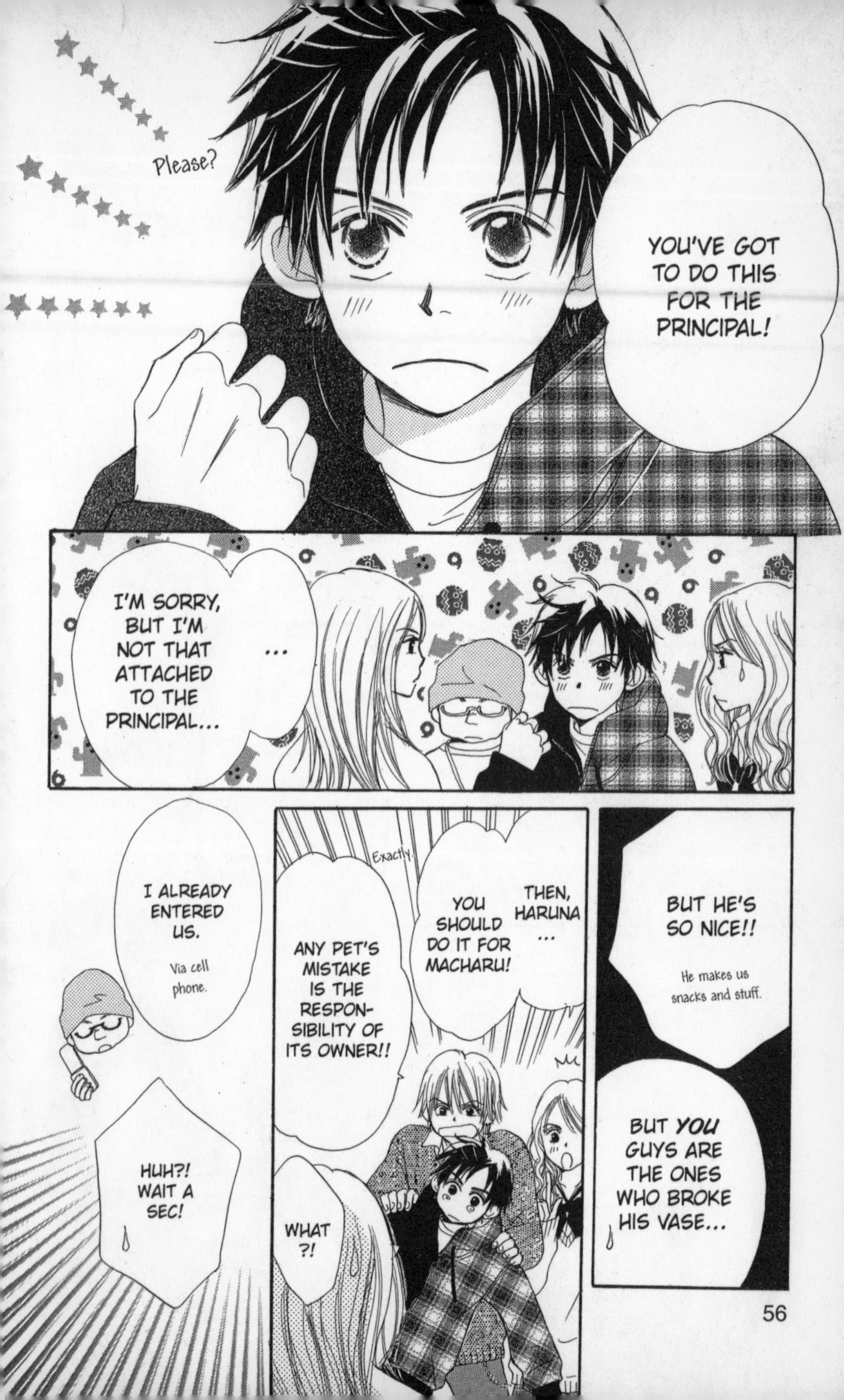
YOU'VE GOT TO DO THIS FOR THE PRINCIPAL!
Please?
...
I'M SORRY, BUT I'M NOT THAT ATTACHED TO THE PRINCIPAL...
BUT HE'S SO NICE!!
He makes us snacks and stuff.
BUT *YOU* GUYS ARE THE ONES WHO BROKE HIS VASE...
THEN, HARUNA...
YOU SHOULD DO IT FOR MACHARU!
Exactly.
ANY PET'S MISTAKE IS THE RESPONSIBILITY OF ITS OWNER!!
WHAT?!
I ALREADY ENTERED US.
Via cell phone.
HUH?! WAIT A SEC!

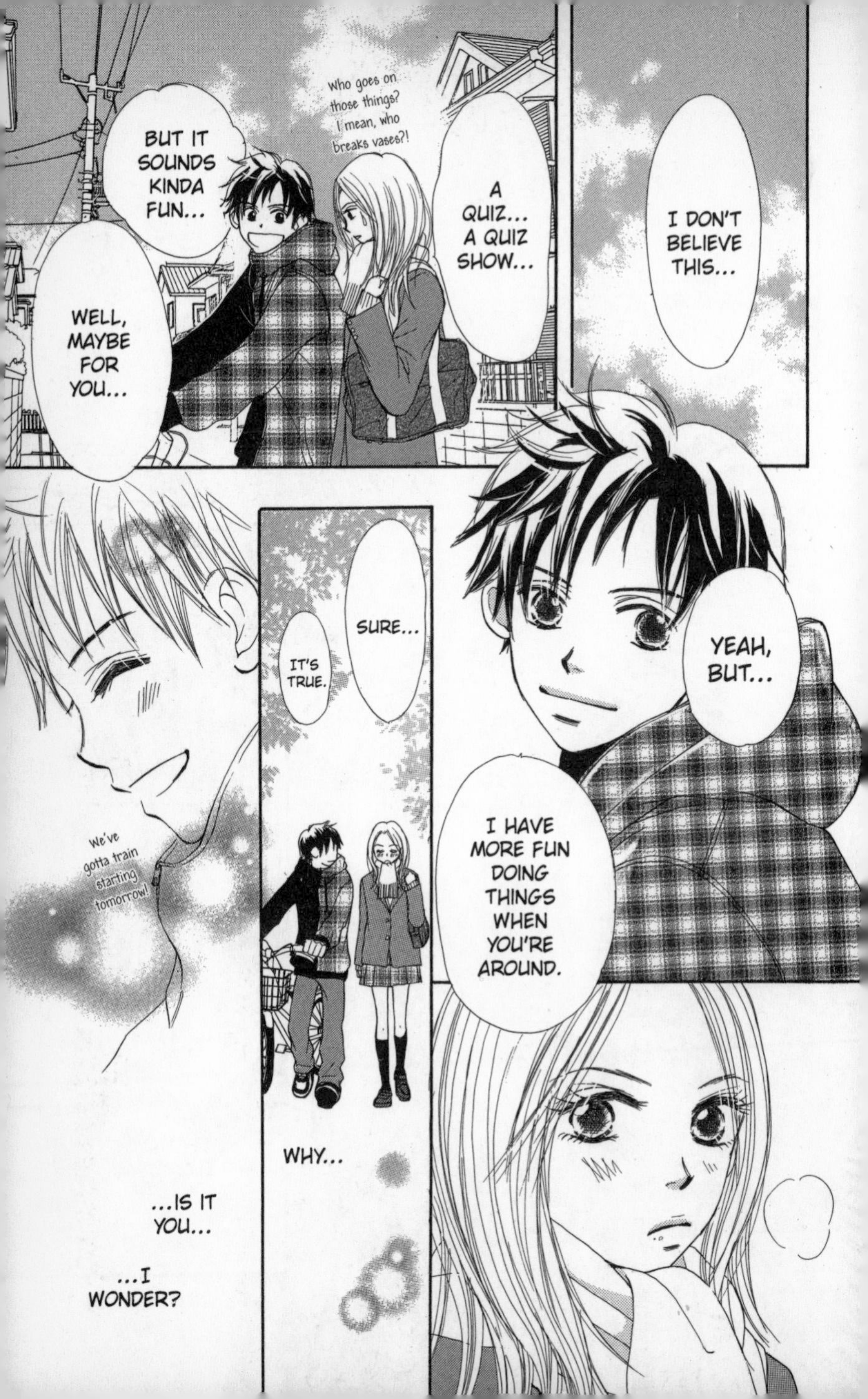
I DON'T BELIEVE THIS...
A QUIZ... A QUIZ SHOW...
Who goes on those things? I mean, who breaks vases?!
BUT IT SOUNDS KINDA FUN...
WELL, MAYBE FOR YOU...
YEAH, BUT...
I HAVE MORE FUN DOING THINGS WHEN YOU'RE AROUND.
SURE...
IT'S TRUE.
We've gotta train starting tomorrow!
WHY...
...IS IT YOU...
...I WONDER?

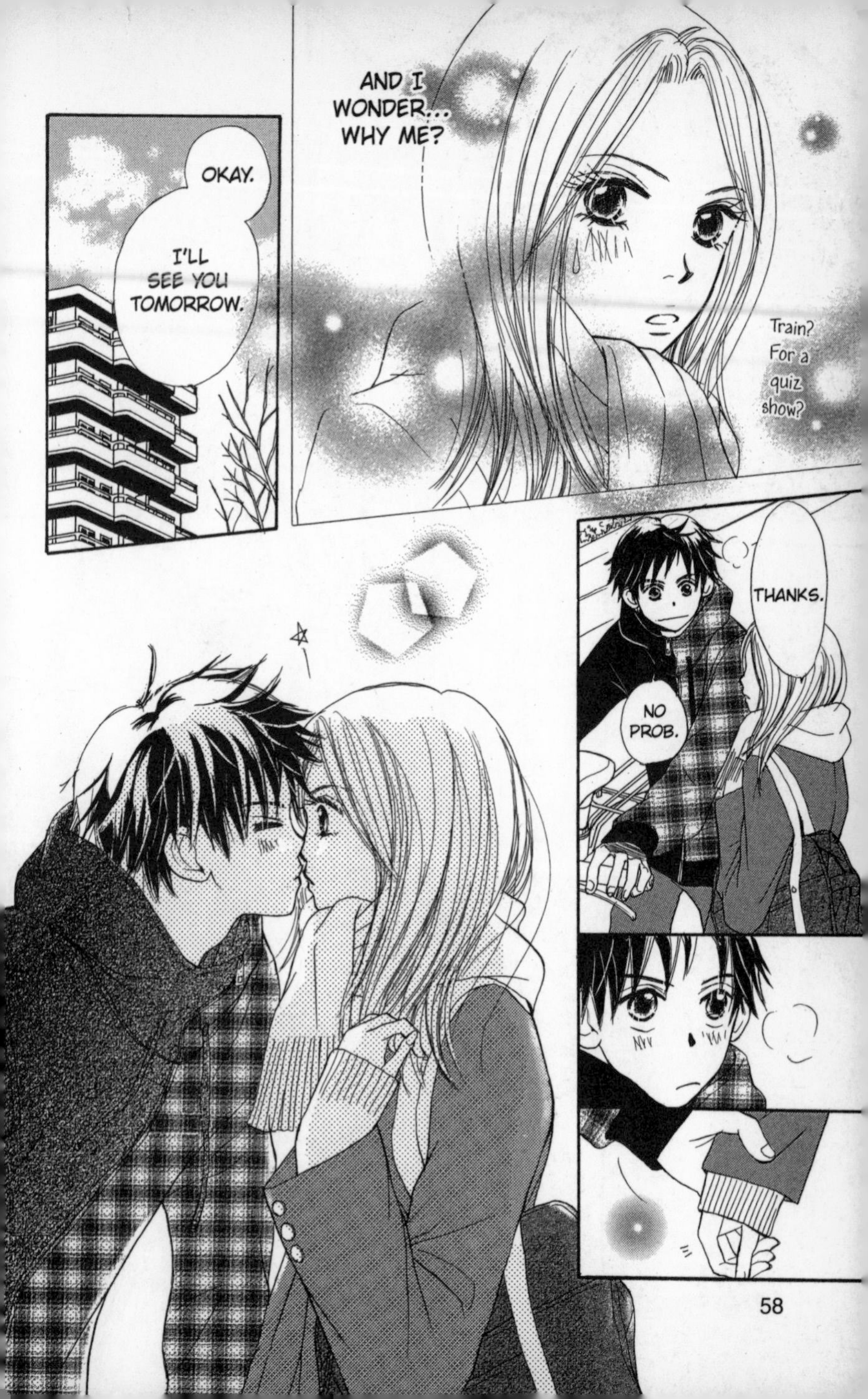
AND I WONDER... WHY ME?
Train? For a quiz show?
OKAY.
I'LL SEE YOU TOMORROW.
THANKS.
NO PROB.

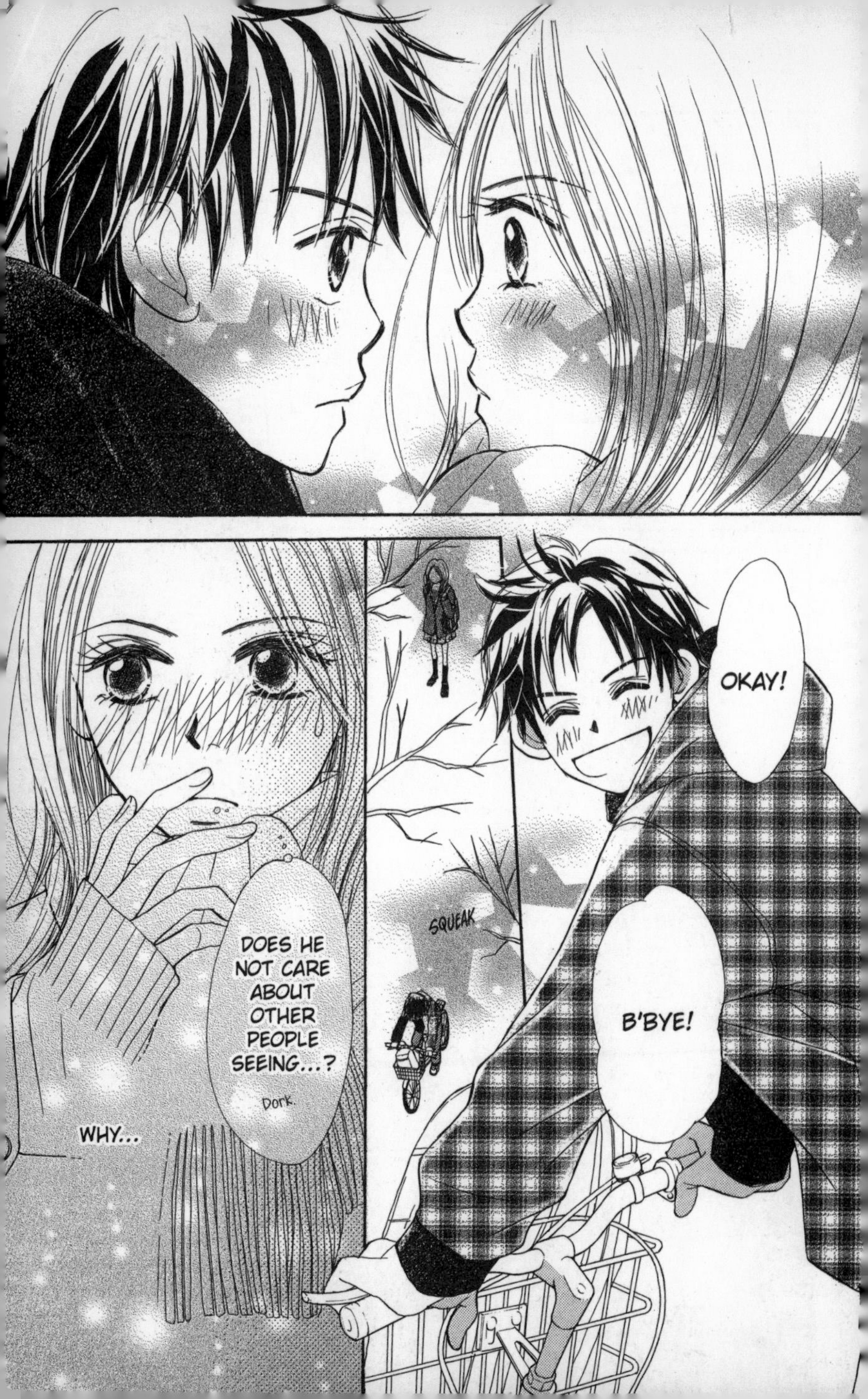
OKAY!
SQUEAK
B'BYE!
DOES HE NOT CARE ABOUT OTHER PEOPLE SEEING...?
Dork.
WHY...

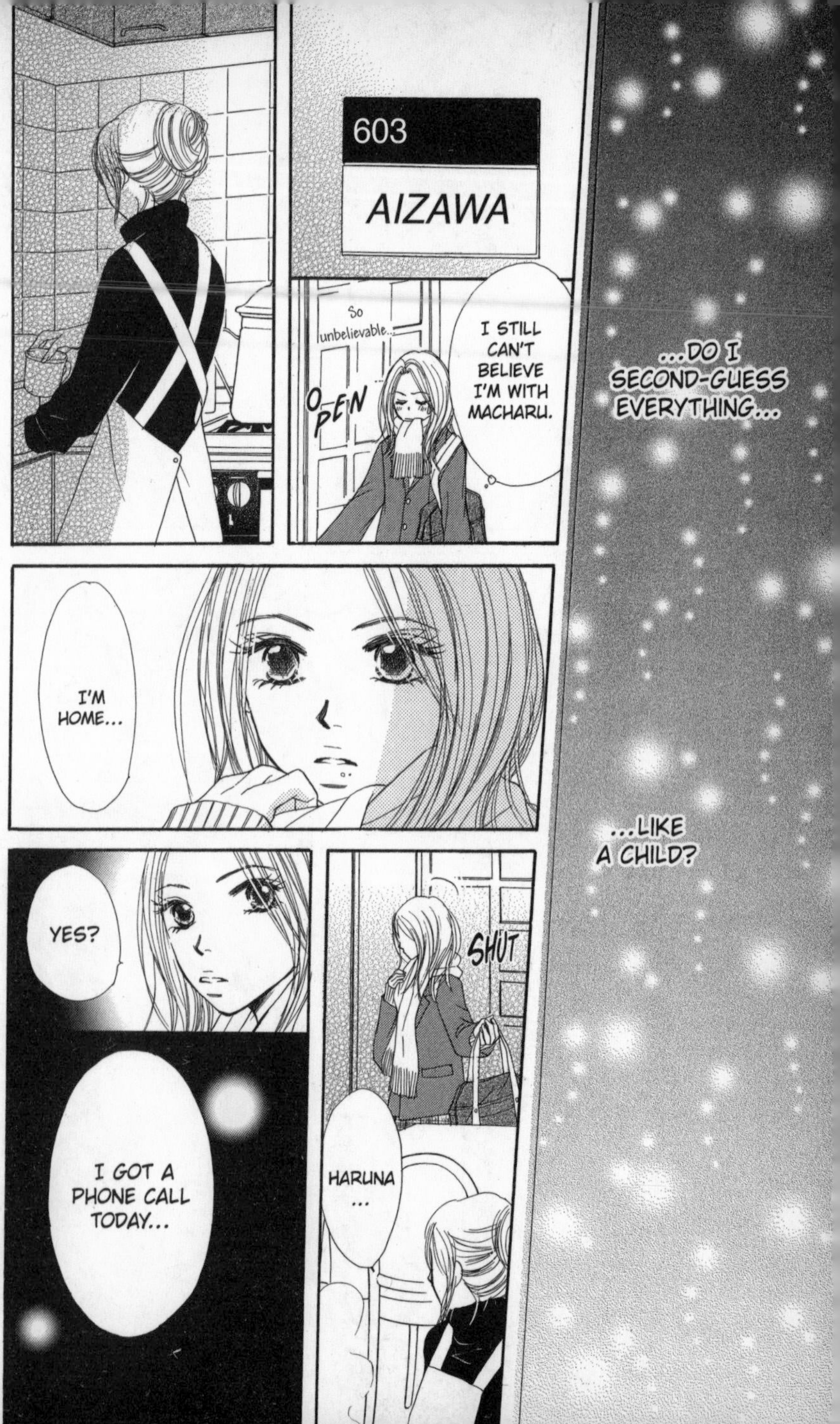
...DO I SECOND-GUESS EVERYTHING...
...LIKE A CHILD?
603
AIZAWA
I STILL CAN'T BELIEVE I'M WITH MACHARU.
So unbelievable...
OPEN
I'M HOME...
SHUT
HARUNA ...
YES?
I GOT A PHONE CALL TODAY...

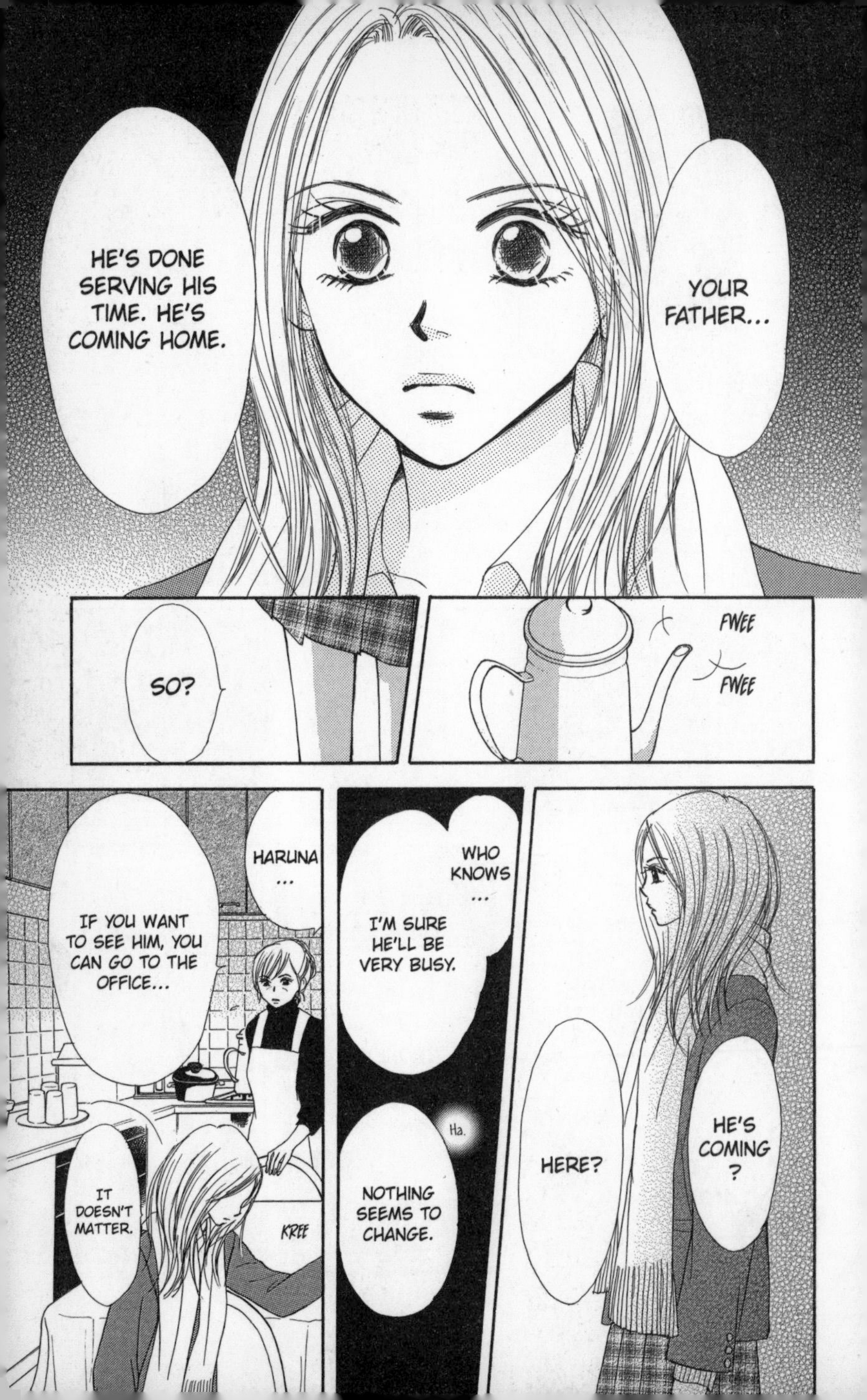
YOUR FATHER...
HE'S DONE SERVING HIS TIME. HE'S COMING HOME.
FWEE
FWEE
SO?
HE'S COMING?
HERE?
WHO KNOWS...
I'M SURE HE'LL BE VERY BUSY.
Ha.
NOTHING SEEMS TO CHANGE.
HARUNA...
IF YOU WANT TO SEE HIM, YOU CAN GO TO THE OFFICE...
IT DOESN'T MATTER.
KREE

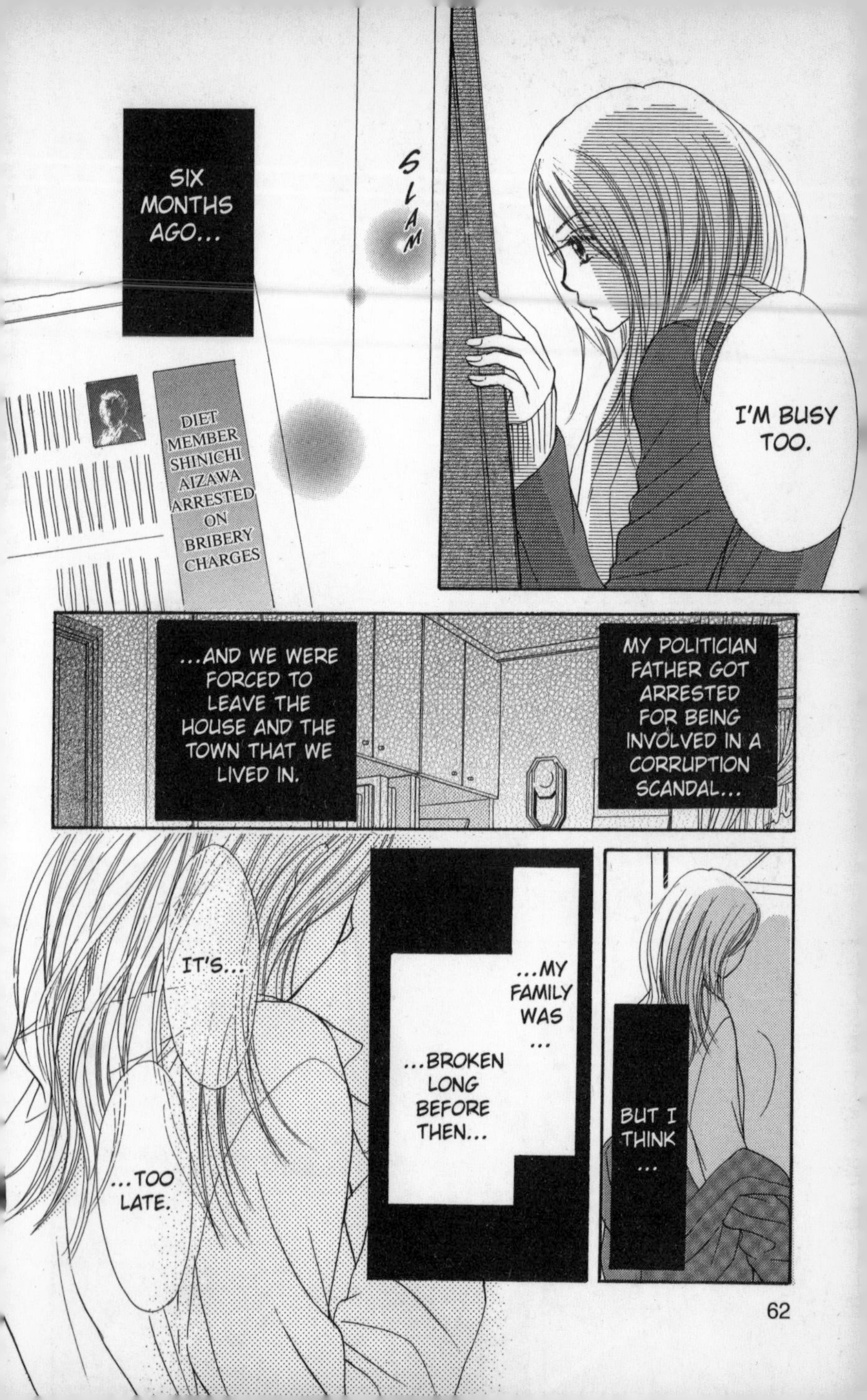
I'M BUSY TOO.
SLAM
SIX MONTHS AGO...
DIET MEMBER SHINICHI AIZAWA ARRESTED ON BRIBERY CHARGES
MY POLITICIAN FATHER GOT ARRESTED FOR BEING INVOLVED IN A CORRUPTION SCANDAL...
...AND WE WERE FORCED TO LEAVE THE HOUSE AND THE TOWN THAT WE LIVED IN.
BUT I THINK ...
...MY FAMILY WAS ...
...BROKEN LONG BEFORE THEN...
IT'S...
...TOO LATE.

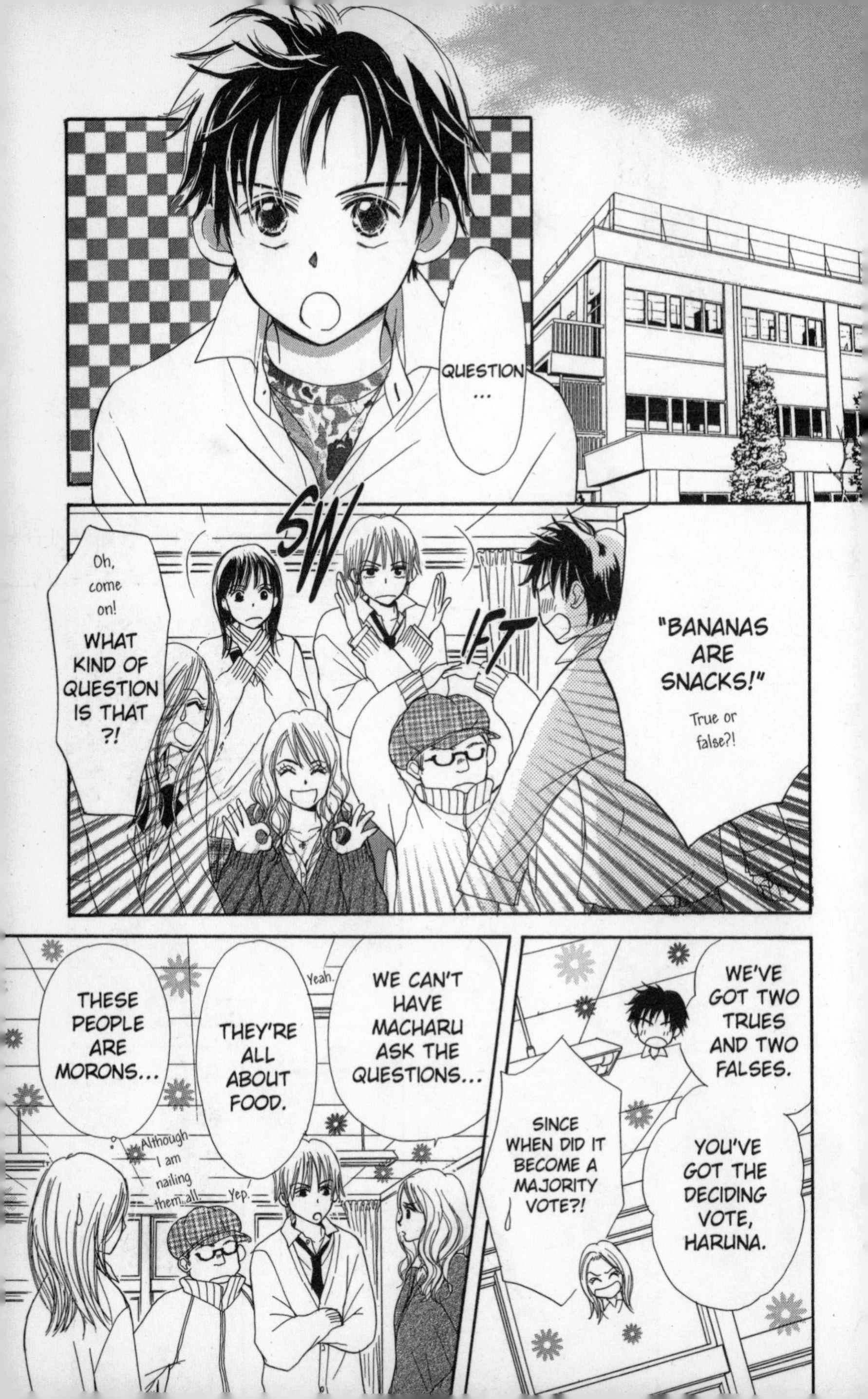
QUESTION ...
"BANANAS ARE SNACKS!"
True or false?!
SWIFT
Oh, come on!
WHAT KIND OF QUESTION IS THAT?!
WE'VE GOT TWO TRUES AND TWO FALSES.
YOU'VE GOT THE DECIDING VOTE, HARUNA.
SINCE WHEN DID IT BECOME A MAJORITY VOTE?!
WE CAN'T HAVE MACHARU ASK THE QUESTIONS...
Yeah.
THEY'RE ALL ABOUT FOOD.
Yep.
THESE PEOPLE ARE MORONS...
Although I am nailing them all.

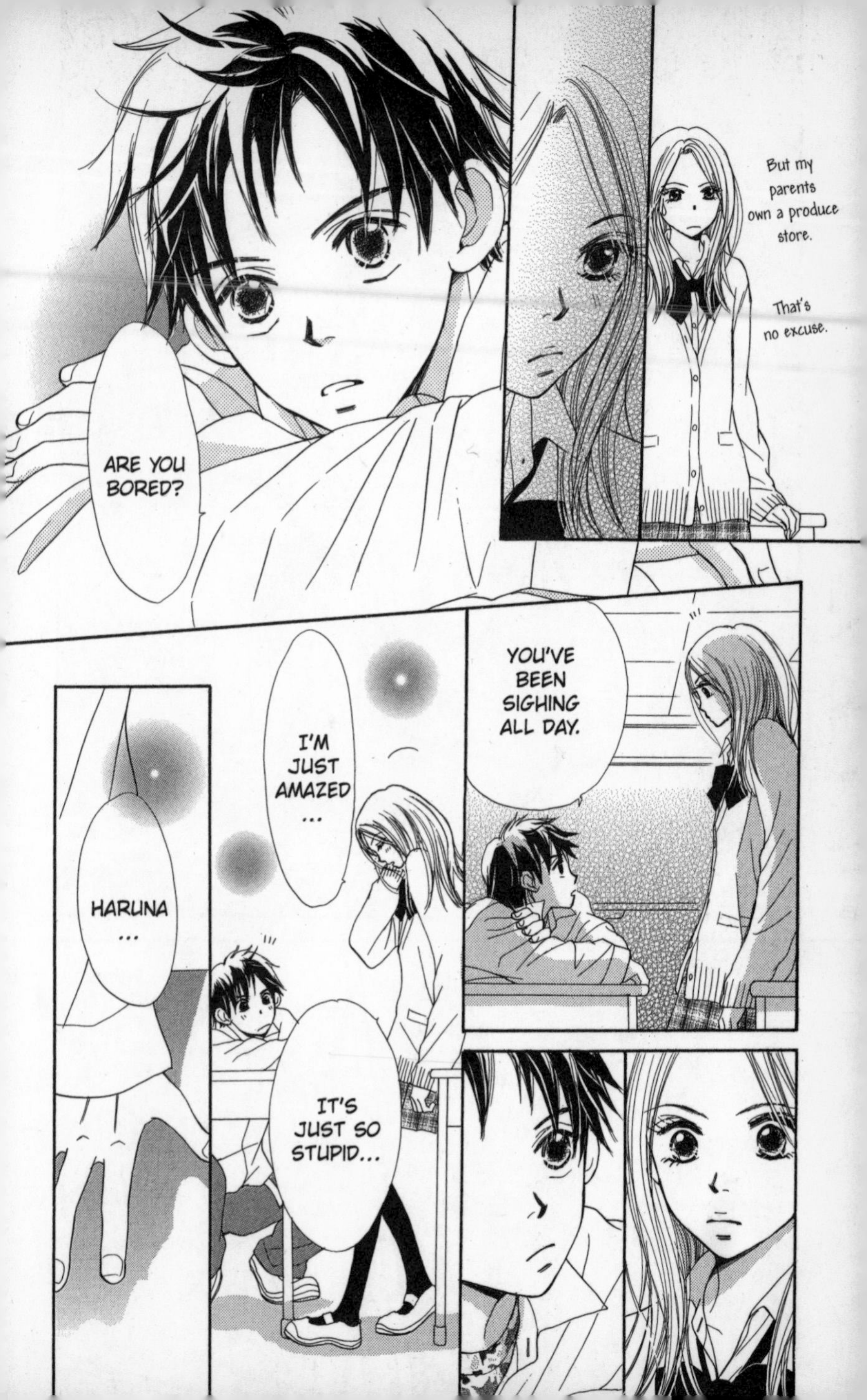
But my parents own a produce store.
That's no excuse.
ARE YOU BORED?
YOU'VE BEEN SIGHING ALL DAY.
I'M JUST AMAZED...
IT'S JUST SO STUPID...
HARUNA...

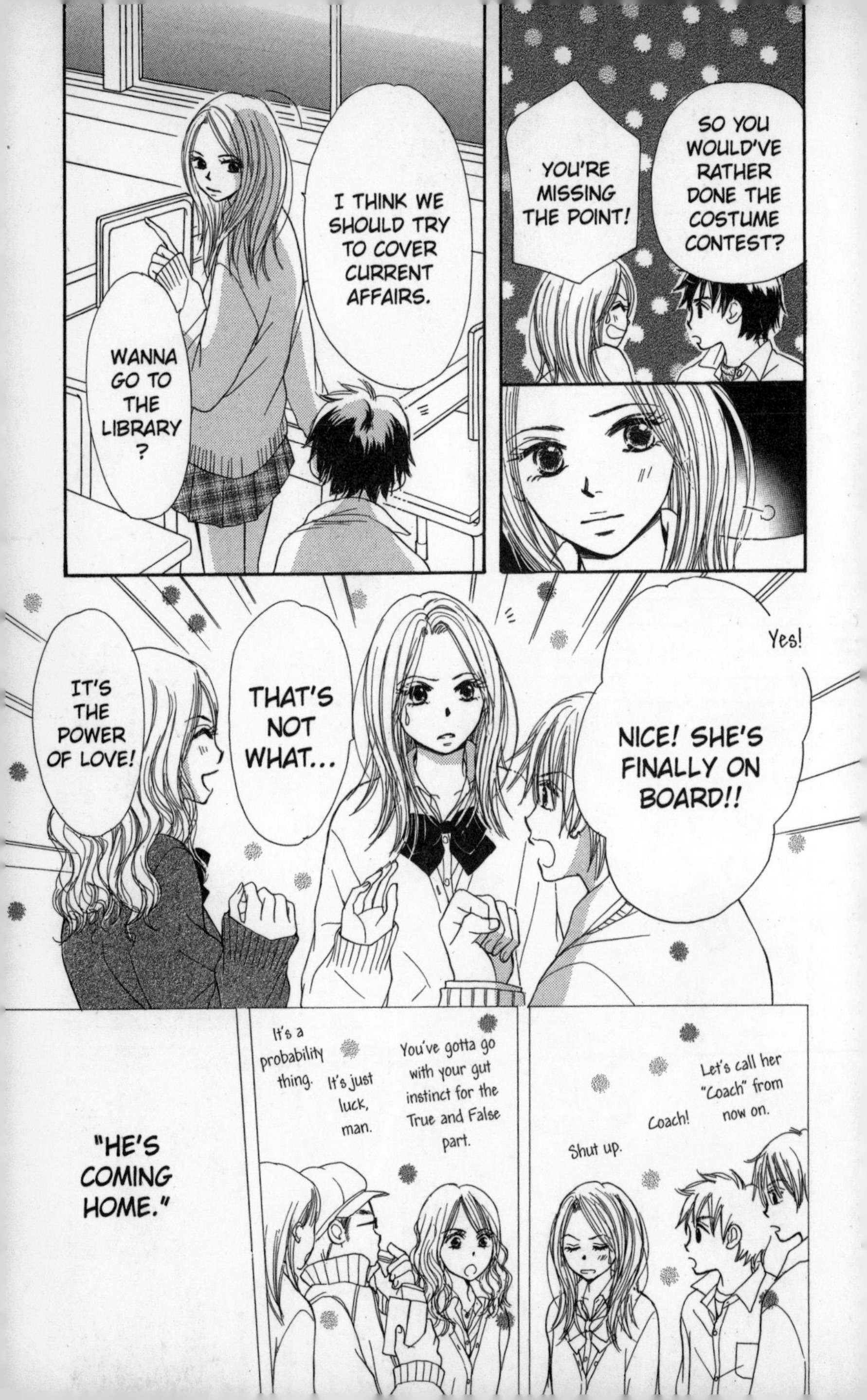
SO YOU WOULD'VE RATHER DONE THE COSTUME CONTEST?
YOU'RE MISSING THE POINT!
I THINK WE SHOULD TRY TO COVER CURRENT AFFAIRS.
WANNA GO TO THE LIBRARY?
Yes!
NICE! SHE'S FINALLY ON BOARD!!
THAT'S NOT WHAT...
IT'S THE POWER OF LOVE!
Let's call her "Coach" from now on.
Coach!
Shut up.
You've gotta go with your gut instinct for the True and False part.
It's just luck, man.
It's a probability thing.
"HE'S COMING HOME."

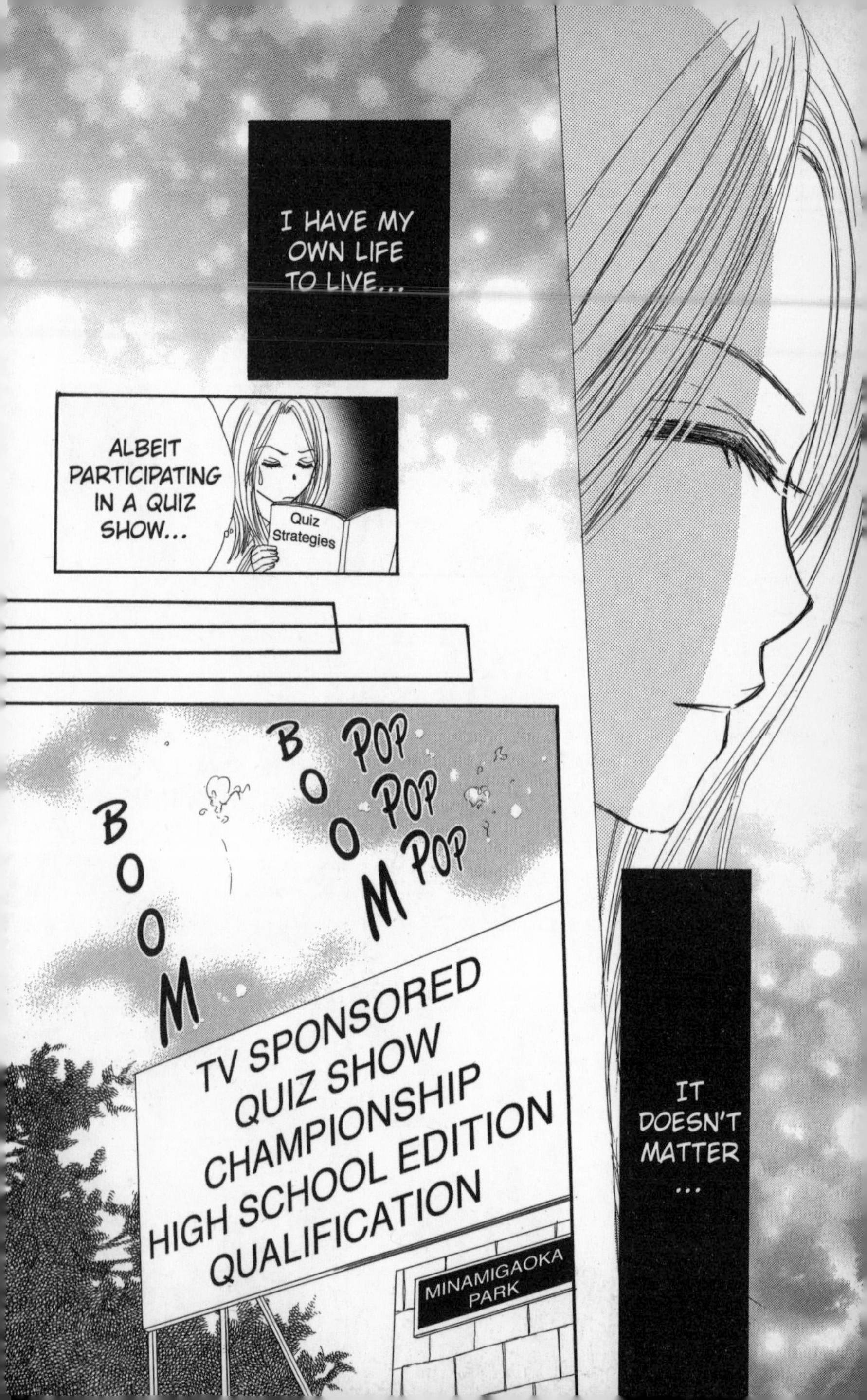
IT DOESN'T MATTER ...
I HAVE MY OWN LIFE TO LIVE...
ALBEIT PARTICIPATING IN A QUIZ SHOW...
Quiz Strategies
BOOM
BOOM
POP POP POP
TV SPONSORED QUIZ SHOW CHAMPIONSHIP HIGH SCHOOL EDITION QUALIFICATION
MINAMIGAOKA PARK

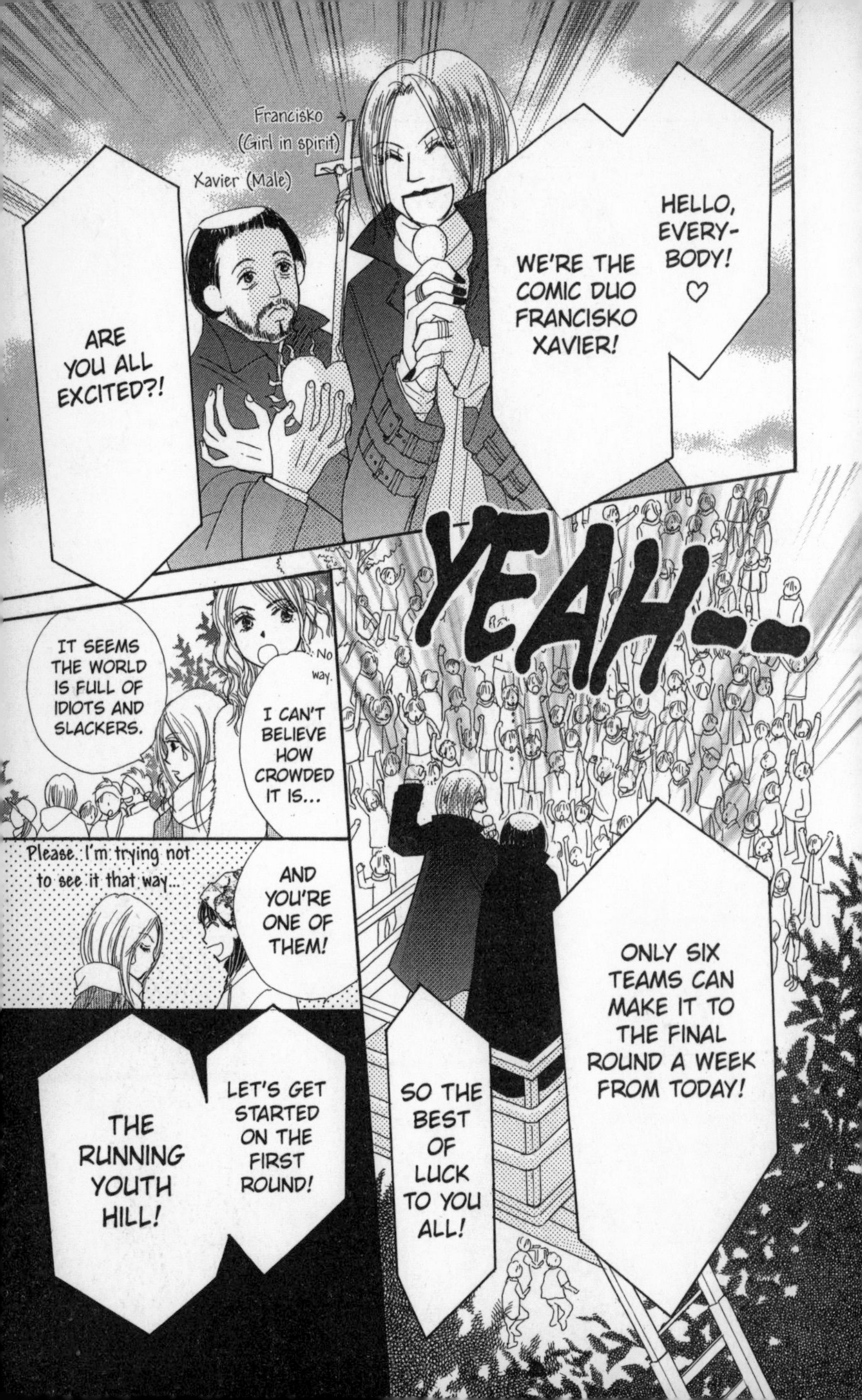
Francisko
(Girl in spirit)
Xavier (Male)
HELLO, EVERY-BODY! ♡
WE'RE THE COMIC DUO FRANCISKO XAVIER!
ARE YOU ALL EXCITED?!
YEAH--
ONLY SIX TEAMS CAN MAKE IT TO THE FINAL ROUND A WEEK FROM TODAY!
SO THE BEST OF LUCK TO YOU ALL!
...No way.
I CAN'T BELIEVE HOW CROWDED IT IS...
IT SEEMS THE WORLD IS FULL OF IDIOTS AND SLACKERS.
AND YOU'RE ONE OF THEM!
Please. I'm trying not to see it that way...
LET'S GET STARTED ON THE FIRST ROUND!
THE RUNNING YOUTH HILL!

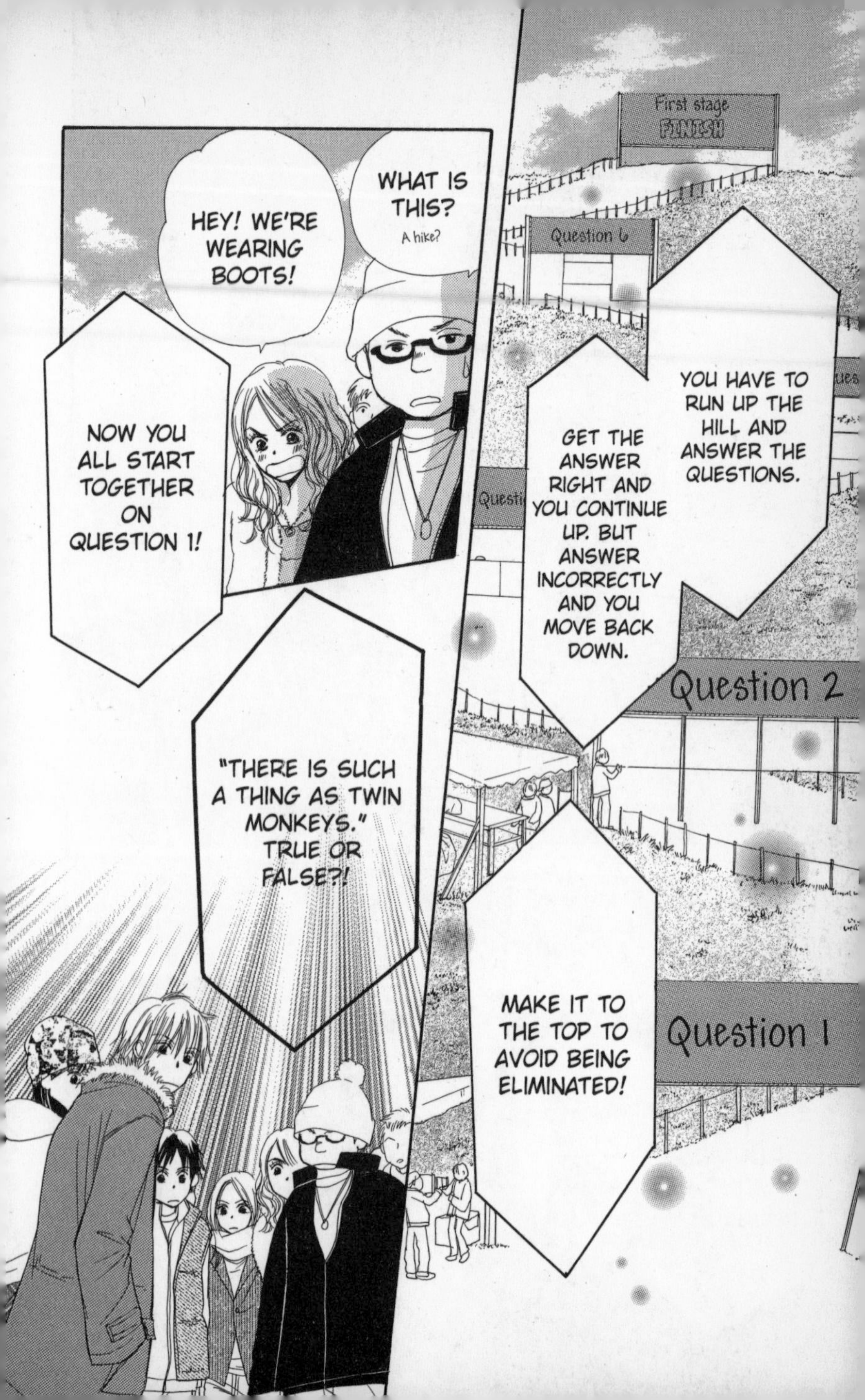
First stage
FINISH
Question 6
YOU HAVE TO RUN UP THE HILL AND ANSWER THE QUESTIONS.
GET THE ANSWER RIGHT AND YOU CONTINUE UP. BUT ANSWER INCORRECTLY AND YOU MOVE BACK DOWN.
Question 2
Question 1
MAKE IT TO THE TOP TO AVOID BEING ELIMINATED!
WHAT IS THIS?
A hike?
HEY! WE'RE WEARING BOOTS!
NOW YOU ALL START TOGETHER ON QUESTION 1!
"THERE IS SUCH A THING AS TWIN MONKEYS." TRUE OR FALSE?!

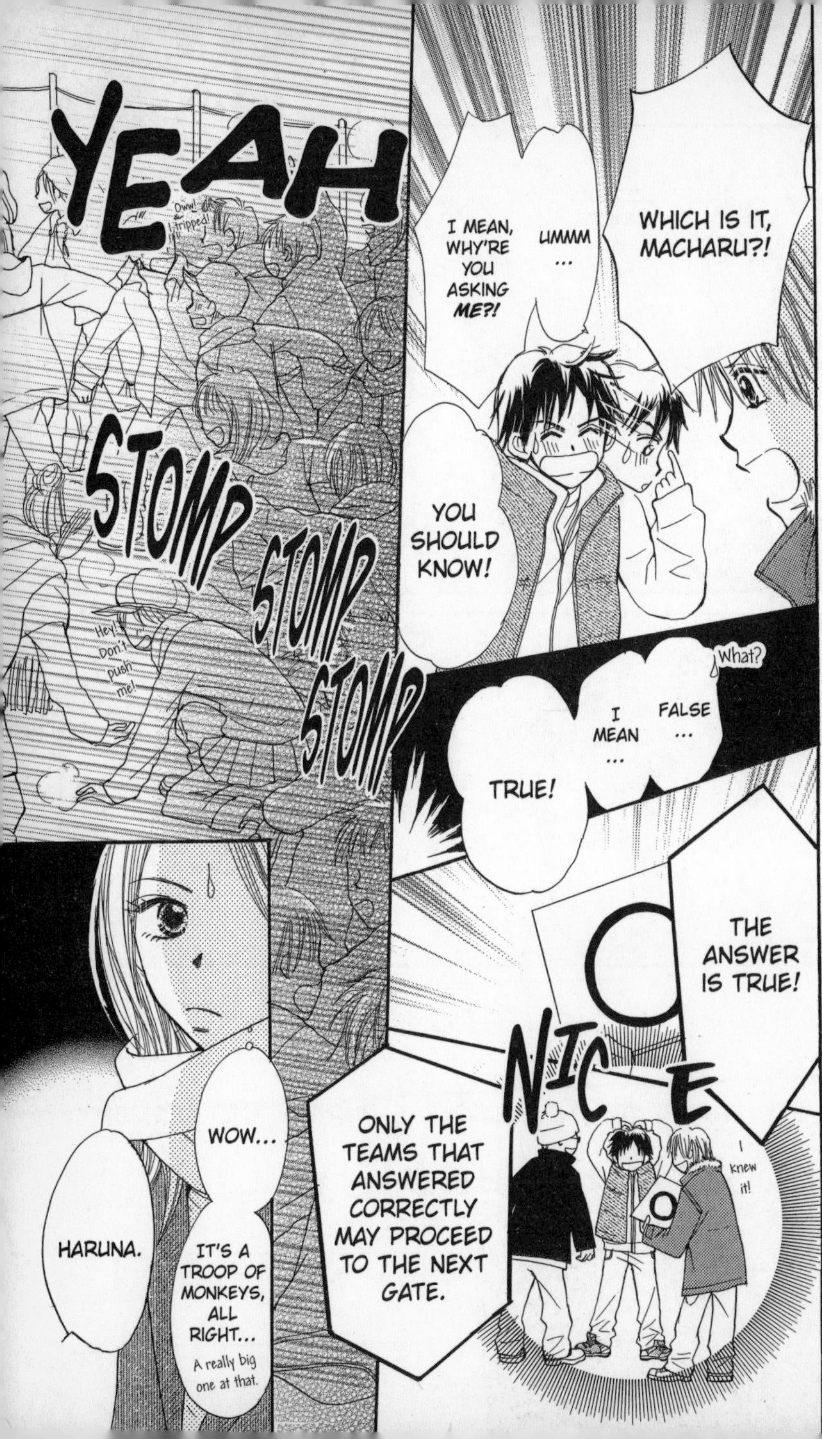
WHICH IS IT, MACHARU?!
UMMM...
I MEAN, WHY'RE YOU ASKING ME?!
YOU SHOULD KNOW!
What?
FALSE...
I MEAN...
TRUE!
THE ANSWER IS TRUE!
NICE
I knew it!
ONLY THE TEAMS THAT ANSWERED CORRECTLY MAY PROCEED TO THE NEXT GATE.
YEAH
Oww! I tripped!
STOMP STOMP STOMP
Hey! Don't push me!
WOW...
IT'S A TROOP OF MONKEYS, ALL RIGHT...
A really big one at that.
HARUNA.

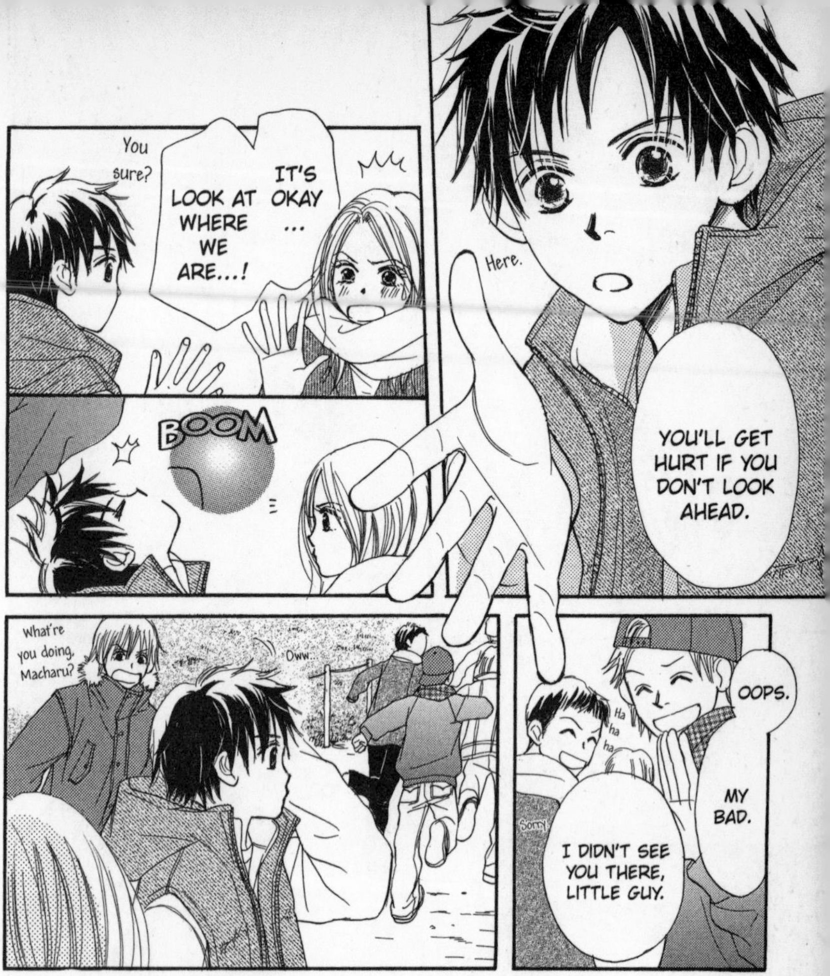
Here.
YOU'LL GET HURT IF YOU DON'T LOOK AHEAD.
IT'S OKAY ...
LOOK AT WHERE WE ARE...!
You sure?
BOOM
OOPS.
Ha ha ha
MY BAD.
Sorry
I DIDN'T SEE YOU THERE, LITTLE GUY.
Oww
What're you doing, Macharu?

QUESTION TWO

TRANSLATE THE FOLLOWING PHRASE INTO ENGLISH:

「終わりよければすべてよし」

A

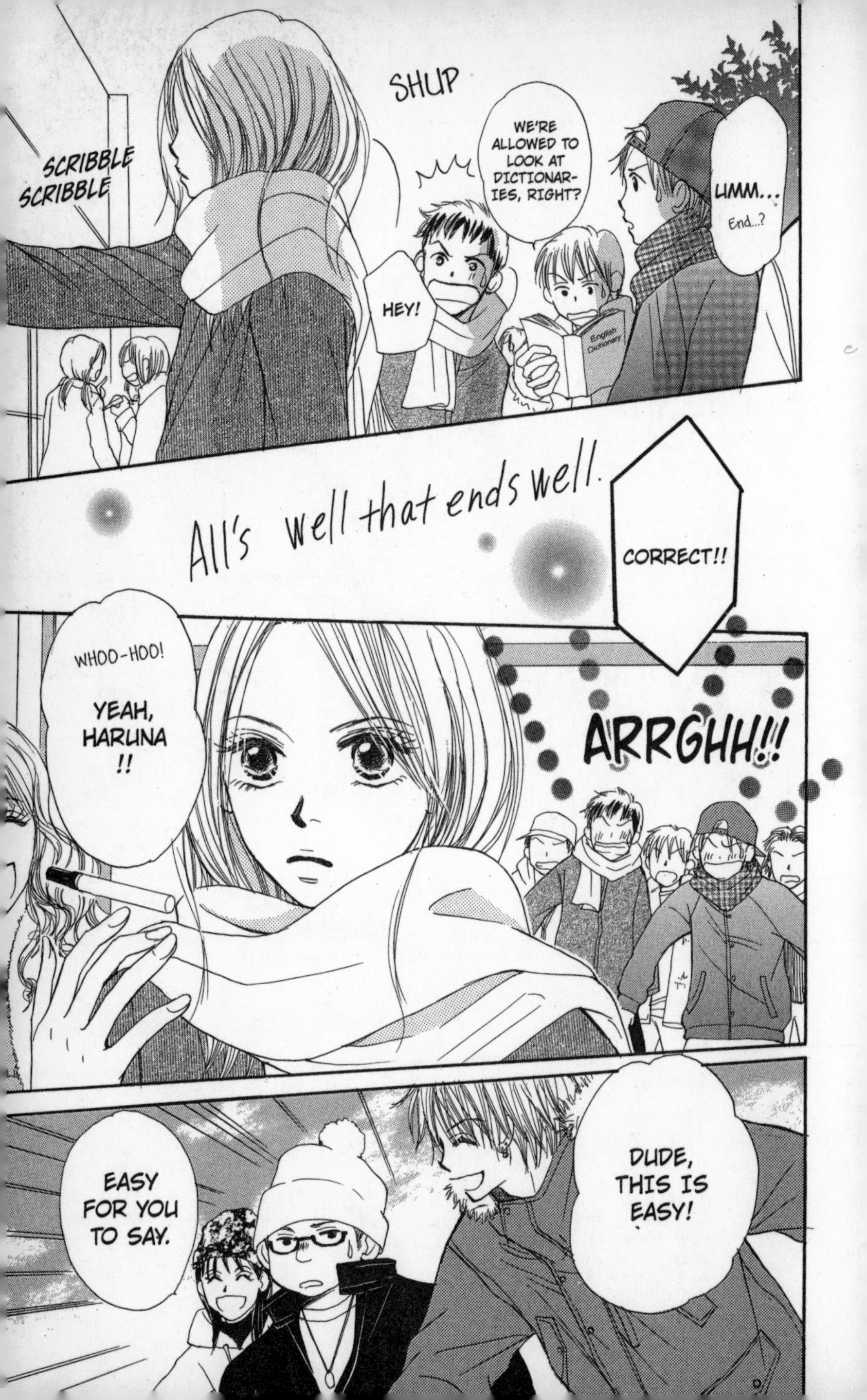
UMM...
End...?
SHUP
WE'RE ALLOWED TO LOOK AT DICTIONARIES, RIGHT?
English Dictionary
HEY!
SCRIBBLE SCRIBBLE
All's well that ends well.
CORRECT!!
ARRGHH!!
WHOO-HOO!
YEAH, HARUNA!!
DUDE, THIS IS EASY!
EASY FOR YOU TO SAY.

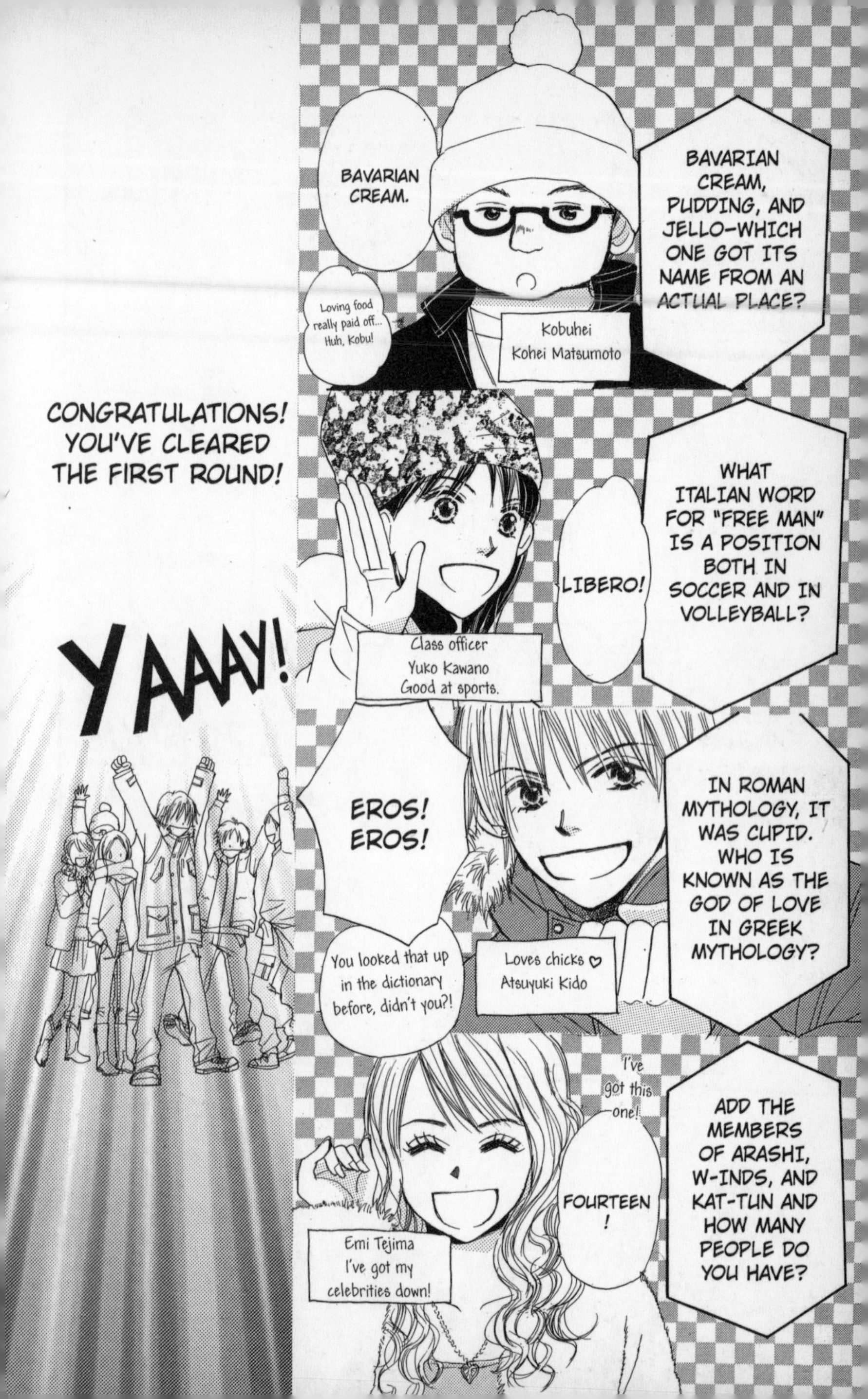
BAVARIAN CREAM, PUDDING, AND JELLO—WHICH ONE GOT ITS NAME FROM AN ACTUAL PLACE?
BAVARIAN CREAM.
Loving food really paid off... Huh, Kobu!
Kobuhei
Kohei Matsumoto
WHAT ITALIAN WORD FOR "FREE MAN" IS A POSITION BOTH IN SOCCER AND IN VOLLEYBALL?
LIBERO!
Class officer
Yuko Kawano
Good at sports.
IN ROMAN MYTHOLOGY, IT WAS CUPID. WHO IS KNOWN AS THE GOD OF LOVE IN GREEK MYTHOLOGY?
EROS! EROS!
Loves chicks ♡
Atsuyuki Kido
You looked that up in the dictionary before, didn't you?!
ADD THE MEMBERS OF ARASHI, W-INDS, AND KAT-TUN AND HOW MANY PEOPLE DO YOU HAVE?
I've got this one!
FOURTEEN!
Emi Tejima
I've got my celebrities down!
CONGRATULATIONS! YOU'VE CLEARED THE FIRST ROUND!
YAAAY!

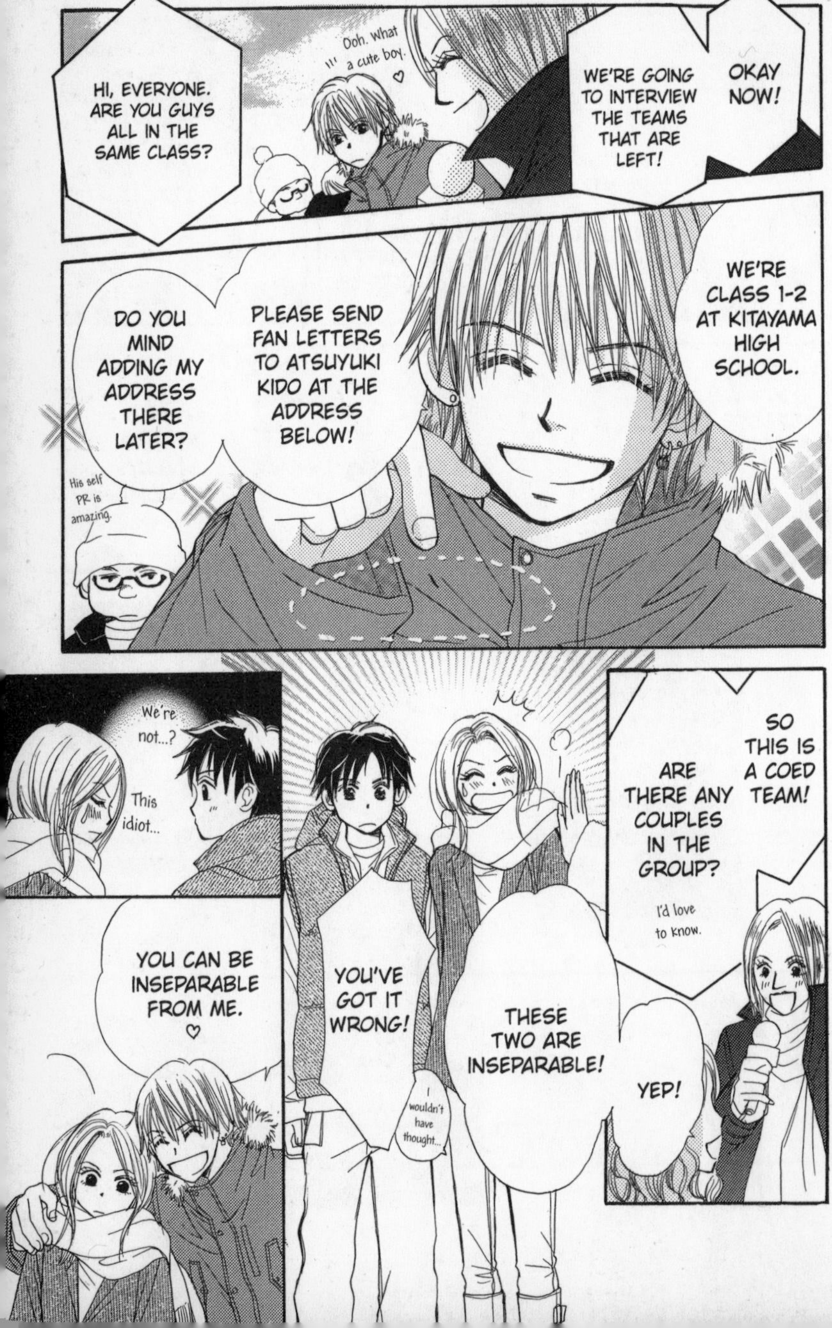
OKAY NOW!
WE'RE GOING TO INTERVIEW THE TEAMS THAT ARE LEFT!
Ooh. What a cute boy. ♡
HI, EVERYONE. ARE YOU GUYS ALL IN THE SAME CLASS?
WE'RE CLASS 1-2 AT KITAYAMA HIGH SCHOOL.
PLEASE SEND FAN LETTERS TO ATSUYUKI KIDO AT THE ADDRESS BELOW!
DO YOU MIND ADDING MY ADDRESS THERE LATER?
His self PR is amazing.
SO THIS IS A COED TEAM!
ARE THERE ANY COUPLES IN THE GROUP?
I'd love to know.
YEP!
THESE TWO ARE INSEPARABLE!
I wouldn't have thought...
YOU'VE GOT IT WRONG!
We're not...?
This idiot...
YOU CAN BE INSEPARABLE FROM ME. ♡

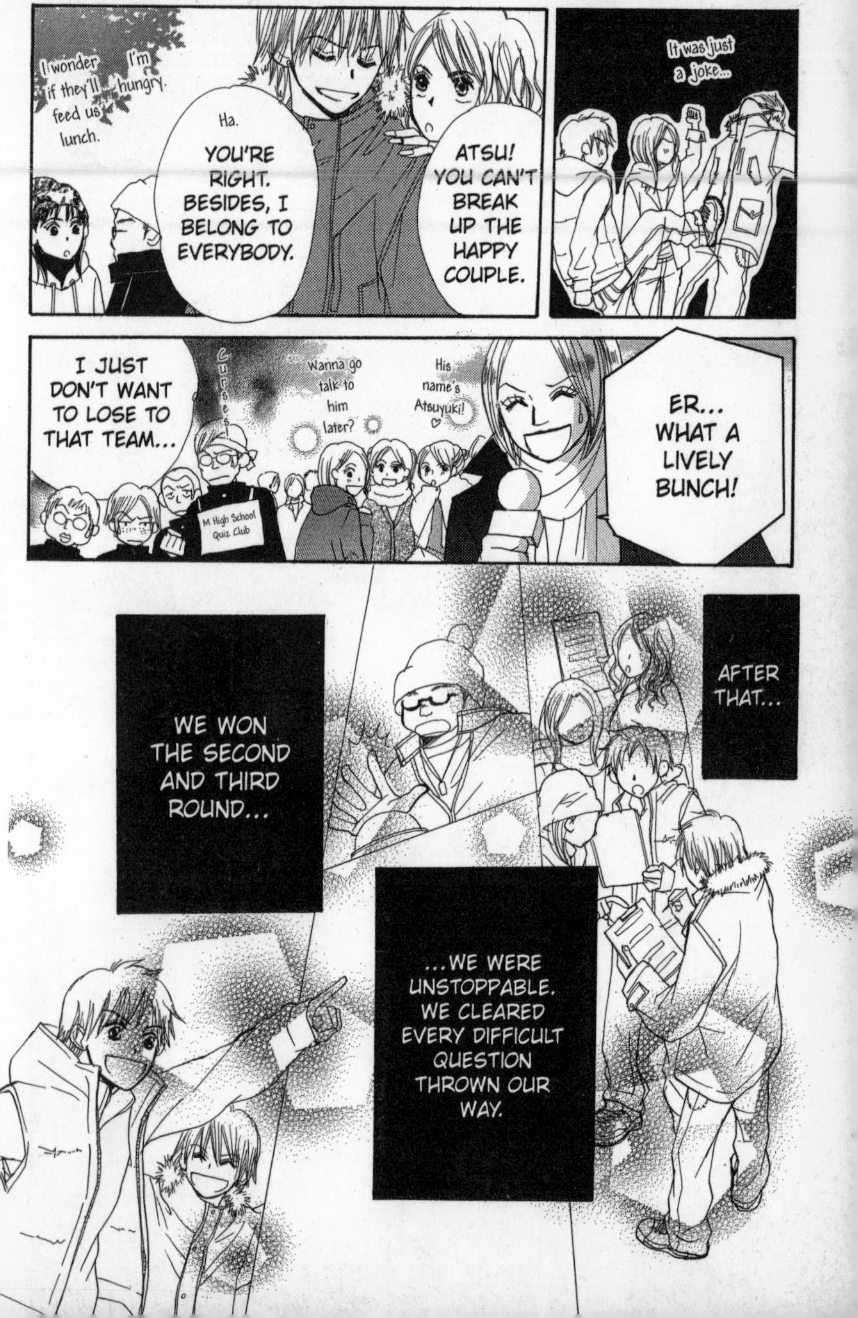
It was just a joke...
ATSU! YOU CAN'T BREAK UP THE HAPPY COUPLE.
Ha.
YOU'RE RIGHT. BESIDES, I BELONG TO EVERYBODY.
I'm hungry.
I wonder if they'll feed us lunch.
ER... WHAT A LIVELY BUNCH!
His name's Atsuyuki!
Wanna go talk to him later?
Curses
M High School Quiz Club
I JUST DON'T WANT TO LOSE TO THAT TEAM...
AFTER THAT...
WE WON THE SECOND AND THIRD ROUND...
...WE WERE UNSTOPPABLE. WE CLEARED EVERY DIFFICULT QUESTION THROWN OUR WAY.

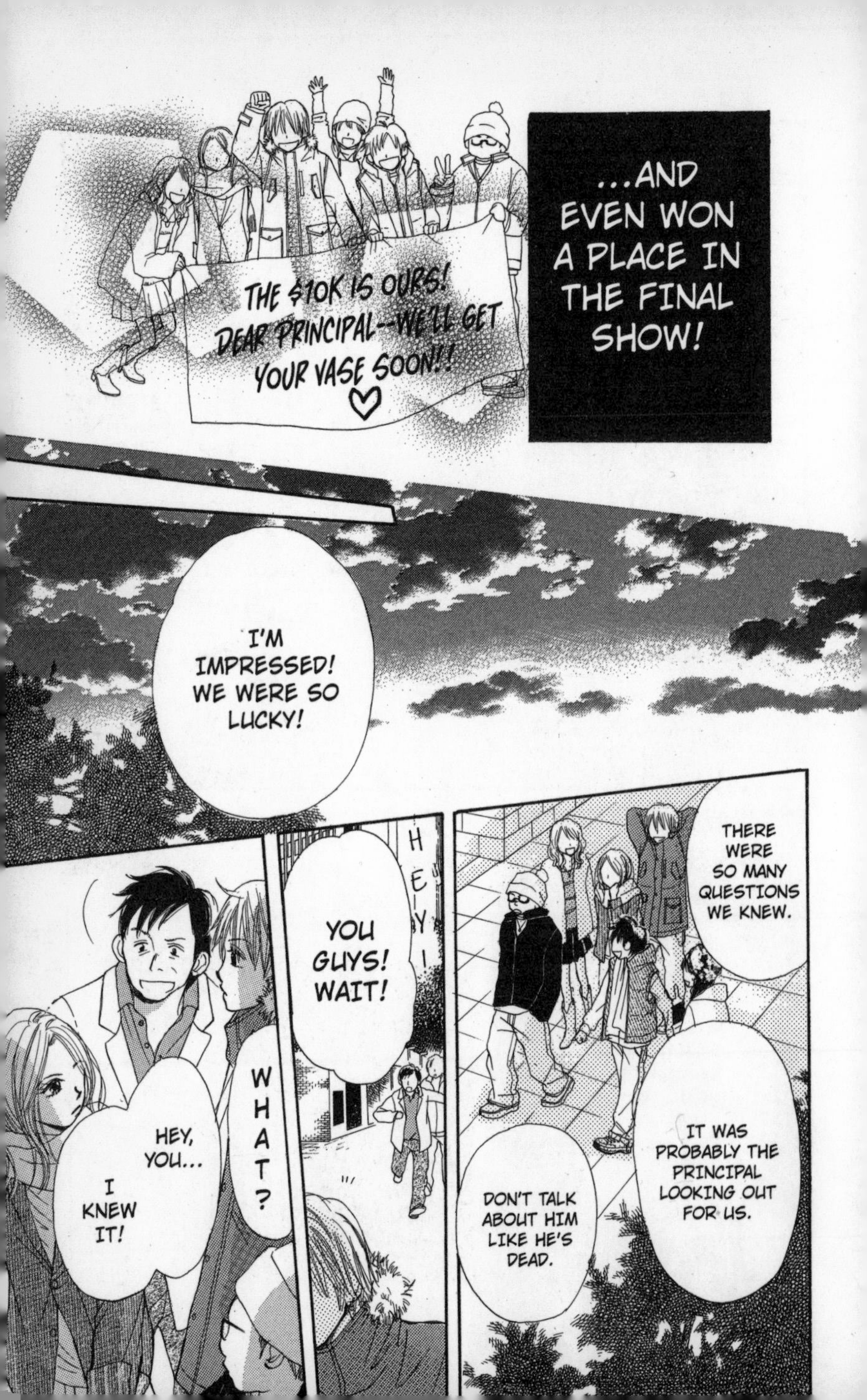
...AND EVEN WON A PLACE IN THE FINAL SHOW!
THE $10K IS OURS! DEAR PRINCIPAL--WE'LL GET YOUR VASE SOON!!
I'M IMPRESSED! WE WERE SO LUCKY!
THERE WERE SO MANY QUESTIONS WE KNEW.
IT WAS PROBABLY THE PRINCIPAL LOOKING OUT FOR US.
DON'T TALK ABOUT HIM LIKE HE'S DEAD.
HEY!
YOU GUYS! WAIT!
WHAT?
HEY, YOU...
I KNEW IT!

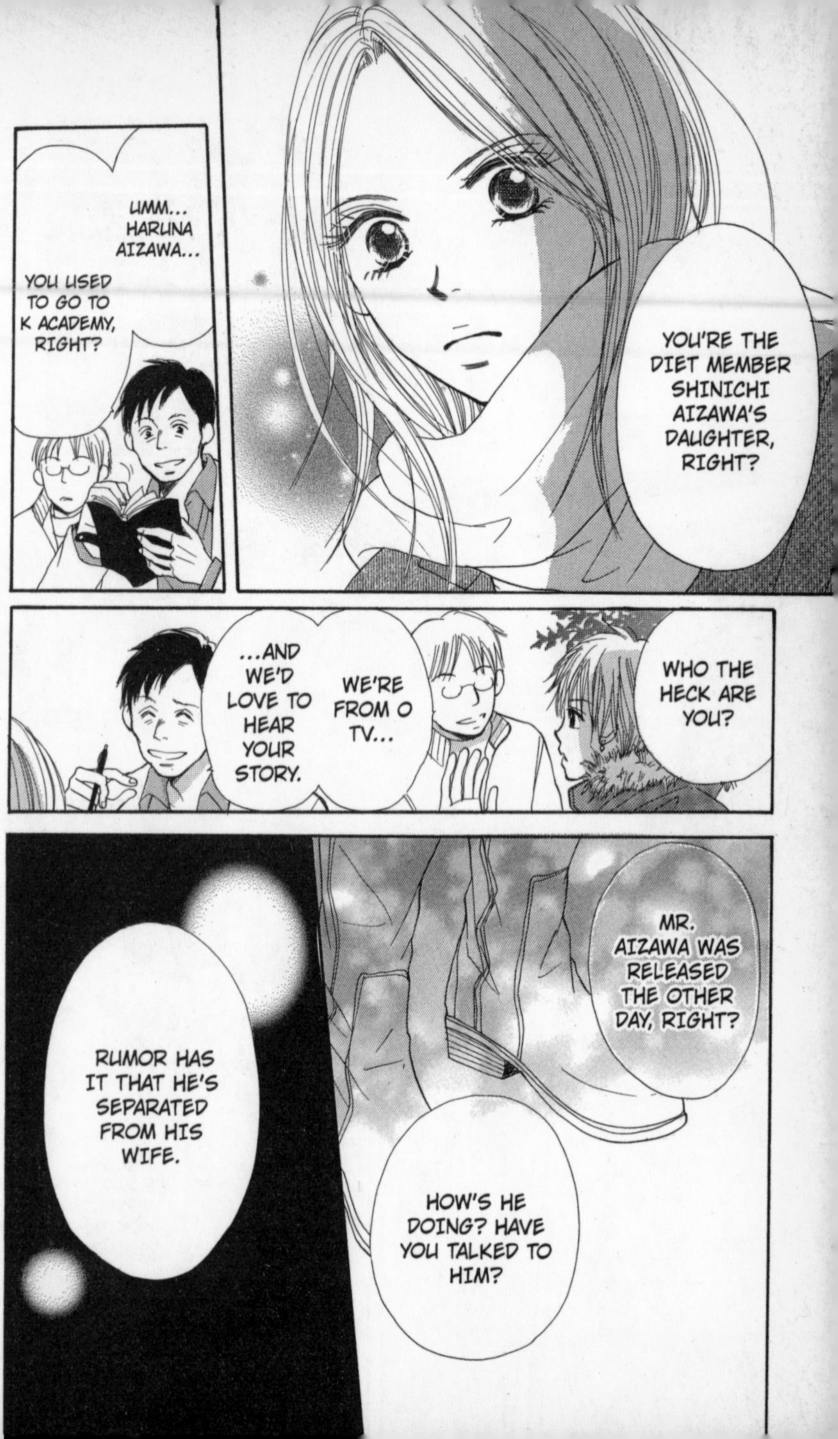
YOU'RE THE DIET MEMBER SHINICHI AIZAWA'S DAUGHTER, RIGHT?
UMM... HARUNA AIZAWA...
YOU USED TO GO TO K ACADEMY, RIGHT?
WHO THE HECK ARE YOU?
WE'RE FROM O TV...
...AND WE'D LOVE TO HEAR YOUR STORY.
MR. AIZAWA WAS RELEASED THE OTHER DAY, RIGHT?
HOW'S HE DOING? HAVE YOU TALKED TO HIM?
RUMOR HAS IT THAT HE'S SEPARATED FROM HIS WIFE.

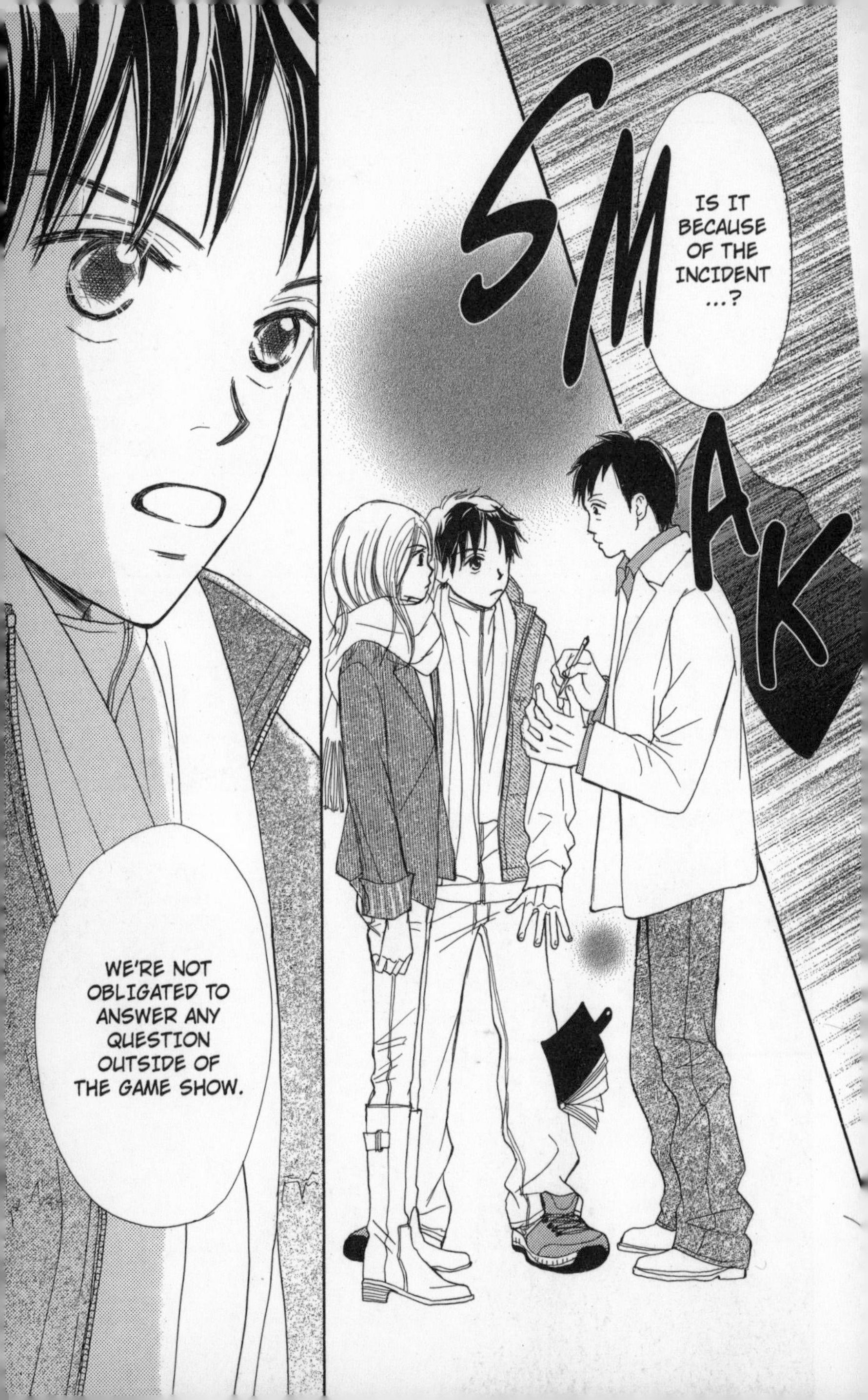
SMAK
IS IT BECAUSE OF THE INCIDENT ...?
WE'RE NOT OBLIGATED TO ANSWER ANY QUESTION OUTSIDE OF THE GAME SHOW.

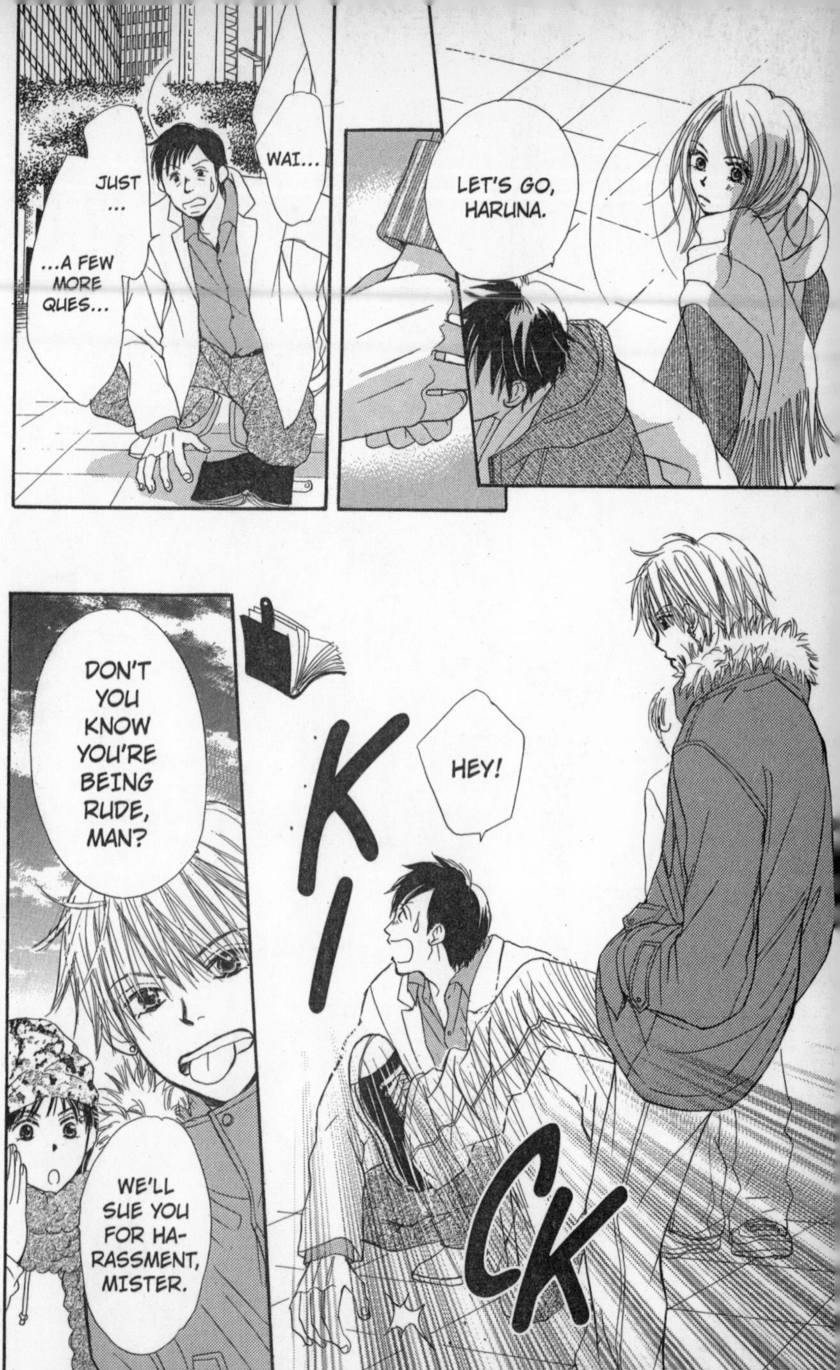
LET'S GO, HARUNA.
WAI...
JUST ...
...A FEW MORE QUES...
HEY!
KICK
DON'T YOU KNOW YOU'RE BEING RUDE, MAN?
WE'LL SUE YOU FOR HA-RASSMENT, MISTER.

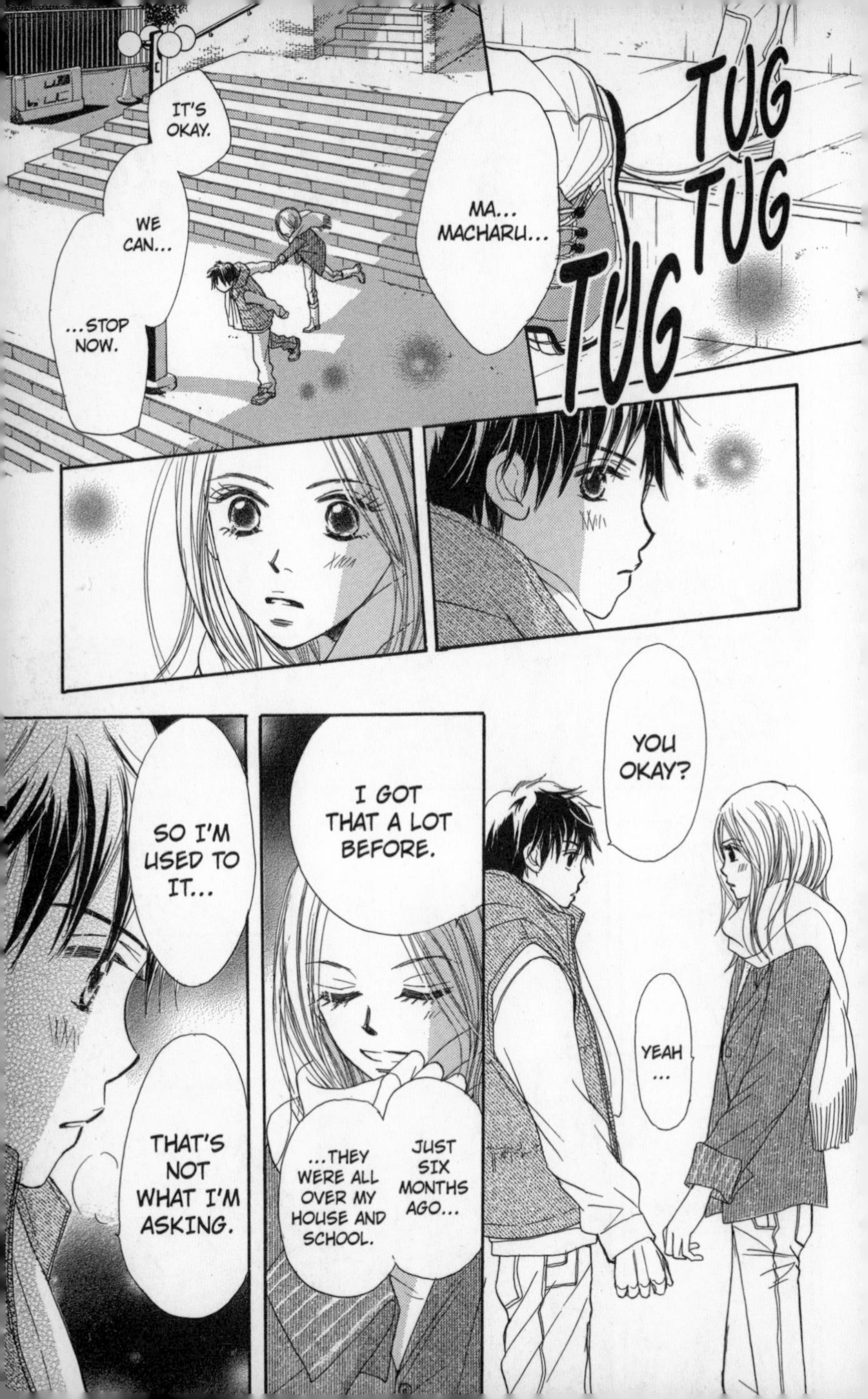
TUG TUG TUG
MA... MACHARU...
IT'S OKAY.
WE CAN...
...STOP NOW.
YOU OKAY?
YEAH...
I GOT THAT A LOT BEFORE.
JUST SIX MONTHS AGO...
...THEY WERE ALL OVER MY HOUSE AND SCHOOL.
SO I'M USED TO IT...
THAT'S NOT WHAT I'M ASKING.

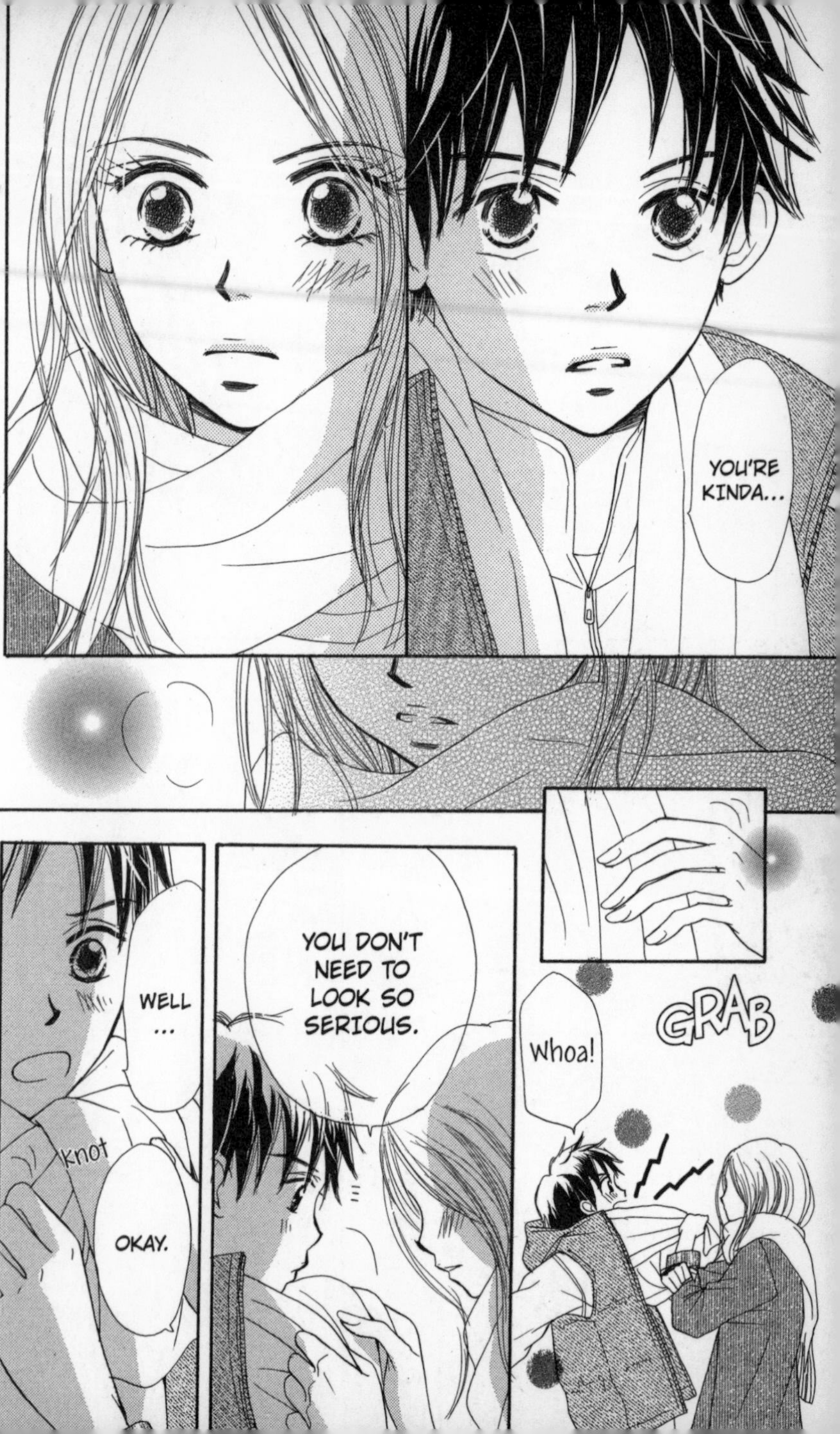
YOU'RE KINDA...
GRAB
Whoa!
YOU DON'T NEED TO LOOK SO SERIOUS.
WELL ...
knot
OKAY.

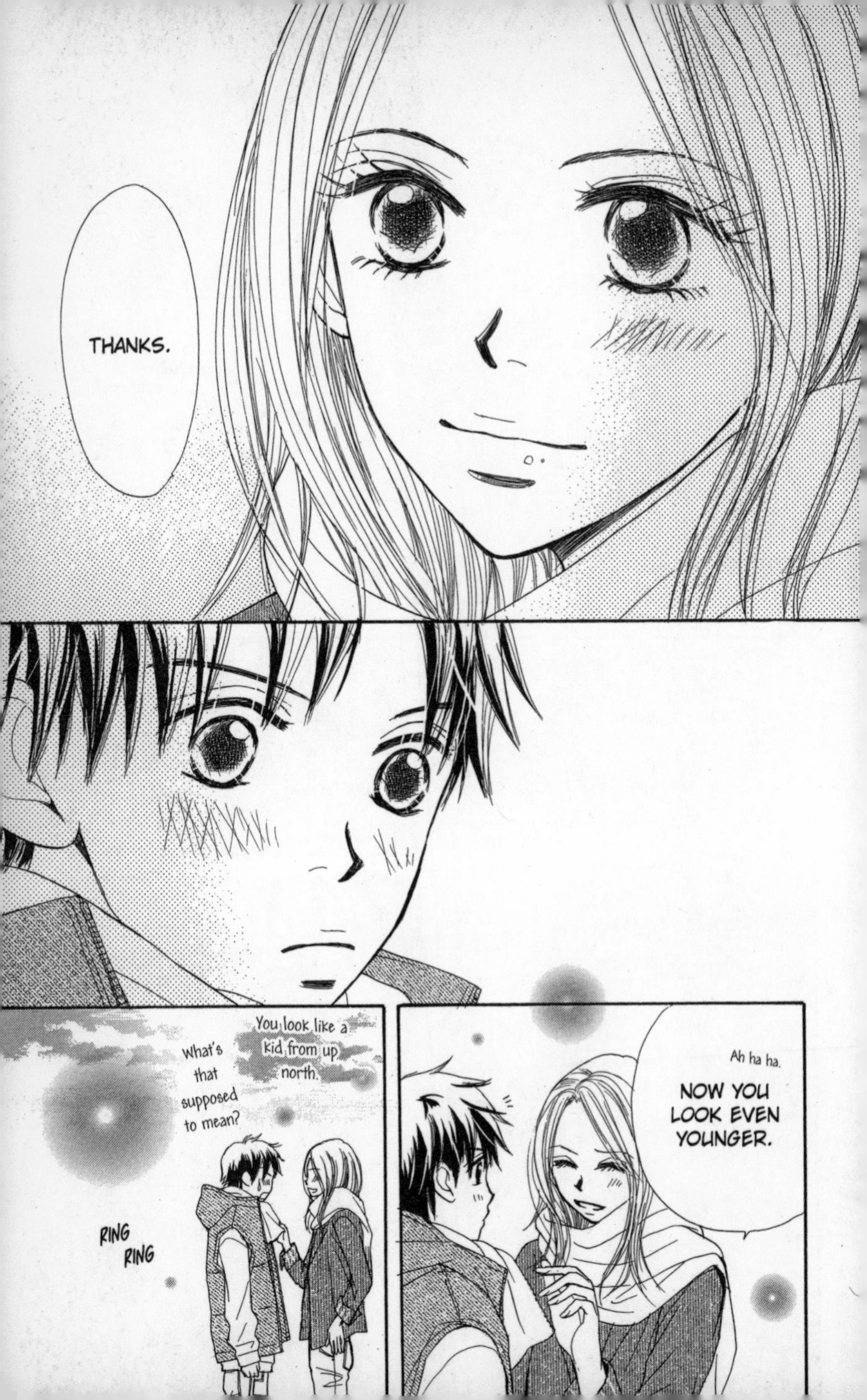
THANKS.
Ah ha ha.
NOW YOU LOOK EVEN YOUNGER.
You look like a kid from up north.
What's that supposed to mean?
RING RING

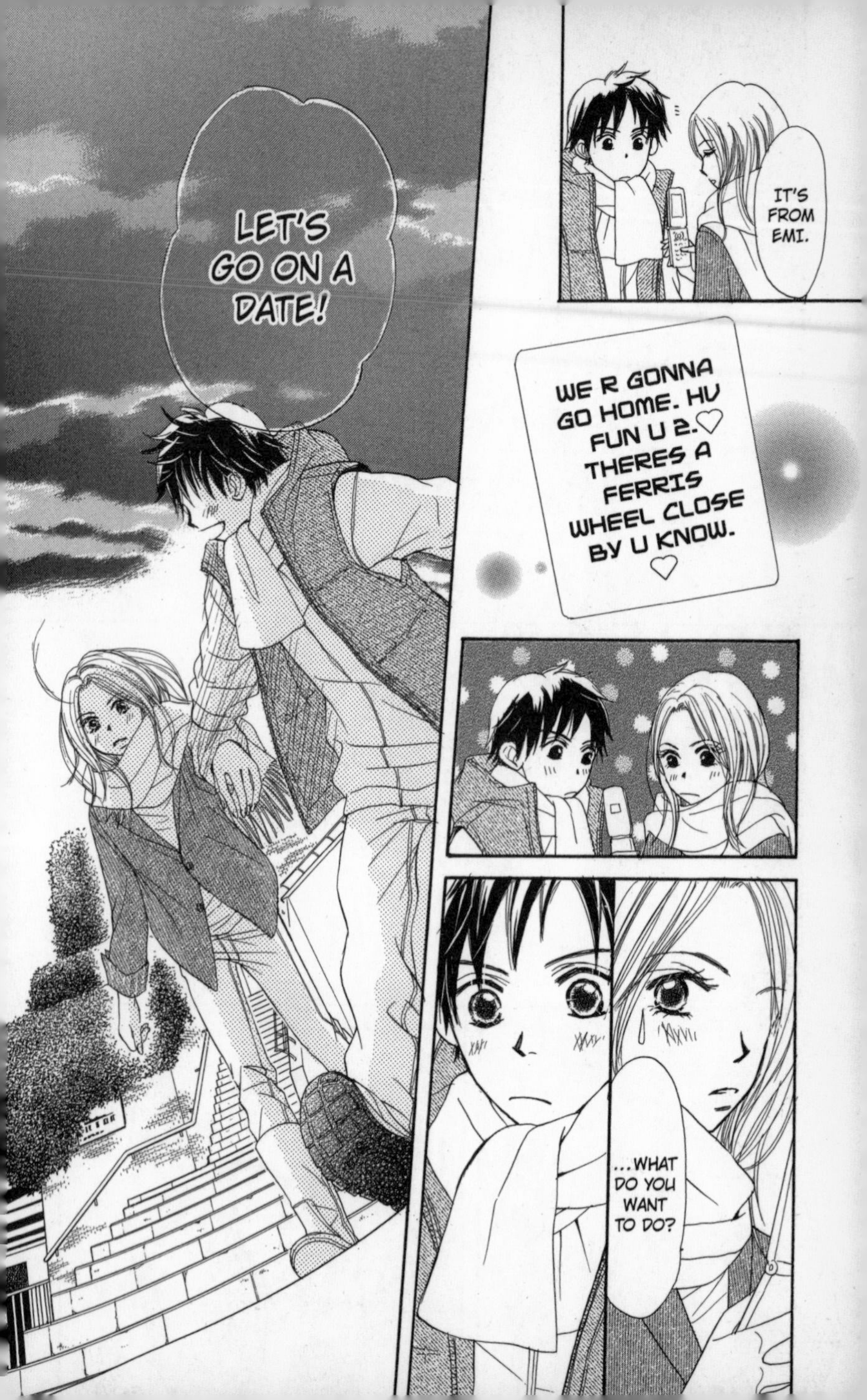
IT'S FROM EMI.
WE R GONNA GO HOME. HV FUN U 2.♡ THERES A FERRIS WHEEL CLOSE BY U KNOW. ♡
...WHAT DO YOU WANT TO DO?
LET'S GO ON A DATE!

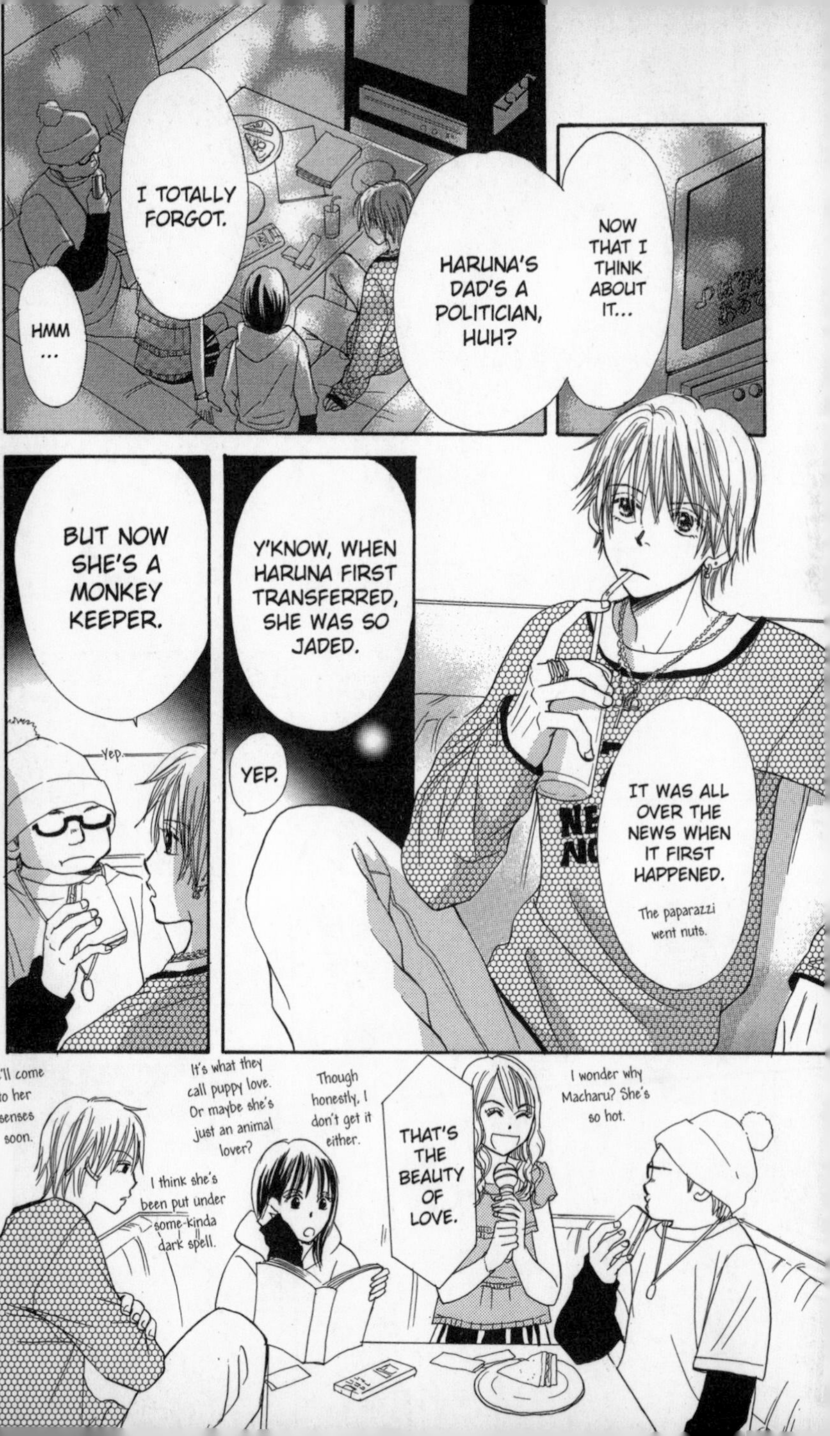
NOW THAT I THINK ABOUT IT...
HARUNA'S DAD'S A POLITICIAN, HUH?
I TOTALLY FORGOT.
HMM ...
IT WAS ALL OVER THE NEWS WHEN IT FIRST HAPPENED.
The paparazzi went nuts.
Y'KNOW, WHEN HARUNA FIRST TRANSFERRED, SHE WAS SO JADED.
YEP.
BUT NOW SHE'S A MONKEY KEEPER.
Yep.
I wonder why Macharu? She's so hot.
THAT'S THE BEAUTY OF LOVE.
Though honestly, I don't get it either.
It's what they call puppy love. Or maybe she's just an animal lover?
I think she's been put under some-kinda dark spell.
She'll come to her senses soon.

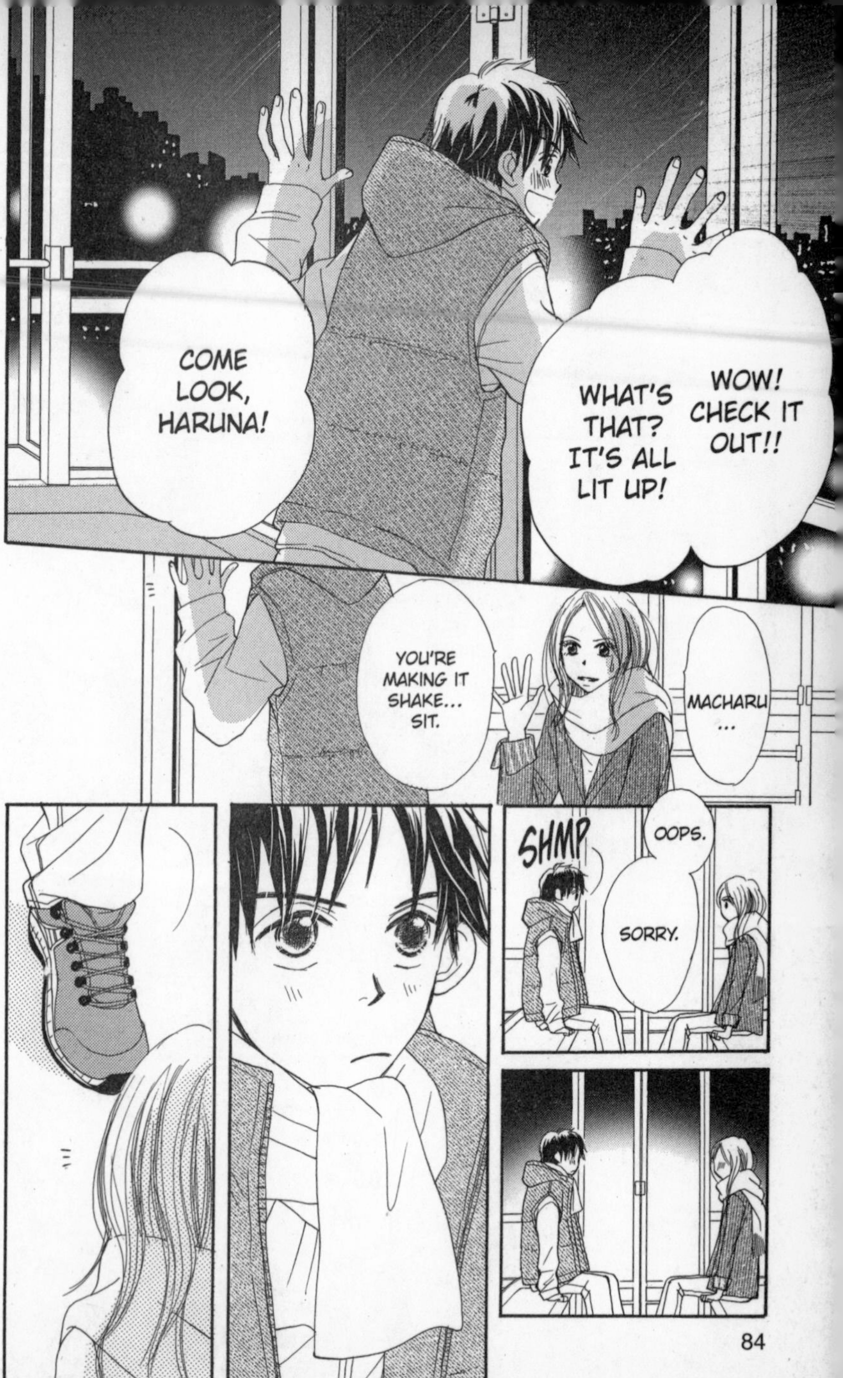
WOW! CHECK IT OUT!!
WHAT'S THAT? IT'S ALL LIT UP!
COME LOOK, HARUNA!
MACHARU ...
YOU'RE MAKING IT SHAKE... SIT.
OOPS.
SHMP
SORRY.

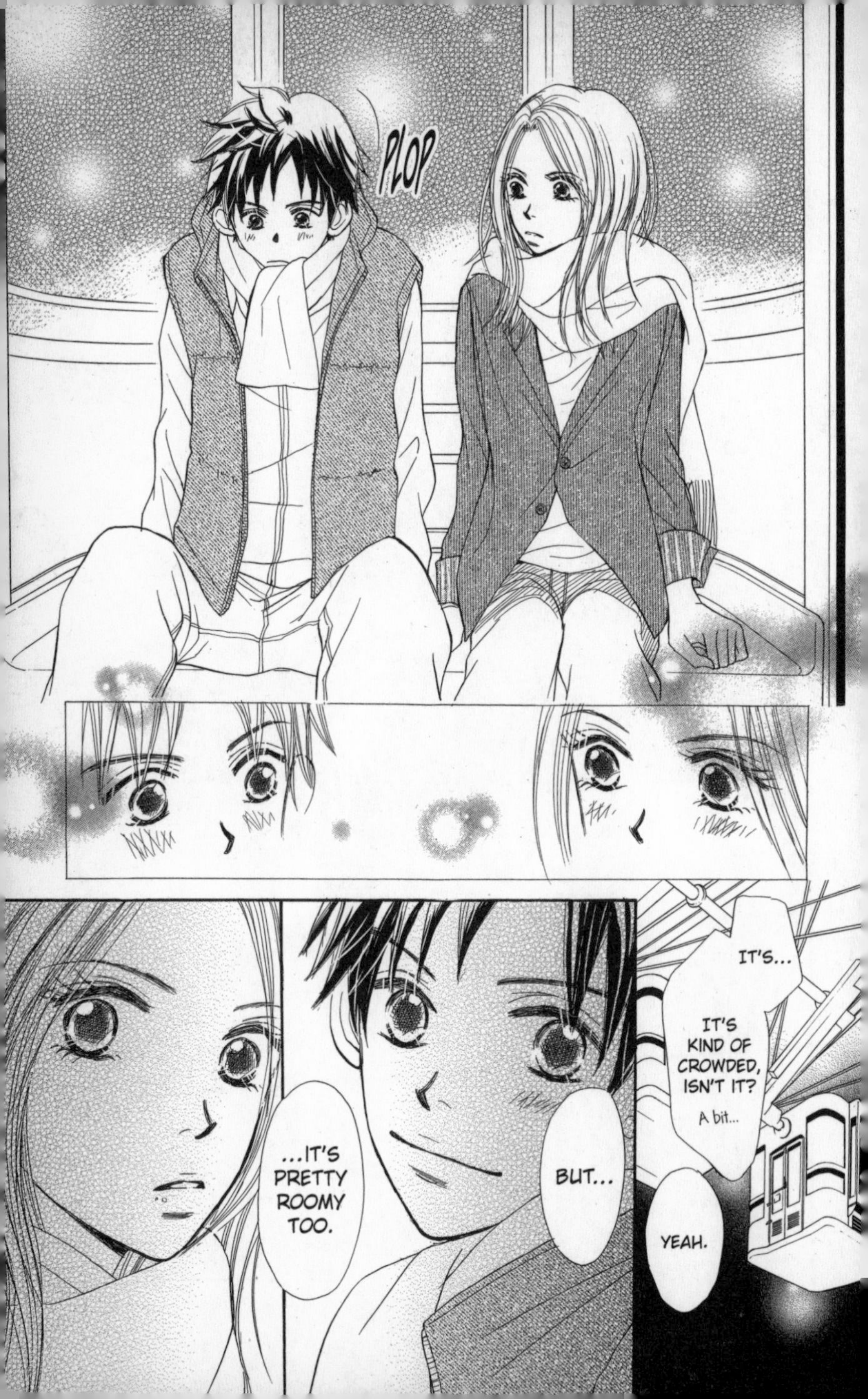
PLOP
IT'S...
IT'S KIND OF CROWDED, ISN'T IT?
A bit...
YEAH.
BUT...
...IT'S PRETTY ROOMY TOO.

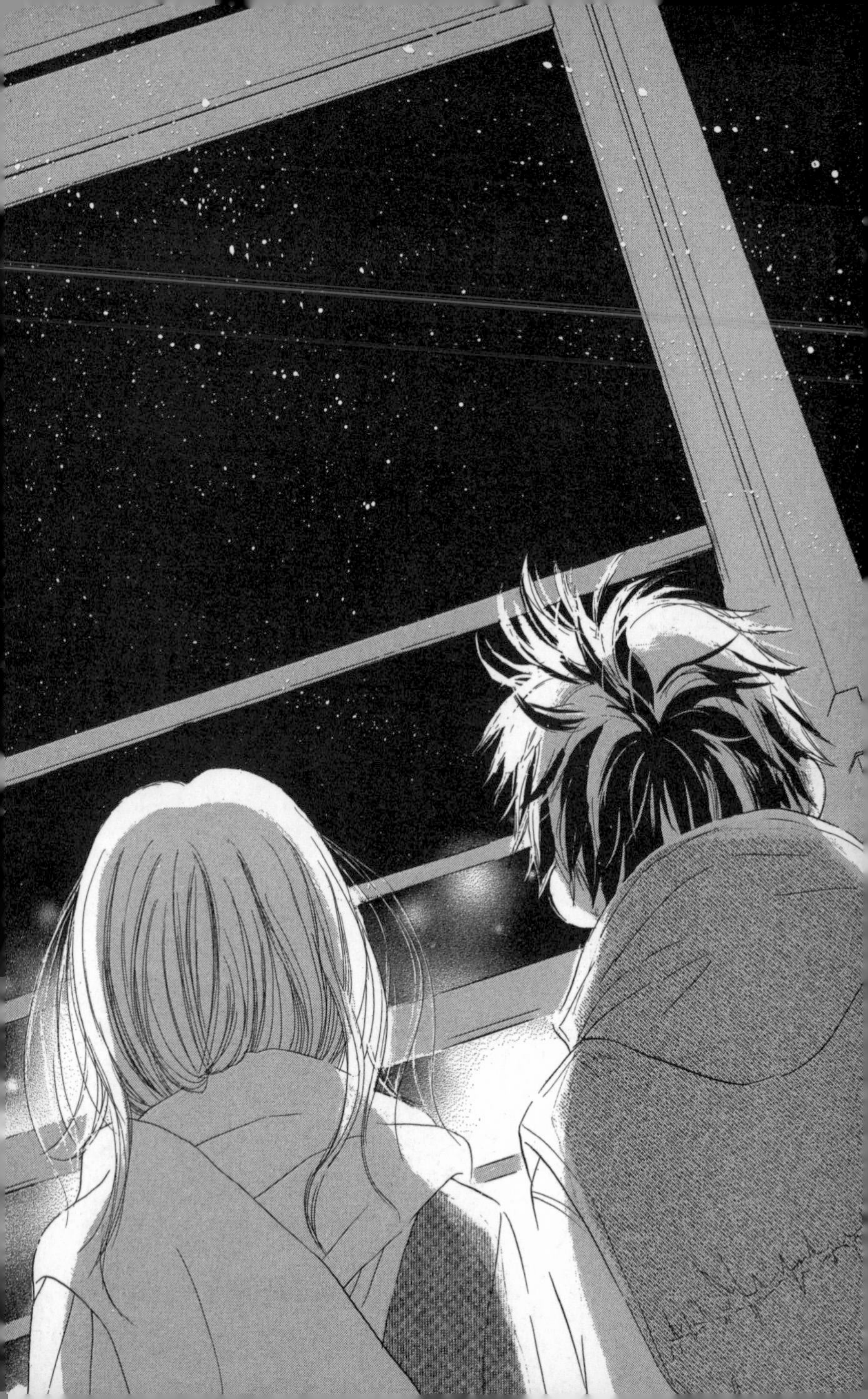

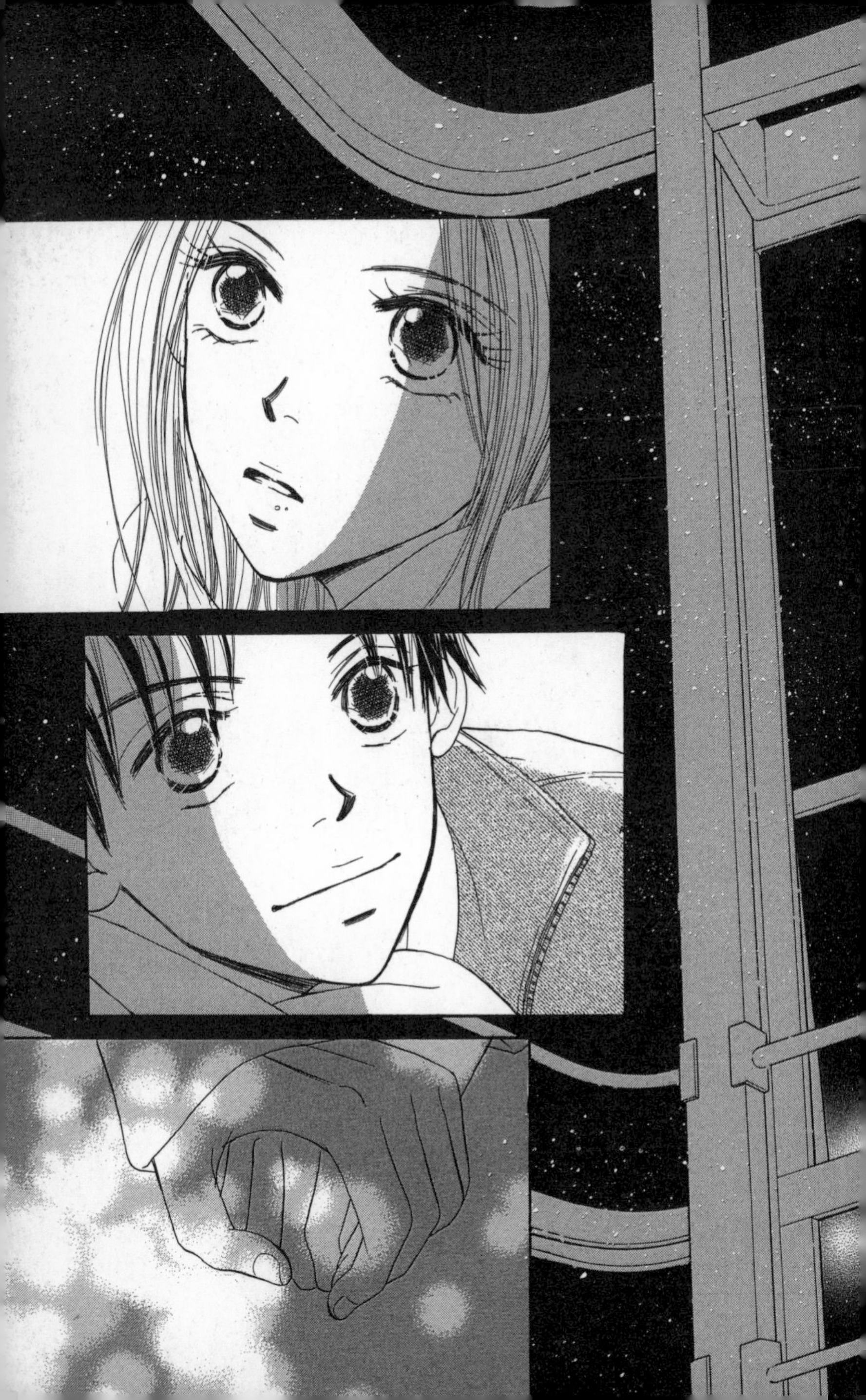

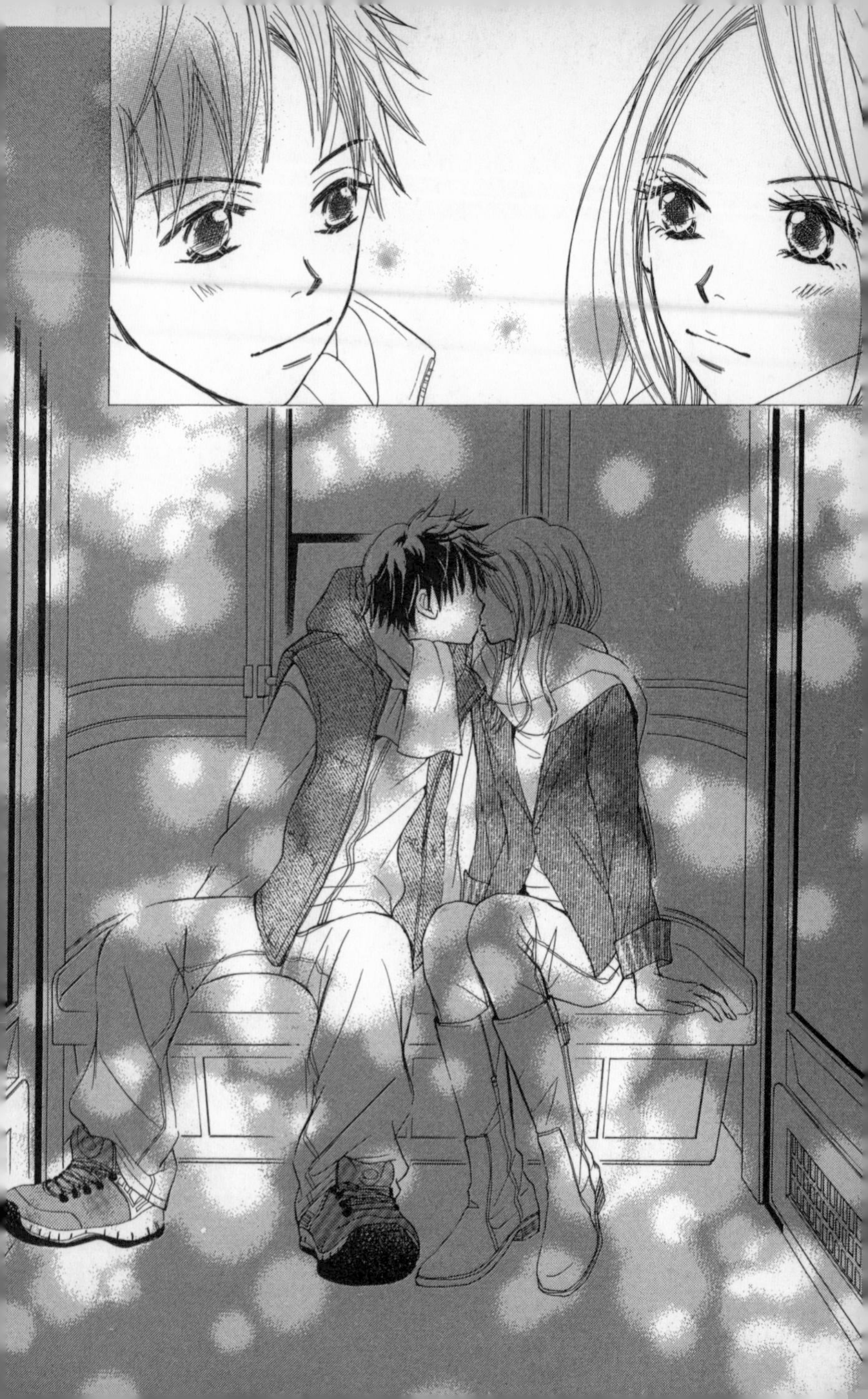

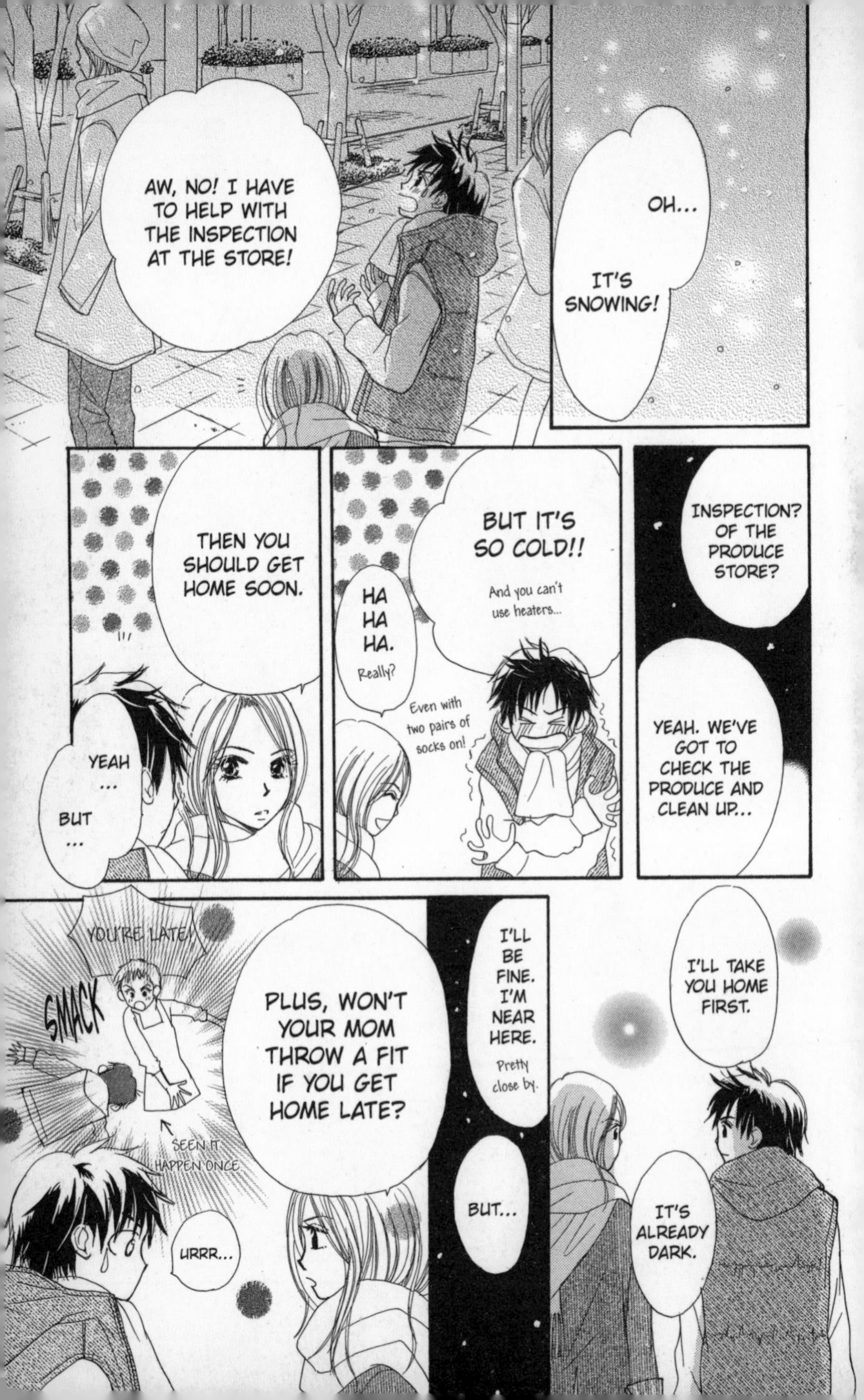
OH...
IT'S SNOWING!
AW, NO! I HAVE TO HELP WITH THE INSPECTION AT THE STORE!
INSPECTION? OF THE PRODUCE STORE?
YEAH. WE'VE GOT TO CHECK THE PRODUCE AND CLEAN UP...
BUT IT'S SO COLD!!
And you can't use heaters...
HA HA HA.
Really?
Even with two pairs of socks on!
THEN YOU SHOULD GET HOME SOON.
YEAH... BUT...
I'LL TAKE YOU HOME FIRST.
IT'S ALREADY DARK.
I'LL BE FINE. I'M NEAR HERE.
Pretty close by.
BUT...
PLUS, WON'T YOUR MOM THROW A FIT IF YOU GET HOME LATE?
YOU'RE LATE!
SMACK
SEEN IT HAPPEN ONCE
URRR...

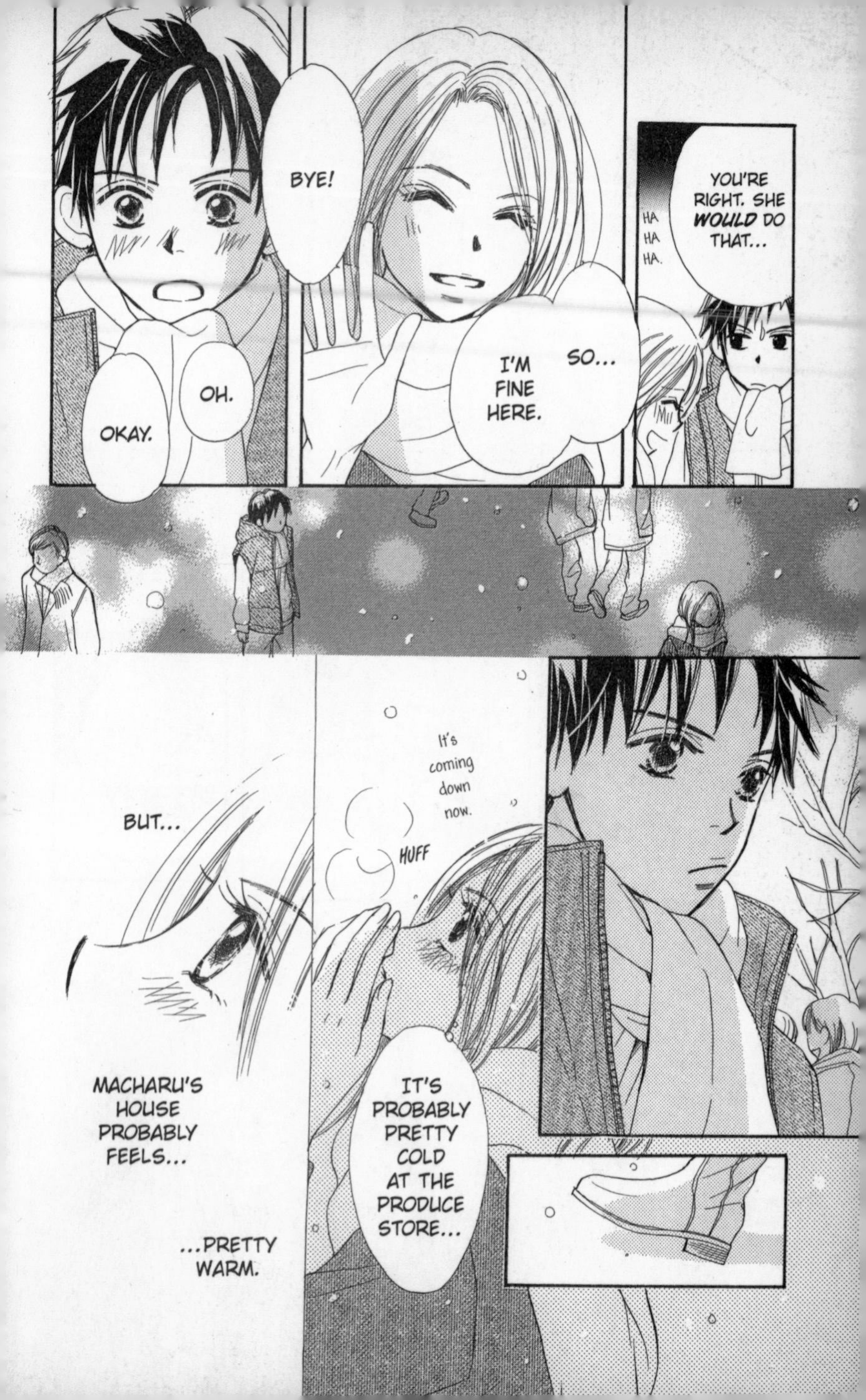
YOU'RE RIGHT. SHE WOULD DO THAT...
HA HA HA.
SO...
I'M FINE HERE.
BYE!
OH.
OKAY.
It's coming down now.
HUFF
IT'S PROBABLY PRETTY COLD AT THE PRODUCE STORE...
BUT...
MACHARU'S HOUSE PROBABLY FEELS...
...PRETTY WARM.

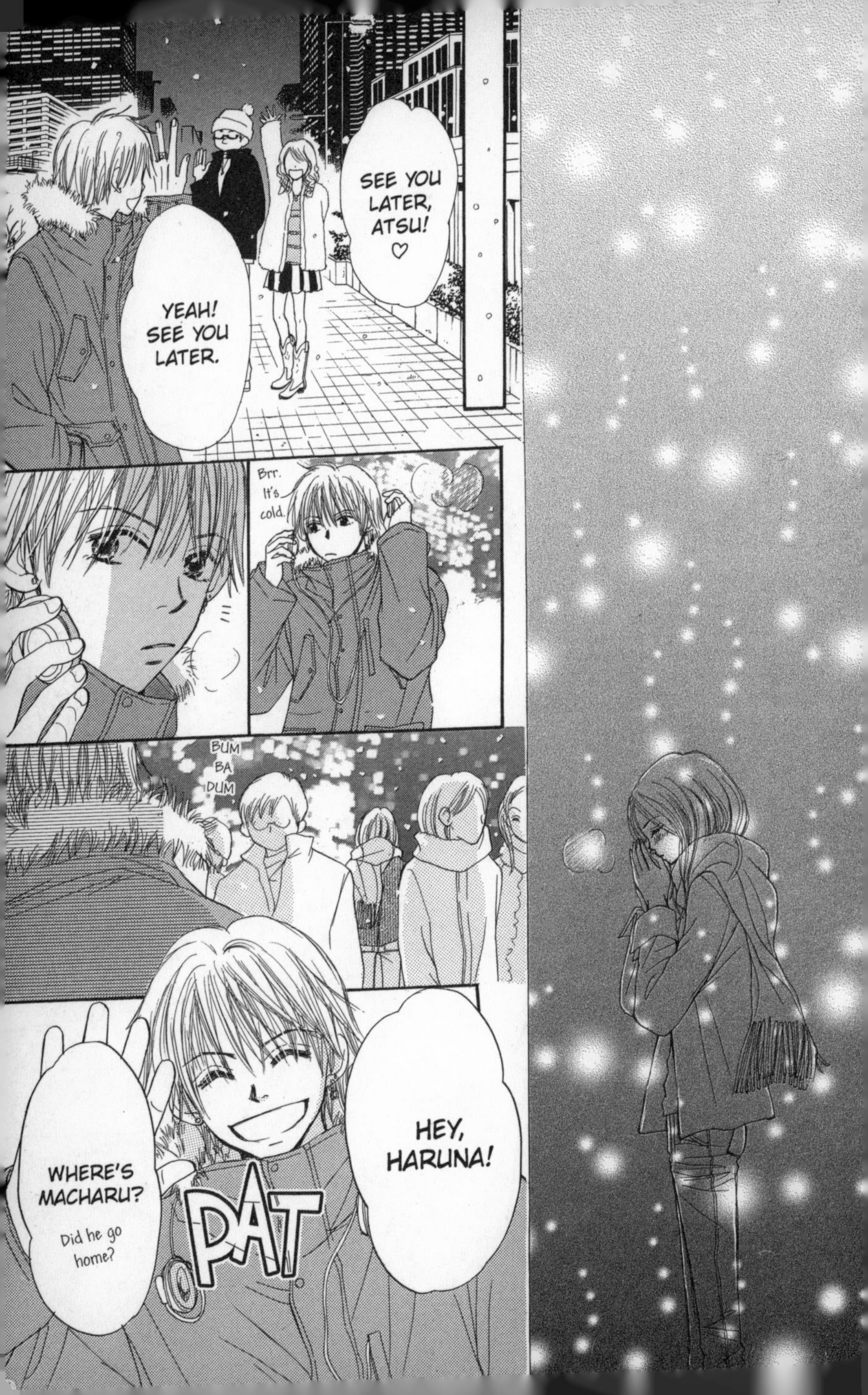
SEE YOU LATER, ATSU! ♡
YEAH! SEE YOU LATER.
Brr. It's cold.
BUM BA DUM
HEY, HARUNA!
PAT
WHERE'S MACHARU?
Did he go home?

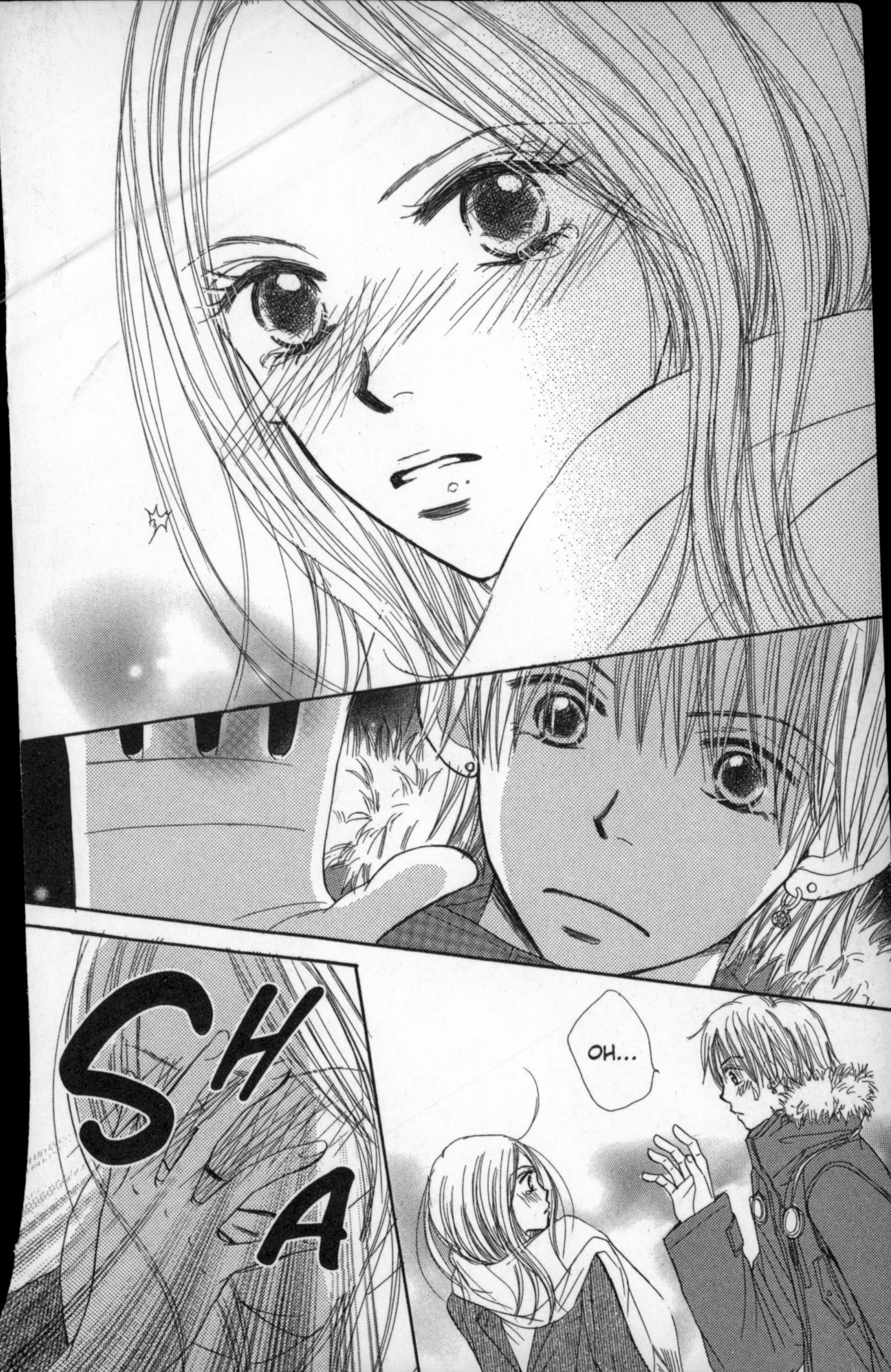
OH...
SHA

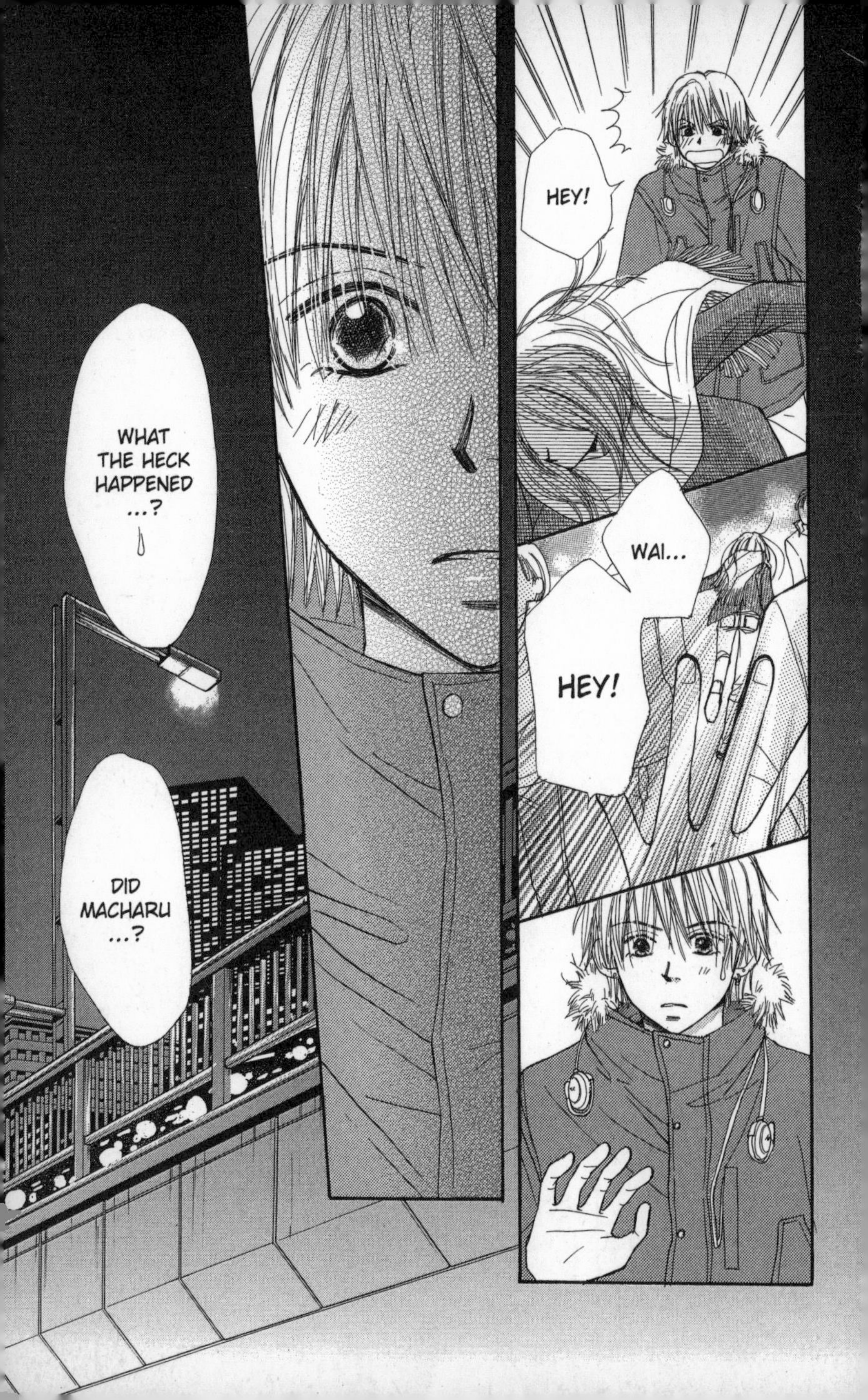
HEY!
WAI...
HEY!
WHAT THE HECK HAPPENED ...?
DID MACHARU ...?

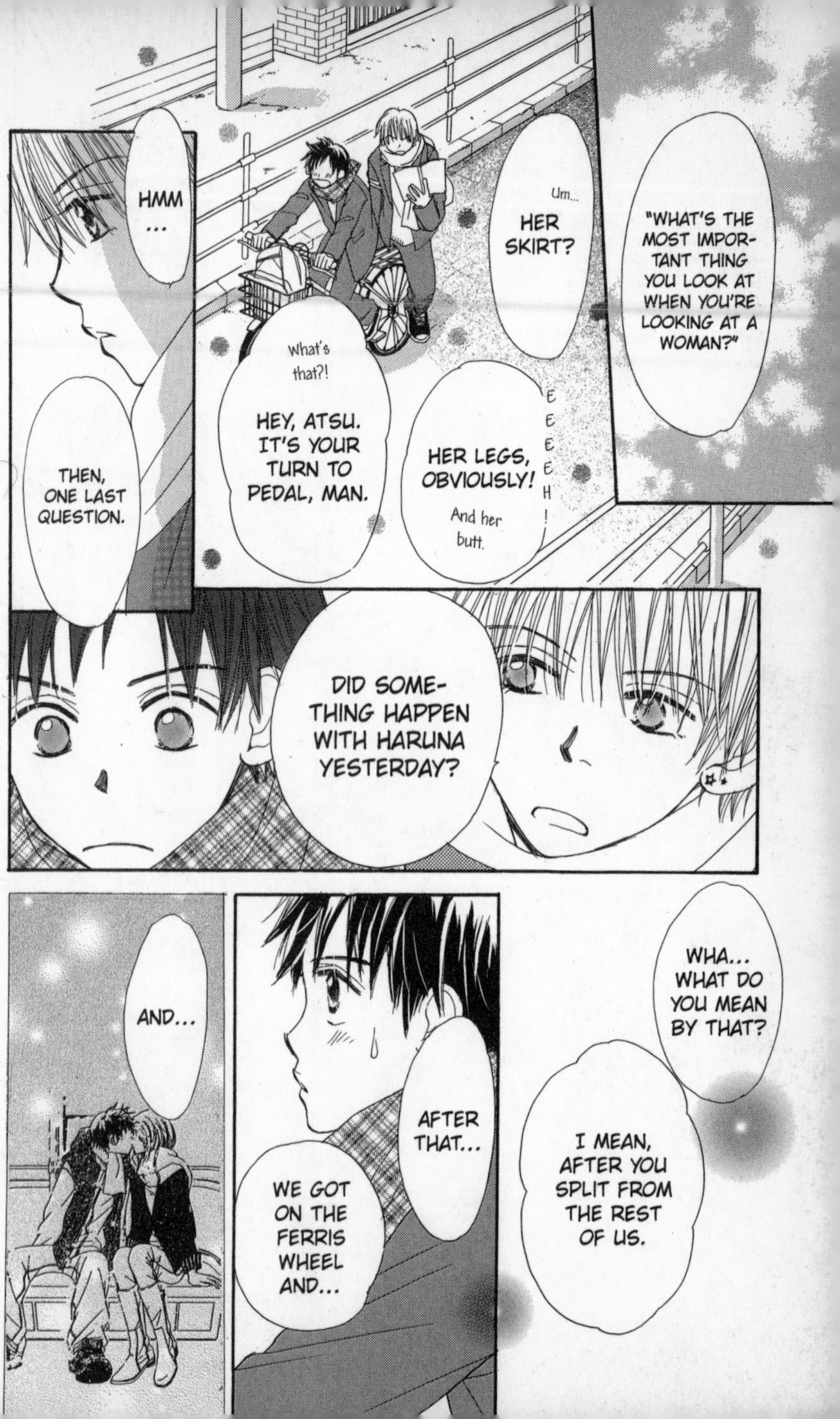
"WHAT'S THE MOST IMPORTANT THING YOU LOOK AT WHEN YOU'RE LOOKING AT A WOMAN?"
Um... HER SKIRT?
HER LEGS, OBVIOUSLY!
EEEEH!
And her butt.
What's that?!
HEY, ATSU. IT'S YOUR TURN TO PEDAL, MAN.
HMM...
THEN, ONE LAST QUESTION.
DID SOMETHING HAPPEN WITH HARUNA YESTERDAY?
WHA... WHAT DO YOU MEAN BY THAT?
I MEAN, AFTER YOU SPLIT FROM THE REST OF US.
AFTER THAT...
WE GOT ON THE FERRIS WHEEL AND...
AND...

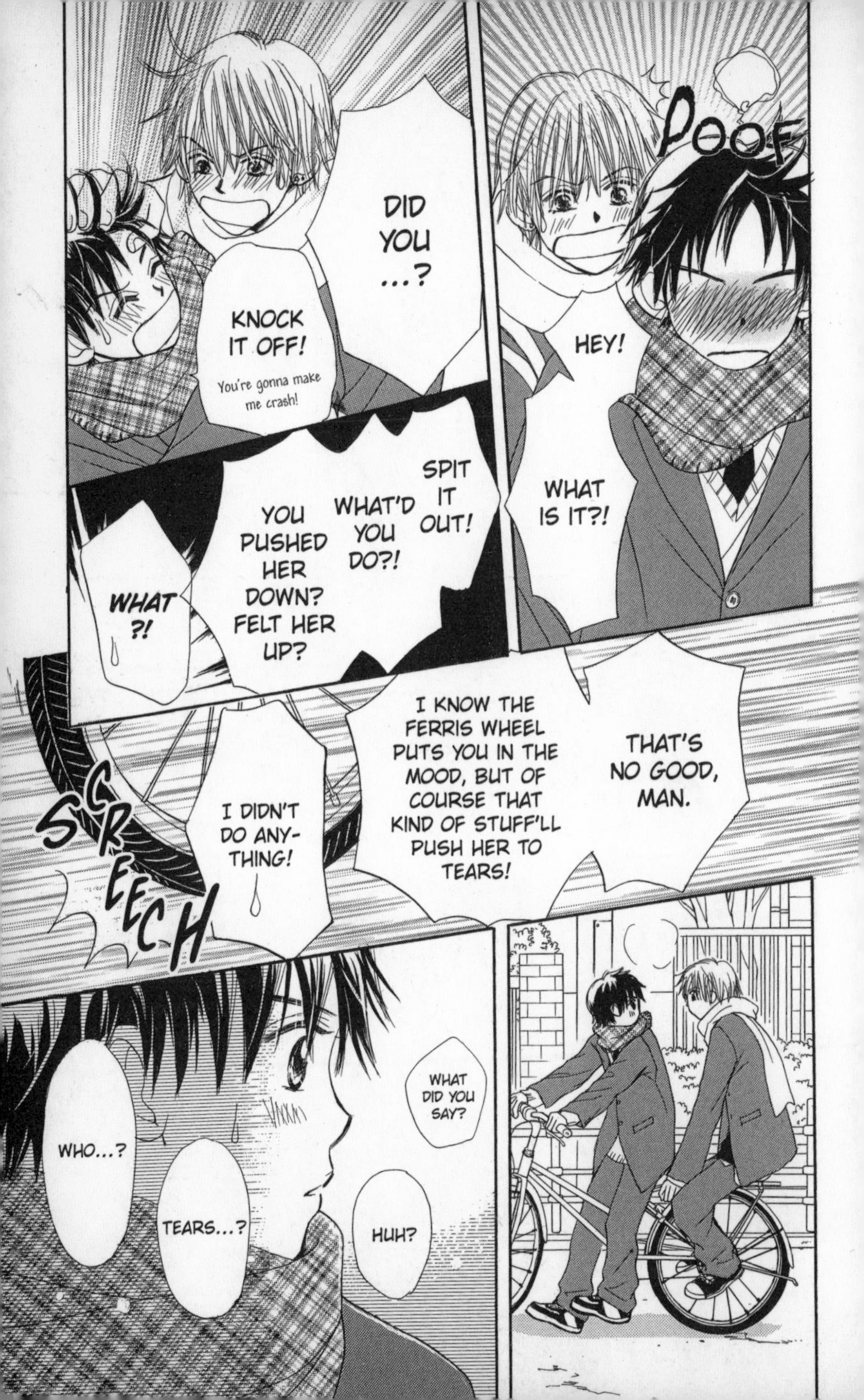
POOF
HEY!
WHAT IS IT?!
DID YOU ...?
KNOCK IT OFF!
You're gonna make me crash!
SPIT IT OUT!
WHAT'D YOU DO?!
YOU PUSHED HER DOWN? FELT HER UP?
WHAT ?!
THAT'S NO GOOD, MAN.
I KNOW THE FERRIS WHEEL PUTS YOU IN THE MOOD, BUT OF COURSE THAT KIND OF STUFF'LL PUSH HER TO TEARS!
I DIDN'T DO ANY-THING!
SCREECH
WHAT DID YOU SAY?
HUH?
TEARS...?
WHO...?

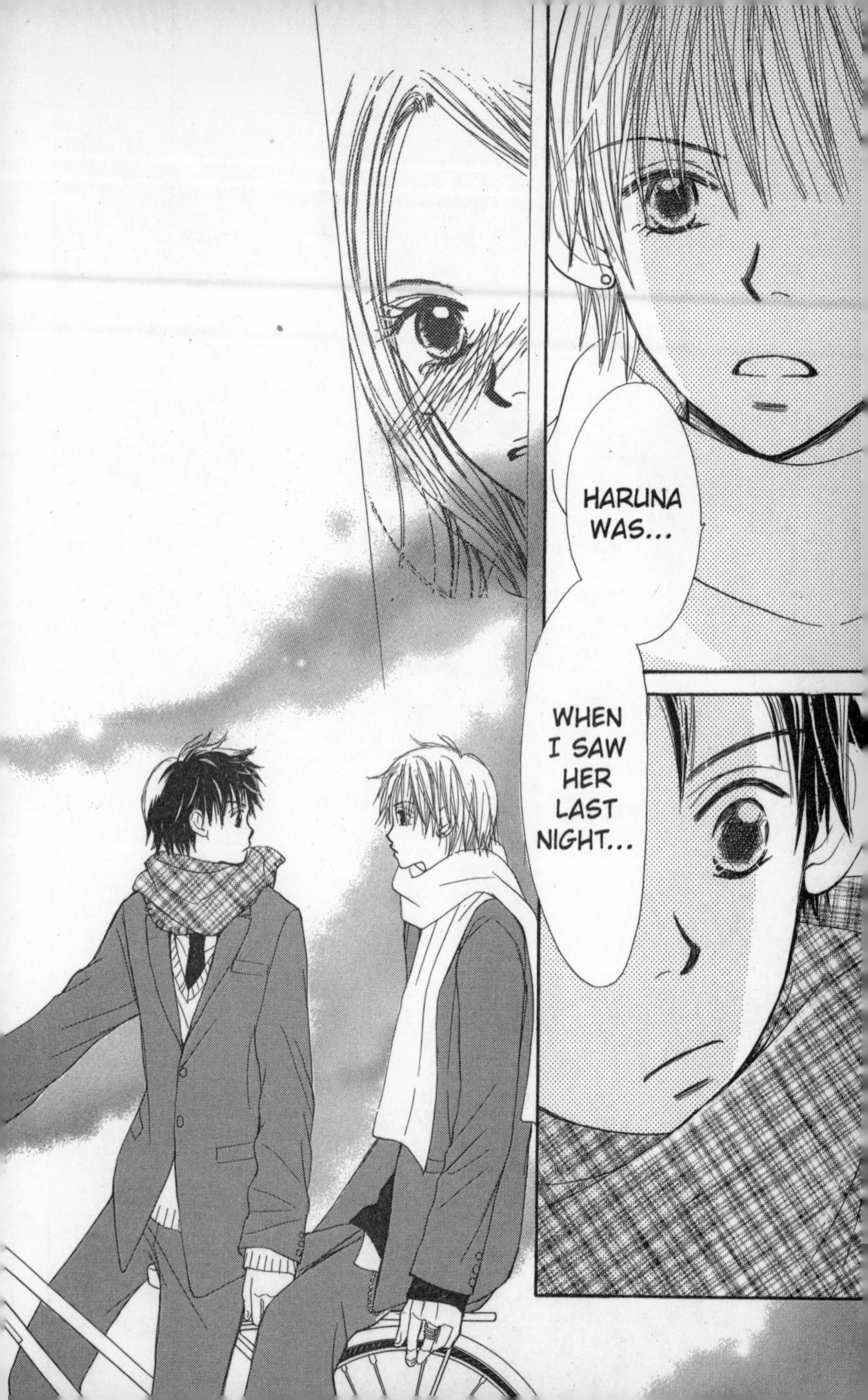
HARUNA WAS...
WHEN I SAW HER LAST NIGHT...

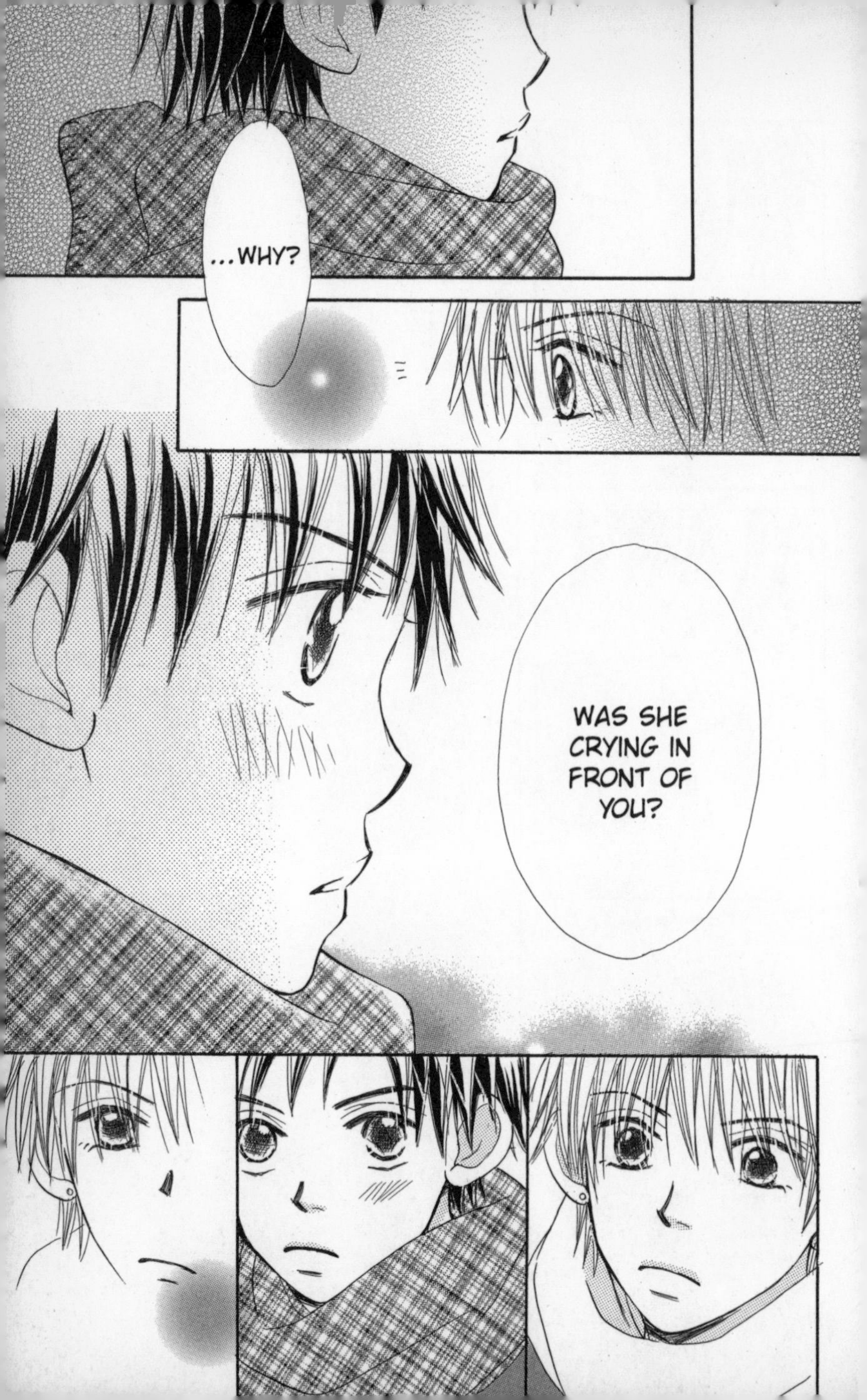
...WHY?
WAS SHE CRYING IN FRONT OF YOU?

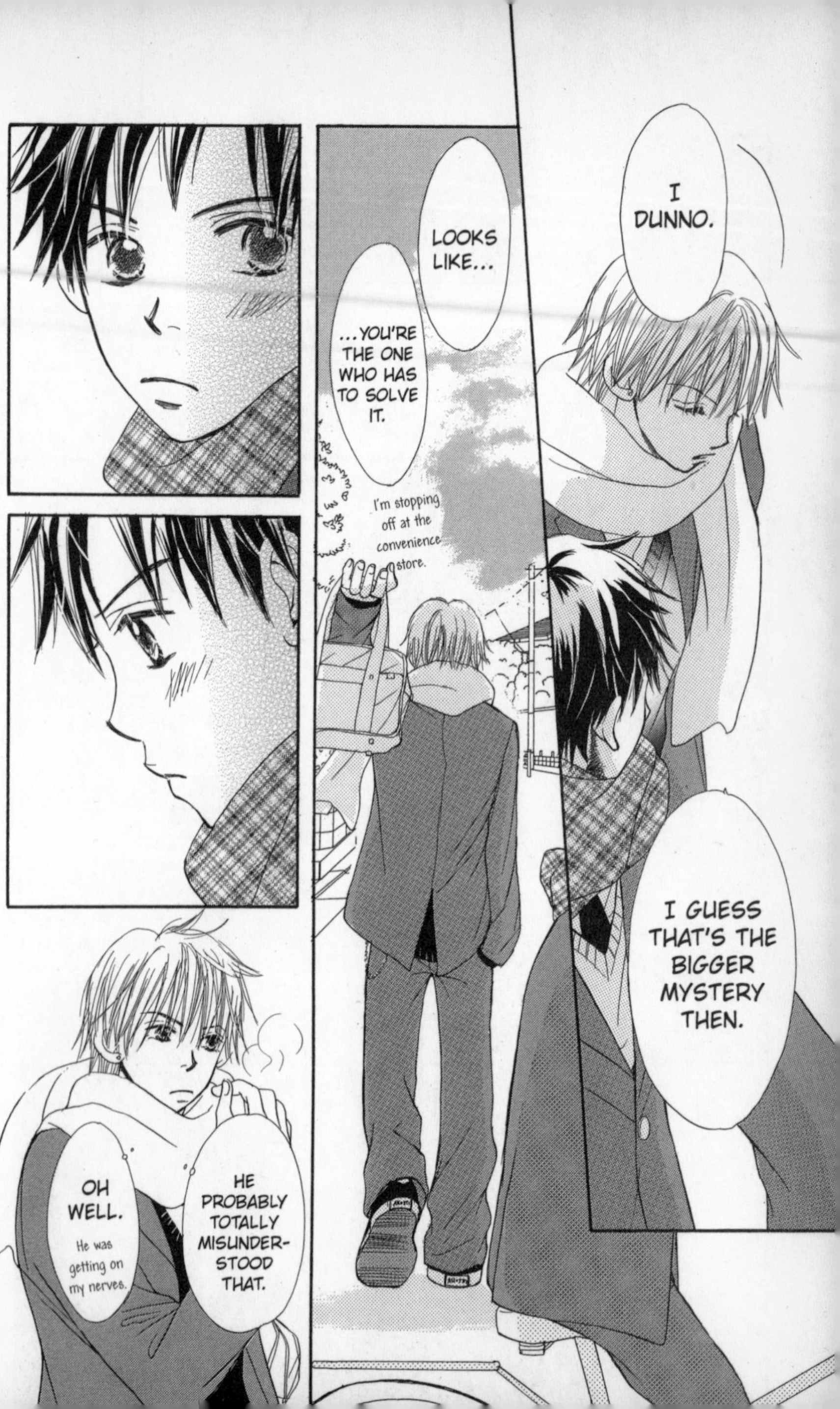
I DUNNO.
I GUESS THAT'S THE BIGGER MYSTERY THEN.
LOOKS LIKE...
...YOU'RE THE ONE WHO HAS TO SOLVE IT.
I'm stopping off at the convenience store.
HE PROBABLY TOTALLY MISUNDERSTOOD THAT.
OH WELL.
He was getting on my nerves.

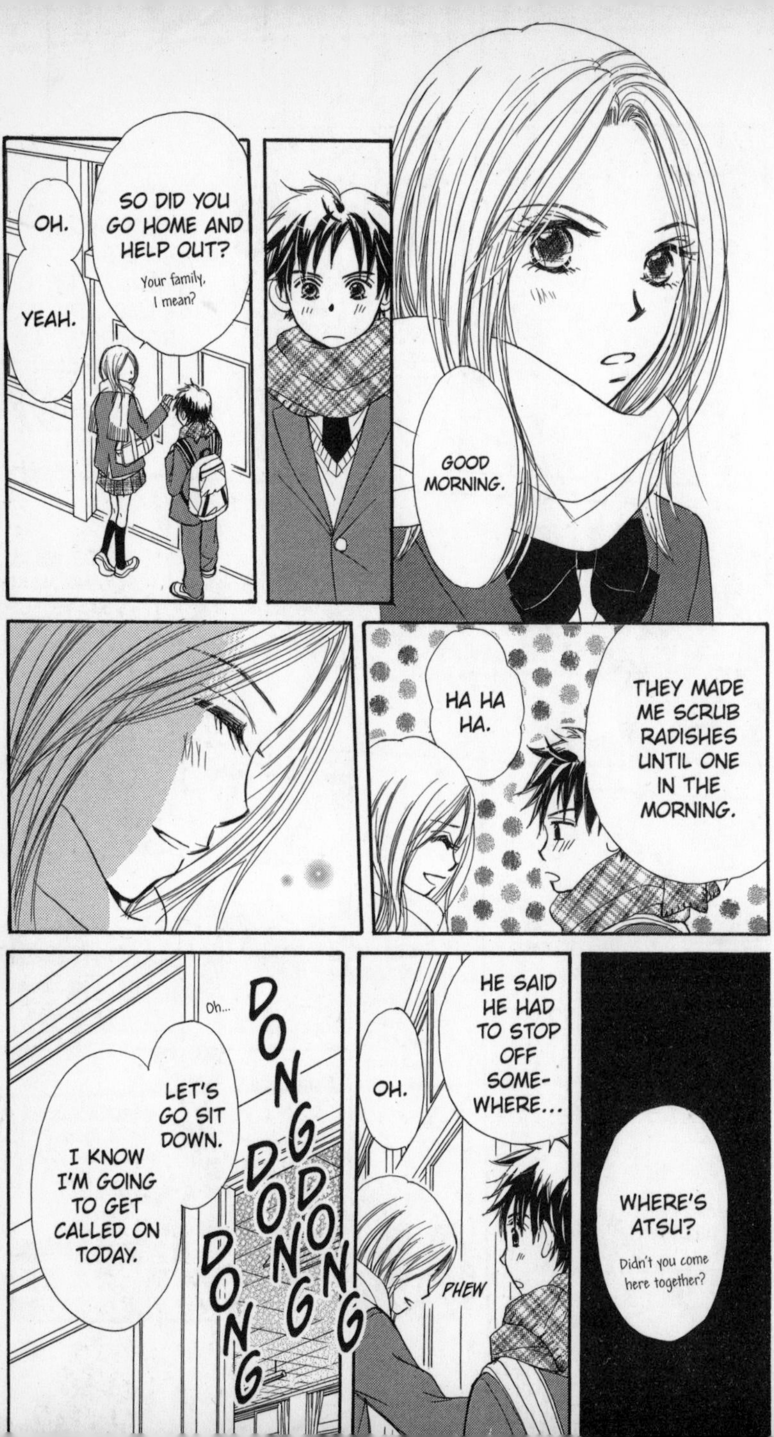
GOOD MORNING.
SO DID YOU GO HOME AND HELP OUT?
Your family, I mean?
OH.
YEAH.
THEY MADE ME SCRUB RADISHES UNTIL ONE IN THE MORNING.
HA HA HA.
WHERE'S ATSU?
Didn't you come here together?
HE SAID HE HAD TO STOP OFF SOME-WHERE...
OH.
PHEW
Oh...
DONG DONG DONG DONG
LET'S GO SIT DOWN.
I KNOW I'M GOING TO GET CALLED ON TODAY.

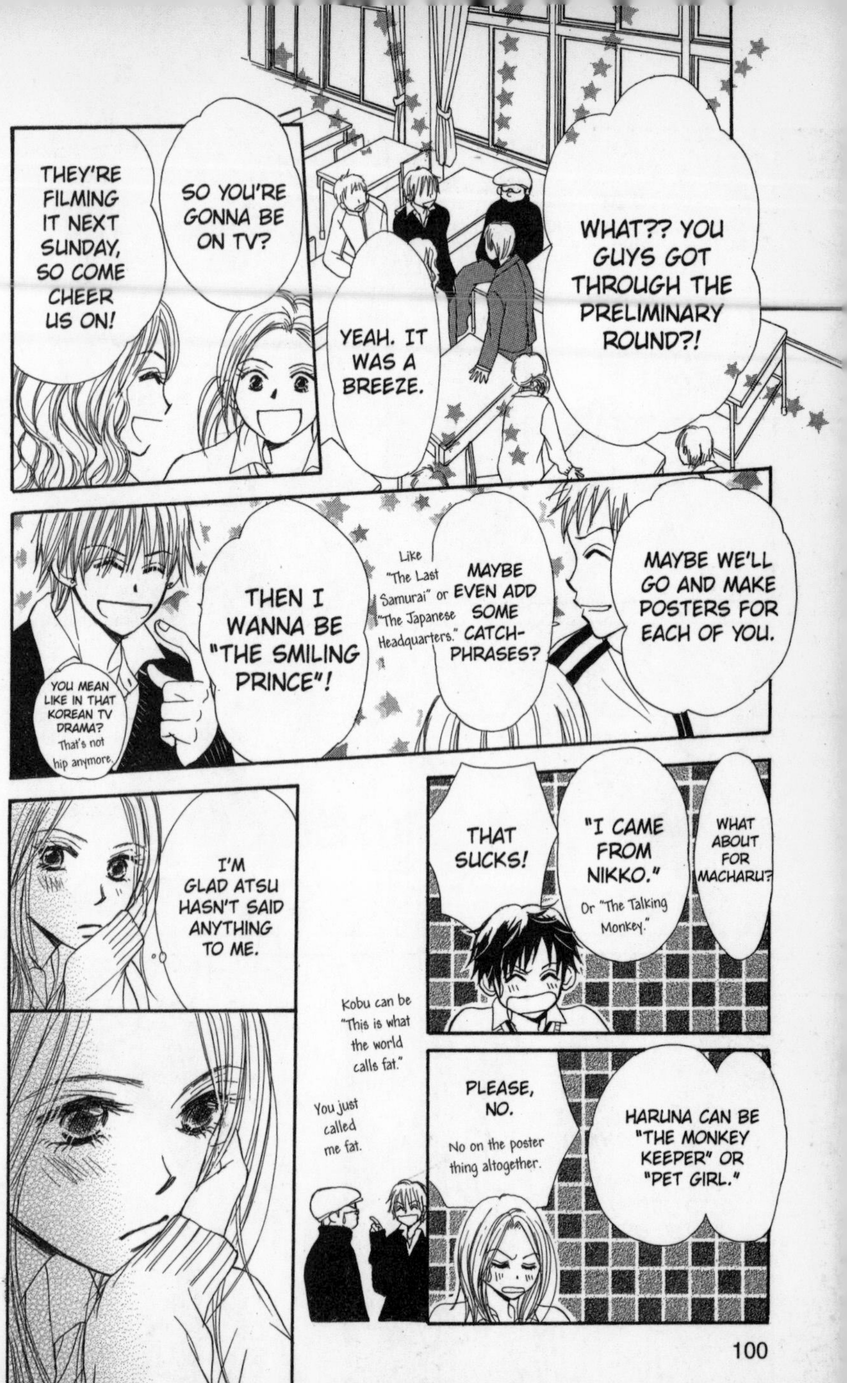
WHAT?? YOU GUYS GOT THROUGH THE PRELIMINARY ROUND?!
YEAH. IT WAS A BREEZE.
SO YOU'RE GONNA BE ON TV?
THEY'RE FILMING IT NEXT SUNDAY, SO COME CHEER US ON!
MAYBE WE'LL GO AND MAKE POSTERS FOR EACH OF YOU.
MAYBE EVEN ADD SOME CATCH-PHRASES?
Like "The Last Samurai" or "The Japanese Headquarters."
THEN I WANNA BE "THE SMILING PRINCE"!
YOU MEAN LIKE IN THAT KOREAN TV DRAMA? That's not hip anymore.
WHAT ABOUT FOR MACHARU?
"I CAME FROM NIKKO."
Or "The Talking Monkey."
THAT SUCKS!
HARUNA CAN BE "THE MONKEY KEEPER" OR "PET GIRL."
PLEASE, NO.
No on the poster thing altogether.
Kobu can be "This is what the world calls fat."
You just called me fat.
I'M GLAD ATSU HASN'T SAID ANYTHING TO ME.

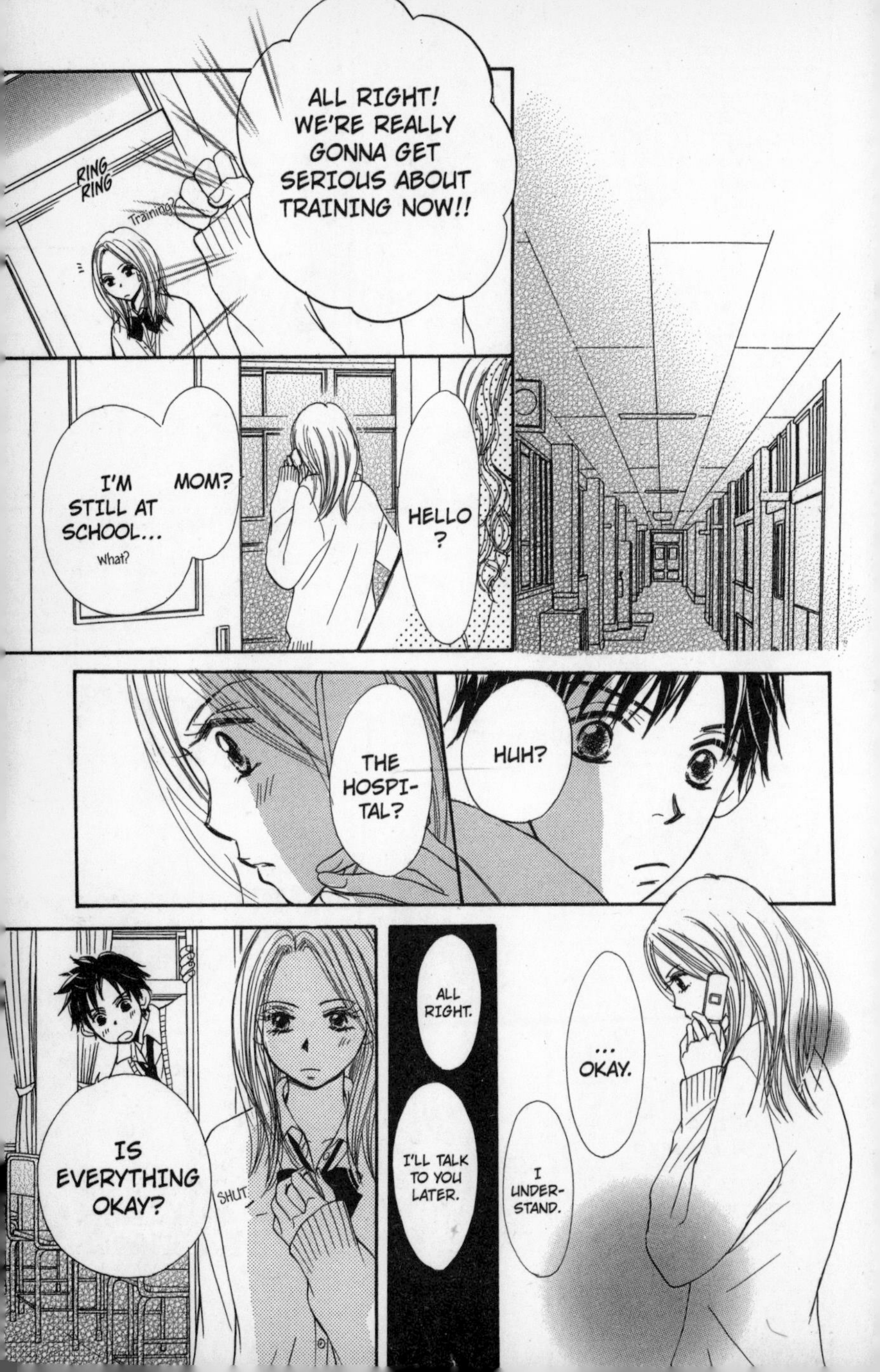
ALL RIGHT! WE'RE REALLY GONNA GET SERIOUS ABOUT TRAINING NOW!!
RING RING
Training?
HELLO ?
MOM?
I'M STILL AT SCHOOL...
What?
THE HOSPI-TAL?
HUH?
... OKAY.
I UNDER-STAND.
ALL RIGHT.
I'LL TALK TO YOU LATER.
SHUT
IS EVERYTHING OKAY?

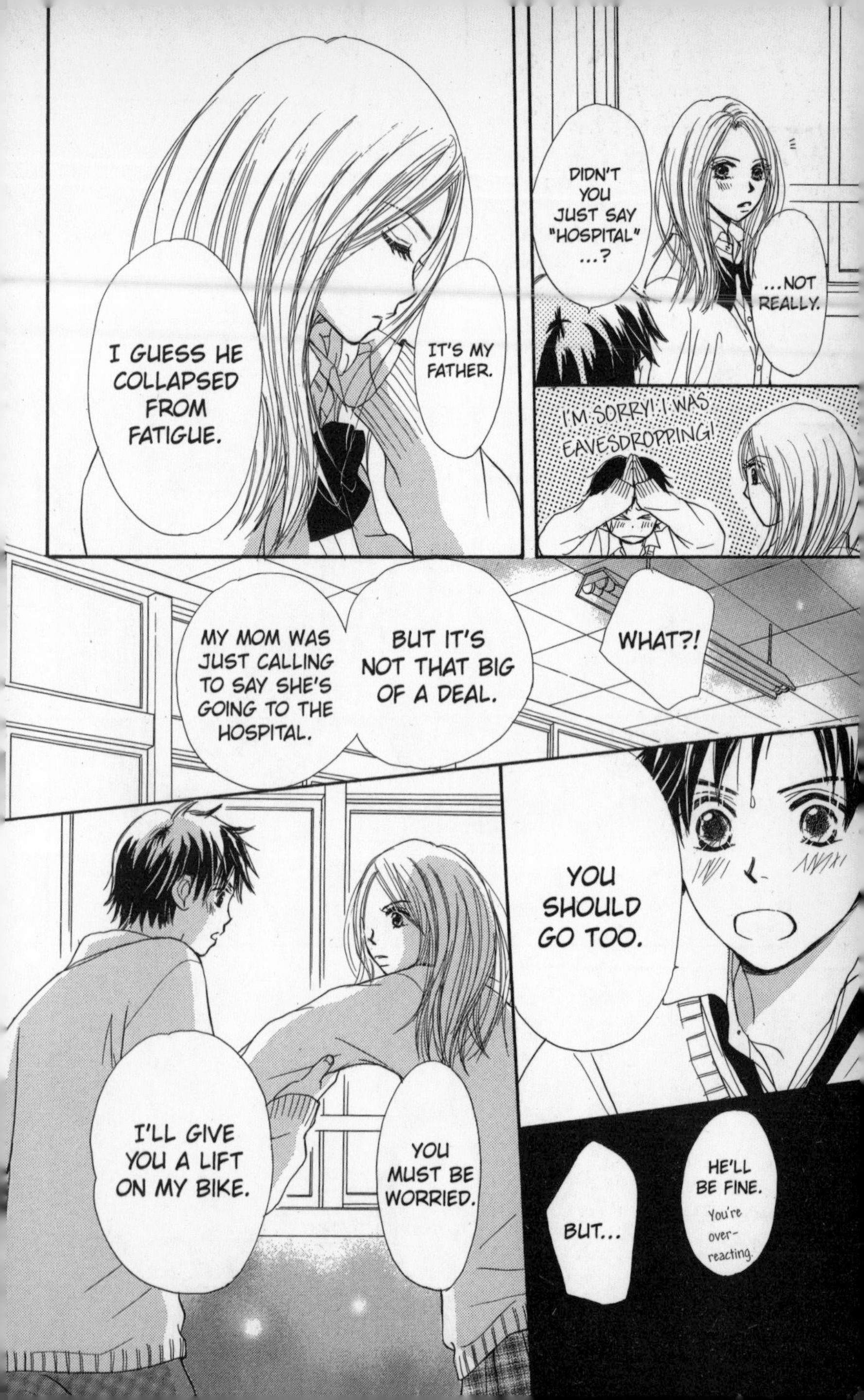
DIDN'T YOU JUST SAY "HOSPITAL" ...?
...NOT REALLY.
I'M SORRY! I WAS EAVESDROPPING!
IT'S MY FATHER.
I GUESS HE COLLAPSED FROM FATIGUE.
WHAT?!
BUT IT'S NOT THAT BIG OF A DEAL.
MY MOM WAS JUST CALLING TO SAY SHE'S GOING TO THE HOSPITAL.
YOU SHOULD GO TOO.
HE'LL BE FINE.
You're over-reacting.
BUT...
YOU MUST BE WORRIED.
I'LL GIVE YOU A LIFT ON MY BIKE.

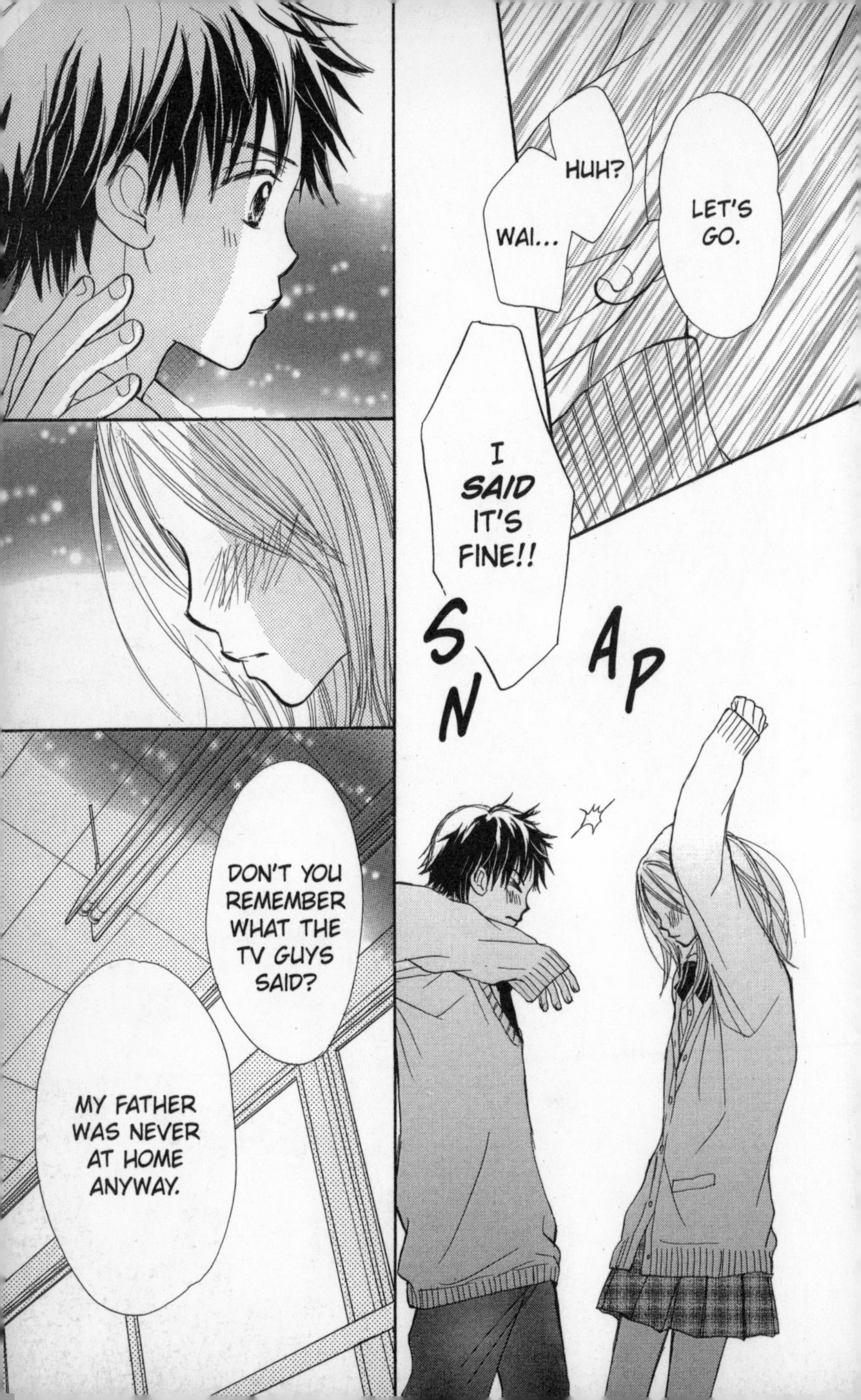
LET'S GO.
HUH?
WAI...
I SAID IT'S FINE!!
SNAP
DON'T YOU REMEMBER WHAT THE TV GUYS SAID?
MY FATHER WAS NEVER AT HOME ANYWAY.

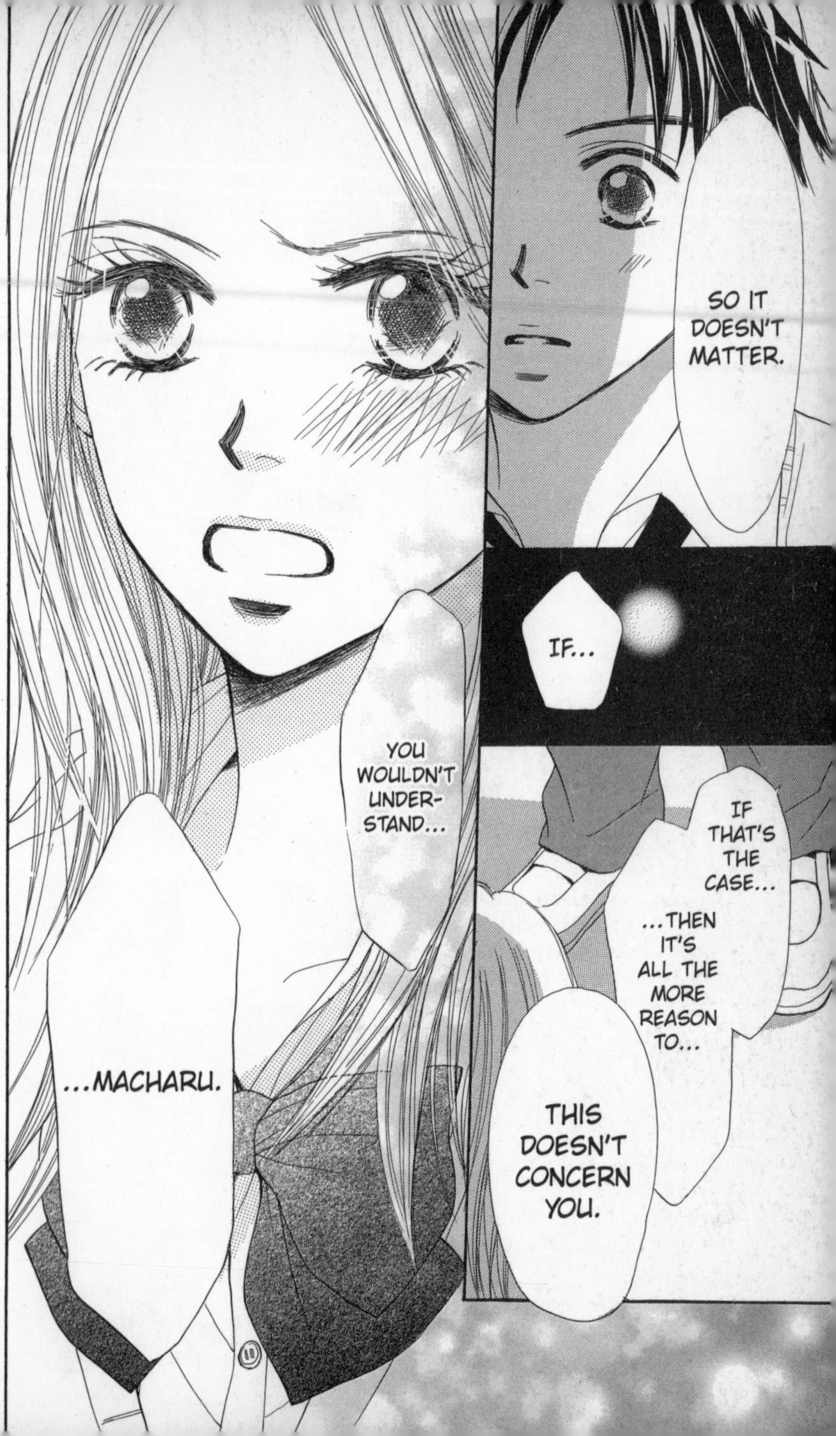
SO IT DOESN'T MATTER.
IF...
IF THAT'S THE CASE...
...THEN IT'S ALL THE MORE REASON TO...
THIS DOESN'T CONCERN YOU.
YOU WOULDN'T UNDER-STAND...
...MACHARU.

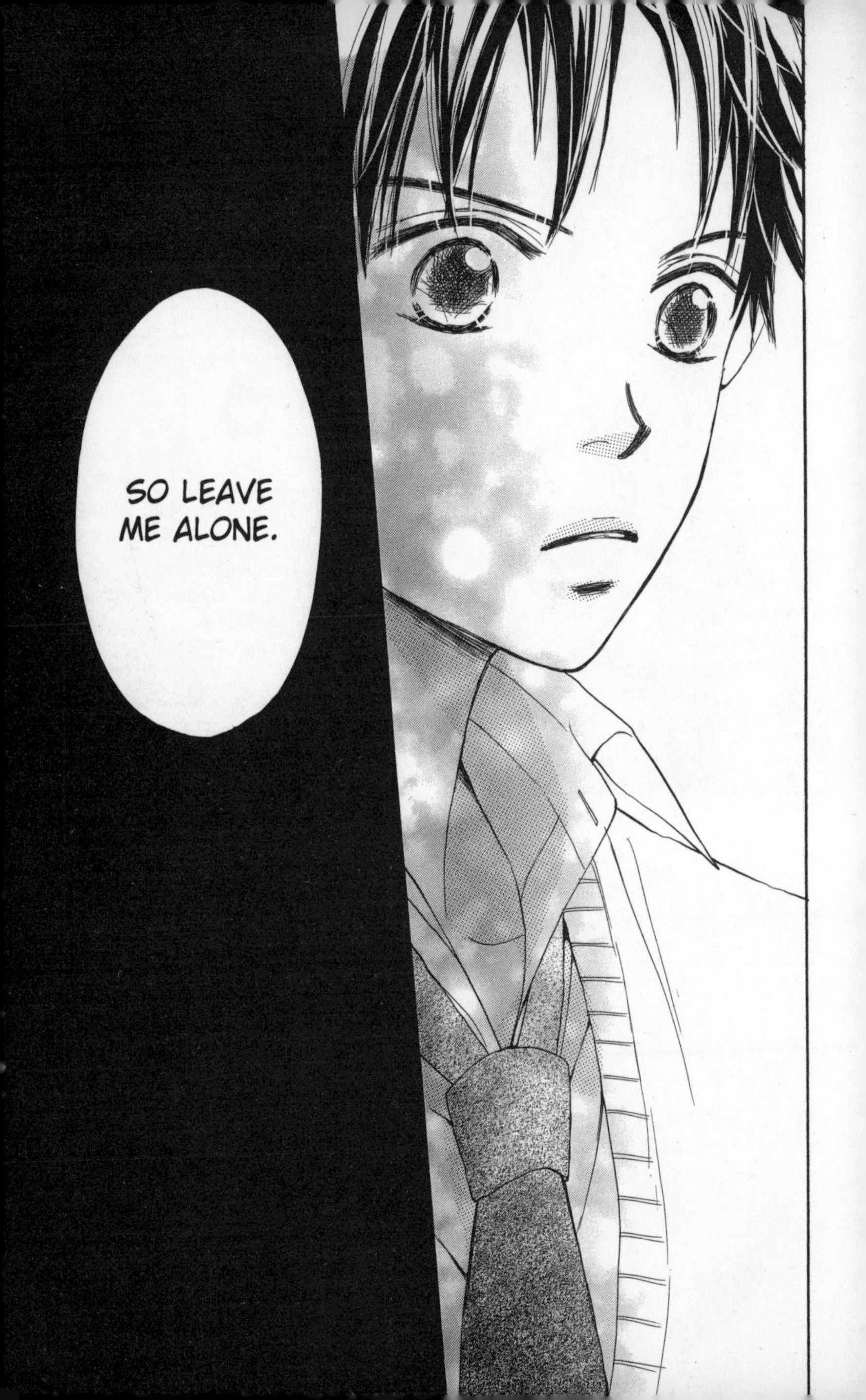
SO LEAVE ME ALONE.

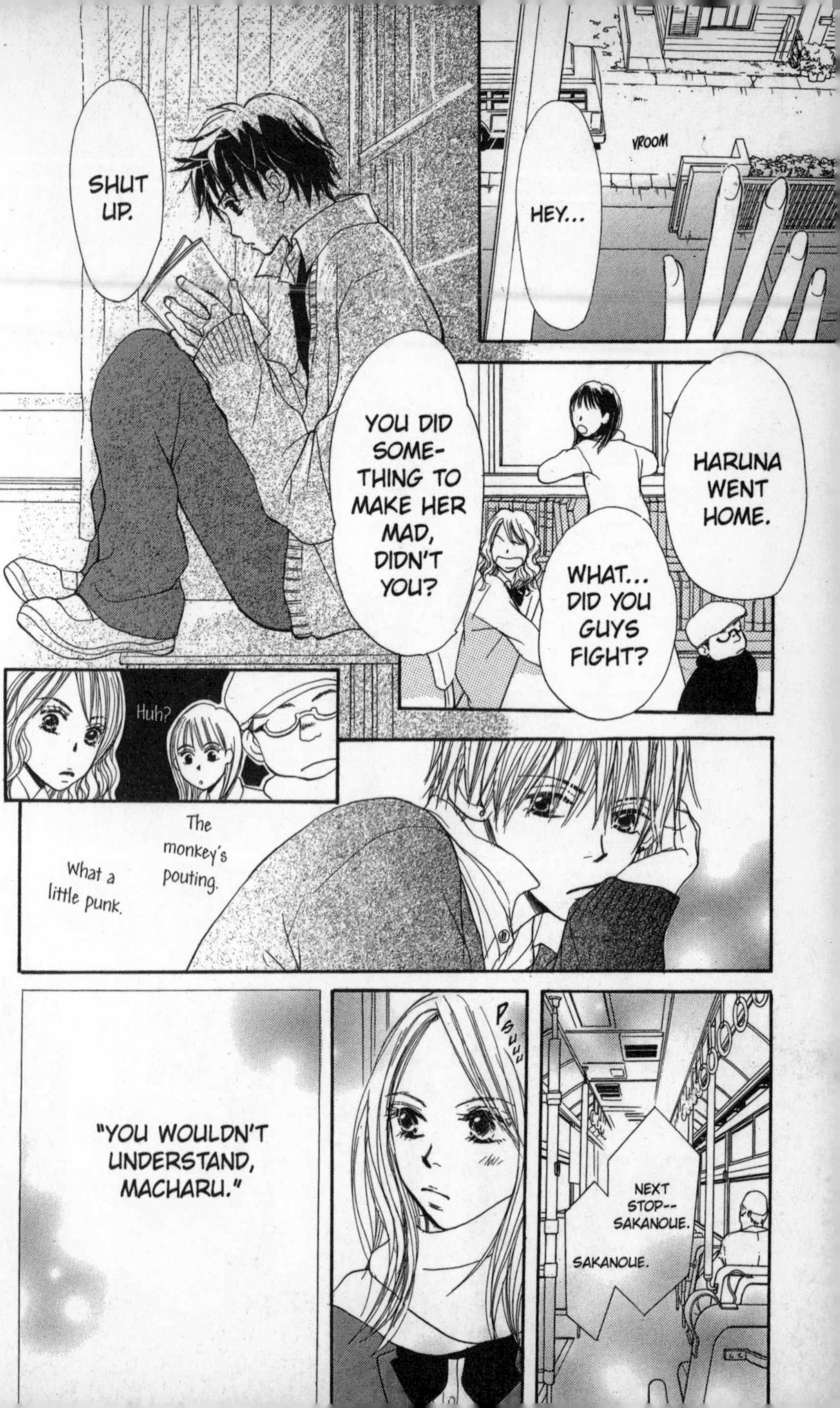
VROOM
HEY...
HARUNA WENT HOME.
WHAT... DID YOU GUYS FIGHT?
YOU DID SOME-THING TO MAKE HER MAD, DIDN'T YOU?
SHUT UP.
Huh?
The monkey's pouting.
What a little punk.
NEXT STOP-- SAKANOUE.
SAKANOUE.
PSUUU
"YOU WOULDN'T UNDERSTAND, MACHARU."

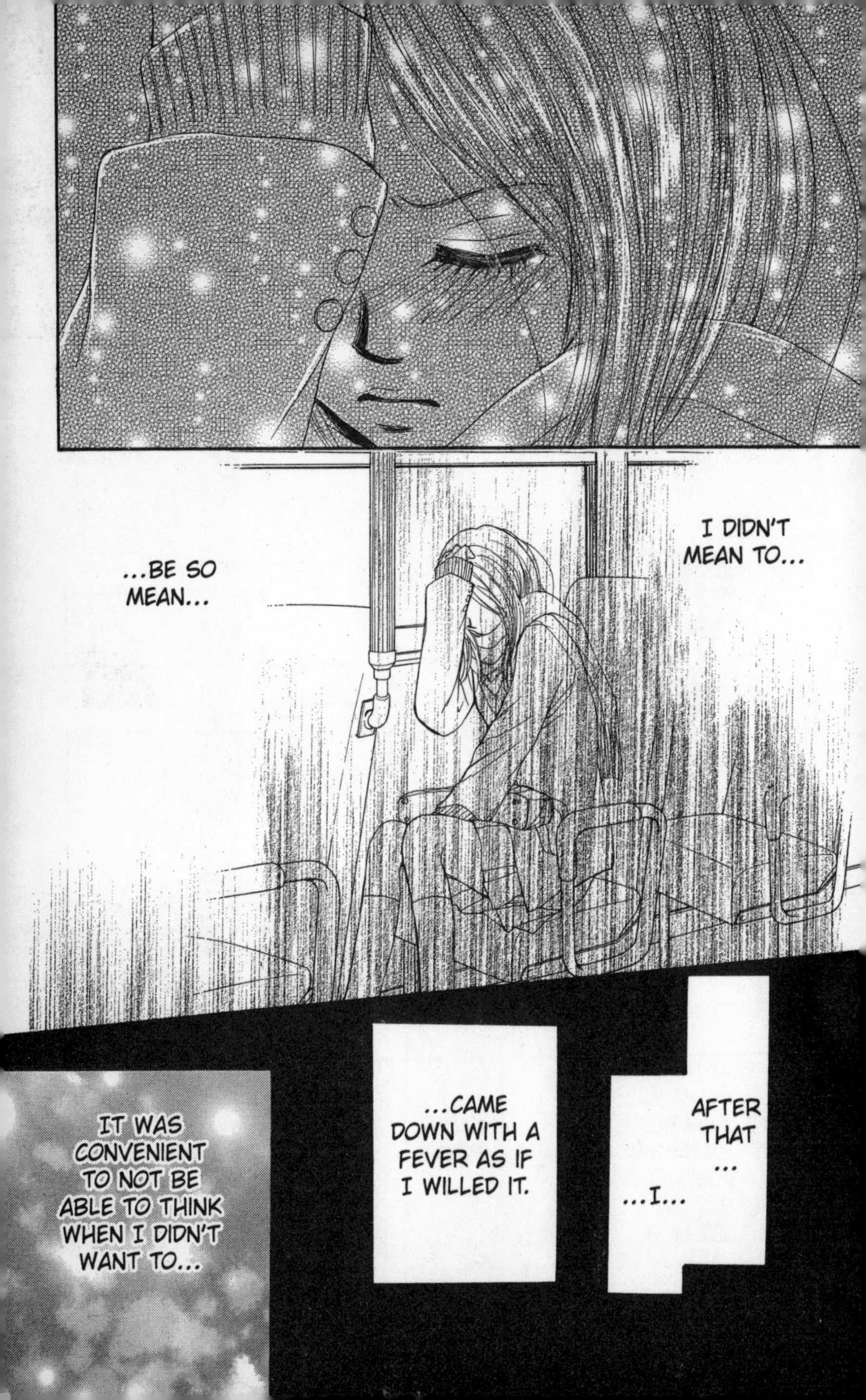
I DIDN'T MEAN TO...
...BE SO MEAN...
AFTER THAT ...
...I...
...CAME DOWN WITH A FEVER AS IF I WILLED IT.
IT WAS CONVENIENT TO NOT BE ABLE TO THINK WHEN I DIDN'T WANT TO...

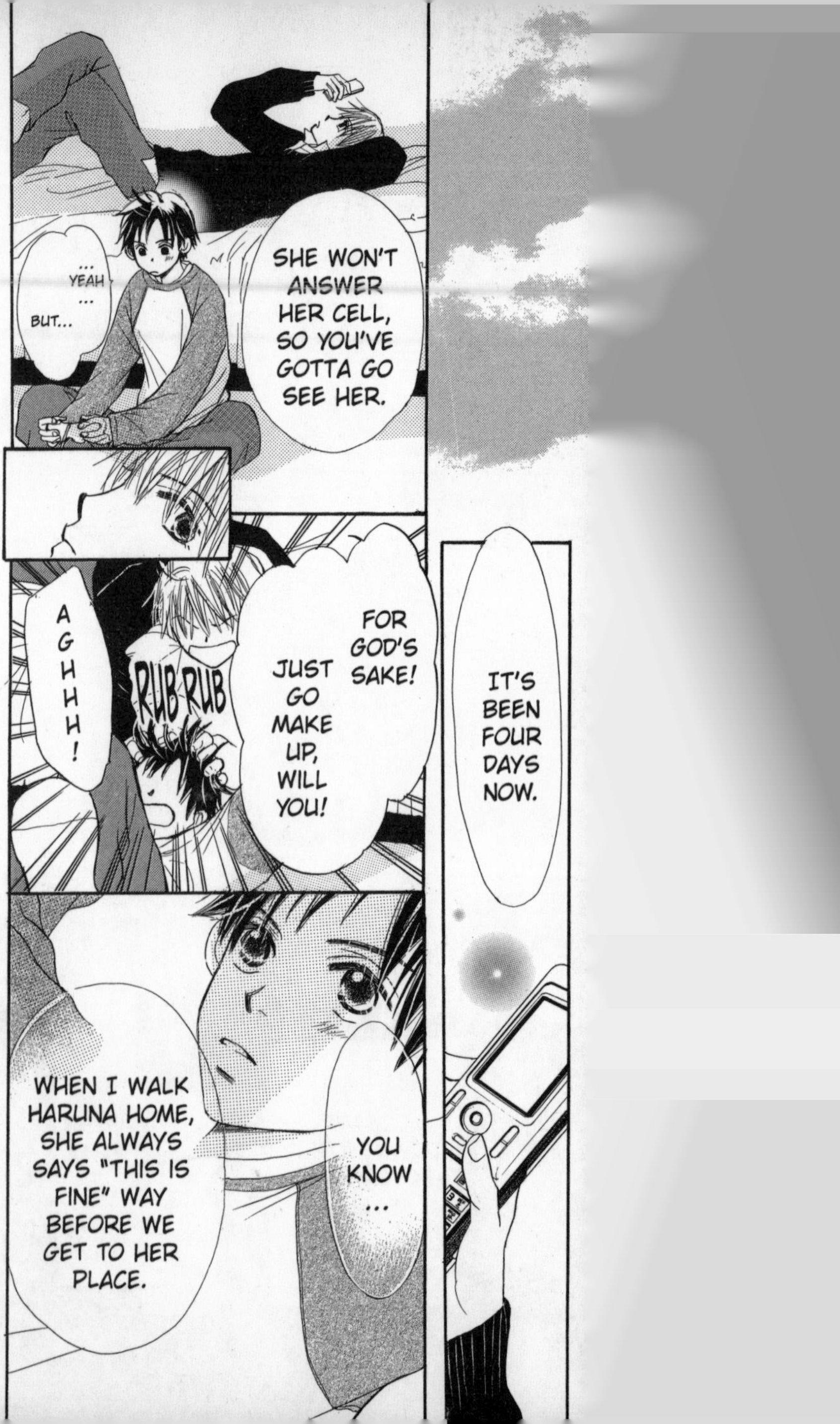

IT'S BEEN FOUR DAYS NOW.
SHE WON'T ANSWER HER CELL, SO YOU'VE GOTTA GO SEE HER.
... YEAH ... BUT...
FOR GOD'S SAKE!
JUST GO MAKE UP, WILL YOU!
RUB RUB
AGHHH!
YOU KNOW ...
WHEN I WALK HARUNA HOME, SHE ALWAYS SAYS "THIS IS FINE" WAY BEFORE WE GET TO HER PLACE.

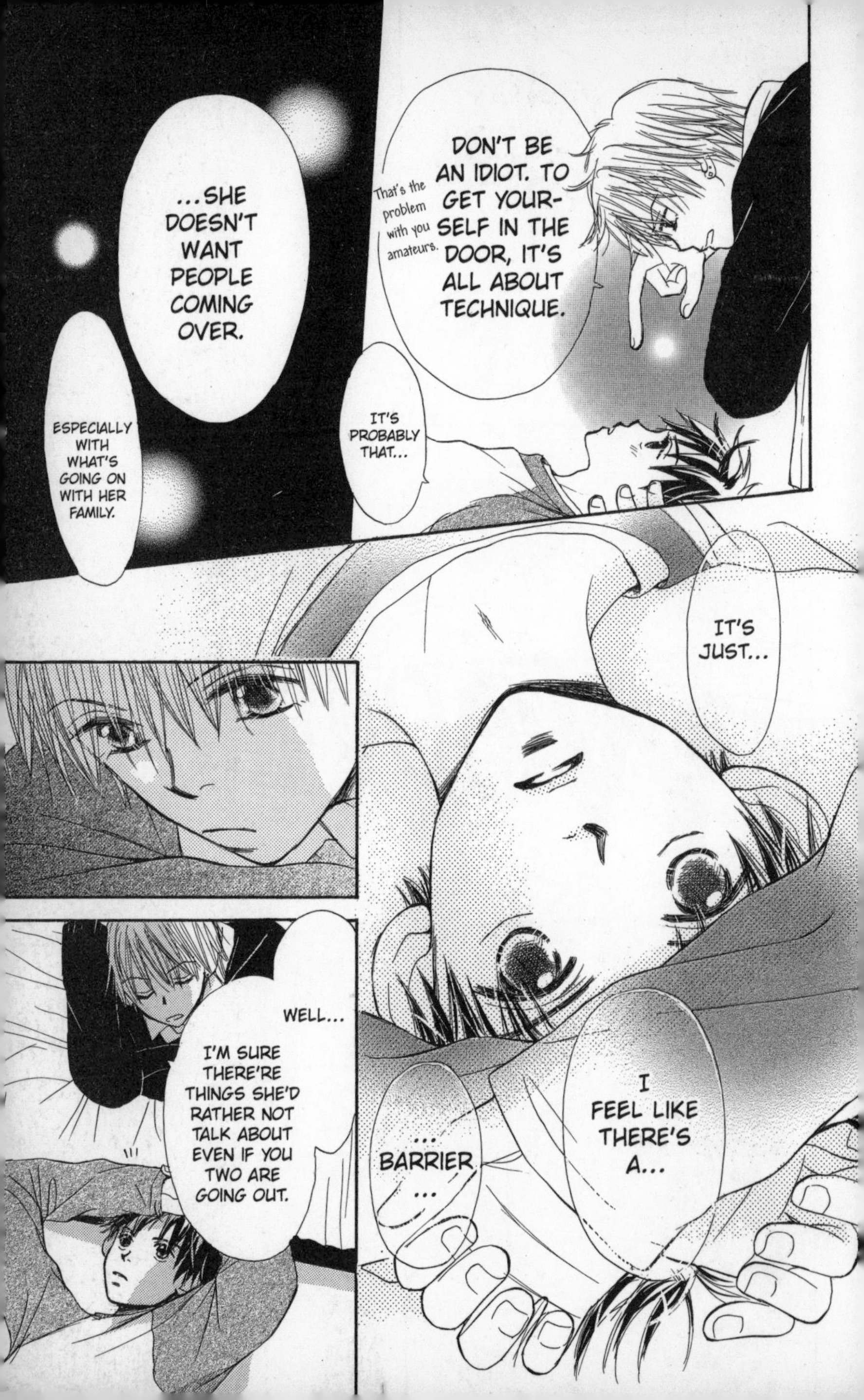
DON'T BE AN IDIOT. TO GET YOURSELF IN THE DOOR, IT'S ALL ABOUT TECHNIQUE.
That's the problem with you amateurs.
IT'S PROBABLY THAT...
...SHE DOESN'T WANT PEOPLE COMING OVER.
ESPECIALLY WITH WHAT'S GOING ON WITH HER FAMILY.
IT'S JUST...
I FEEL LIKE THERE'S A...
...BARRIER...
WELL...
I'M SURE THERE'RE THINGS SHE'D RATHER NOT TALK ABOUT EVEN IF YOU TWO ARE GOING OUT.

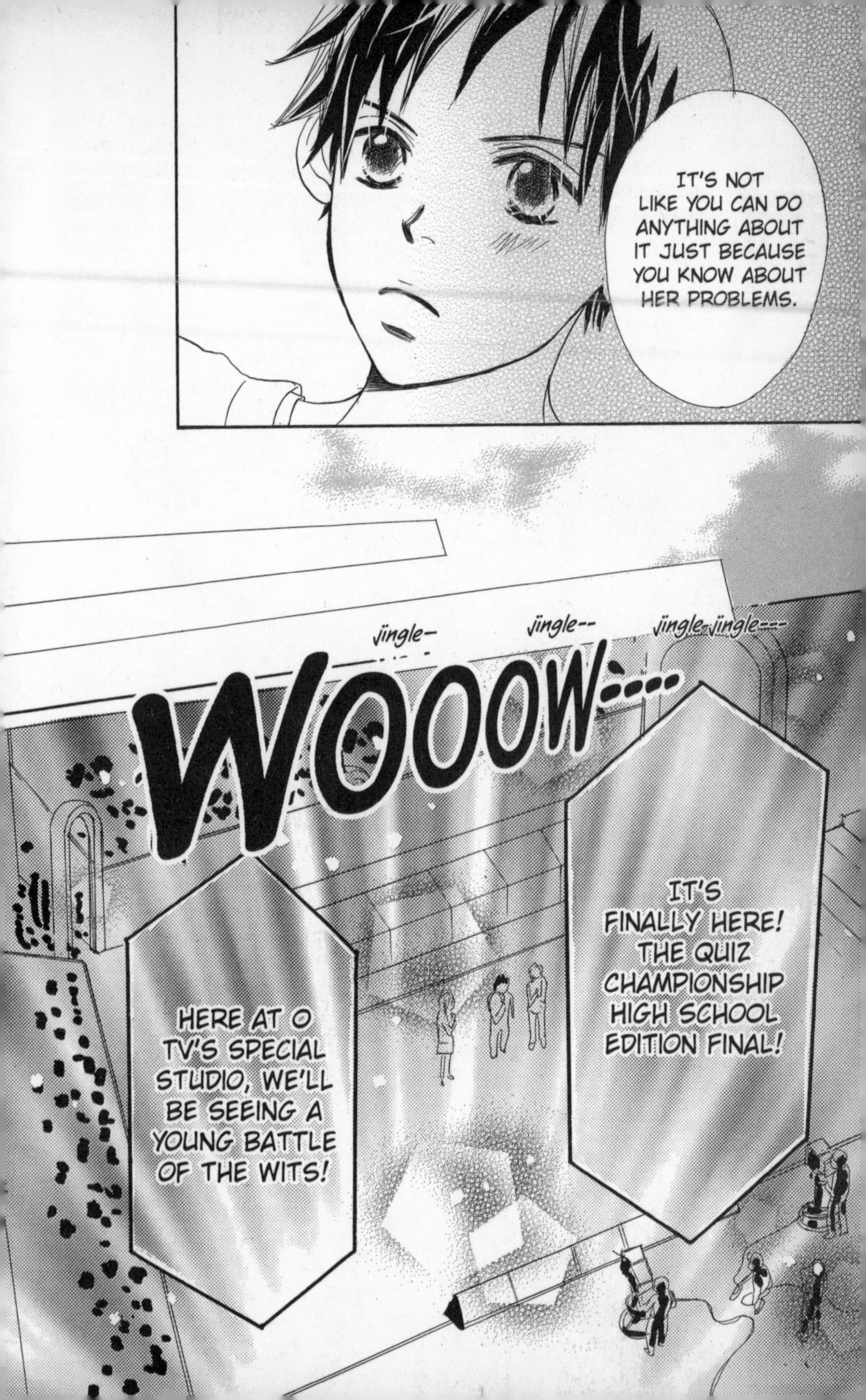
IT'S NOT LIKE YOU CAN DO ANYTHING ABOUT IT JUST BECAUSE YOU KNOW ABOUT HER PROBLEMS.
jingle-jingle---
jingle--
jingle-
WOOOW----
IT'S FINALLY HERE! THE QUIZ CHAMPIONSHIP HIGH SCHOOL EDITION FINAL!
HERE AT O TV'S SPECIAL STUDIO, WE'LL BE SEEING A YOUNG BATTLE OF THE WITS!

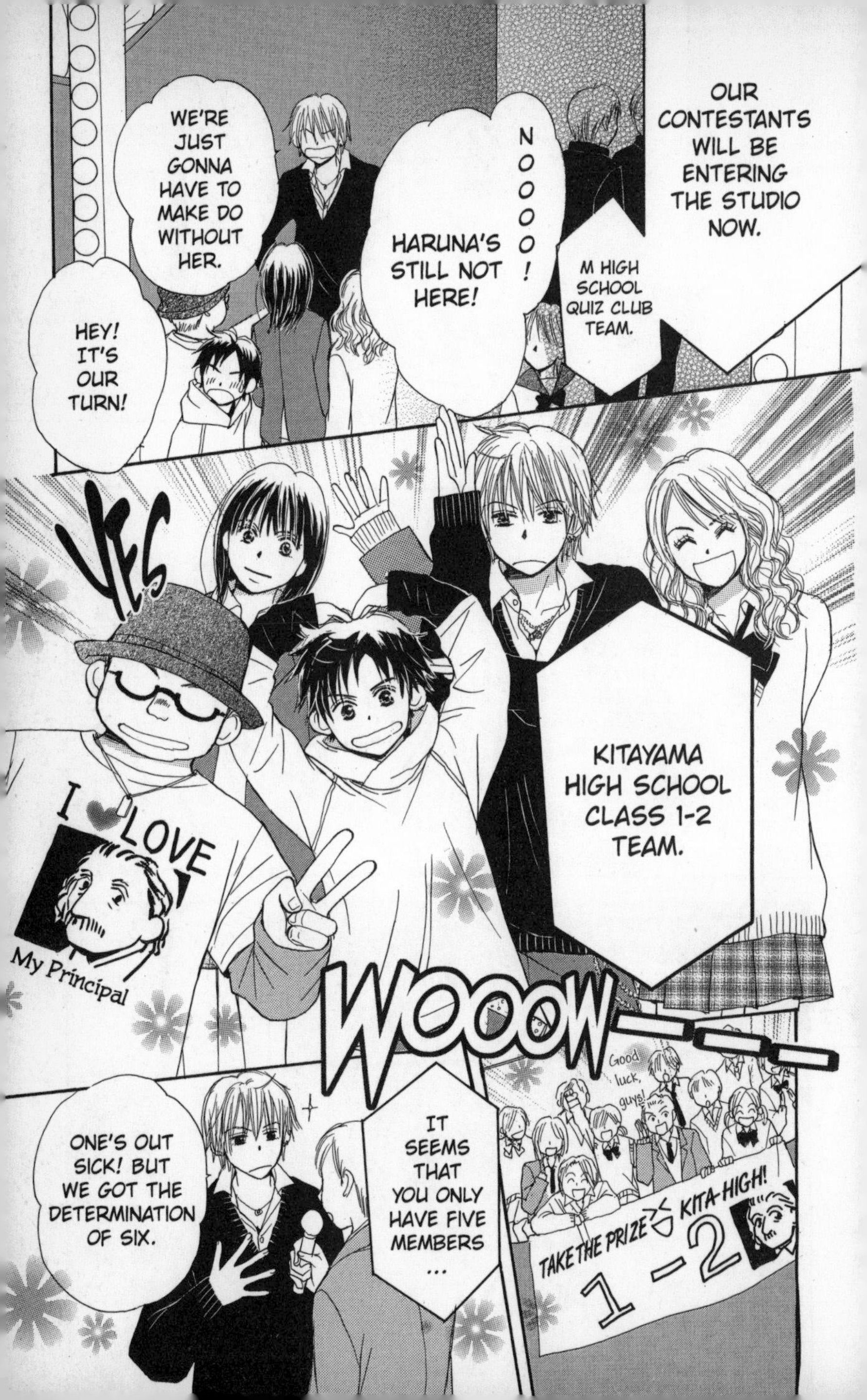
OUR CONTESTANTS WILL BE ENTERING THE STUDIO NOW.
M HIGH SCHOOL QUIZ CLUB TEAM.
NOOOOO!
HARUNA'S STILL NOT HERE!
WE'RE JUST GONNA HAVE TO MAKE DO WITHOUT HER.
HEY! IT'S OUR TURN!
KITAYAMA HIGH SCHOOL CLASS 1-2 TEAM.
YES
I LOVE
My Principal
WOOOW---
Good luck, guys!
TAKE THE PRIZE KITA-HIGH!
1-2
IT SEEMS THAT YOU ONLY HAVE FIVE MEMBERS...
ONE'S OUT SICK! BUT WE GOT THE DETERMINATION OF SIX.

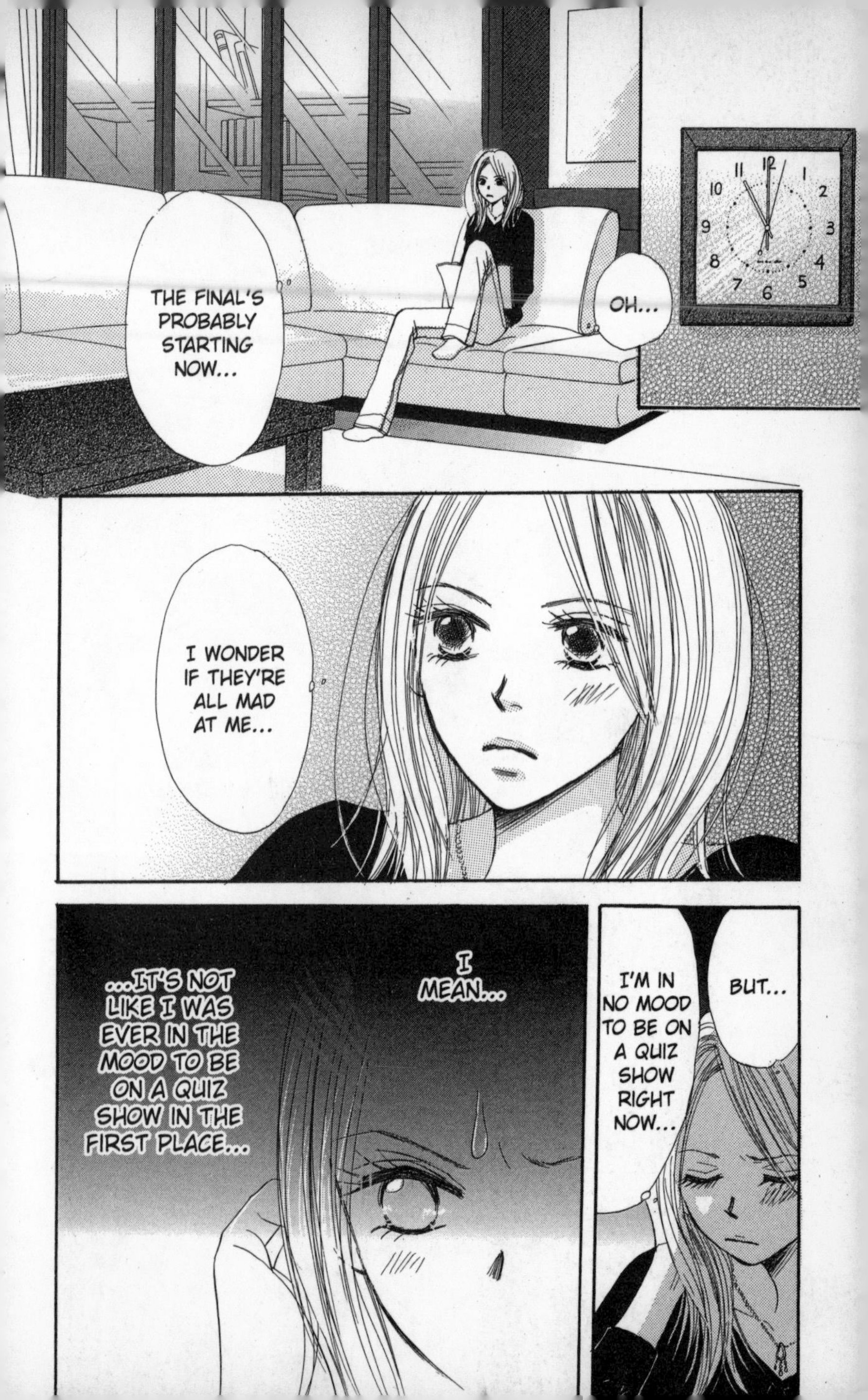
OH...
THE FINAL'S PROBABLY STARTING NOW...
I WONDER IF THEY'RE ALL MAD AT ME...
BUT...
I'M IN NO MOOD TO BE ON A QUIZ SHOW RIGHT NOW...
I MEAN...
...IT'S NOT LIKE I WAS EVER IN THE MOOD TO BE ON A QUIZ SHOW IN THE FIRST PLACE...

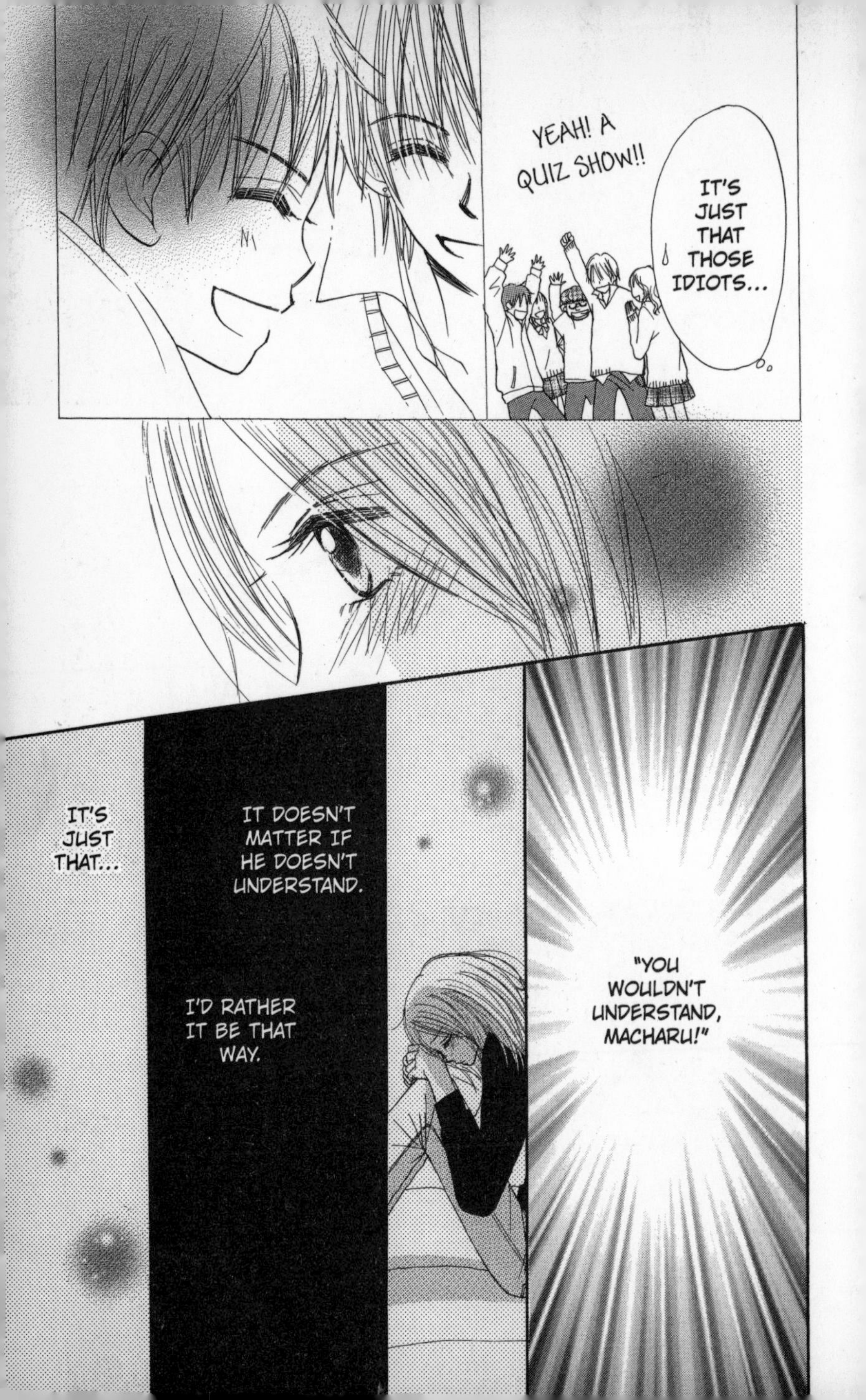
YEAH! A QUIZ SHOW!!
IT'S JUST THAT THOSE IDIOTS...
"YOU WOULDN'T UNDERSTAND, MACHARU!"
IT DOESN'T MATTER IF HE DOESN'T UNDERSTAND.
I'D RATHER IT BE THAT WAY.
IT'S JUST THAT...

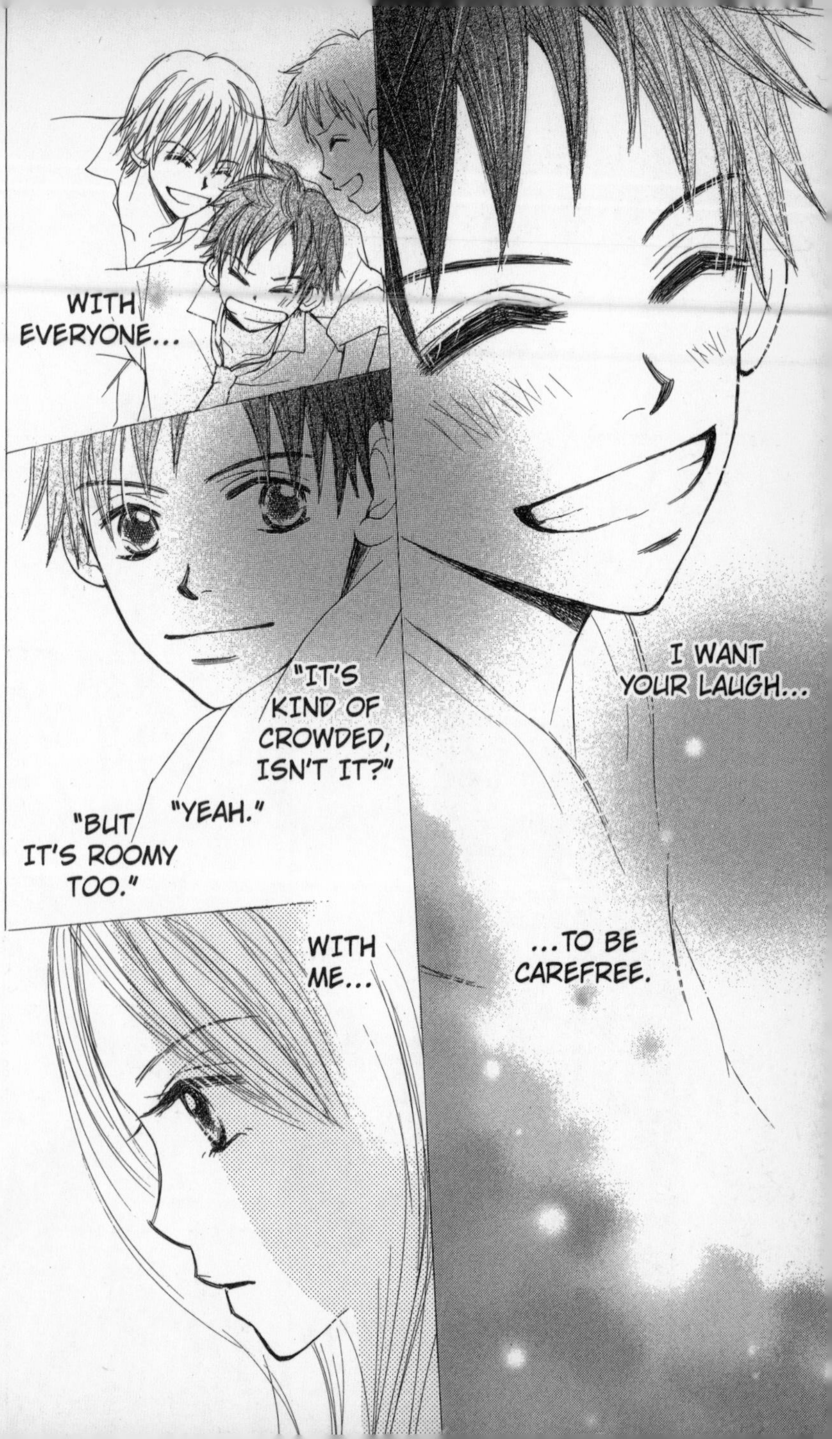
I WANT YOUR LAUGH...
WITH EVERYONE...
"IT'S KIND OF CROWDED, ISN'T IT?"
"YEAH."
"BUT IT'S ROOMY TOO."
WITH ME...
...TO BE CAREFREE.

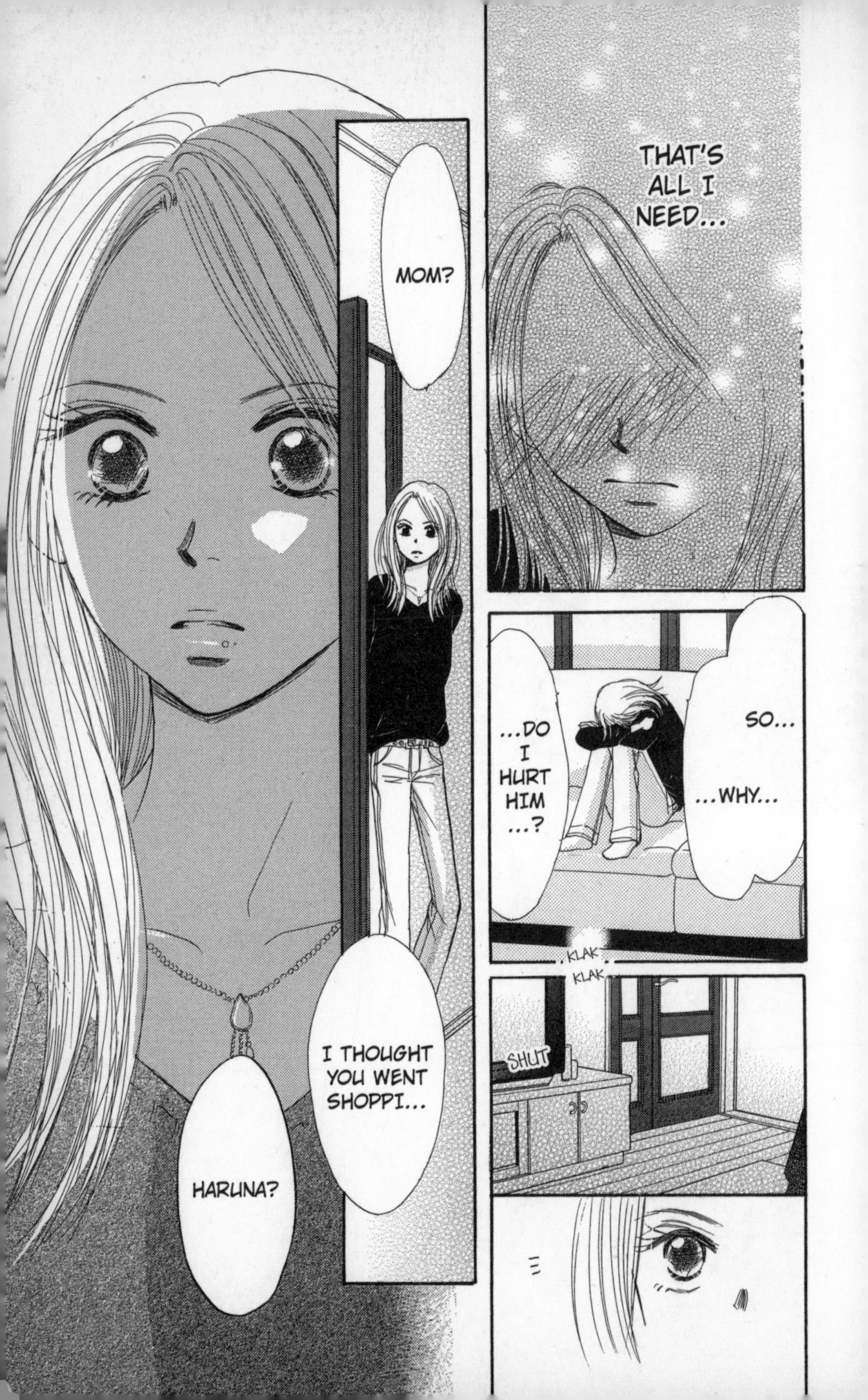
THAT'S ALL I NEED...
SO...
...WHY...
...DO I HURT HIM ...?
KLAK KLAK
SHUT
MOM?
I THOUGHT YOU WENT SHOPPI...
HARUNA?

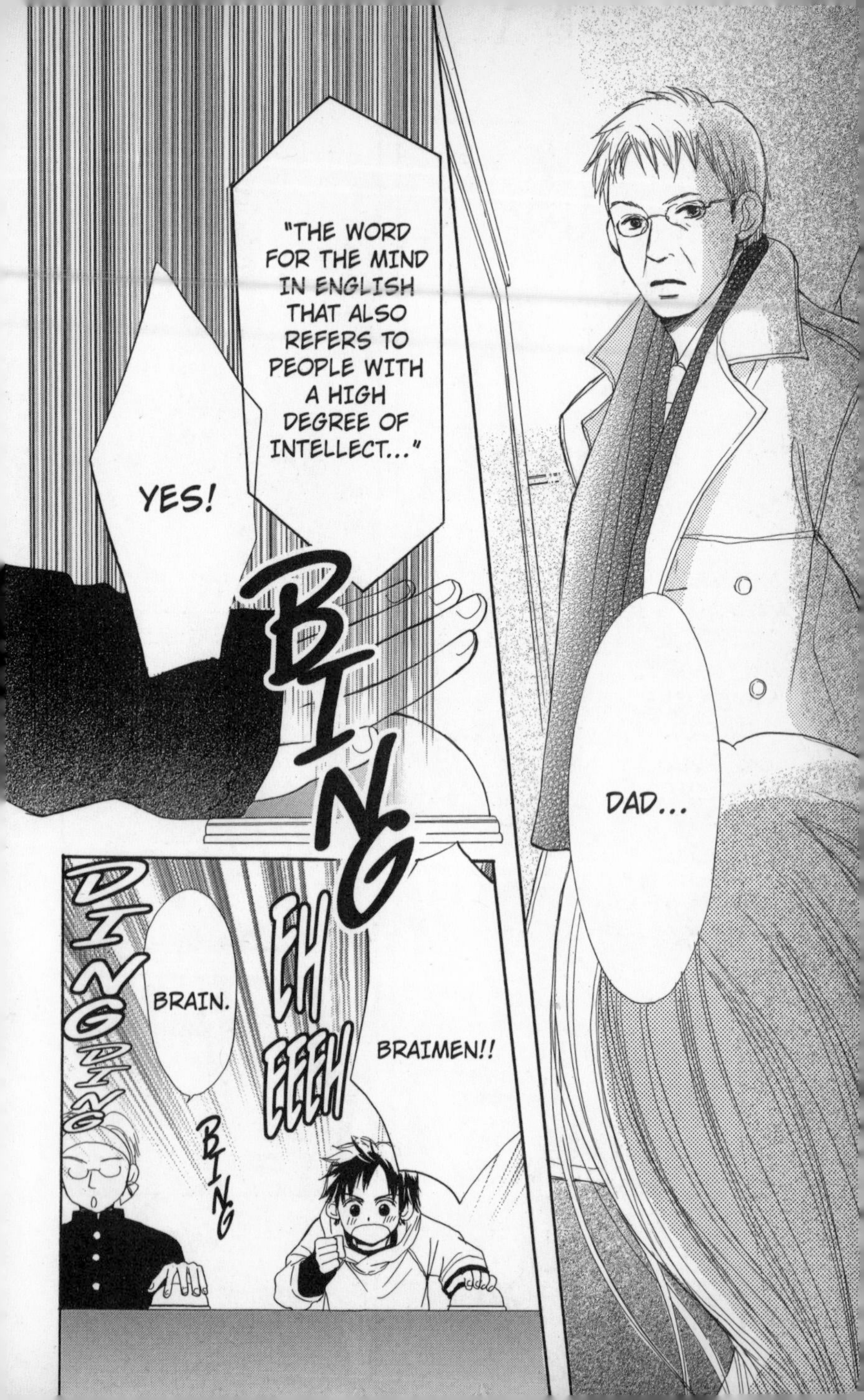
DAD...
"THE WORD FOR THE MIND IN ENGLISH THAT ALSO REFERS TO PEOPLE WITH A HIGH DEGREE OF INTELLECT..."
YES!
BING
EH EEEH
BRAIMEN!!
BRAIN.
DING DING
BING

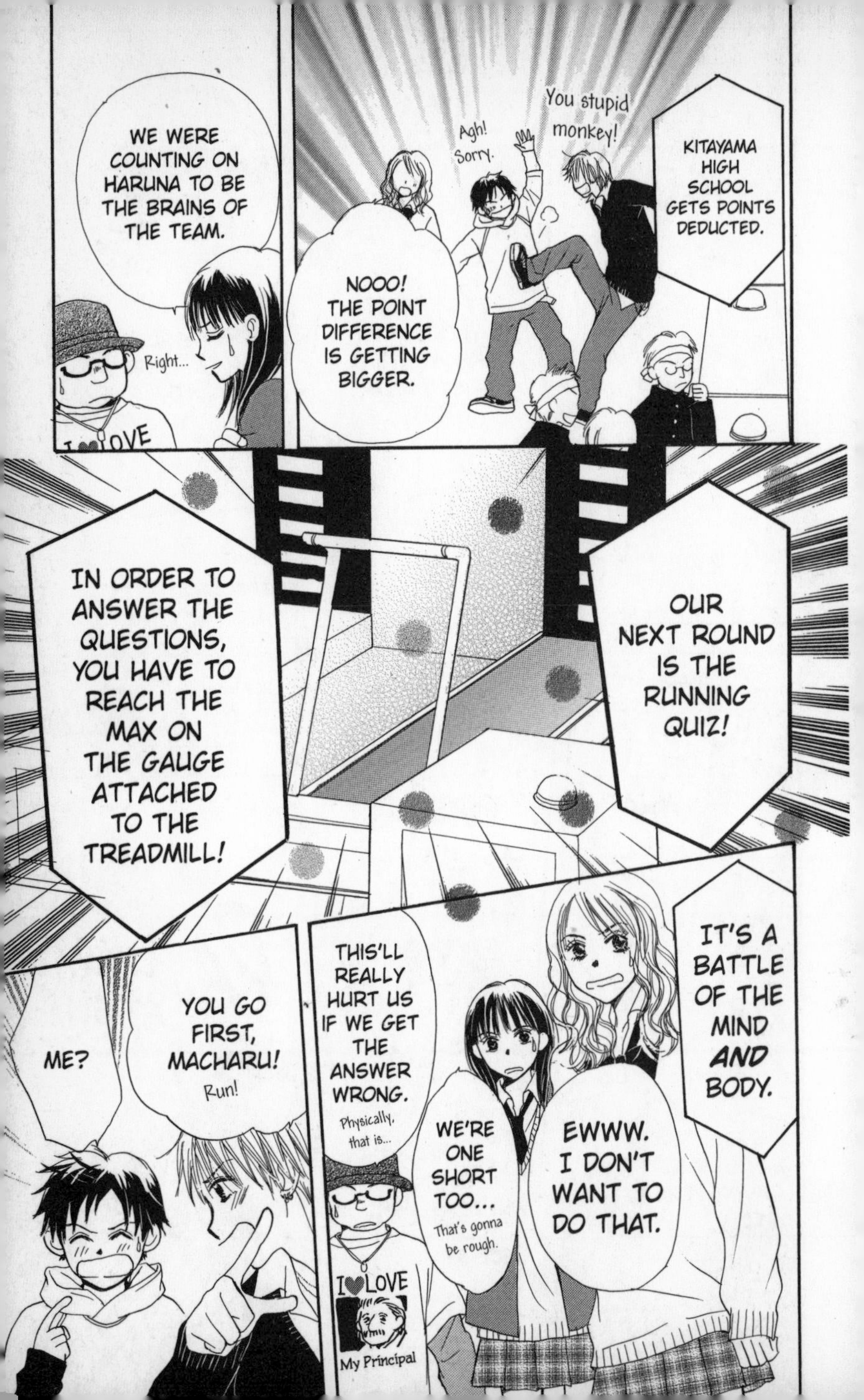
KITAYAMA HIGH SCHOOL GETS POINTS DEDUCTED.
You stupid monkey!
Agh! Sorry.
NOOO! THE POINT DIFFERENCE IS GETTING BIGGER.
WE WERE COUNTING ON HARUNA TO BE THE BRAINS OF THE TEAM.
Right...
I LOVE
OUR NEXT ROUND IS THE RUNNING QUIZ!
IN ORDER TO ANSWER THE QUESTIONS, YOU HAVE TO REACH THE MAX ON THE GAUGE ATTACHED TO THE TREADMILL!
IT'S A BATTLE OF THE MIND *AND* BODY.
EWWW. I DON'T WANT TO DO THAT.
THIS'LL REALLY HURT US IF WE GET THE ANSWER WRONG.
Physically, that is...
WE'RE ONE SHORT TOO...
That's gonna be rough.
I LOVE
My Principal
YOU GO FIRST, MACHARU!
Run!
ME?

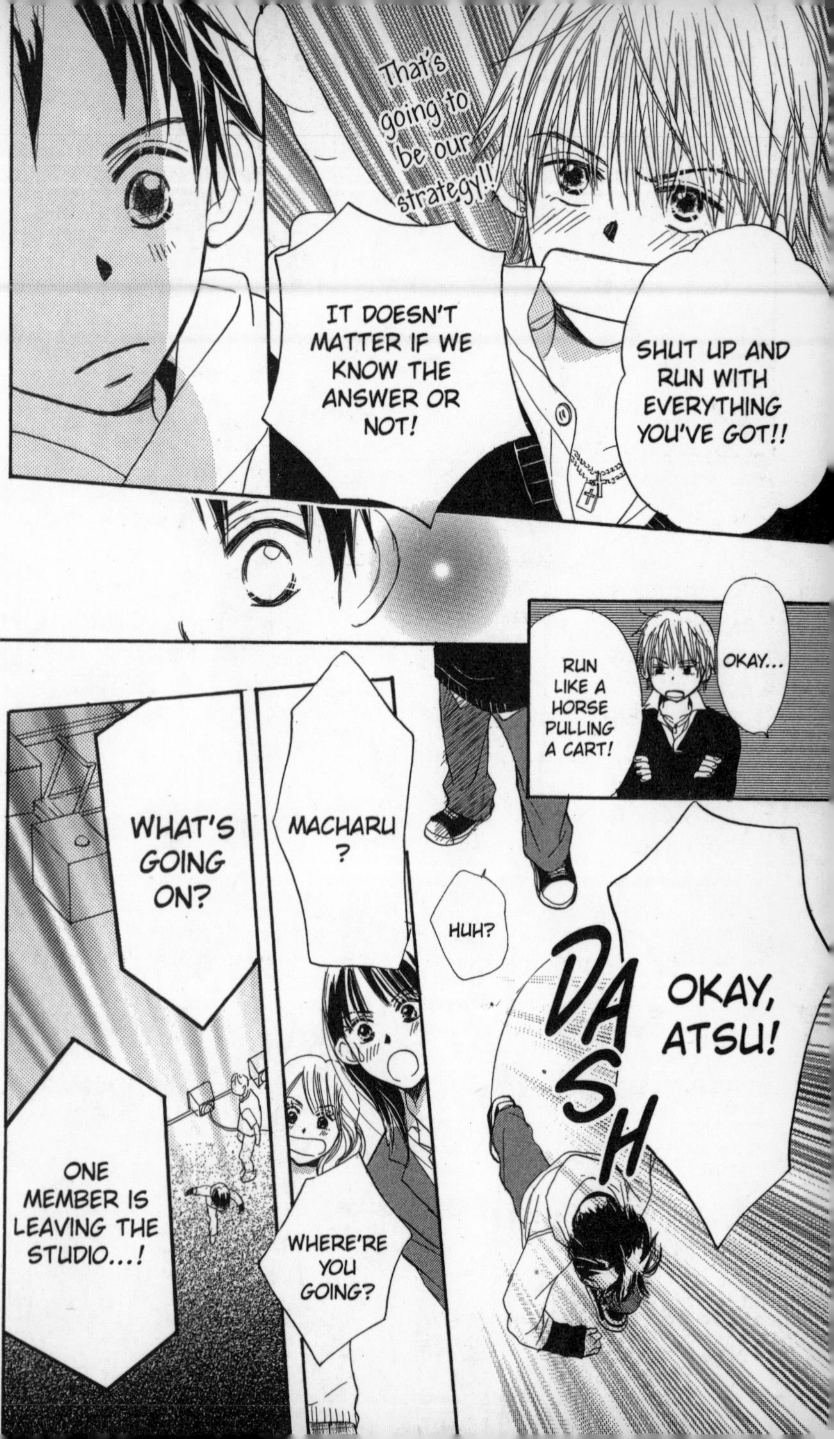
SHUT UP AND RUN WITH EVERYTHING YOU'VE GOT!!
IT DOESN'T MATTER IF WE KNOW THE ANSWER OR NOT!
That's going to be our strategy!!
OKAY...
RUN LIKE A HORSE PULLING A CART!
OKAY, ATSU!
DASH
HUH?
MACHARU?
WHAT'S GOING ON?
WHERE'RE YOU GOING?
ONE MEMBER IS LEAVING THE STUDIO...!

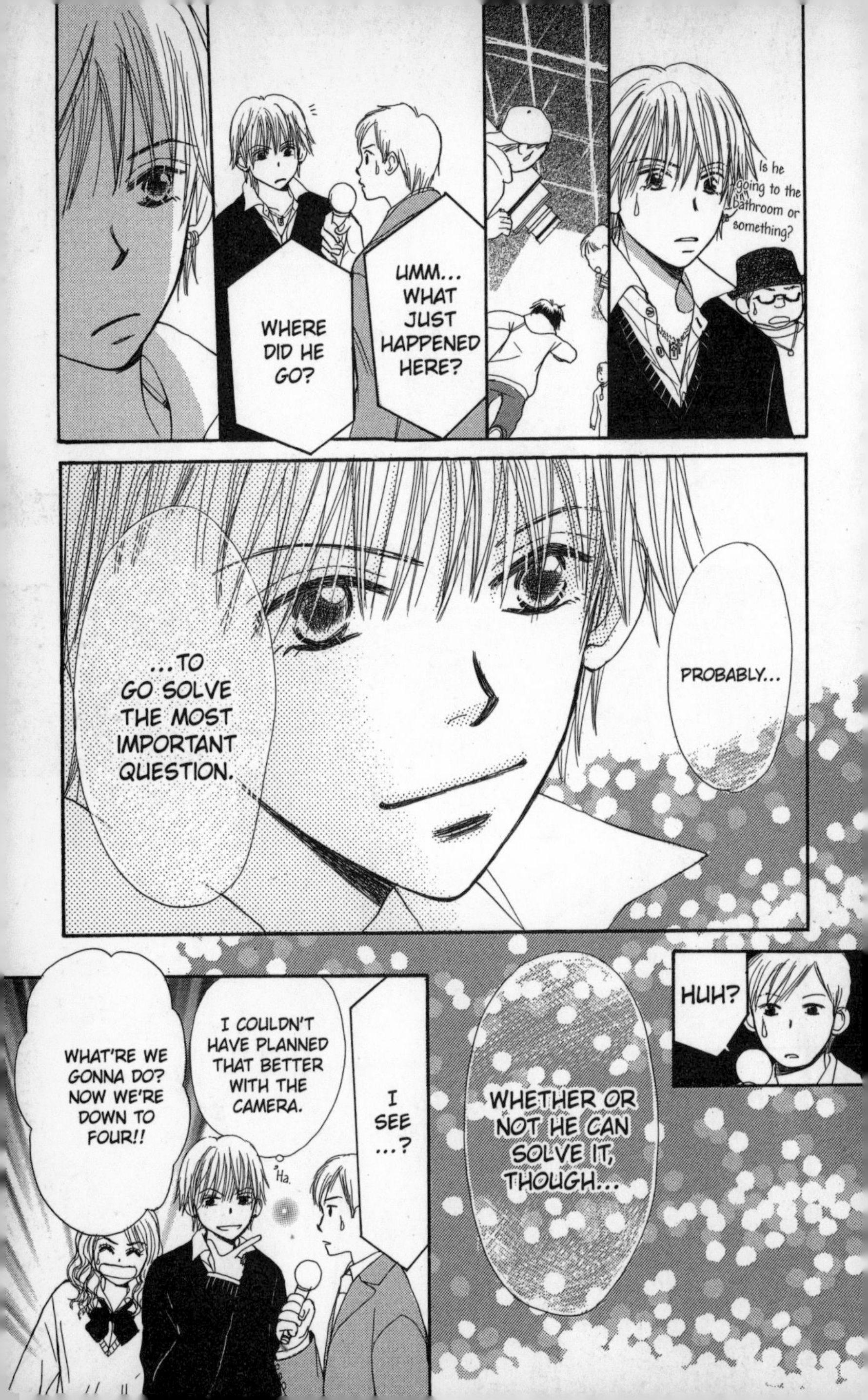
Is he going to the bathroom or something?
UMM... WHAT JUST HAPPENED HERE?
WHERE DID HE GO?
PROBABLY...
...TO GO SOLVE THE MOST IMPORTANT QUESTION.
HUH?
WHETHER OR NOT HE CAN SOLVE IT, THOUGH...
I SEE ...?
I COULDN'T HAVE PLANNED THAT BETTER WITH THE CAMERA.
Ha.
WHAT'RE WE GONNA DO? NOW WE'RE DOWN TO FOUR!!

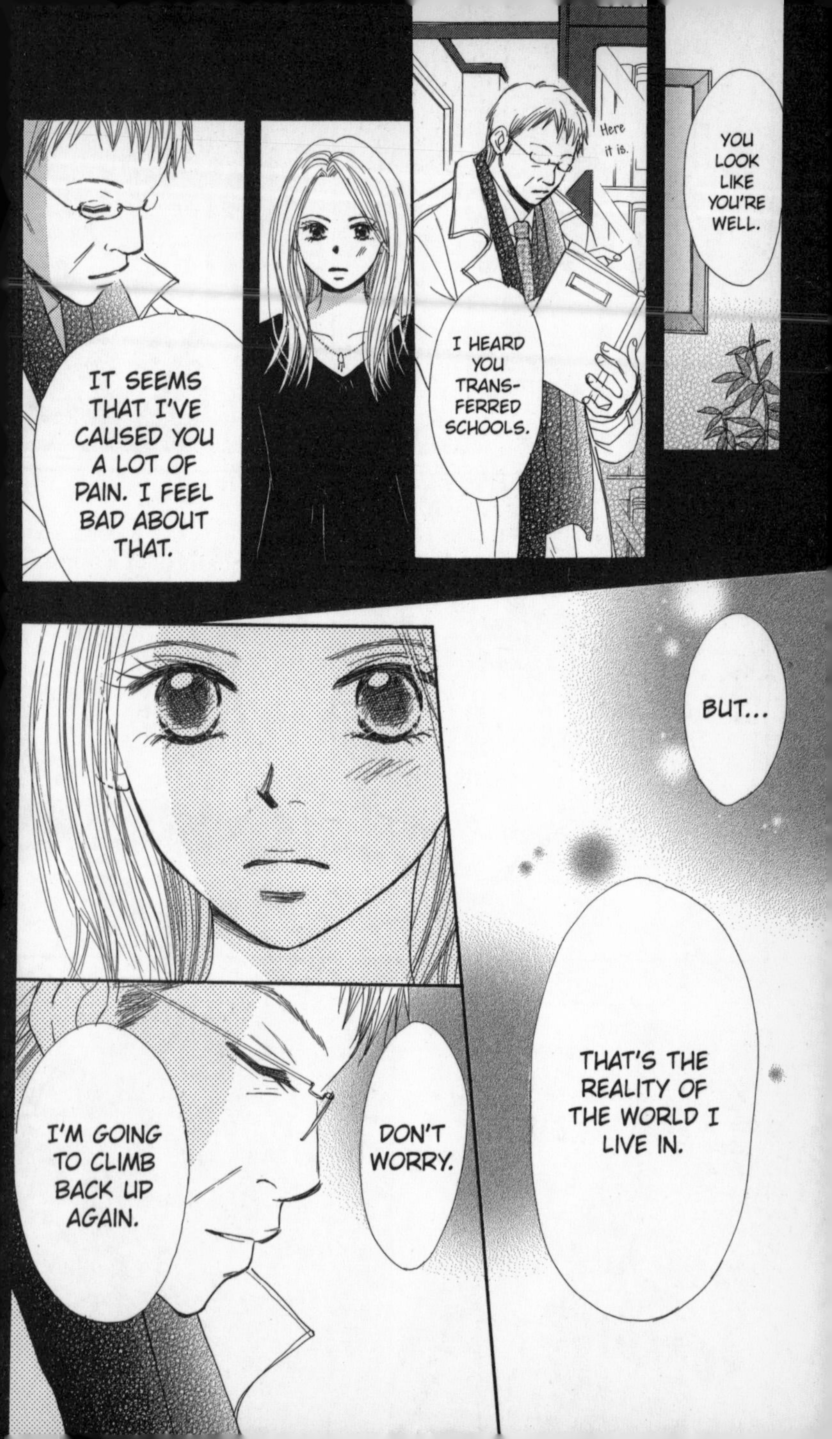
YOU LOOK LIKE YOU'RE WELL.
Here it is.
I HEARD YOU TRANS-FERRED SCHOOLS.
IT SEEMS THAT I'VE CAUSED YOU A LOT OF PAIN. I FEEL BAD ABOUT THAT.
BUT...
THAT'S THE REALITY OF THE WORLD I LIVE IN.
DON'T WORRY.
I'M GOING TO CLIMB BACK UP AGAIN.

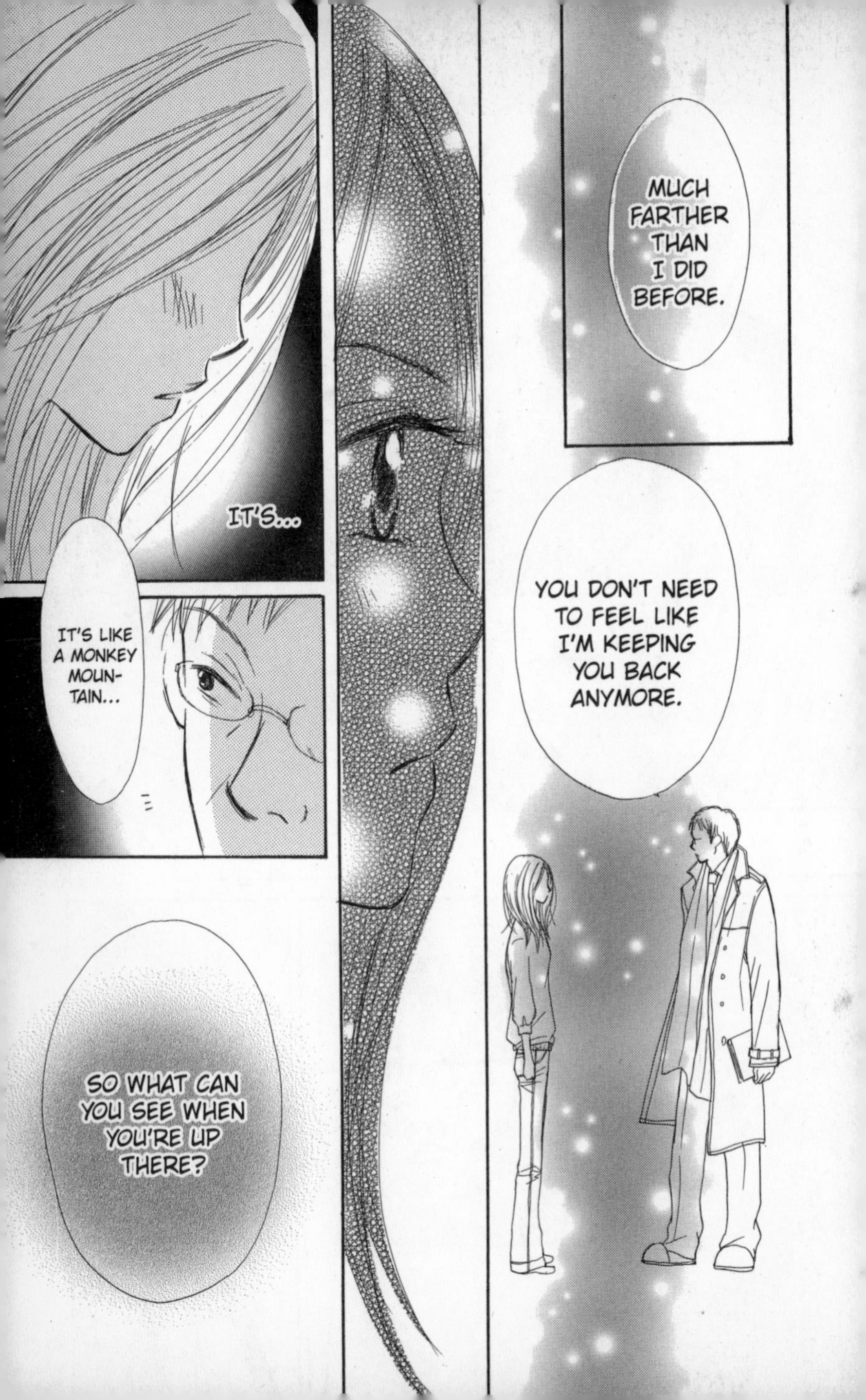
MUCH FARTHER THAN I DID BEFORE.
YOU DON'T NEED TO FEEL LIKE I'M KEEPING YOU BACK ANYMORE.
IT'S...
IT'S LIKE A MONKEY MOUN-TAIN...
SO WHAT CAN YOU SEE WHEN YOU'RE UP THERE?

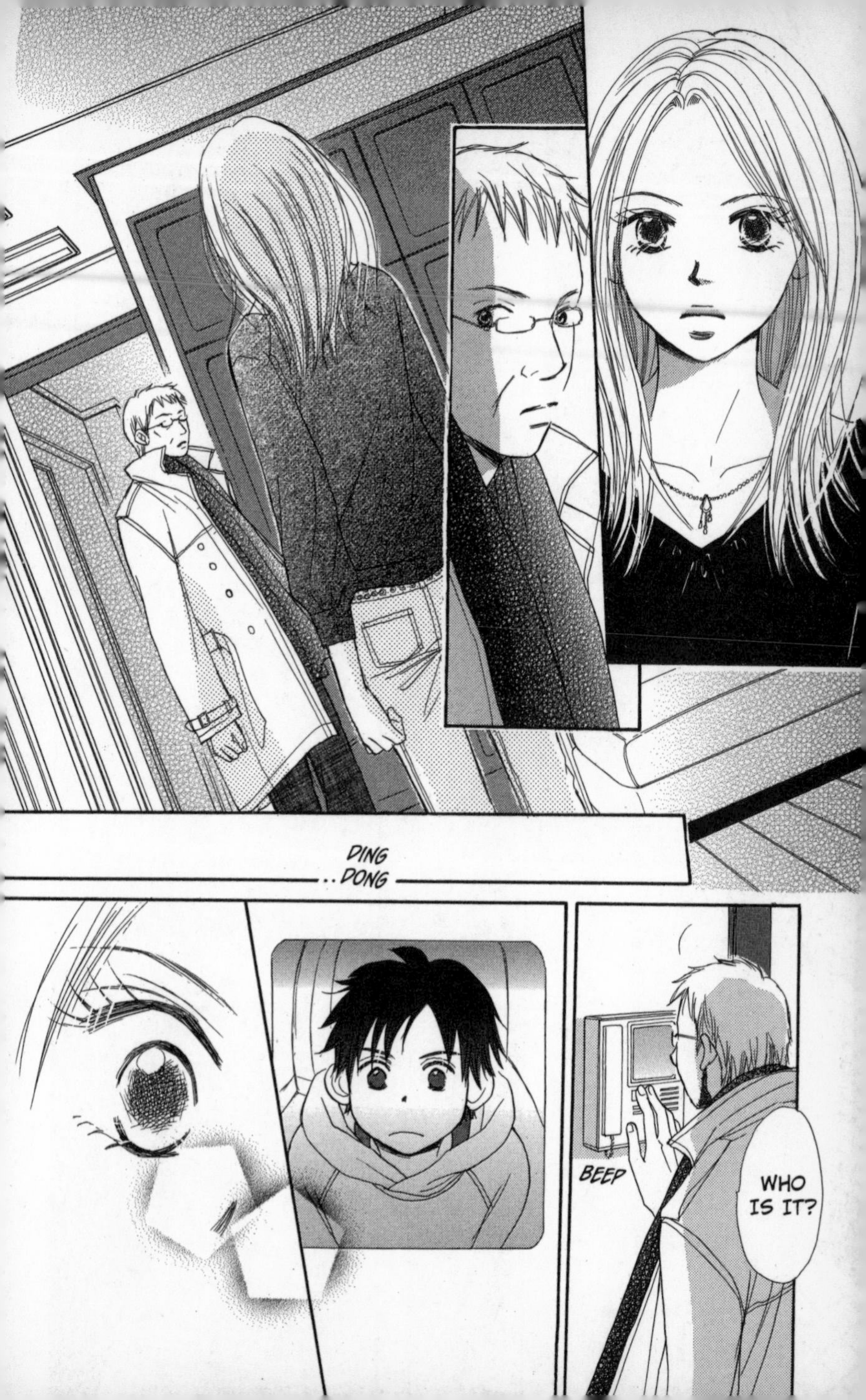
DING
..DONG
WHO IS IT?
BEEP

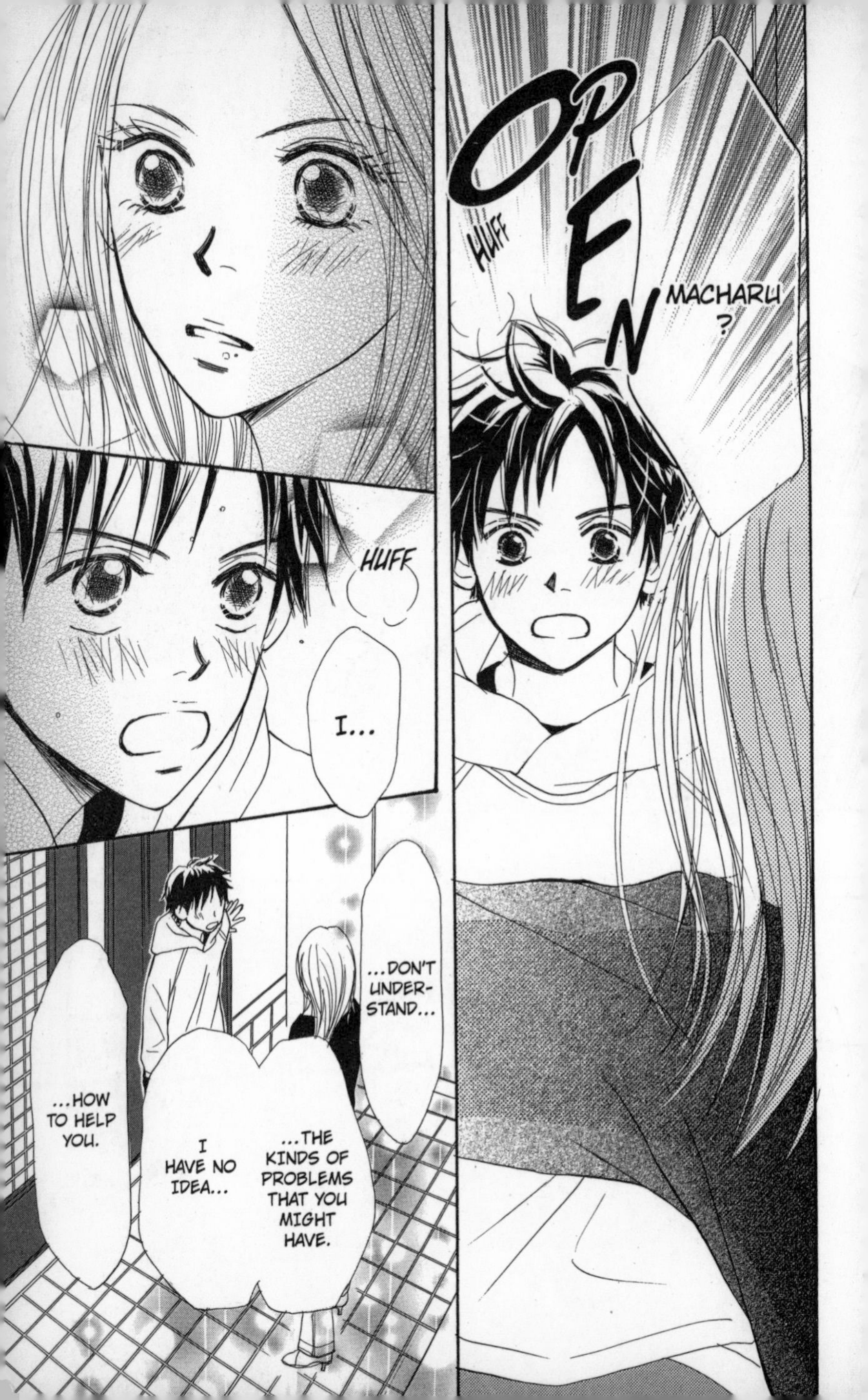
OPEN
HUFF
MACHARU?
HUFF
I...
...DON'T UNDER-STAND...
...THE KINDS OF PROBLEMS THAT YOU MIGHT HAVE.
I HAVE NO IDEA...
...HOW TO HELP YOU.

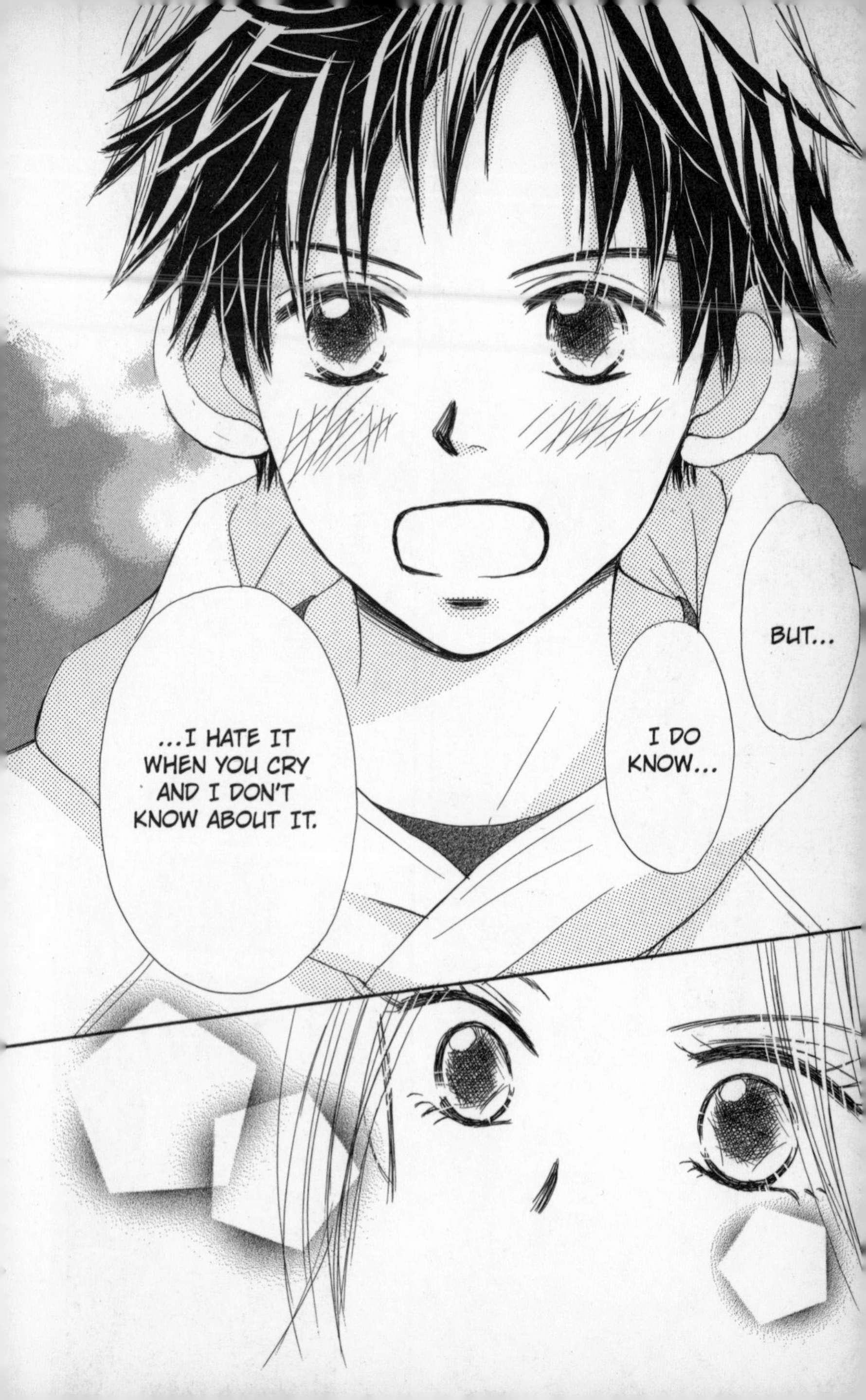
BUT...
I DO KNOW...
...I HATE IT WHEN YOU CRY AND I DON'T KNOW ABOUT IT.

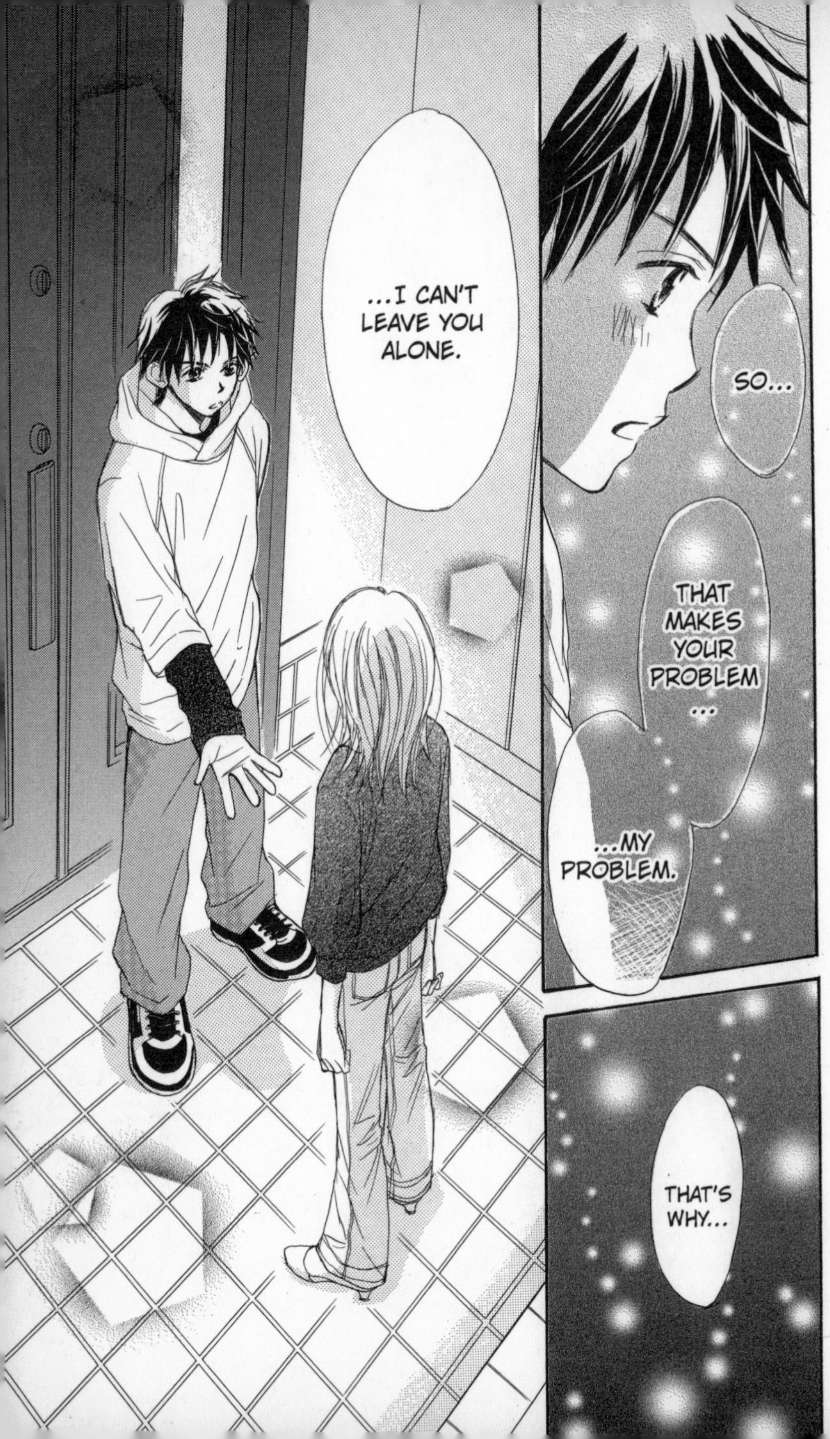
SO...
THAT MAKES YOUR PROBLEM ...
...MY PROBLEM.
THAT'S WHY...
...I CAN'T LEAVE YOU ALONE.

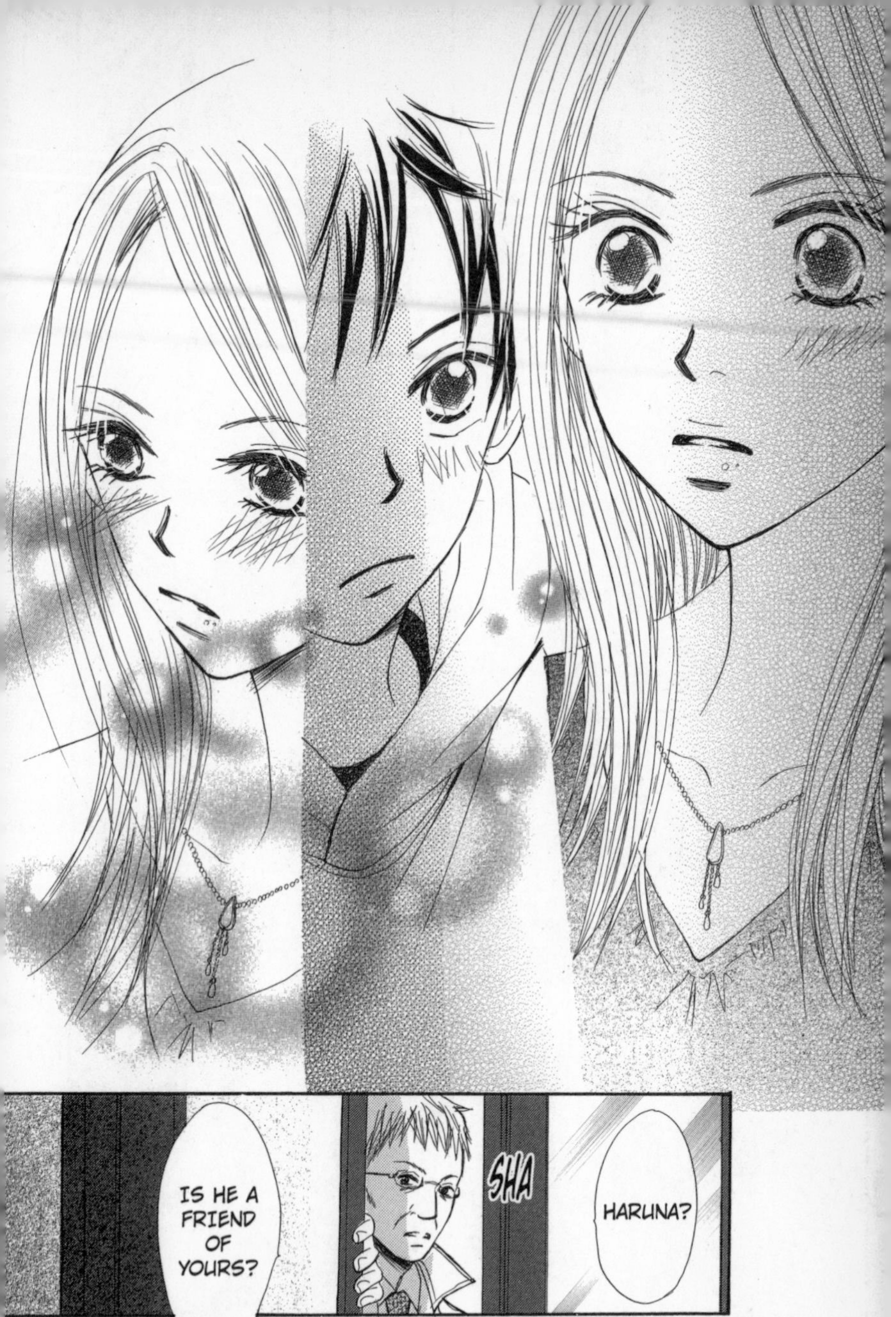
HARUNA?
SHA
IS HE A FRIEND OF YOURS?

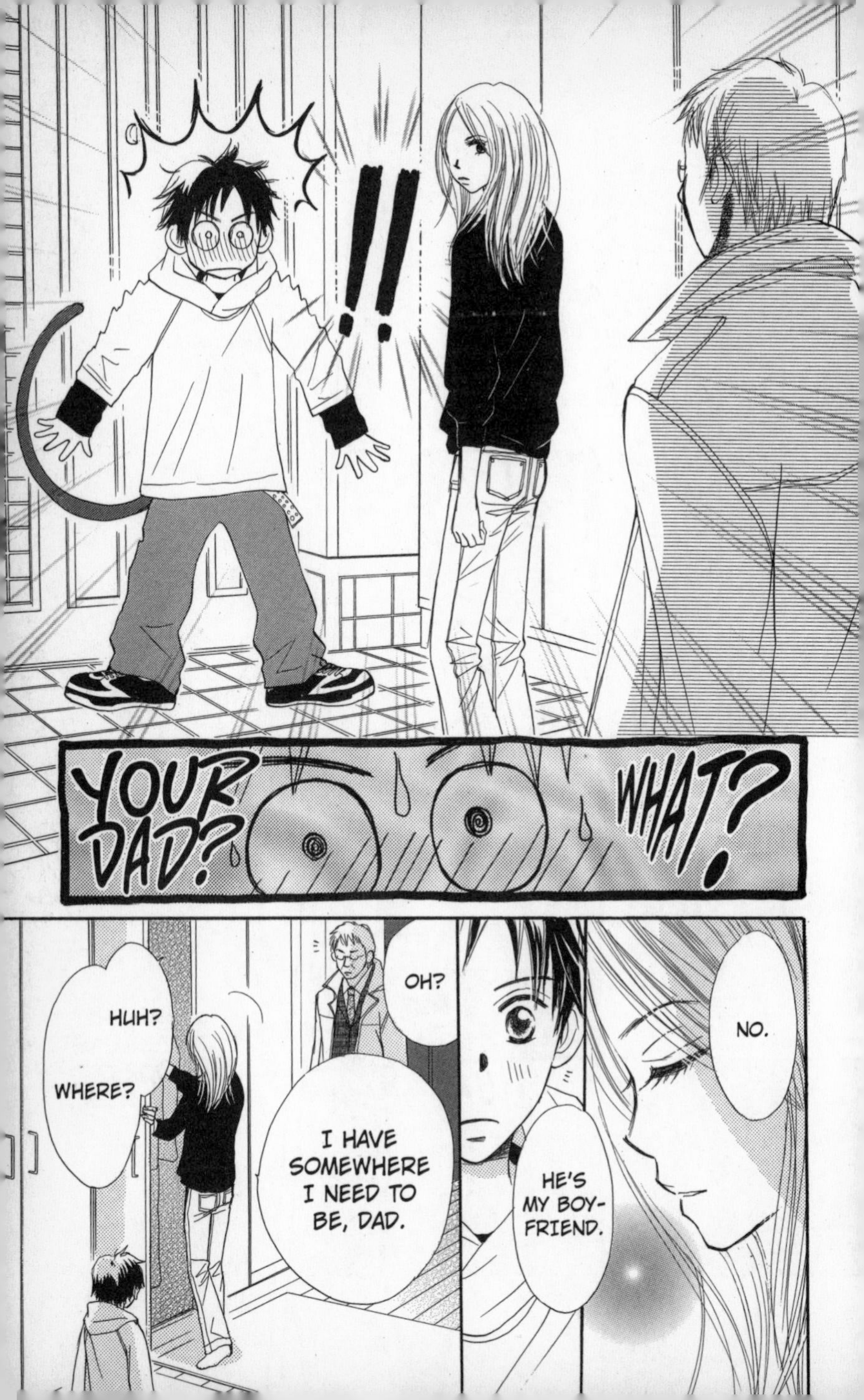
!!
WHAT?
YOUR DAD?
NO.
HE'S MY BOY-FRIEND.
OH?
I HAVE SOMEWHERE I NEED TO BE, DAD.
HUH?
WHERE?

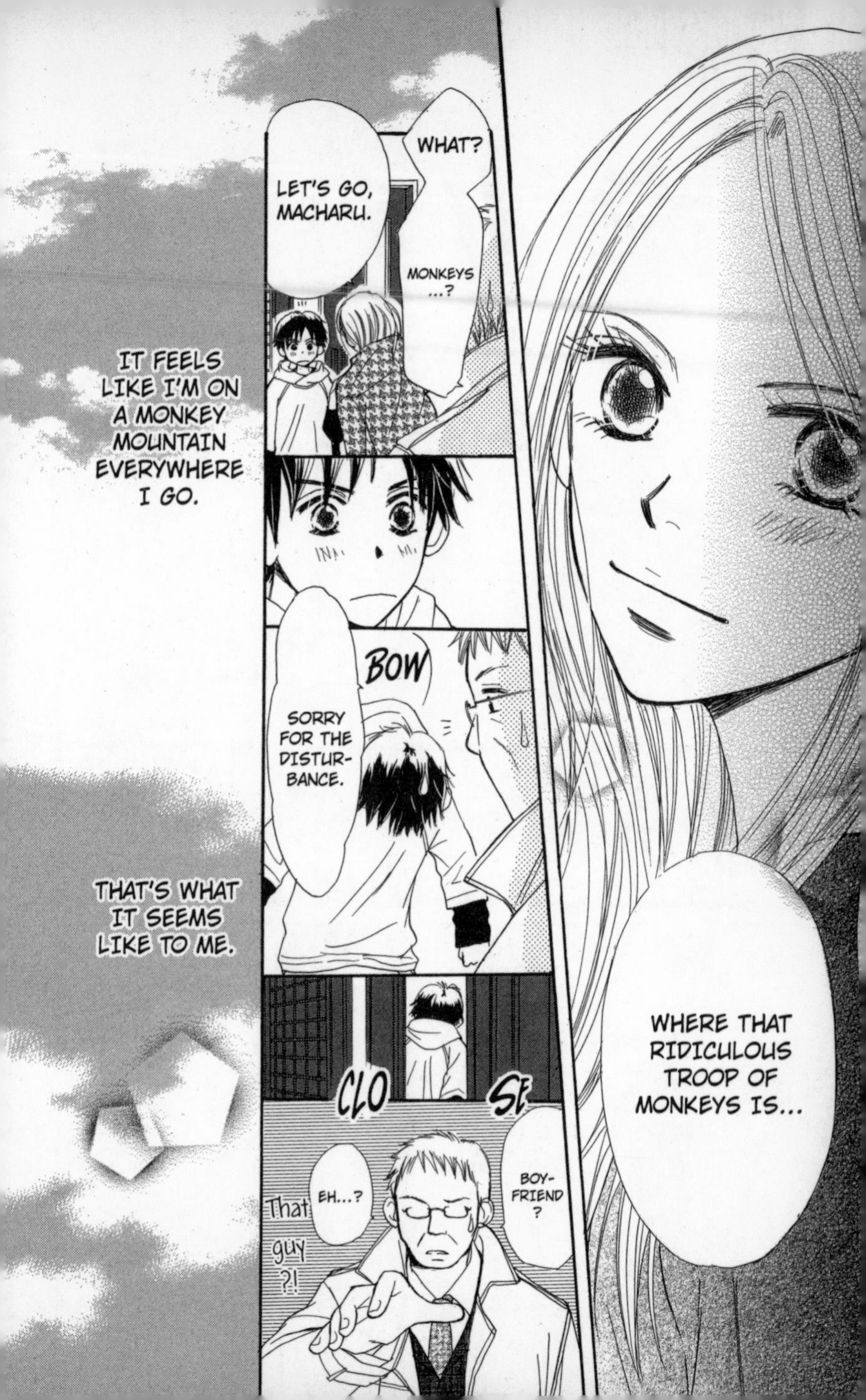
WHERE THAT RIDICULOUS TROOP OF MONKEYS IS...
WHAT?
LET'S GO, MACHARU.
MONKEYS ...?
BOW
SORRY FOR THE DISTUR-BANCE.
CLOSE
BOY-FRIEND ?
EH...?
That guy ?!
IT FEELS LIKE I'M ON A MONKEY MOUNTAIN EVERYWHERE I GO.
THAT'S WHAT IT SEEMS LIKE TO ME.

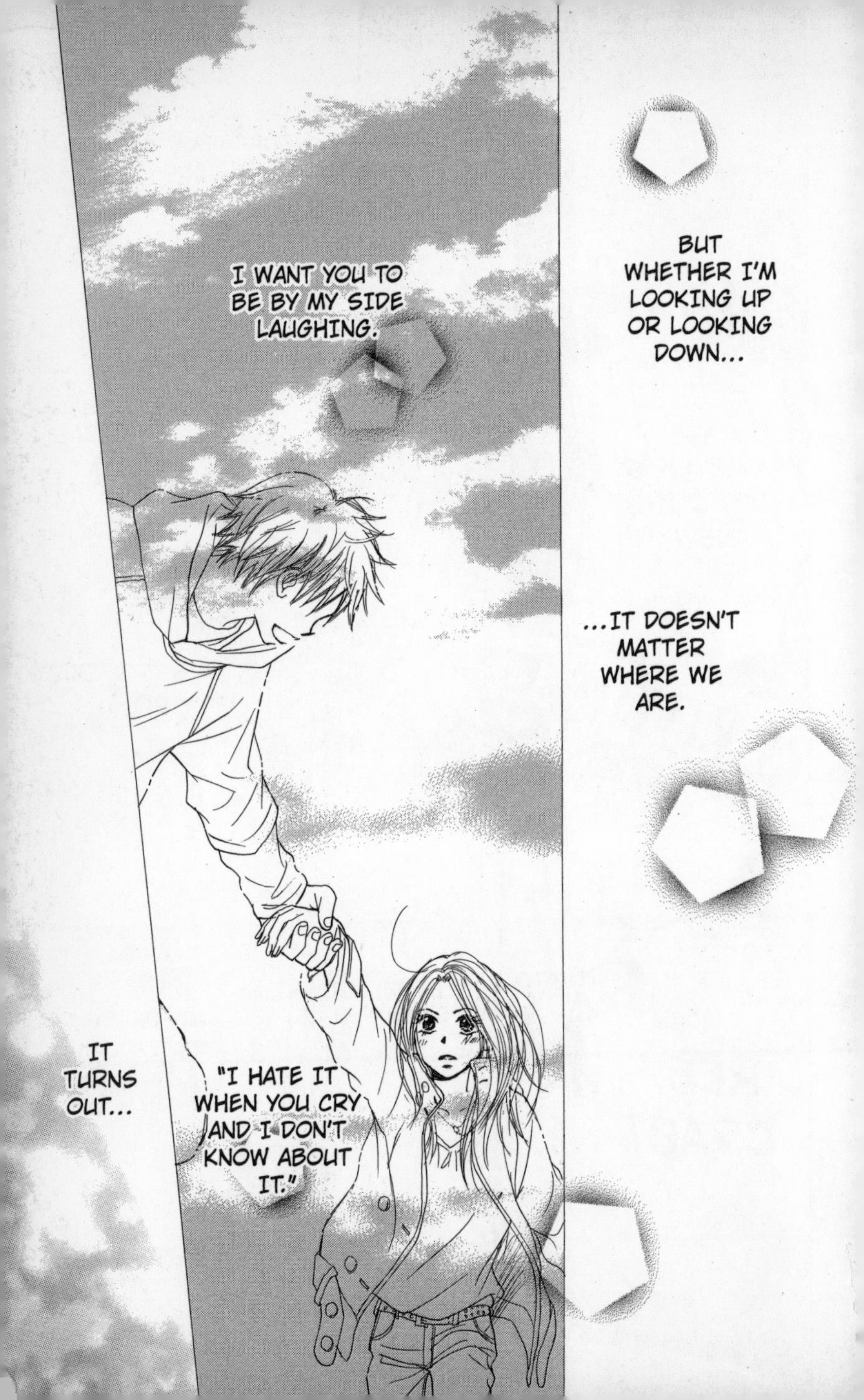
BUT WHETHER I'M LOOKING UP OR LOOKING DOWN...
...IT DOESN'T MATTER WHERE WE ARE.
I WANT YOU TO BE BY MY SIDE LAUGHING.
"I HATE IT WHEN YOU CRY AND I DON'T KNOW ABOUT IT."
IT TURNS OUT...

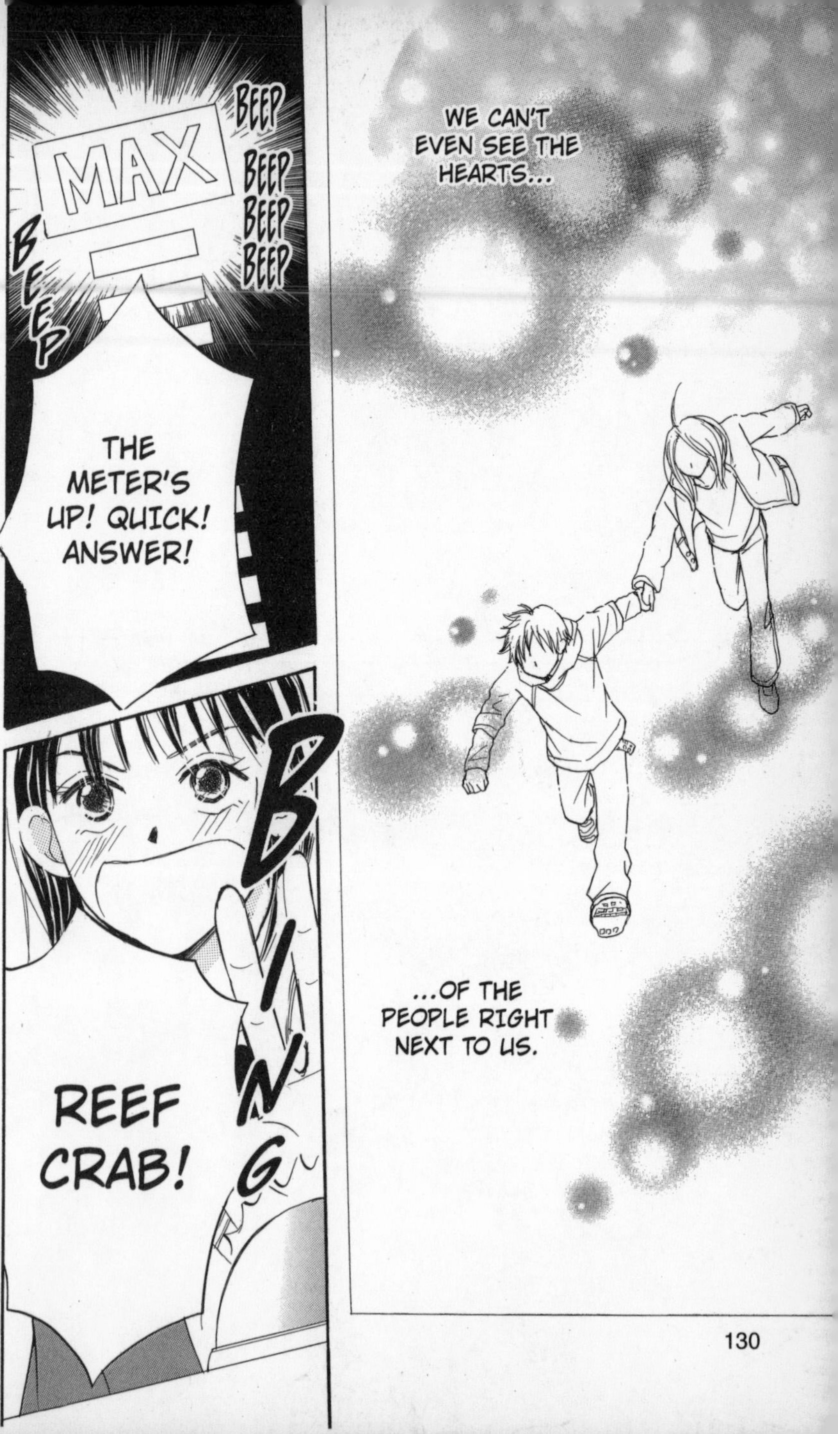
WE CAN'T EVEN SEE THE HEARTS...
...OF THE PEOPLE RIGHT NEXT TO US.
MAX
BEEP BEEP BEEP BEEP
BEEP
THE METER'S UP! QUICK! ANSWER!
BING
REEF CRAB!

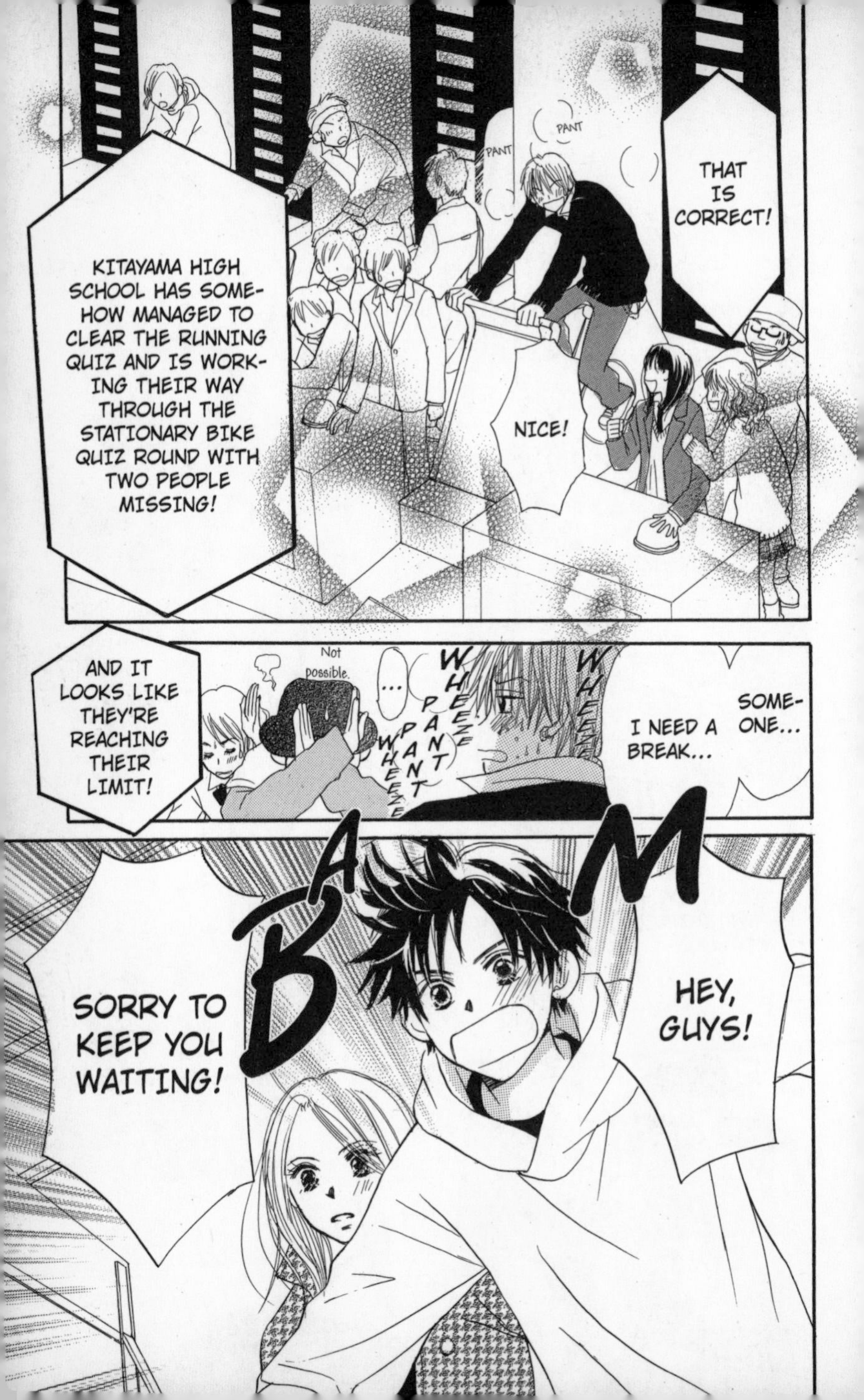
THAT IS CORRECT!
PANT
PANT
NICE!
KITAYAMA HIGH SCHOOL HAS SOME-HOW MANAGED TO CLEAR THE RUNNING QUIZ AND IS WORK-ING THEIR WAY THROUGH THE STATIONARY BIKE QUIZ ROUND WITH TWO PEOPLE MISSING!
SOME-ONE...
I NEED A BREAK...
WHEEZE
WHEEZE
PANT PANT
WHEEZE
...
Not possible.
AND IT LOOKS LIKE THEY'RE REACHING THEIR LIMIT!
HEY, GUYS!
BAM
SORRY TO KEEP YOU WAITING!

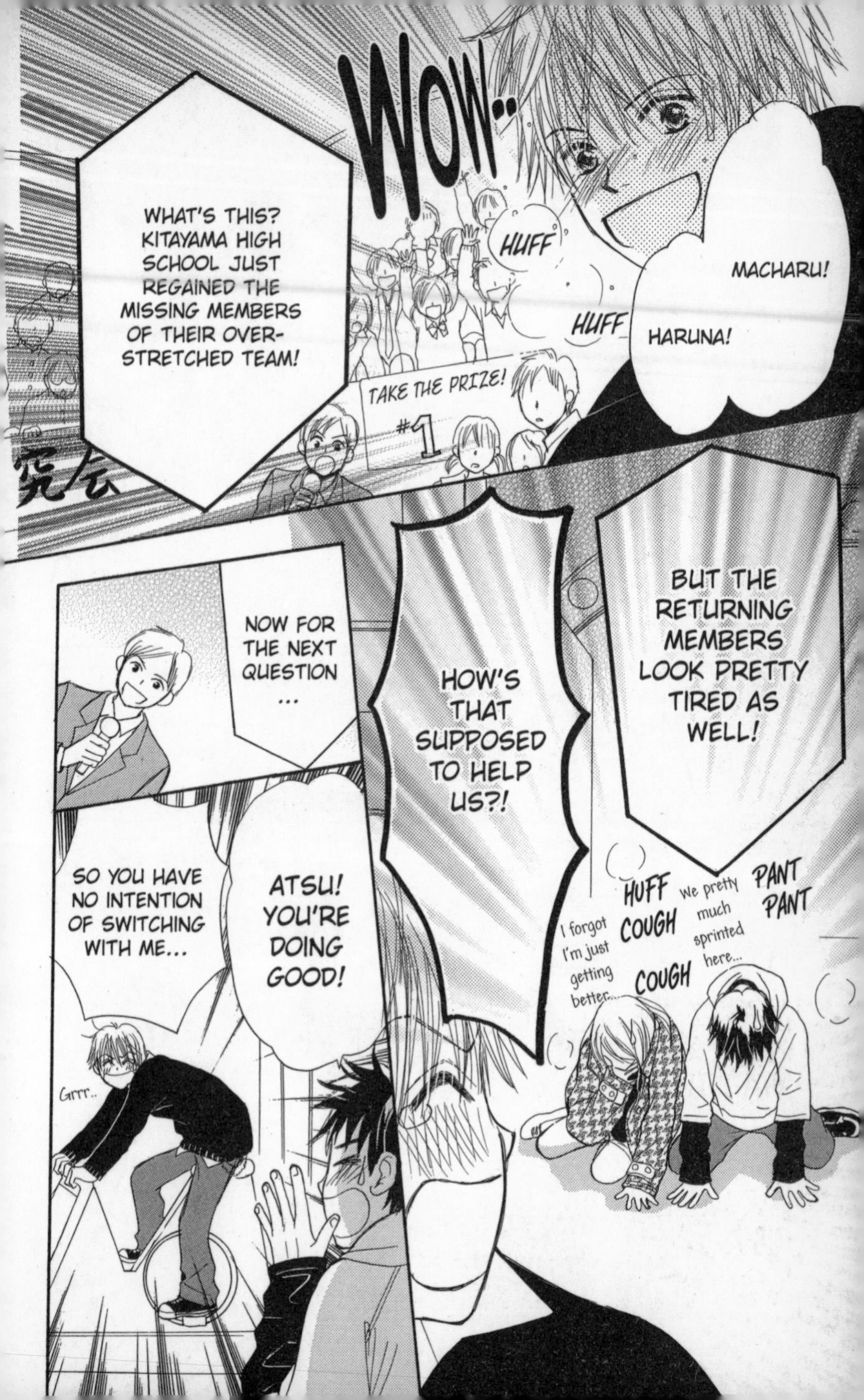
WOW..
MACHARU!
HARUNA!
HUFF
HUFF
TAKE THE PRIZE!
#1
WHAT'S THIS? KITAYAMA HIGH SCHOOL JUST REGAINED THE MISSING MEMBERS OF THEIR OVER-STRETCHED TEAM!
究会
BUT THE RETURNING MEMBERS LOOK PRETTY TIRED AS WELL!
PANT PANT
We pretty much sprinted here...
HUFF
COUGH
COUGH
I forgot I'm just getting better...
HOW'S THAT SUPPOSED TO HELP US?!
NOW FOR THE NEXT QUESTION ...
ATSU! YOU'RE DOING GOOD!
SO YOU HAVE NO INTENTION OF SWITCHING WITH ME...
Grrr..

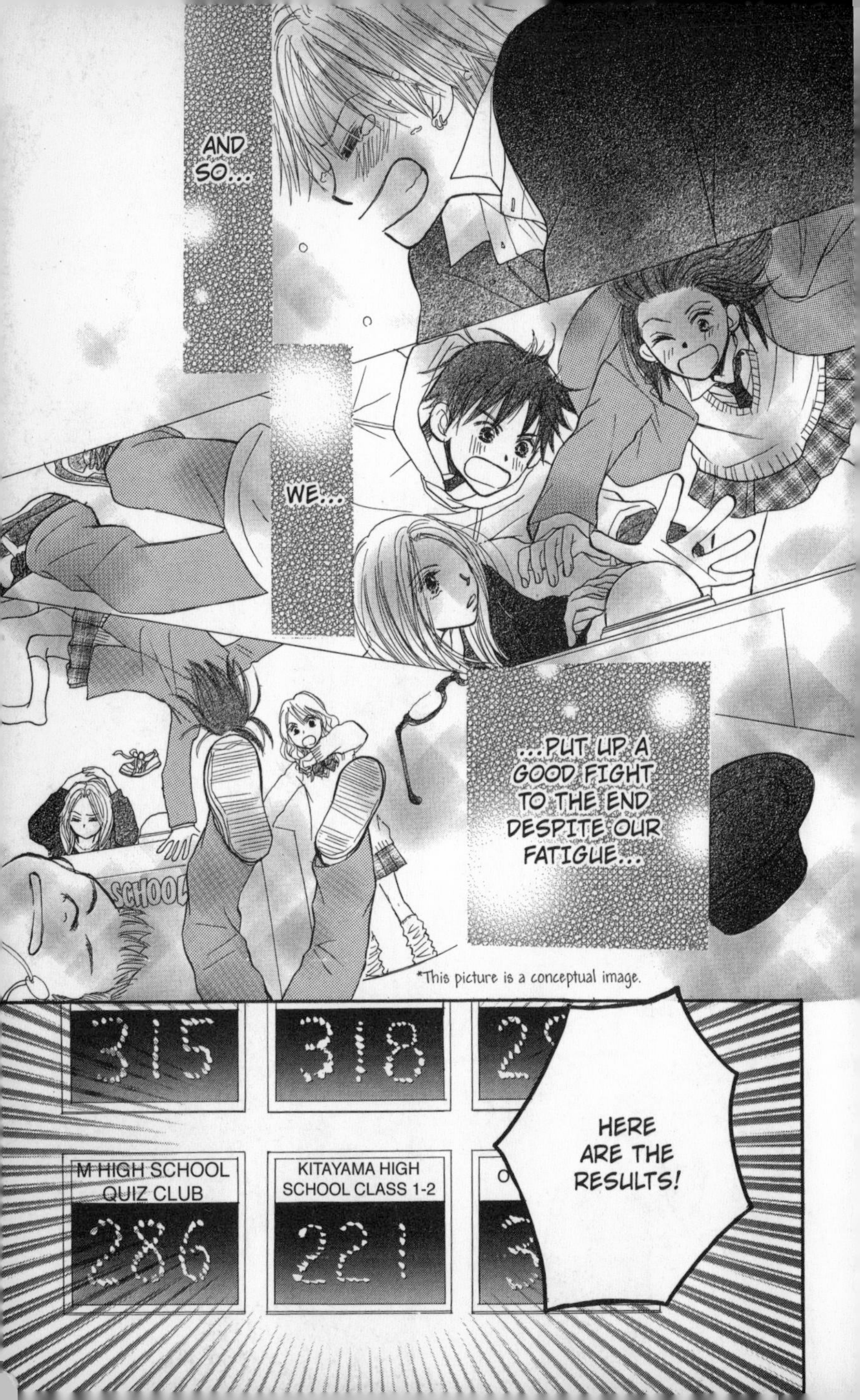
AND SO...
WE...
...PUT UP A GOOD FIGHT TO THE END DESPITE OUR FATIGUE...
SCHOOL
*This picture is a conceptual image.
HERE ARE THE RESULTS!
318
315
KITAYAMA HIGH SCHOOL CLASS 1-2
221
M HIGH SCHOOL QUIZ CLUB
286

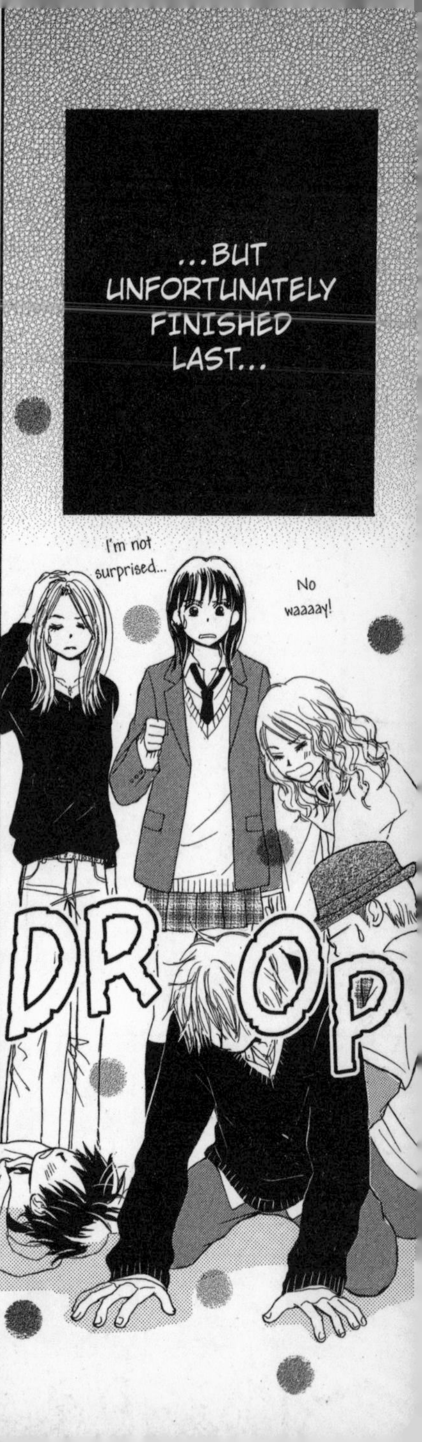
...BUT UNFORTUNATELY FINISHED LAST...
I'm not surprised...
No waaaay!
DROP

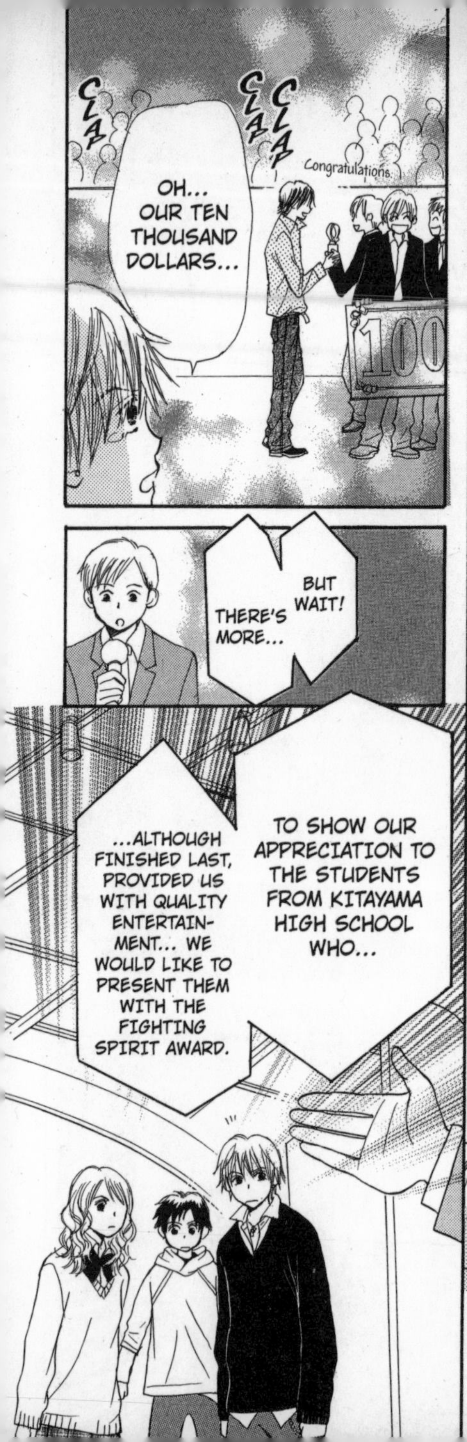
CLAP CLAP
CLAP
Congratulations.
OH... OUR TEN THOUSAND DOLLARS...
100
BUT WAIT!
THERE'S MORE...
TO SHOW OUR APPRECIATION TO THE STUDENTS FROM KITAYAMA HIGH SCHOOL WHO...
...ALTHOUGH FINISHED LAST, PROVIDED US WITH QUALITY ENTERTAIN-MENT... WE WOULD LIKE TO PRESENT THEM WITH THE FIGHTING SPIRIT AWARD.

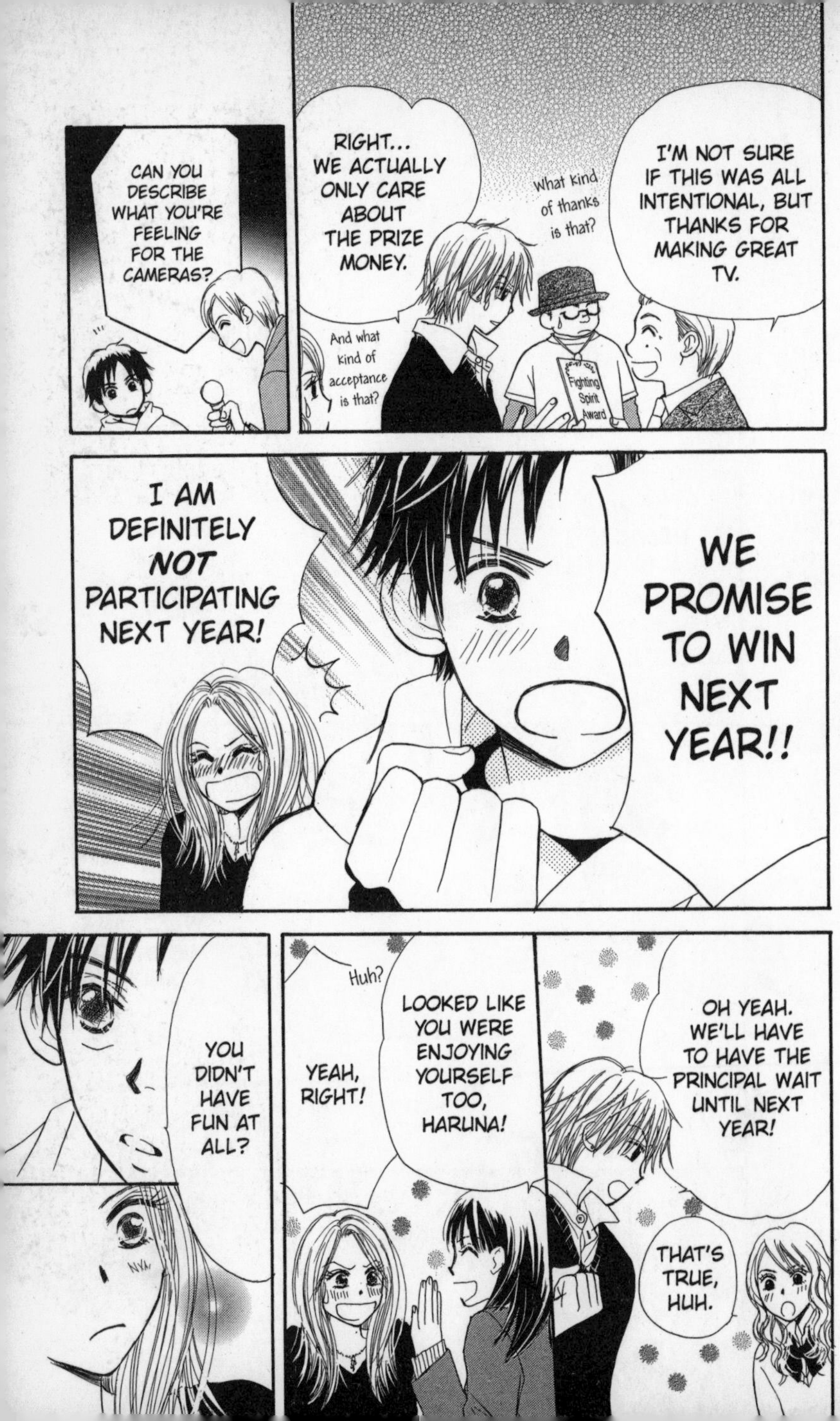
I'M NOT SURE IF THIS WAS ALL INTENTIONAL, BUT THANKS FOR MAKING GREAT TV.
What kind of thanks is that?
RIGHT... WE ACTUALLY ONLY CARE ABOUT THE PRIZE MONEY.
And what kind of acceptance is that?
Fighting Spirit Award
CAN YOU DESCRIBE WHAT YOU'RE FEELING FOR THE CAMERAS?
WE PROMISE TO WIN NEXT YEAR!!
I AM DEFINITELY *NOT* PARTICIPATING NEXT YEAR!
OH YEAH. WE'LL HAVE TO HAVE THE PRINCIPAL WAIT UNTIL NEXT YEAR!
THAT'S TRUE, HUH.
Huh?
LOOKED LIKE YOU WERE ENJOYING YOURSELF TOO, HARUNA!
YEAH, RIGHT!
YOU DIDN'T HAVE FUN AT ALL?

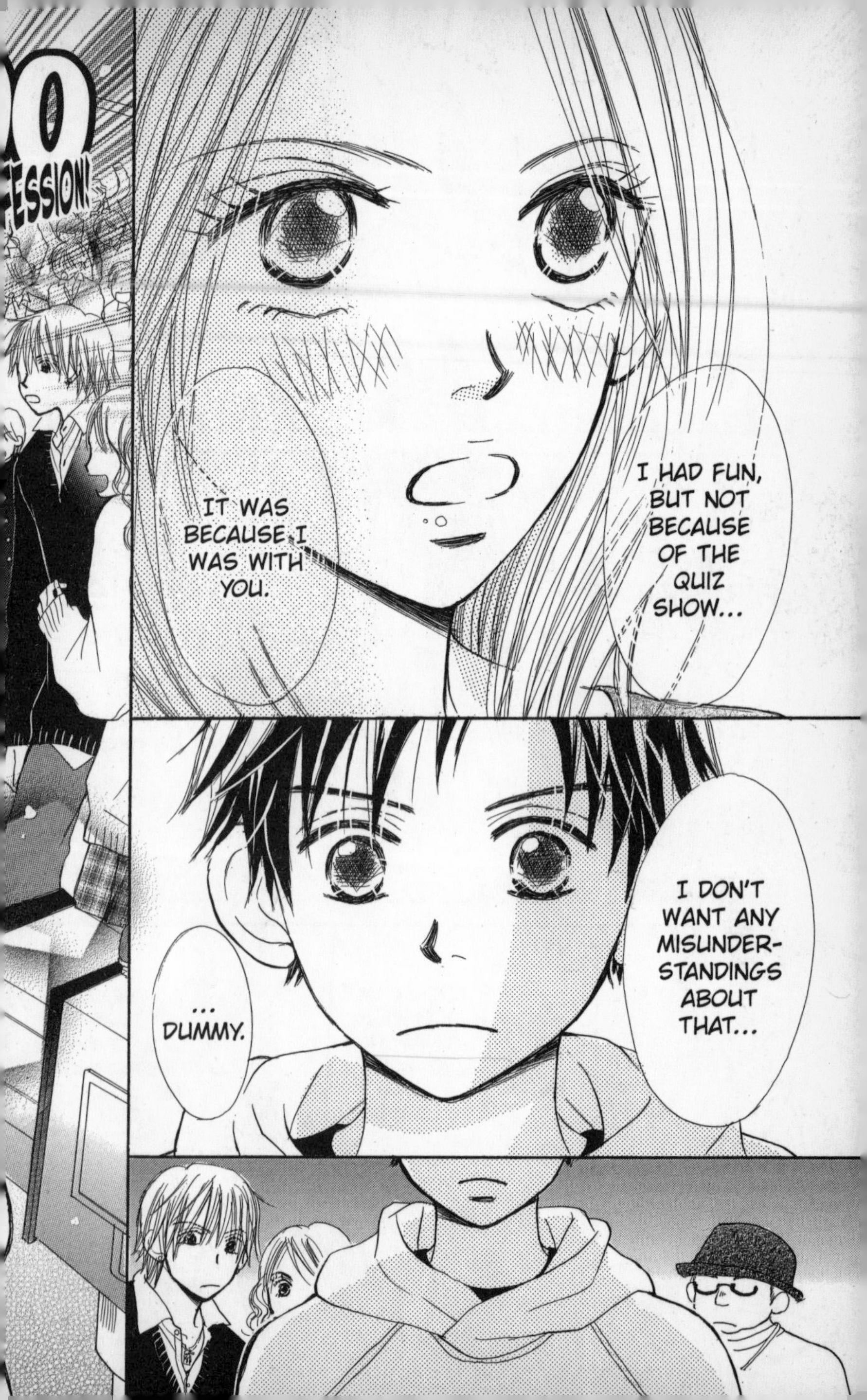
I HAD FUN, BUT NOT BECAUSE OF THE QUIZ SHOW...
IT WAS BECAUSE I WAS WITH YOU.
I DON'T WANT ANY MISUNDER-STANDINGS ABOUT THAT...
... DUMMY.

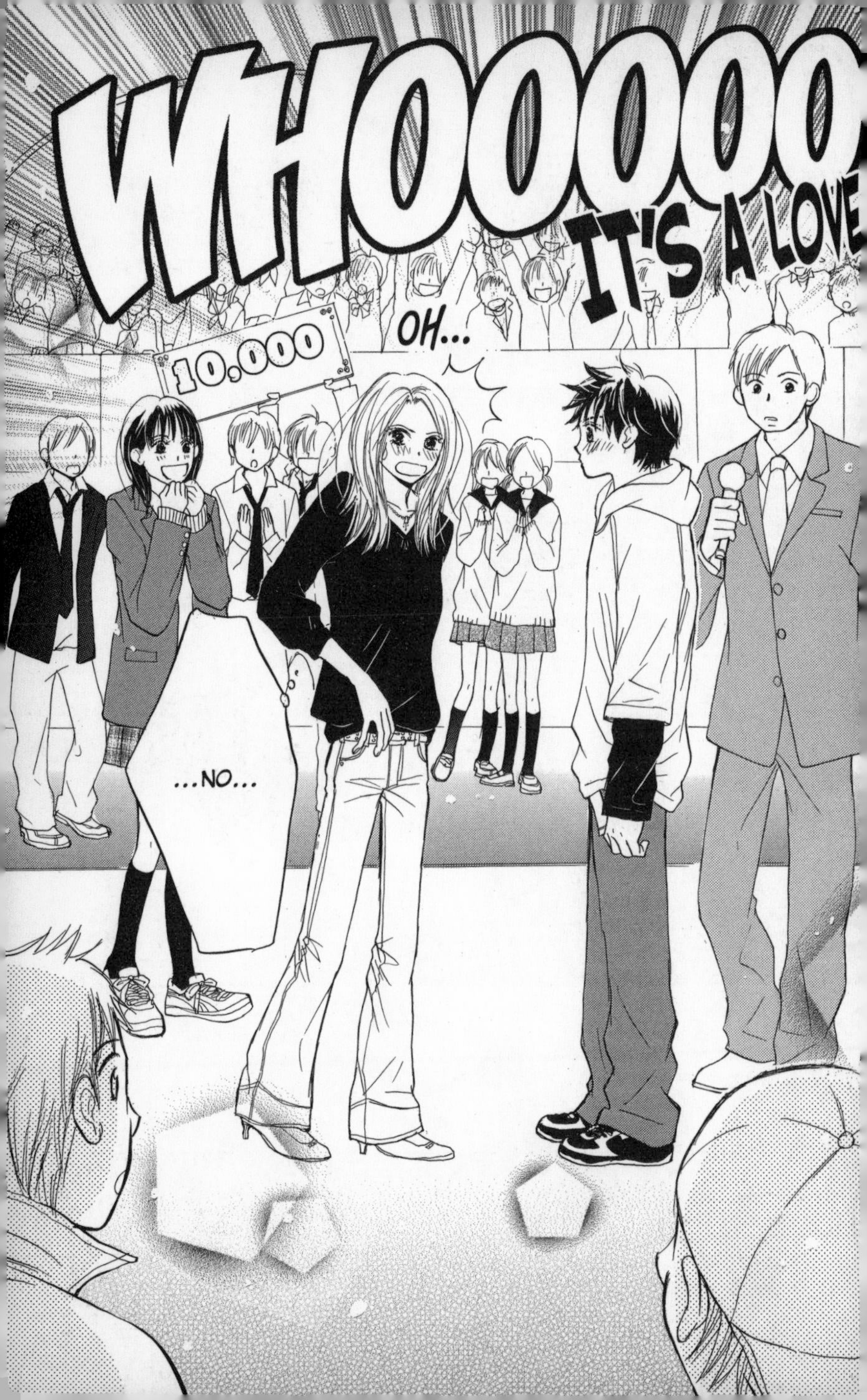
WHOOOOO
IT'S A LOVE
OH...
10,000
...NO...

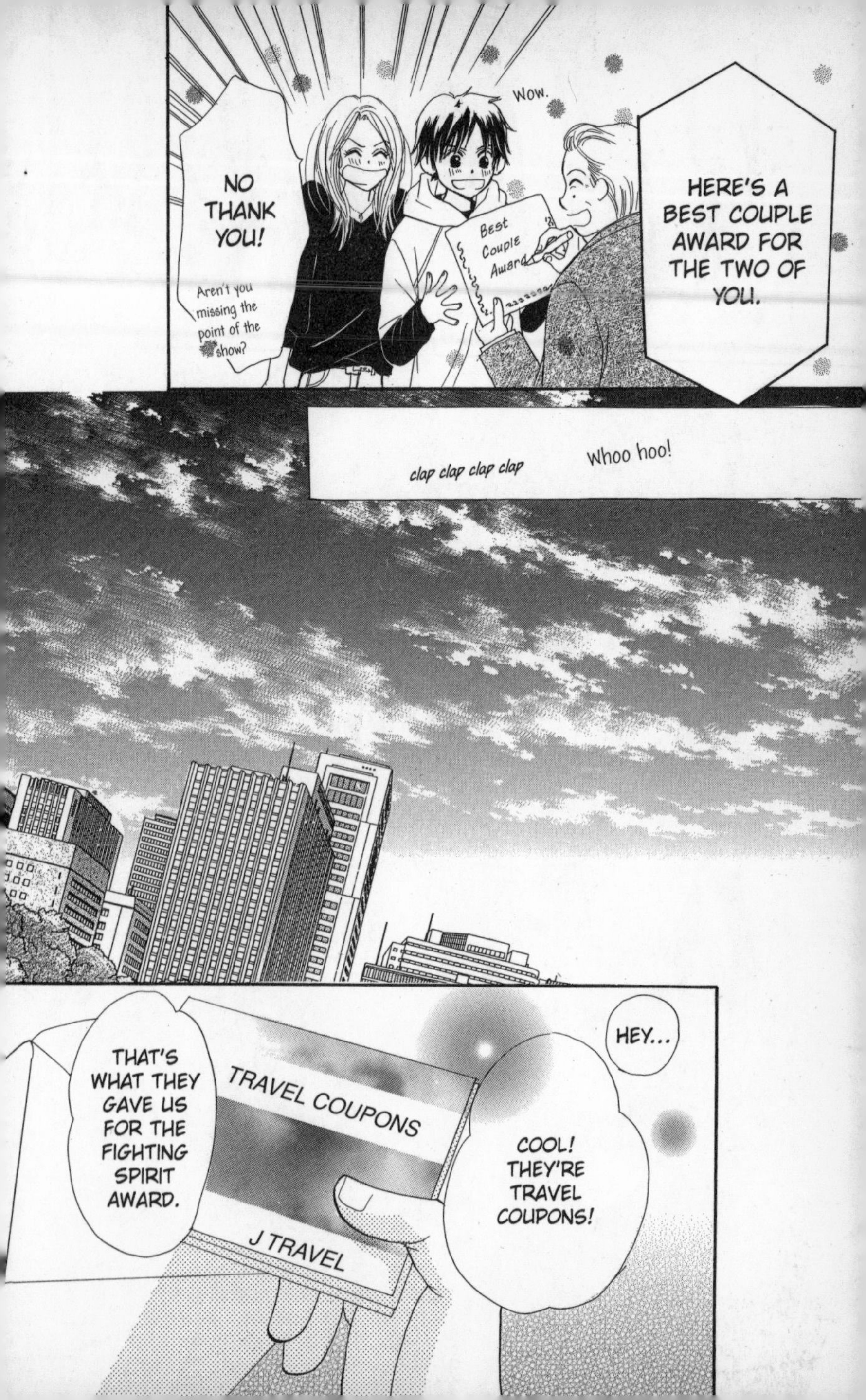
HERE'S A BEST COUPLE AWARD FOR THE TWO OF YOU.
Best Couple Award
Wow.
NO THANK YOU!
Aren't you missing the point of the show?
Whoo hoo!
clap clap clap clap
HEY...
COOL! THEY'RE TRAVEL COUPONS!
TRAVEL COUPONS
J TRAVEL
THAT'S WHAT THEY GAVE US FOR THE FIGHTING SPIRIT AWARD.

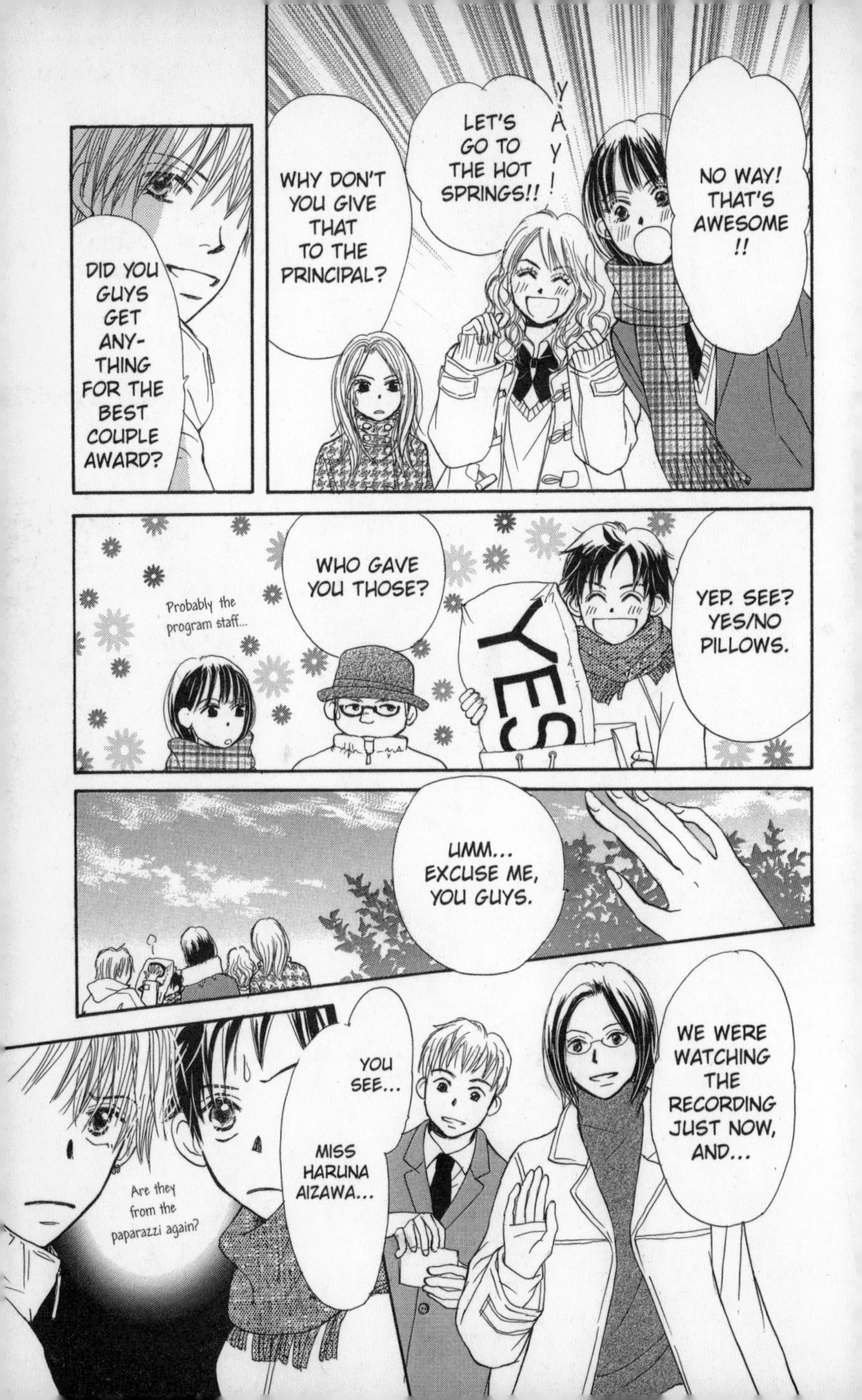
NO WAY! THAT'S AWESOME !!
YAY!
LET'S GO TO THE HOT SPRINGS!!
WHY DON'T YOU GIVE THAT TO THE PRINCIPAL?
DID YOU GUYS GET ANY-THING FOR THE BEST COUPLE AWARD?
YEP. SEE? YES/NO PILLOWS.
YES
WHO GAVE YOU THOSE?
Probably the program staff...
UMM... EXCUSE ME, YOU GUYS.
WE WERE WATCHING THE RECORDING JUST NOW, AND...
YOU SEE...
MISS HARUNA AIZAWA...
Are they from the paparazzi again?

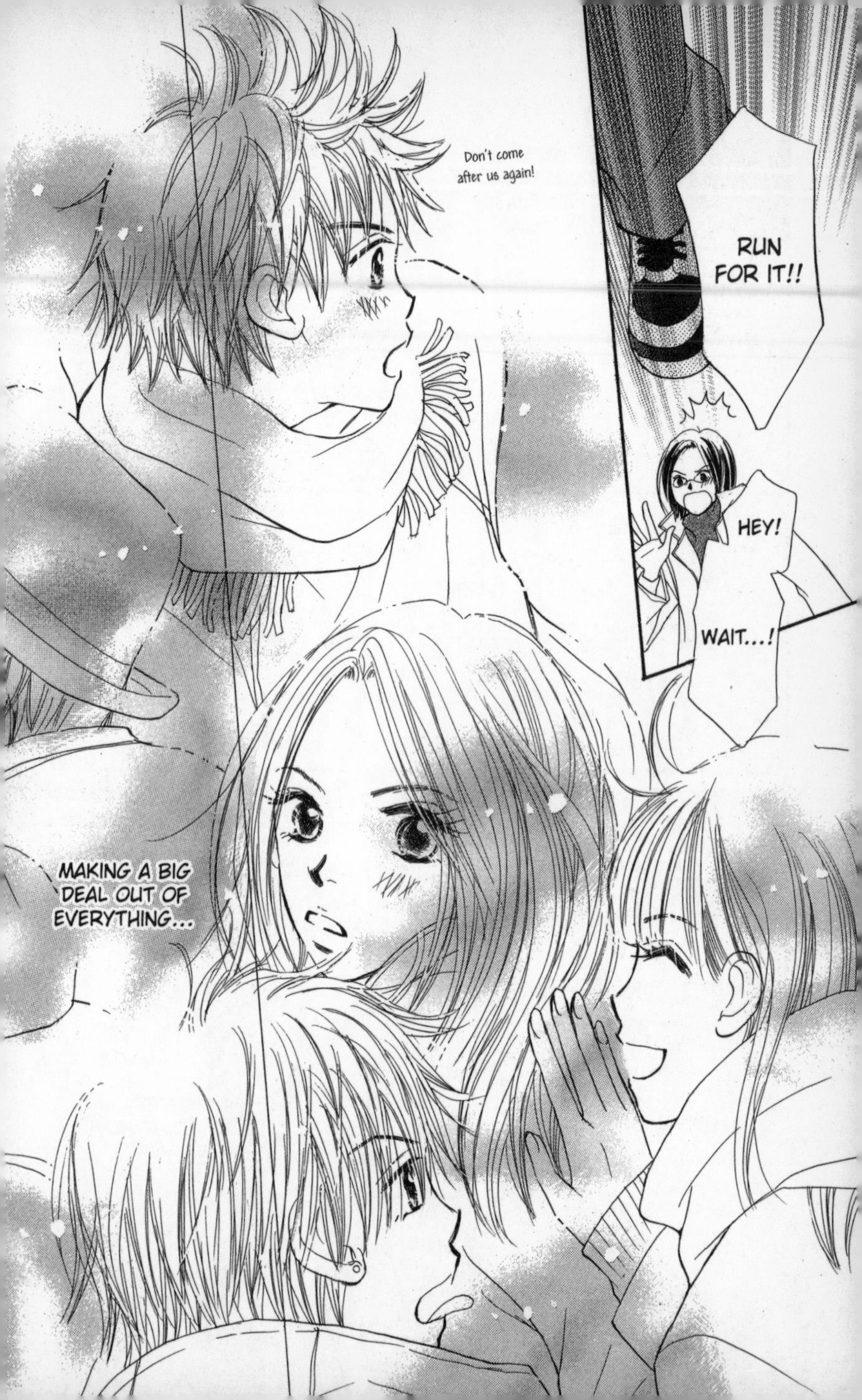
RUN FOR IT!!
HEY!
WAIT...!
Don't come after us again!
MAKING A BIG DEAL OUT OF EVERYTHING...

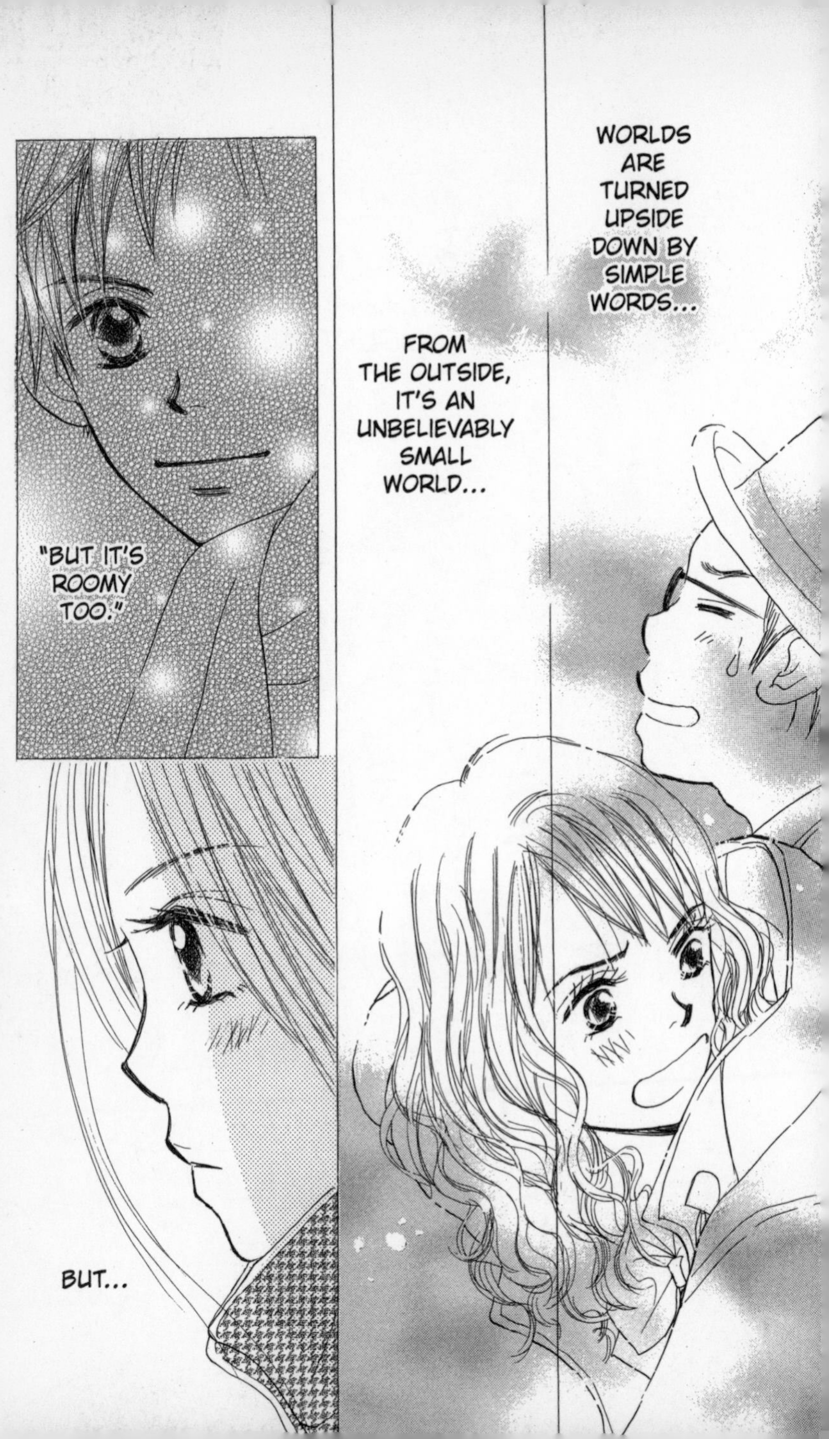
WORLDS ARE TURNED UPSIDE DOWN BY SIMPLE WORDS...
FROM THE OUTSIDE, IT'S AN UNBELIEVABLY SMALL WORLD...
"BUT IT'S ROOMY TOO."
BUT...

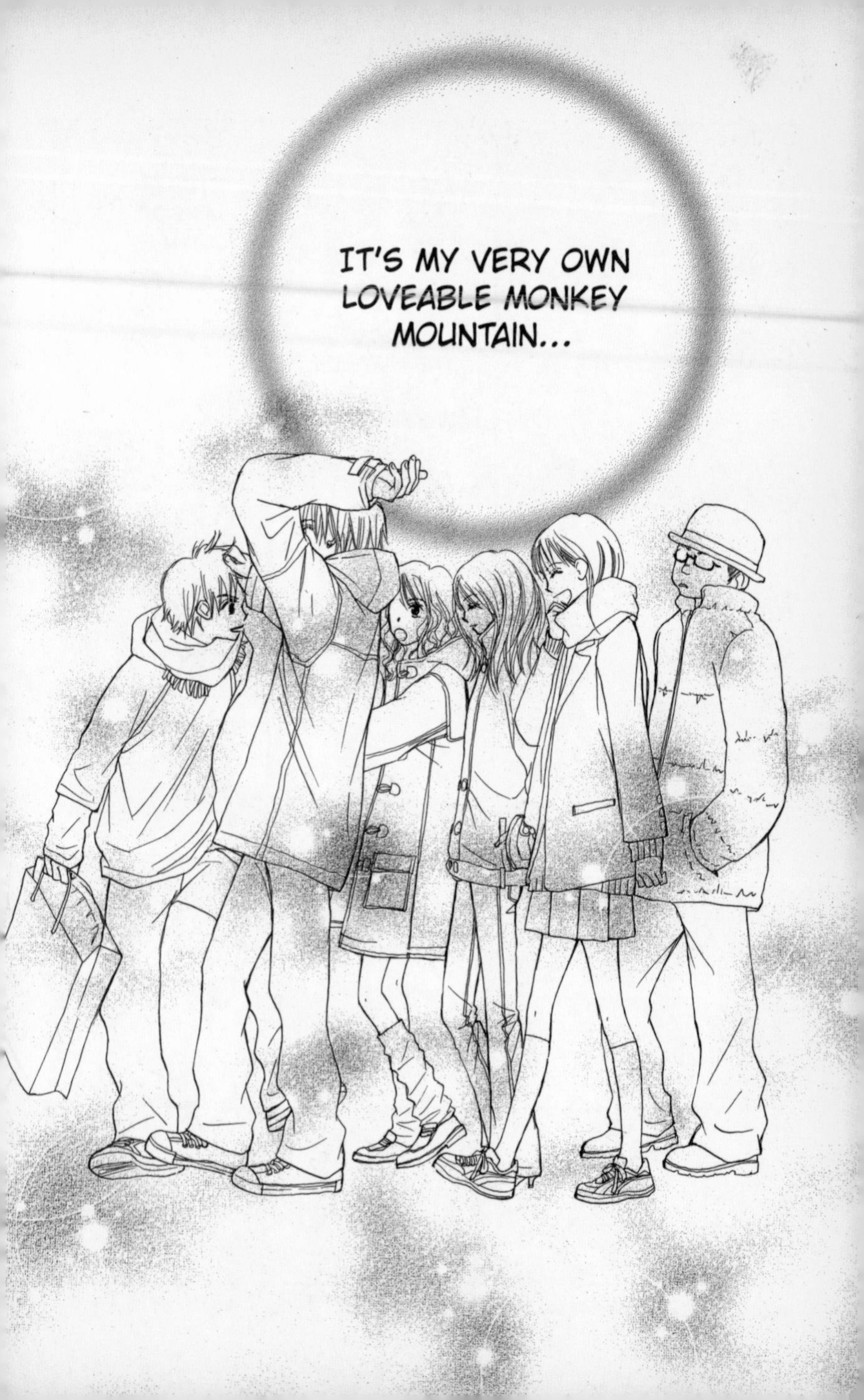
IT'S MY VERY OWN LOVEABLE MONKEY MOUNTAIN...

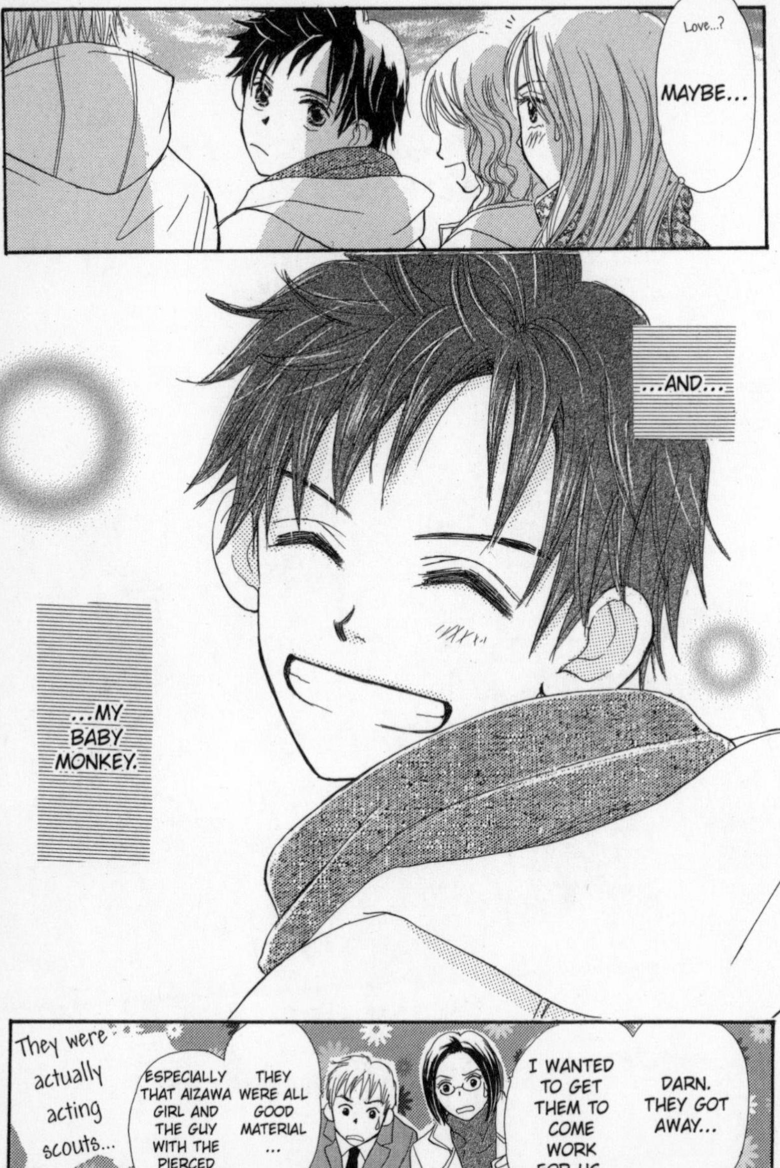
Love...?
MAYBE...
...AND...
...MY BABY MONKEY.
DARN. THEY GOT AWAY...
I WANTED TO GET THEM TO COME WORK FOR US.
THEY WERE ALL GOOD MATERIAL ...
ESPECIALLY THAT AIZAWA GIRL AND THE GUY WITH THE PIERCED EARS...
They were actually acting scouts...

MONKEY HIGH! ② *THE END*

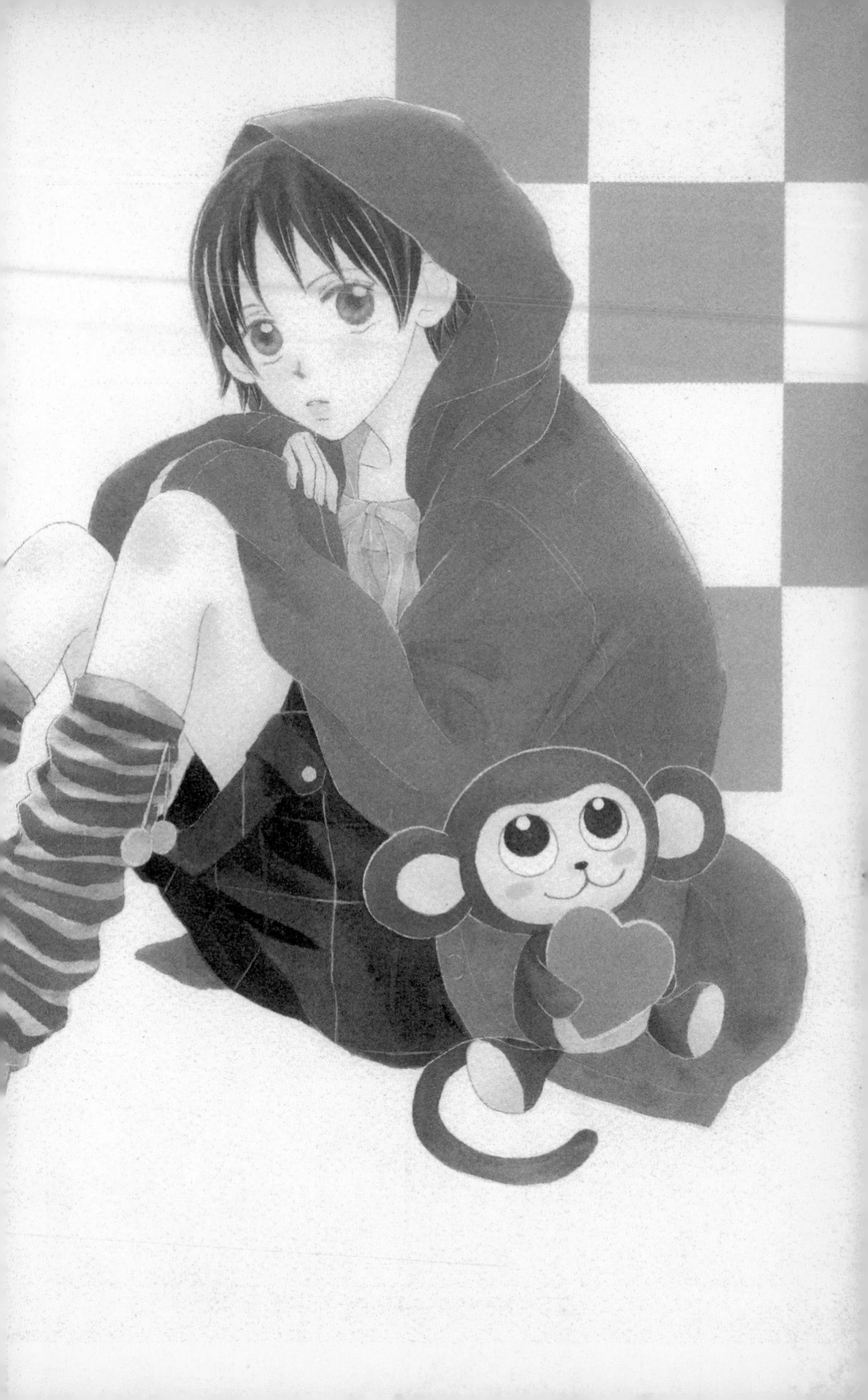

Monkey High!

SPECIAL EDITION

SPECIAL EDITION

SPECIAL EDITION

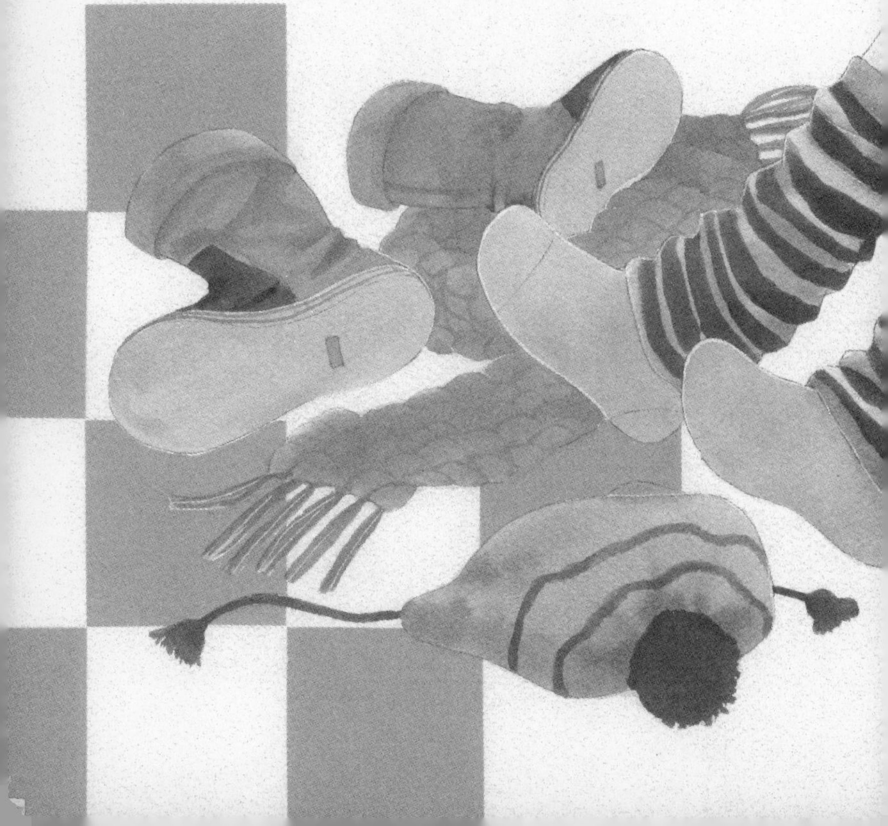

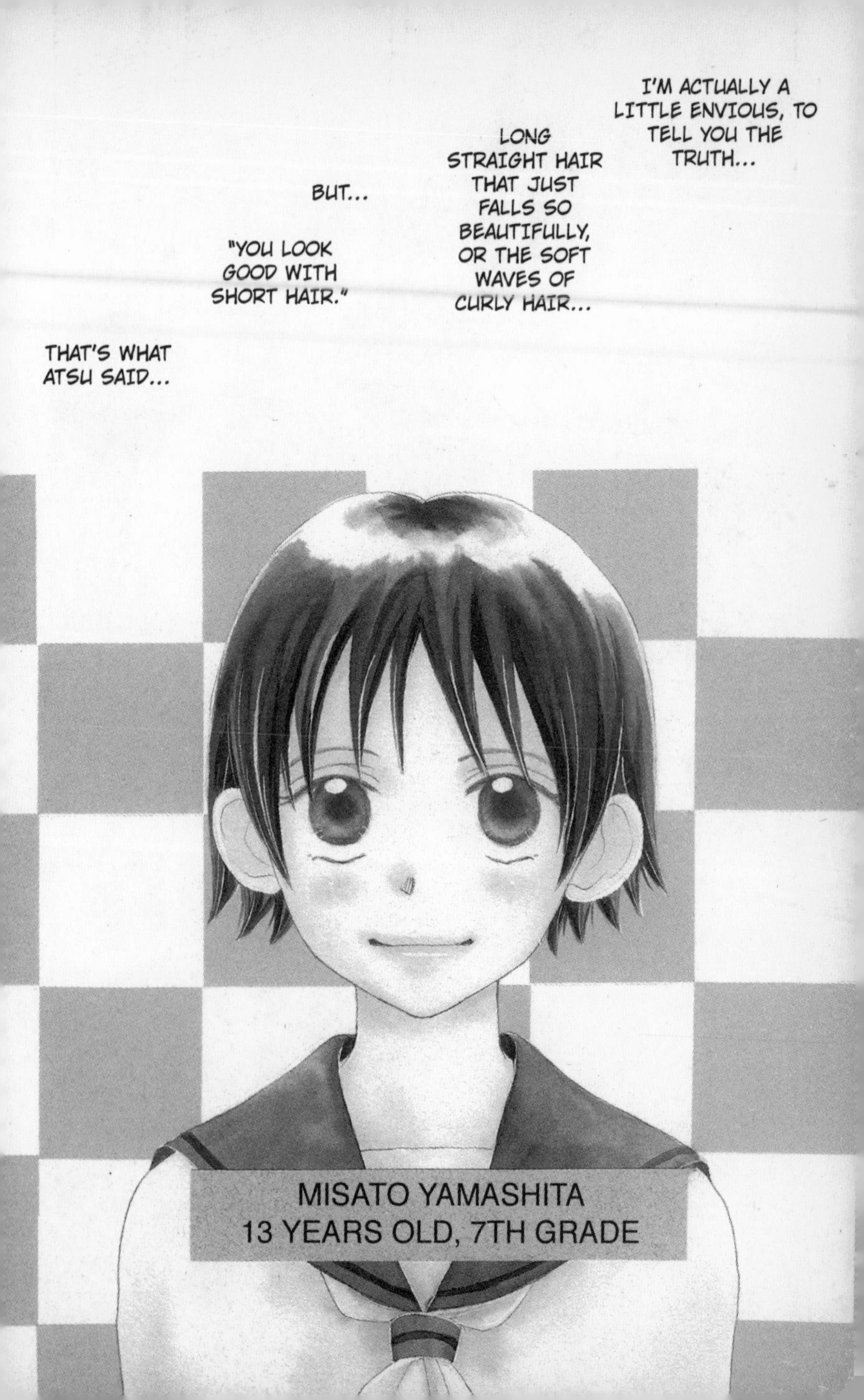
THAT'S WHAT ATSU SAID...
"YOU LOOK GOOD WITH SHORT HAIR."
BUT...
LONG STRAIGHT HAIR THAT JUST FALLS SO BEAUTIFULLY, OR THE SOFT WAVES OF CURLY HAIR...
I'M ACTUALLY A LITTLE ENVIOUS, TO TELL YOU THE TRUTH...
MISATO YAMASHITA
13 YEARS OLD, 7TH GRADE

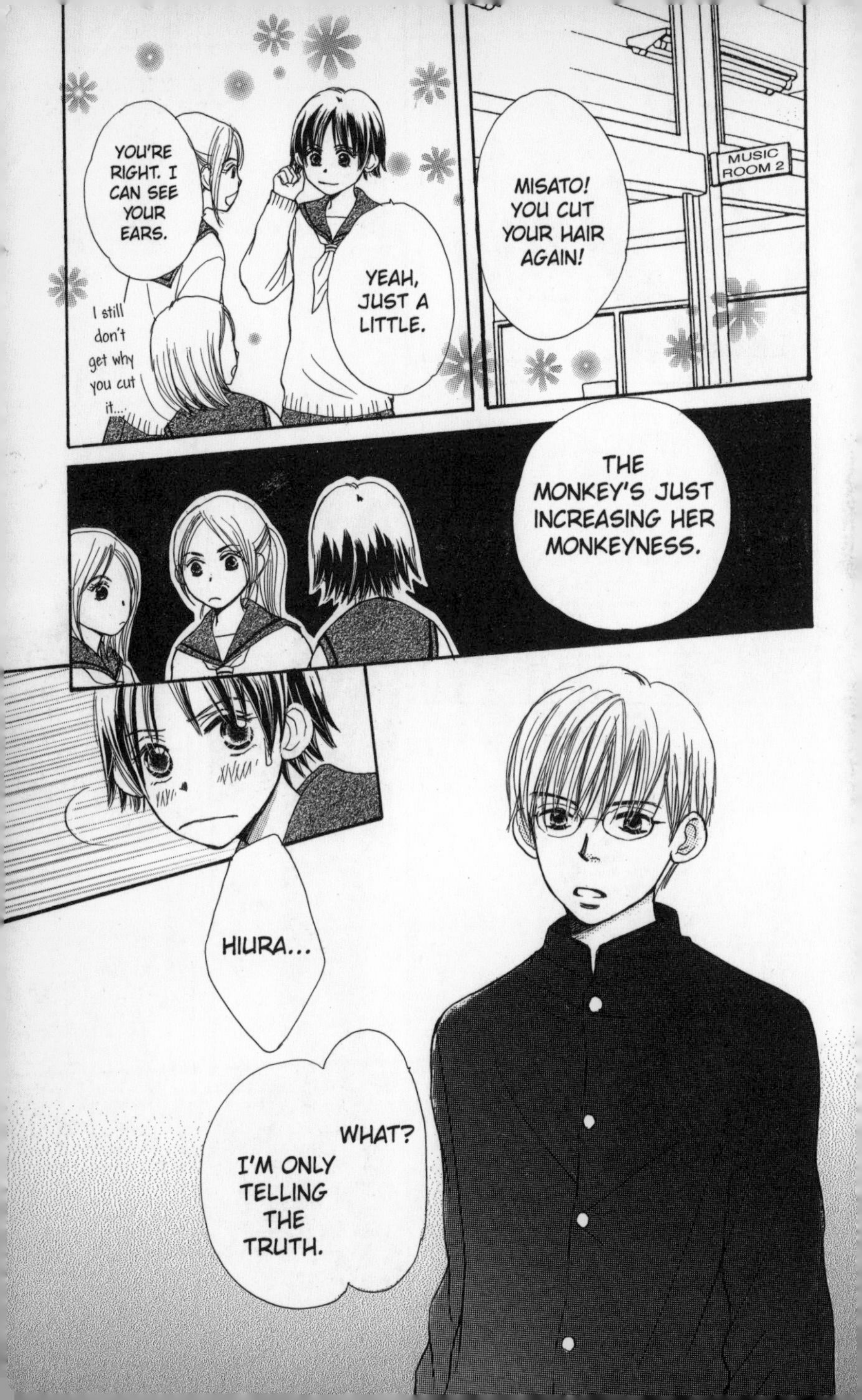
MUSIC ROOM 2
MISATO! YOU CUT YOUR HAIR AGAIN!
YEAH, JUST A LITTLE.
YOU'RE RIGHT. I CAN SEE YOUR EARS.
I still don't get why you cut it...
THE MONKEY'S JUST INCREASING HER MONKEYNESS.
HIURA...
WHAT? I'M ONLY TELLING THE TRUTH.

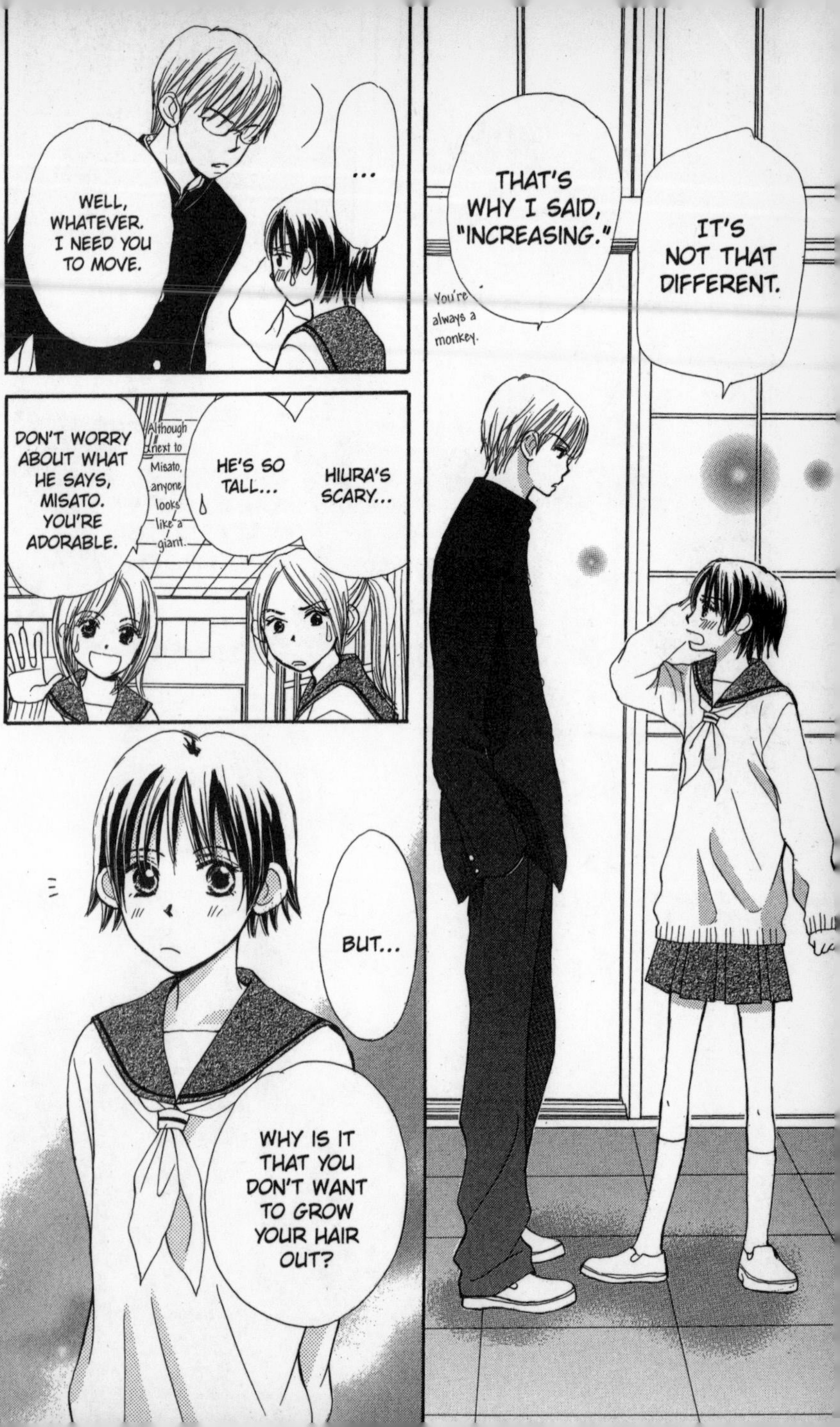
IT'S NOT THAT DIFFERENT.
THAT'S WHY I SAID, "INCREASING."
You're always a monkey.
...
WELL, WHATEVER. I NEED YOU TO MOVE.
HIURA'S SCARY...
HE'S SO TALL...
Although next to Misato, anyone looks like a giant.
DON'T WORRY ABOUT WHAT HE SAYS, MISATO. YOU'RE ADORABLE.
BUT...
WHY IS IT THAT YOU DON'T WANT TO GROW YOUR HAIR OUT?

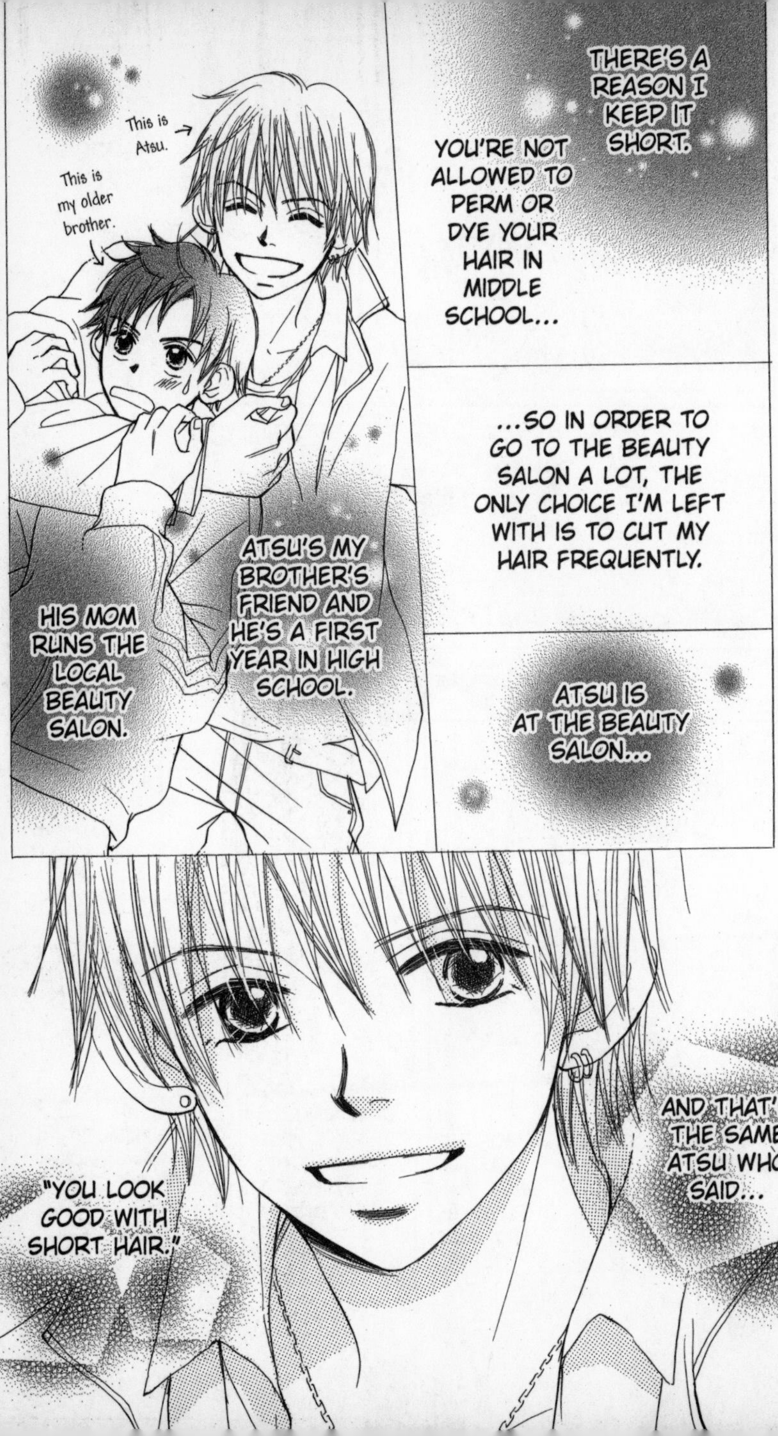
THERE'S A REASON I KEEP IT SHORT.
YOU'RE NOT ALLOWED TO PERM OR DYE YOUR HAIR IN MIDDLE SCHOOL...
...SO IN ORDER TO GO TO THE BEAUTY SALON A LOT, THE ONLY CHOICE I'M LEFT WITH IS TO CUT MY HAIR FREQUENTLY.
ATSU IS AT THE BEAUTY SALON...
This is Atsu.
This is my older brother.
ATSU'S MY BROTHER'S FRIEND AND HE'S A FIRST YEAR IN HIGH SCHOOL.
HIS MOM RUNS THE LOCAL BEAUTY SALON.
AND THAT'S THE SAME ATSU WHO SAID...
"YOU LOOK GOOD WITH SHORT HAIR."

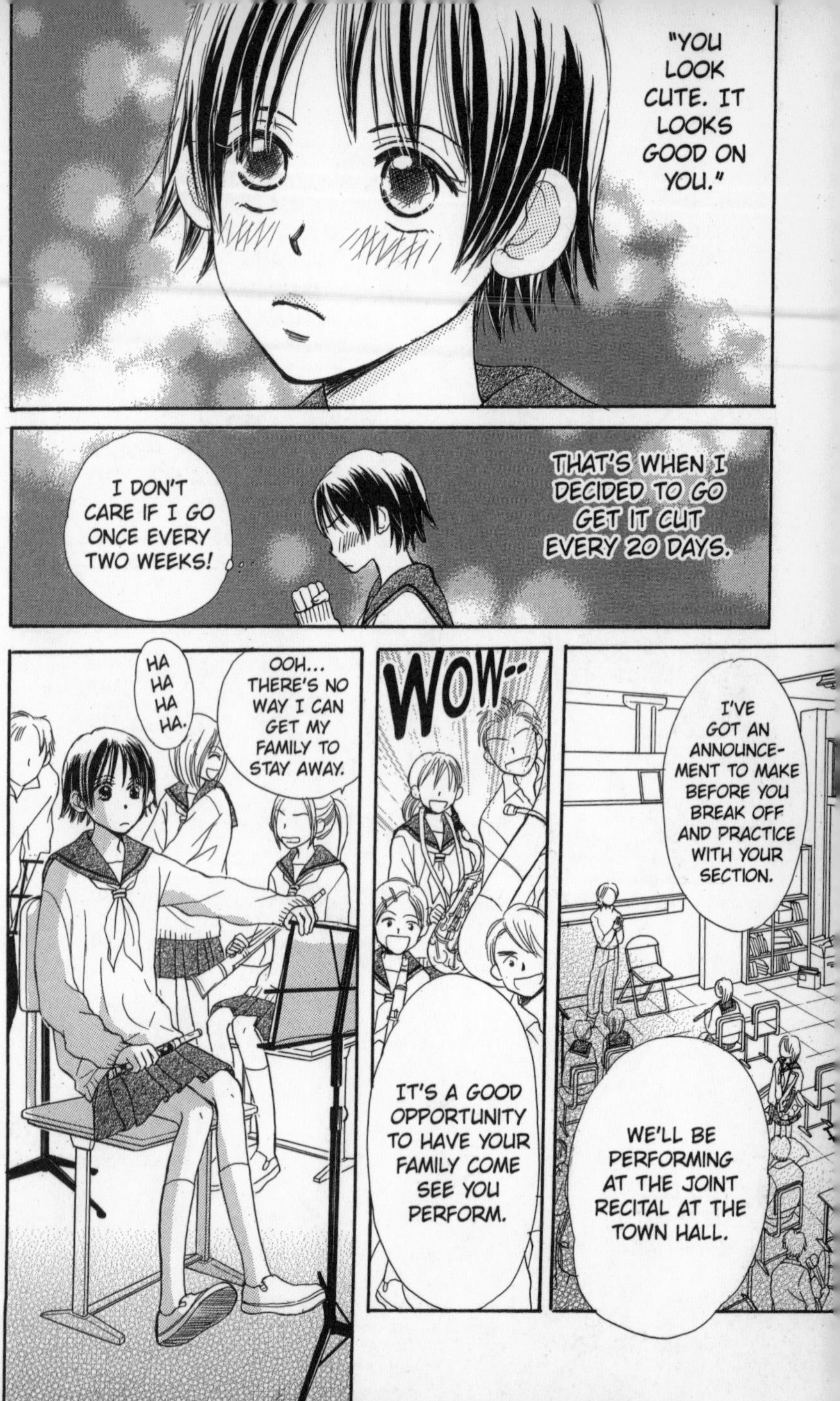
"YOU LOOK CUTE. IT LOOKS GOOD ON YOU."
THAT'S WHEN I DECIDED TO GO GET IT CUT EVERY 20 DAYS.
I DON'T CARE IF I GO ONCE EVERY TWO WEEKS!
I'VE GOT AN ANNOUNCEMENT TO MAKE BEFORE YOU BREAK OFF AND PRACTICE WITH YOUR SECTION.
WE'LL BE PERFORMING AT THE JOINT RECITAL AT THE TOWN HALL.
WOW..
IT'S A GOOD OPPORTUNITY TO HAVE YOUR FAMILY COME SEE YOU PERFORM.
OOH... THERE'S NO WAY I CAN GET MY FAMILY TO STAY AWAY.
HA HA HA HA.

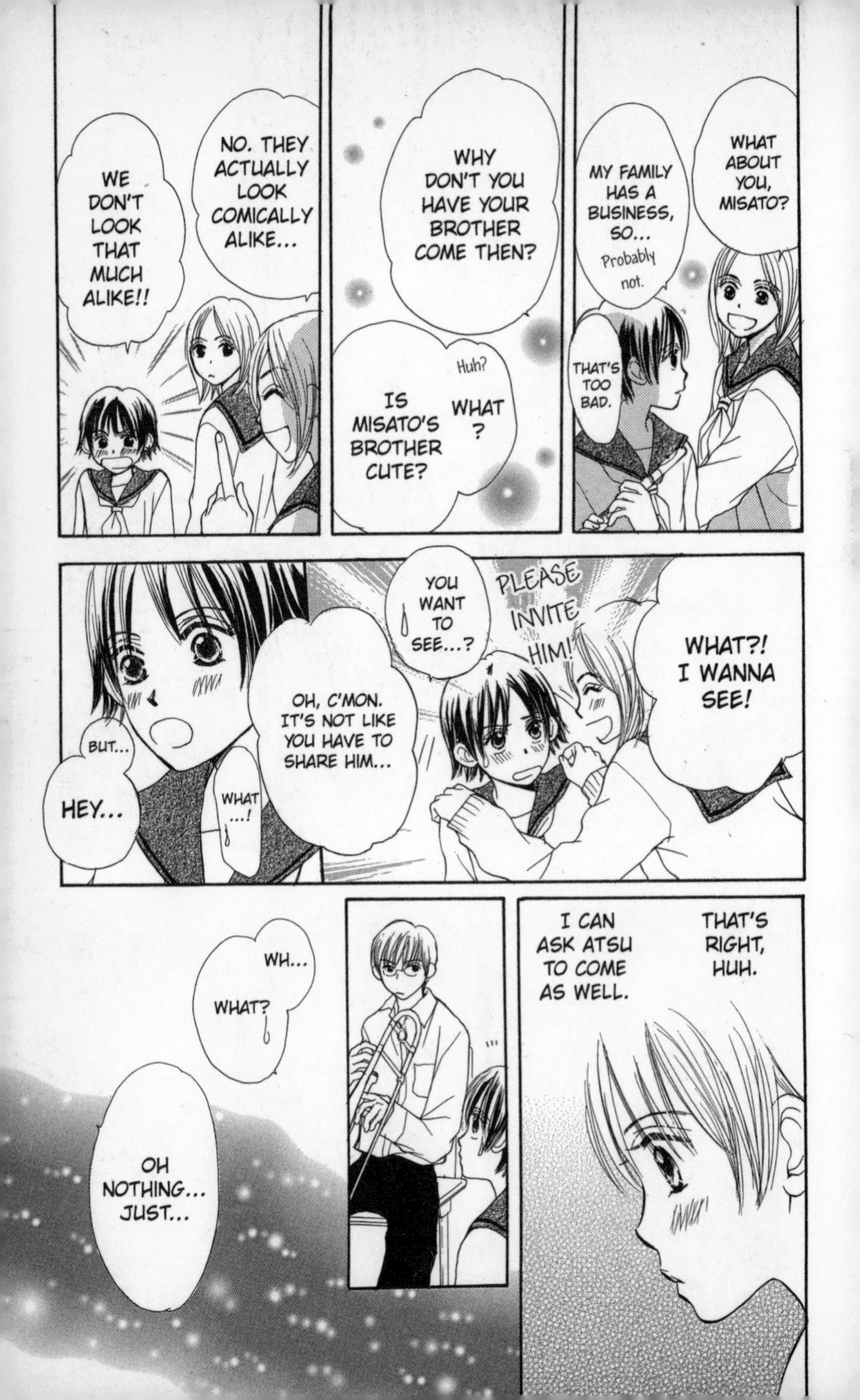
WHAT ABOUT YOU, MISATO?
MY FAMILY HAS A BUSINESS, SO...
Probably not.
THAT'S TOO BAD.
WHY DON'T YOU HAVE YOUR BROTHER COME THEN?
Huh?
WHAT?
IS MISATO'S BROTHER CUTE?
NO. THEY ACTUALLY LOOK COMICALLY ALIKE...
WE DON'T LOOK THAT MUCH ALIKE!!
WHAT?! I WANNA SEE!
PLEASE INVITE HIM!
YOU WANT TO SEE...?
OH, C'MON. IT'S NOT LIKE YOU HAVE TO SHARE HIM...
WHAT...!
BUT...
HEY...
THAT'S RIGHT, HUH.
I CAN ASK ATSU TO COME AS WELL.
WH...
WHAT?
OH NOTHING... JUST...

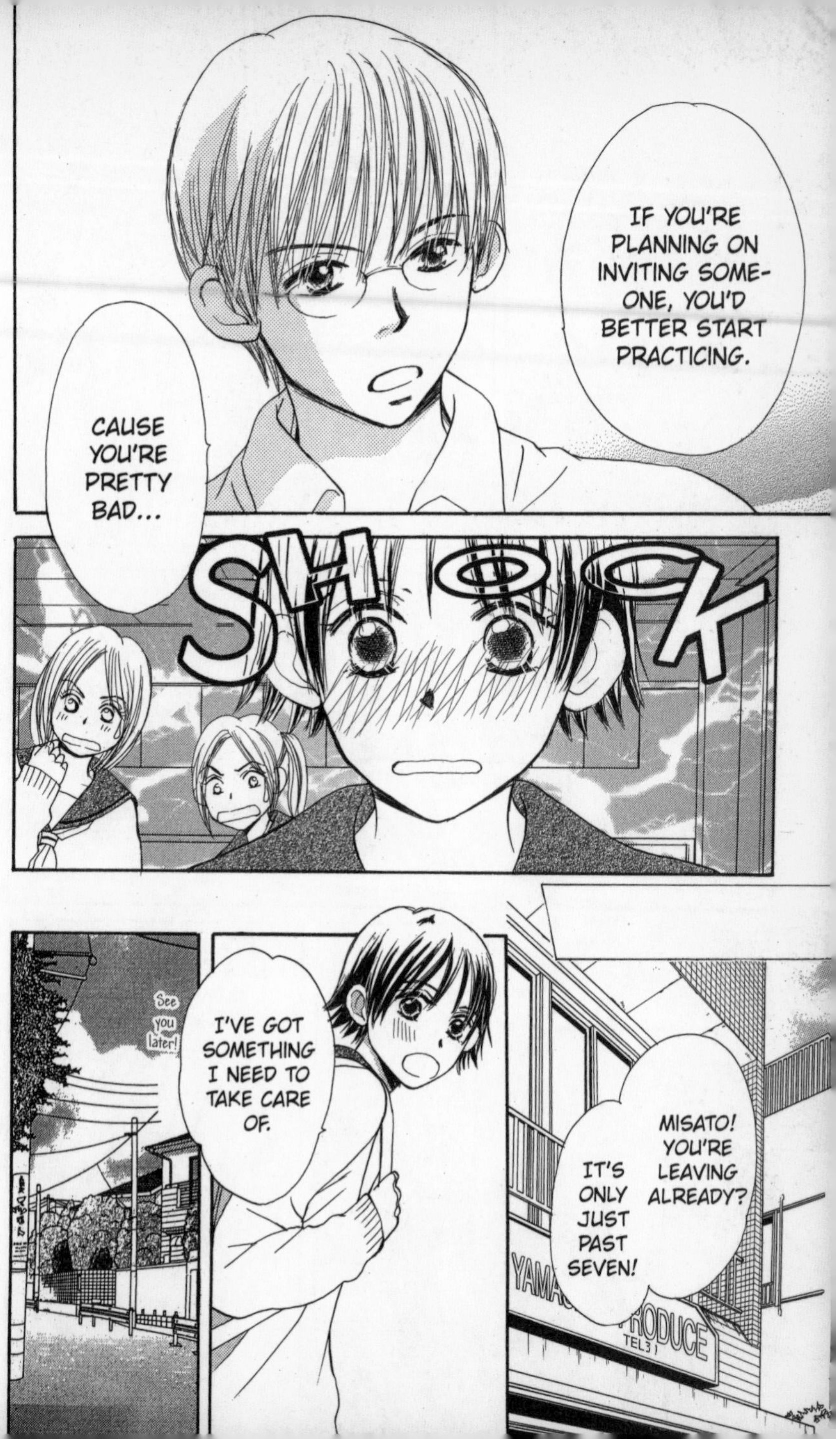
IF YOU'RE PLANNING ON INVITING SOME-ONE, YOU'D BETTER START PRACTICING.
CAUSE YOU'RE PRETTY BAD...
SHOCK
MISATO! YOU'RE LEAVING ALREADY?
IT'S ONLY JUST PAST SEVEN!
I'VE GOT SOMETHING I NEED TO TAKE CARE OF.
See you later!

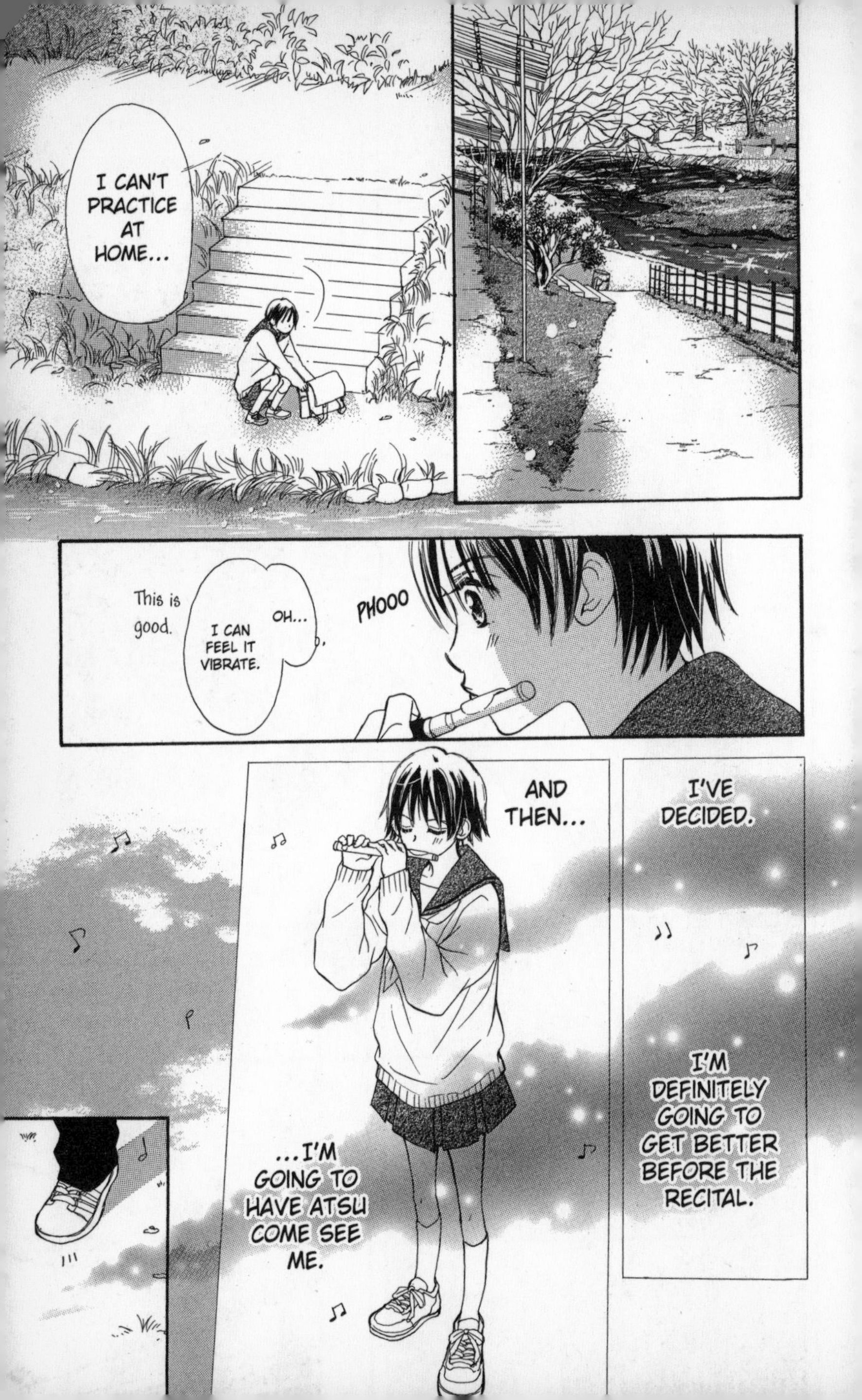
I CAN'T PRACTICE AT HOME...
PHOOO
OH... I CAN FEEL IT VIBRATE.
This is good.
I'VE DECIDED.
I'M DEFINITELY GOING TO GET BETTER BEFORE THE RECITAL.
AND THEN...
...I'M GOING TO HAVE ATSU COME SEE ME.

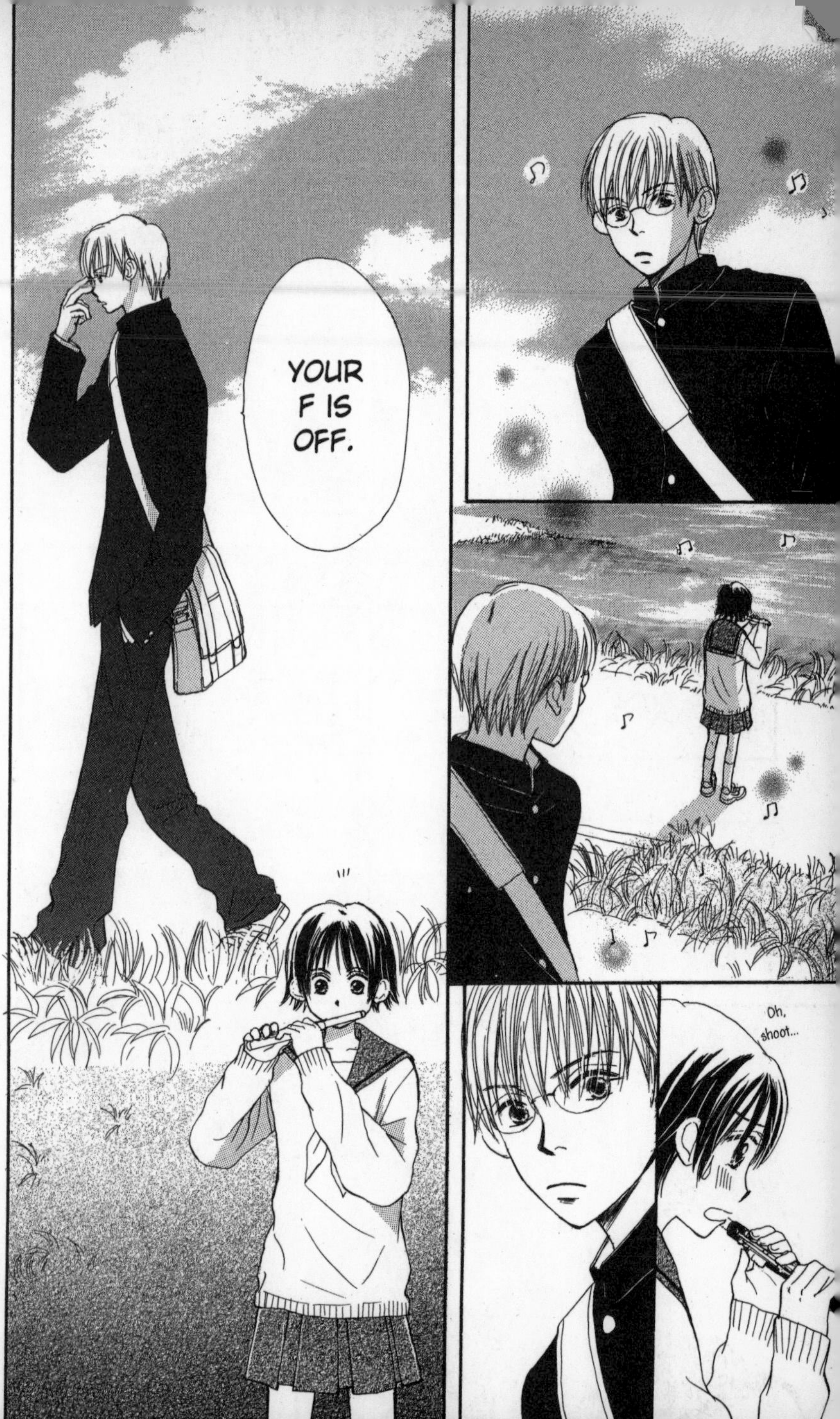
Oh, shoot...
YOUR F IS OFF.

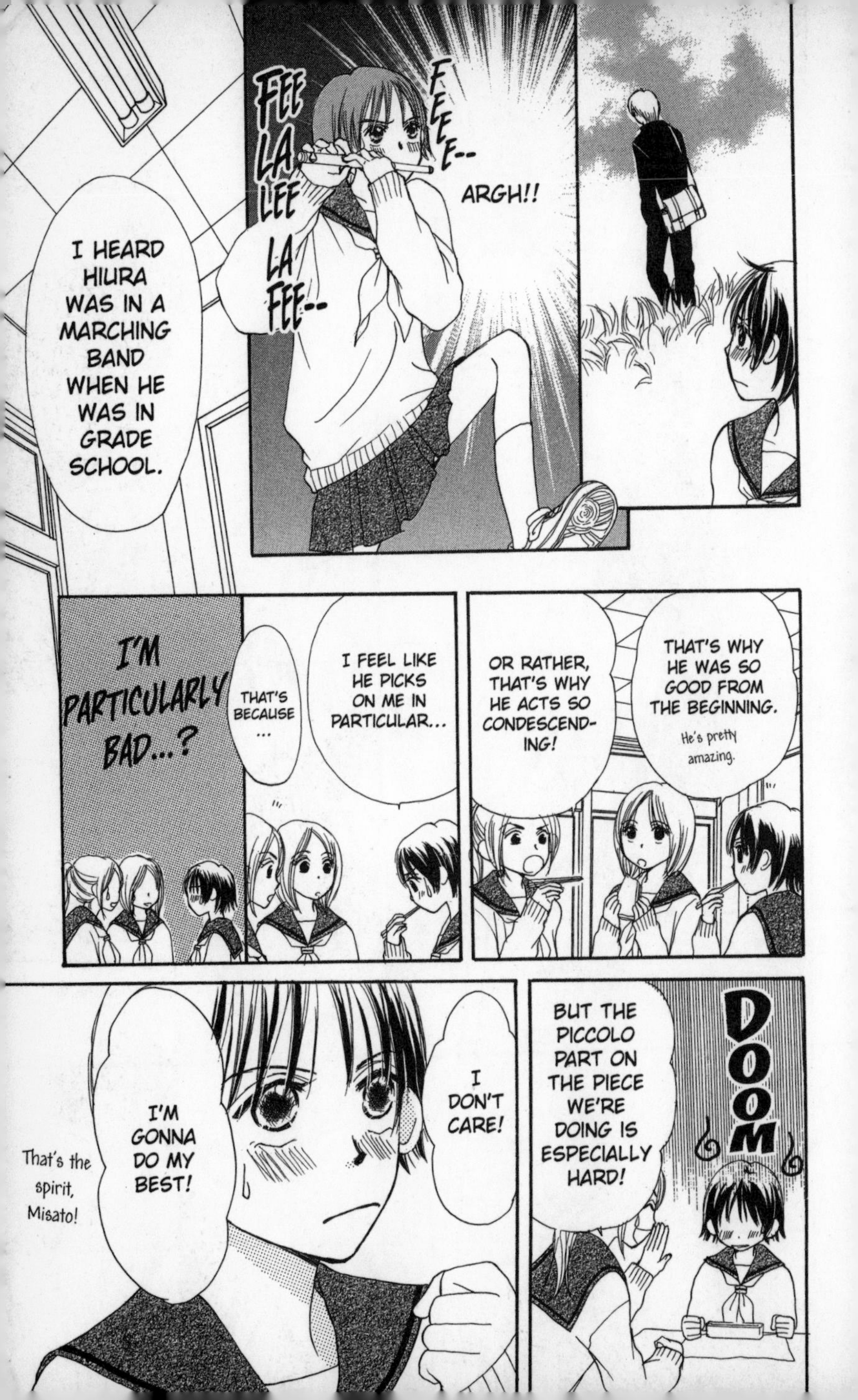
FEEE--
ARGH!!
FEE LA LEE LA FEE--
I HEARD HIURA WAS IN A MARCHING BAND WHEN HE WAS IN GRADE SCHOOL.
THAT'S WHY HE WAS SO GOOD FROM THE BEGINNING.
He's pretty amazing.
OR RATHER, THAT'S WHY HE ACTS SO CONDESCENDING!
I FEEL LIKE HE PICKS ON ME IN PARTICULAR...
THAT'S BECAUSE ...
I'M PARTICULARLY BAD...?
DOOM
BUT THE PICCOLO PART ON THE PIECE WE'RE DOING IS ESPECIALLY HARD!
I DON'T CARE!
I'M GONNA DO MY BEST!
That's the spirit, Misato!

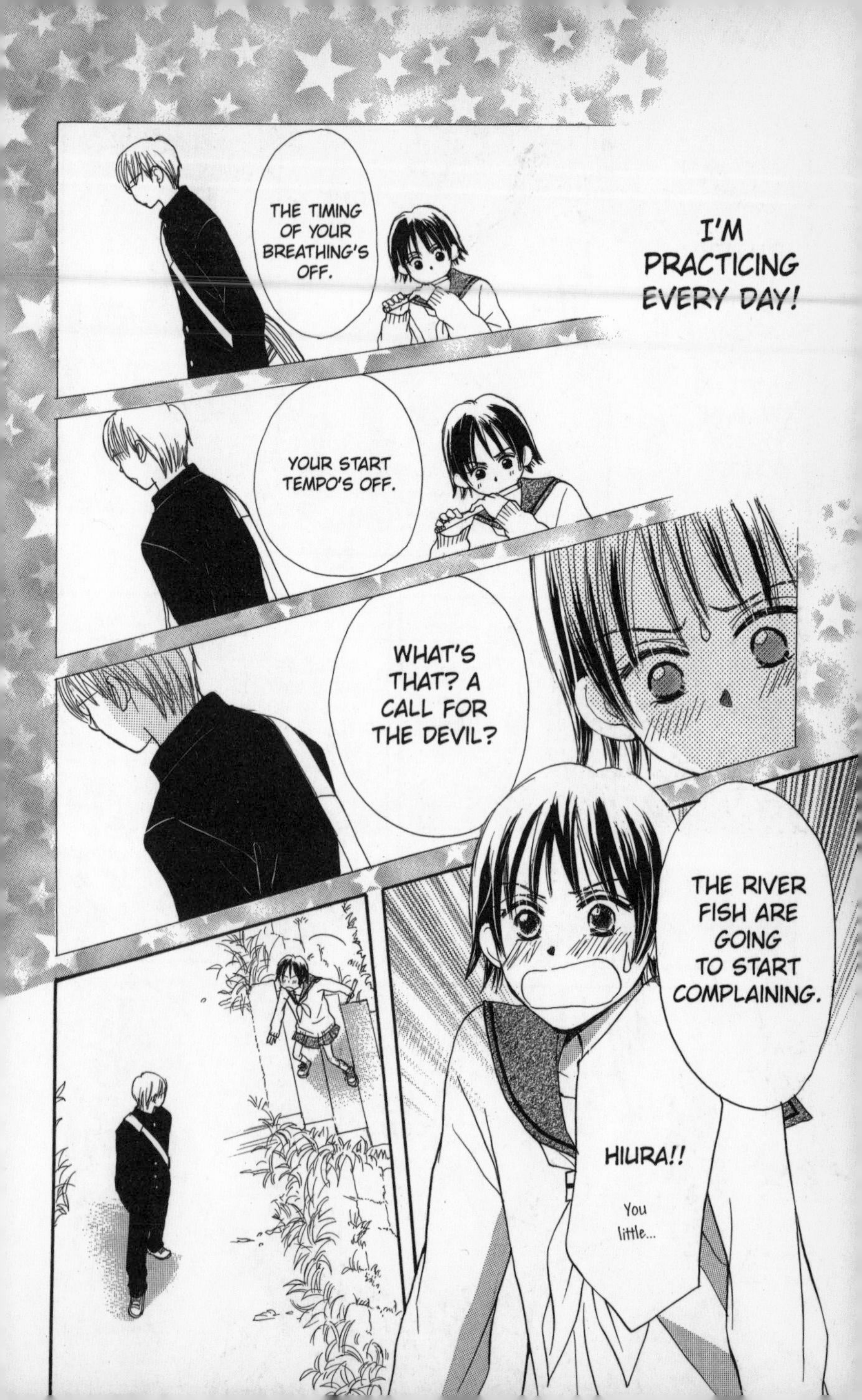
I'M PRACTICING EVERY DAY!
THE TIMING OF YOUR BREATHING'S OFF.
YOUR START TEMPO'S OFF.
WHAT'S THAT? A CALL FOR THE DEVIL?
THE RIVER FISH ARE GOING TO START COMPLAINING.
HIURA!!
You little...

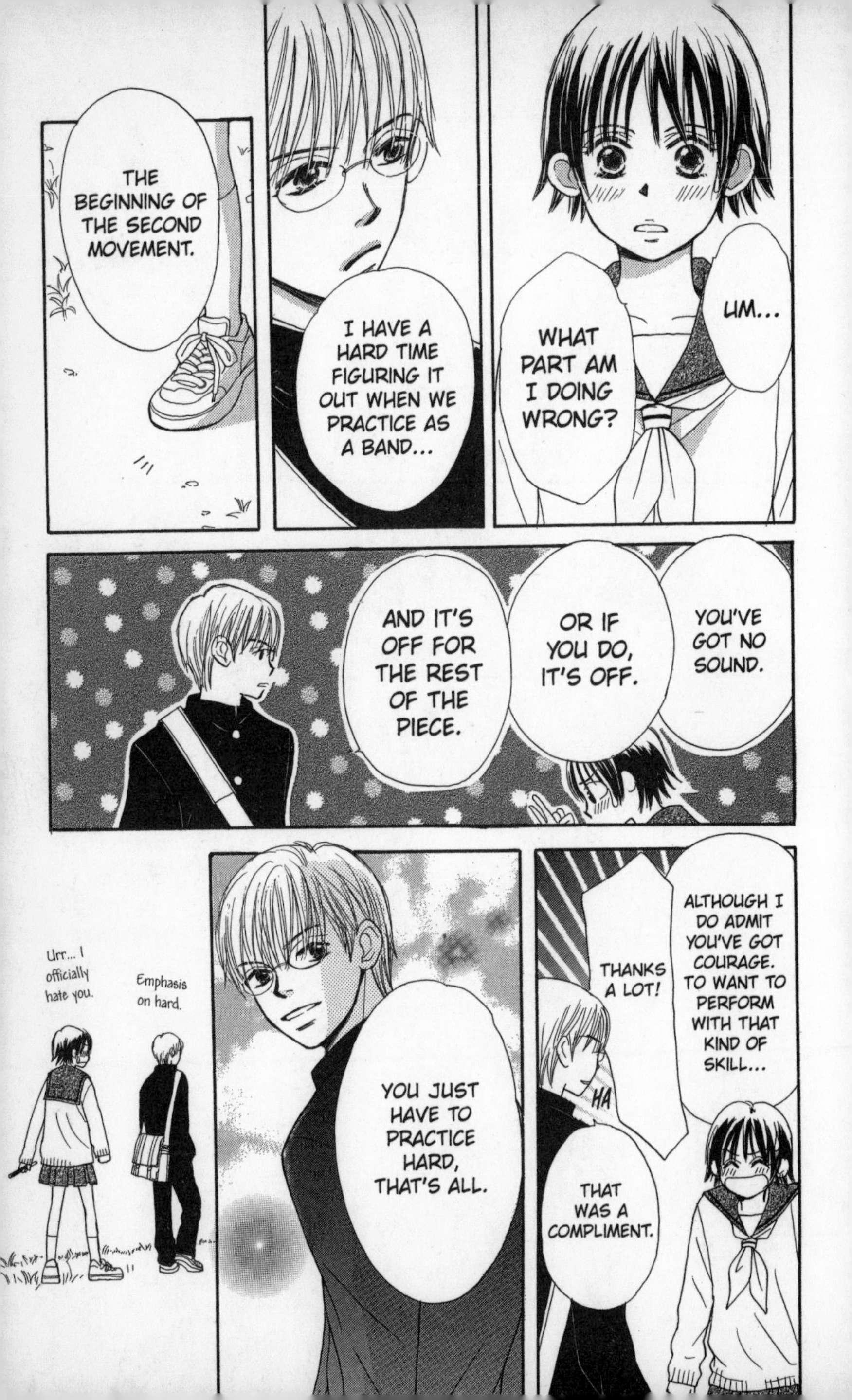
UM...
WHAT PART AM I DOING WRONG?
I HAVE A HARD TIME FIGURING IT OUT WHEN WE PRACTICE AS A BAND...
THE BEGINNING OF THE SECOND MOVEMENT.
YOU'VE GOT NO SOUND.
OR IF YOU DO, IT'S OFF.
AND IT'S OFF FOR THE REST OF THE PIECE.
ALTHOUGH I DO ADMIT YOU'VE GOT COURAGE. TO WANT TO PERFORM WITH THAT KIND OF SKILL...
THANKS A LOT!
HA
THAT WAS A COMPLIMENT.
YOU JUST HAVE TO PRACTICE HARD, THAT'S ALL.
Emphasis on hard.
Urr... I officially hate you.

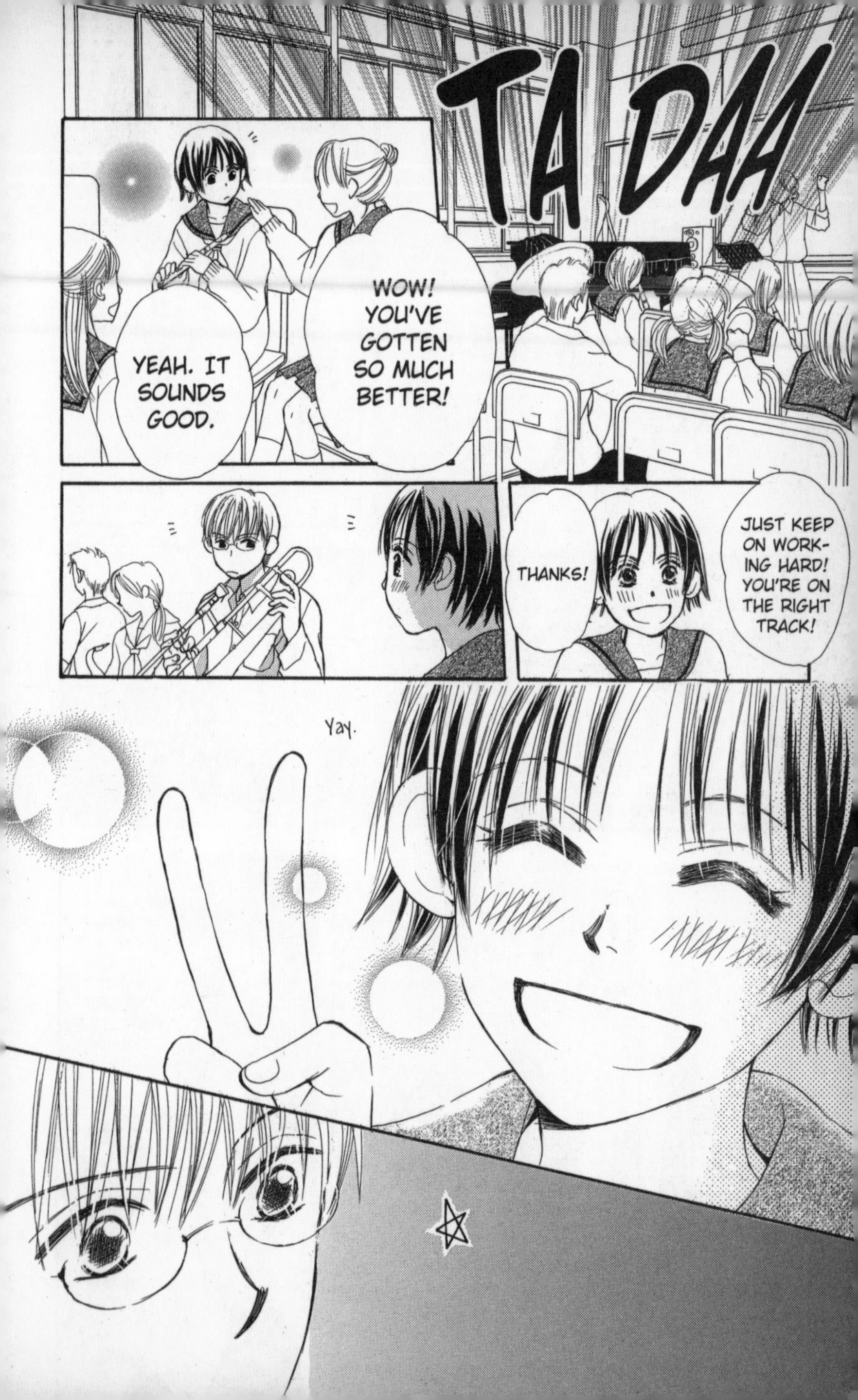
TA DAA
WOW! YOU'VE GOTTEN SO MUCH BETTER!
YEAH. IT SOUNDS GOOD.
JUST KEEP ON WORKING HARD! YOU'RE ON THE RIGHT TRACK!
THANKS!
Yay.

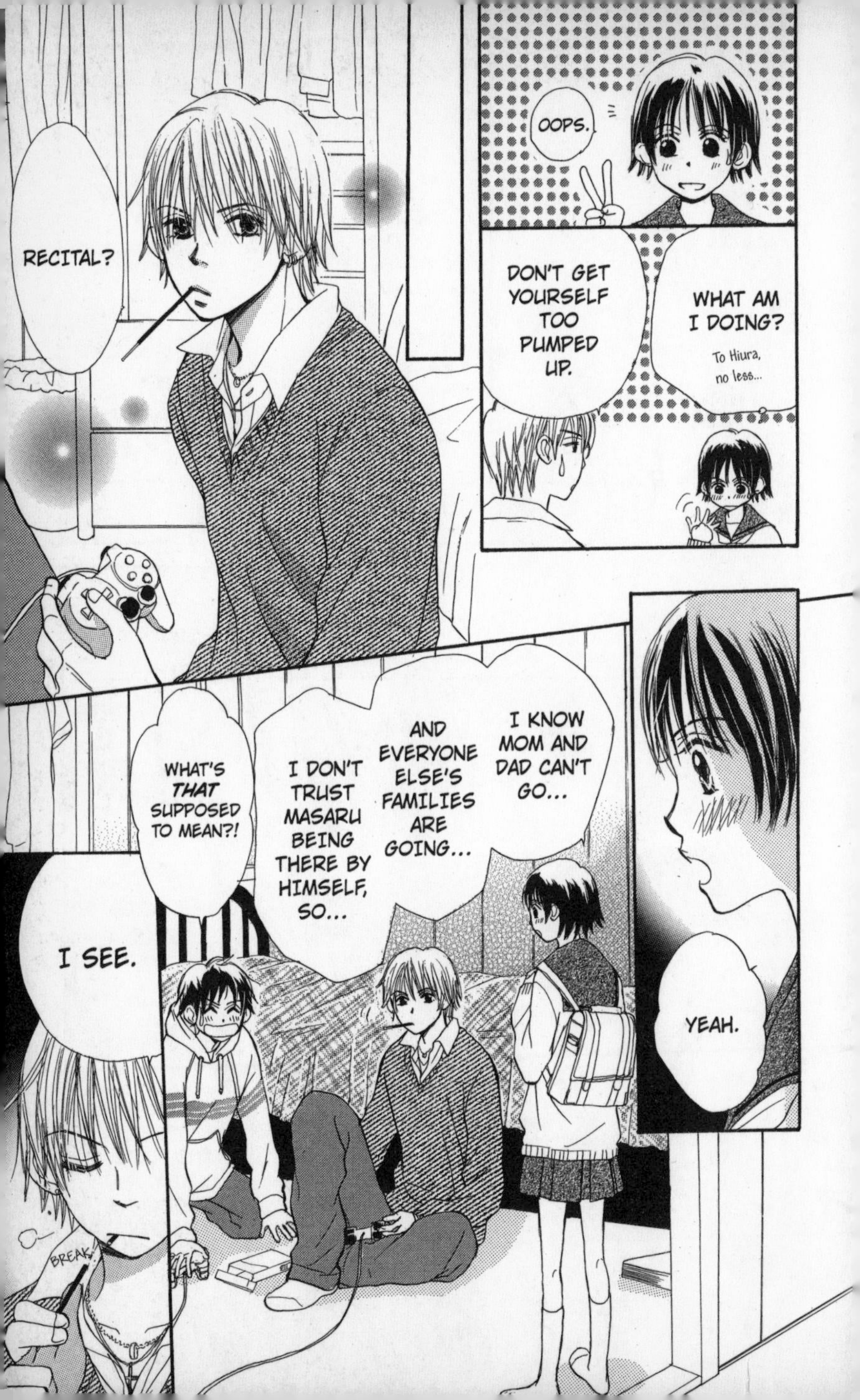
OOPS.
WHAT AM I DOING?
To Hiura, no less...
DON'T GET YOURSELF TOO PUMPED UP.
RECITAL?
YEAH.
I KNOW MOM AND DAD CAN'T GO...
AND EVERYONE ELSE'S FAMILIES ARE GOING...
I DON'T TRUST MASARU BEING THERE BY HIMSELF, SO...
WHAT'S *THAT* SUPPOSED TO MEAN?!
I SEE.
BREAK

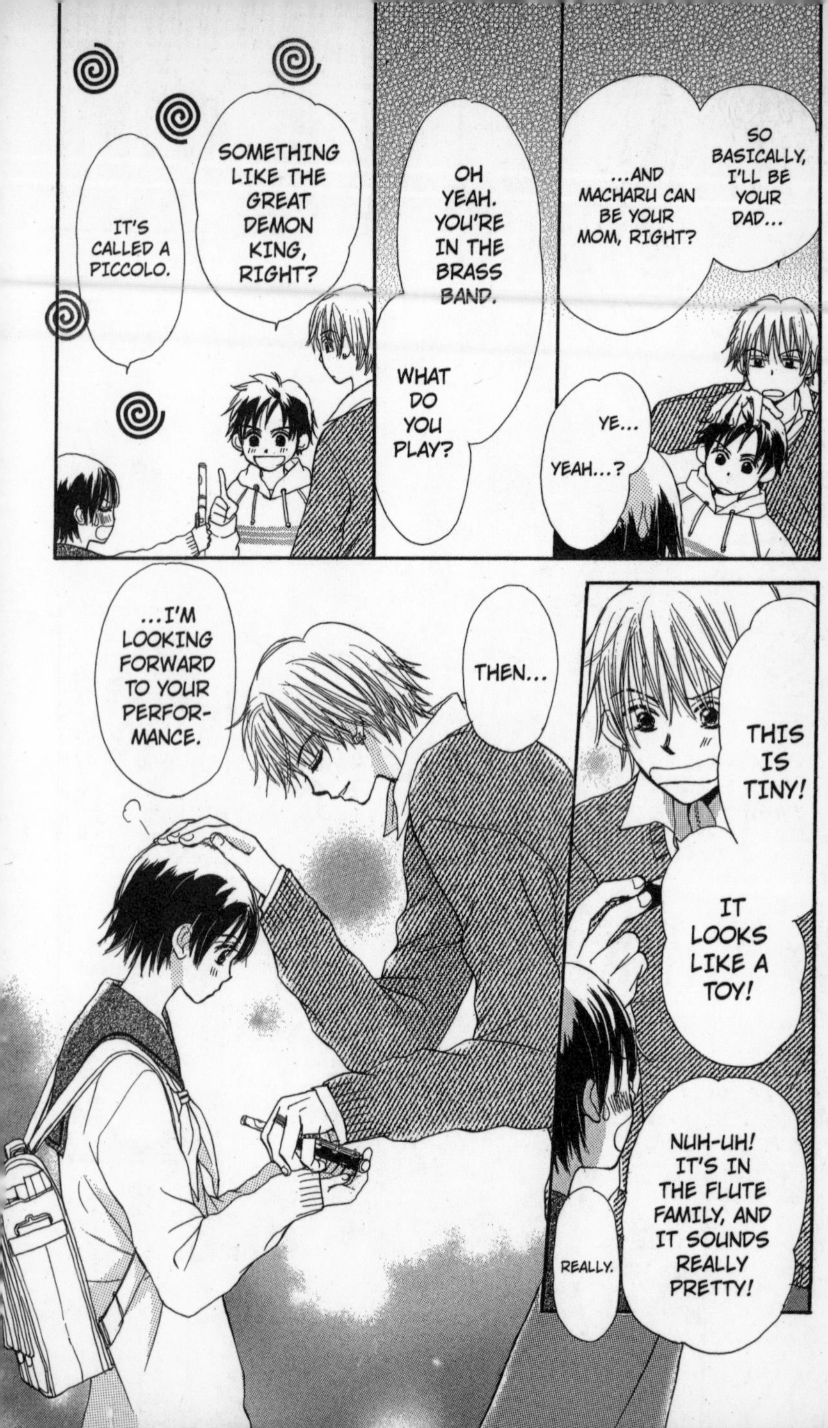
SO BASICALLY, I'LL BE YOUR DAD...
...AND MACHARU CAN BE YOUR MOM, RIGHT?
YE... YEAH...?
OH YEAH. YOU'RE IN THE BRASS BAND.
WHAT DO YOU PLAY?
SOMETHING LIKE THE GREAT DEMON KING, RIGHT?
IT'S CALLED A PICCOLO.
THIS IS TINY!
IT LOOKS LIKE A TOY!
NUH-UH! IT'S IN THE FLUTE FAMILY, AND IT SOUNDS REALLY PRETTY!
REALLY.
THEN...
...I'M LOOKING FORWARD TO YOUR PERFORMANCE.

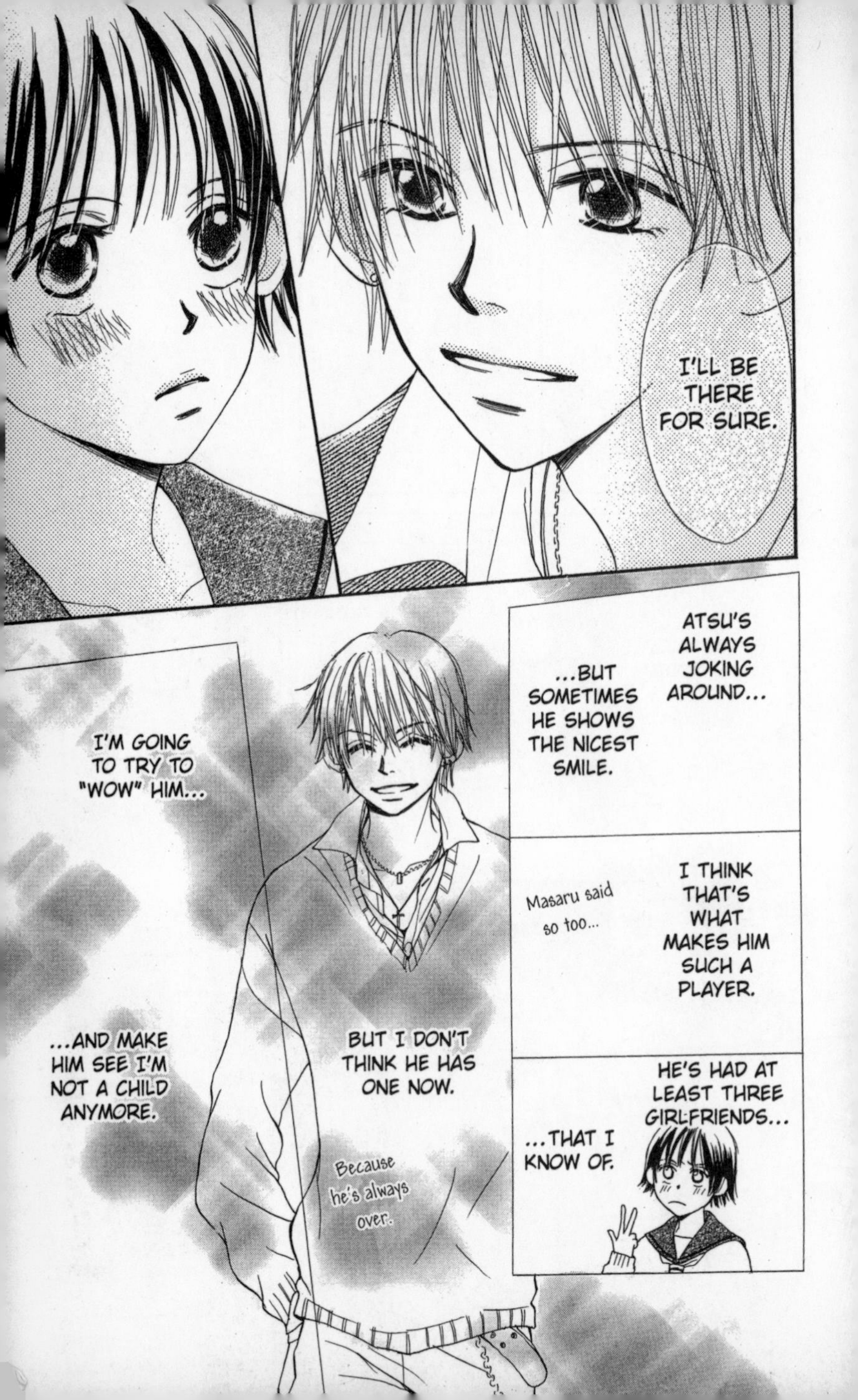
I'LL BE THERE FOR SURE.
ATSU'S ALWAYS JOKING AROUND...
...BUT SOMETIMES HE SHOWS THE NICEST SMILE.
I THINK THAT'S WHAT MAKES HIM SUCH A PLAYER.
Masaru said so too...
HE'S HAD AT LEAST THREE GIRLFRIENDS...
...THAT I KNOW OF.
BUT I DON'T THINK HE HAS ONE NOW.
Because he's always over.
I'M GOING TO TRY TO "WOW" HIM...
...AND MAKE HIM SEE I'M NOT A CHILD ANYMORE.

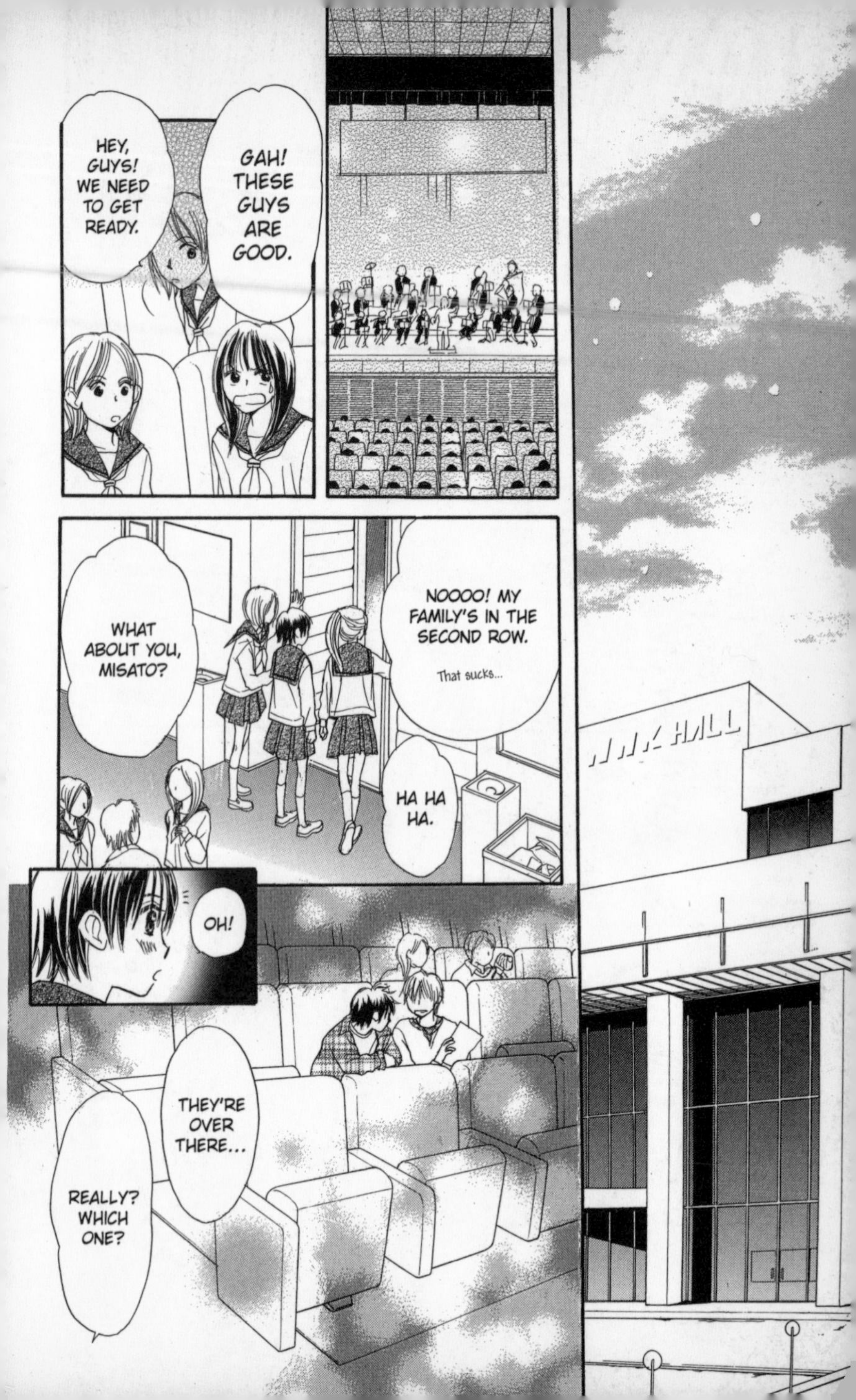
GAH! THESE GUYS ARE GOOD.
HEY, GUYS! WE NEED TO GET READY.
NOOOO! MY FAMILY'S IN THE SECOND ROW.
That sucks...
HA HA HA.
WHAT ABOUT YOU, MISATO?
OH!
THEY'RE OVER THERE...
REALLY? WHICH ONE?

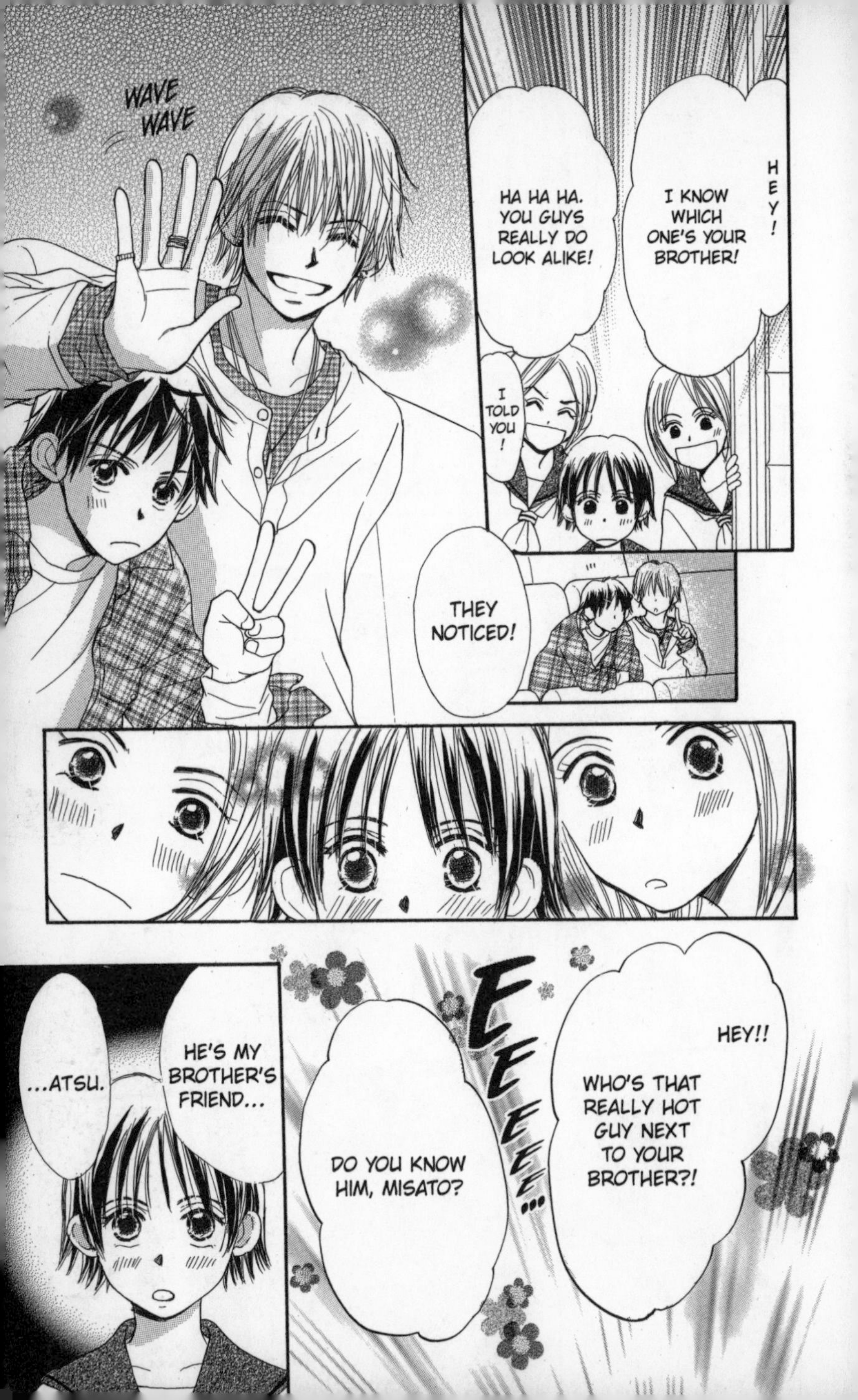
HEY!
I KNOW WHICH ONE'S YOUR BROTHER!
HA HA HA. YOU GUYS REALLY DO LOOK ALIKE!
I TOLD YOU!
THEY NOTICED!
WAVE WAVE
HEY!!
WHO'S THAT REALLY HOT GUY NEXT TO YOUR BROTHER?!
EEEEE...
DO YOU KNOW HIM, MISATO?
HE'S MY BROTHER'S FRIEND...
...ATSU.

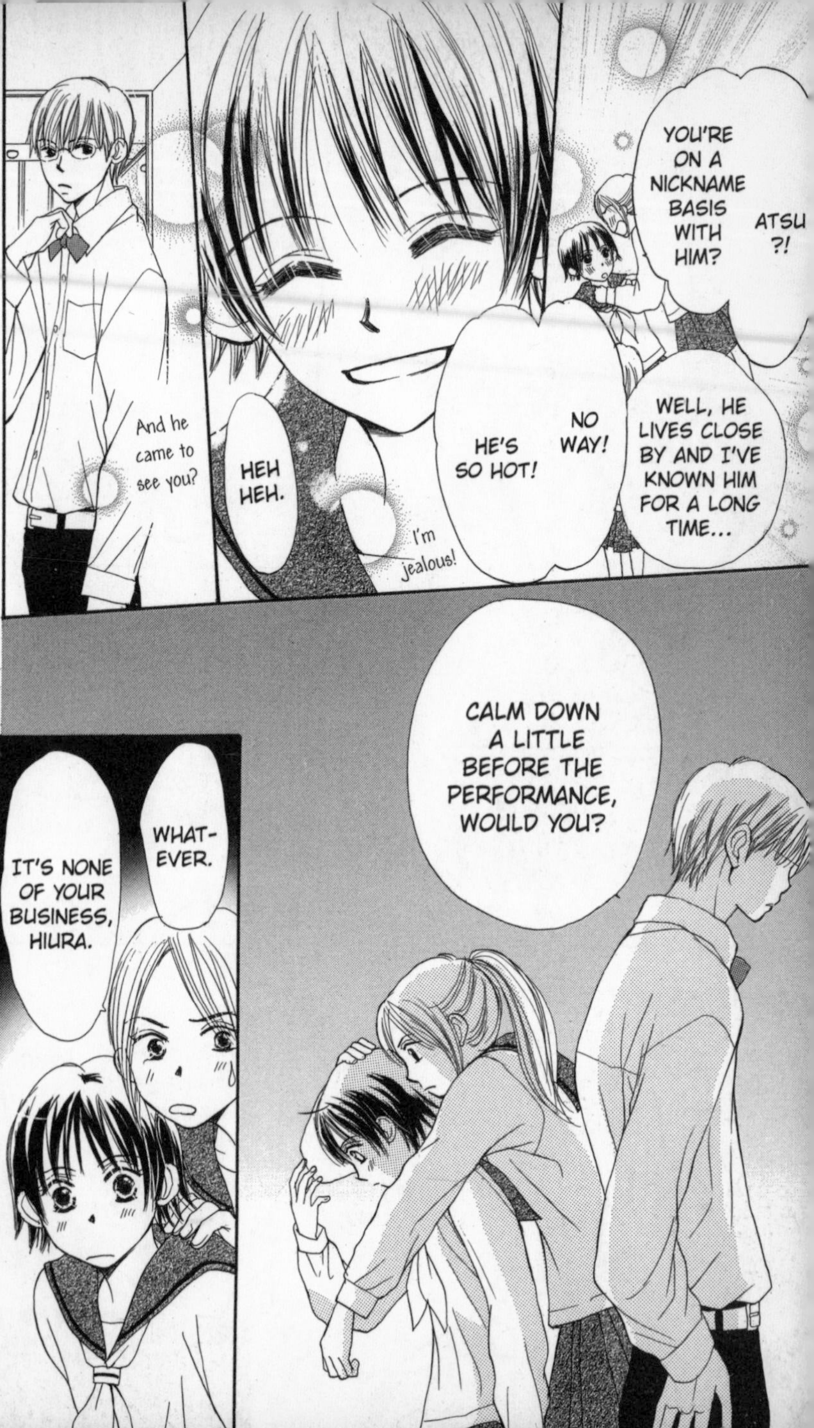
ATSU ?!
YOU'RE ON A NICKNAME BASIS WITH HIM?
WELL, HE LIVES CLOSE BY AND I'VE KNOWN HIM FOR A LONG TIME...
NO WAY!
HE'S SO HOT!
I'm jealous!
HEH HEH.
And he came to see you?
CALM DOWN A LITTLE BEFORE THE PERFORMANCE, WOULD YOU?
WHAT-EVER.
IT'S NONE OF YOUR BUSINESS, HIURA.

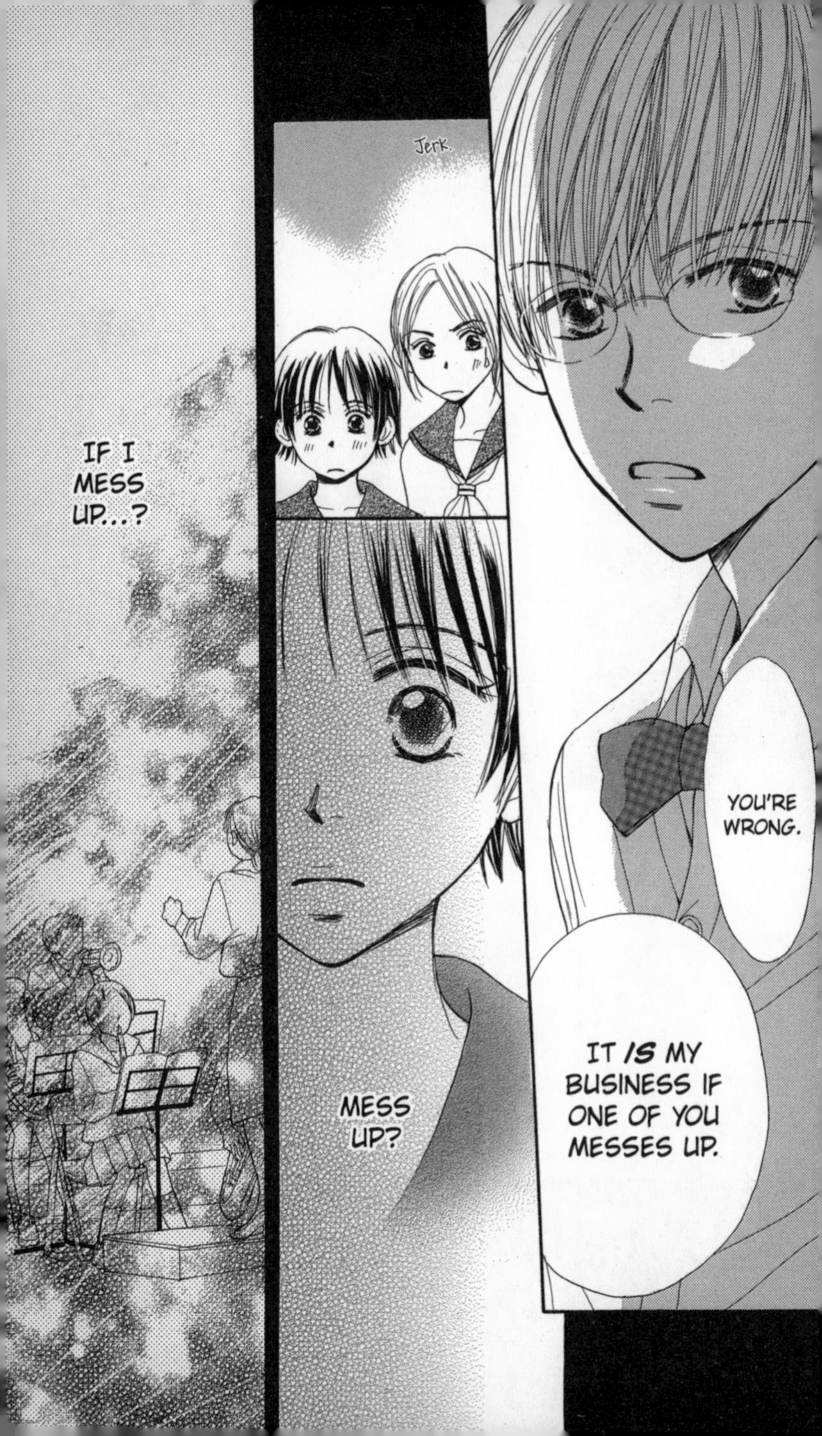
YOU'RE WRONG.
IT *IS* MY BUSINESS IF ONE OF YOU MESSES UP.
Jerk.
MESS UP?
IF I MESS UP...?

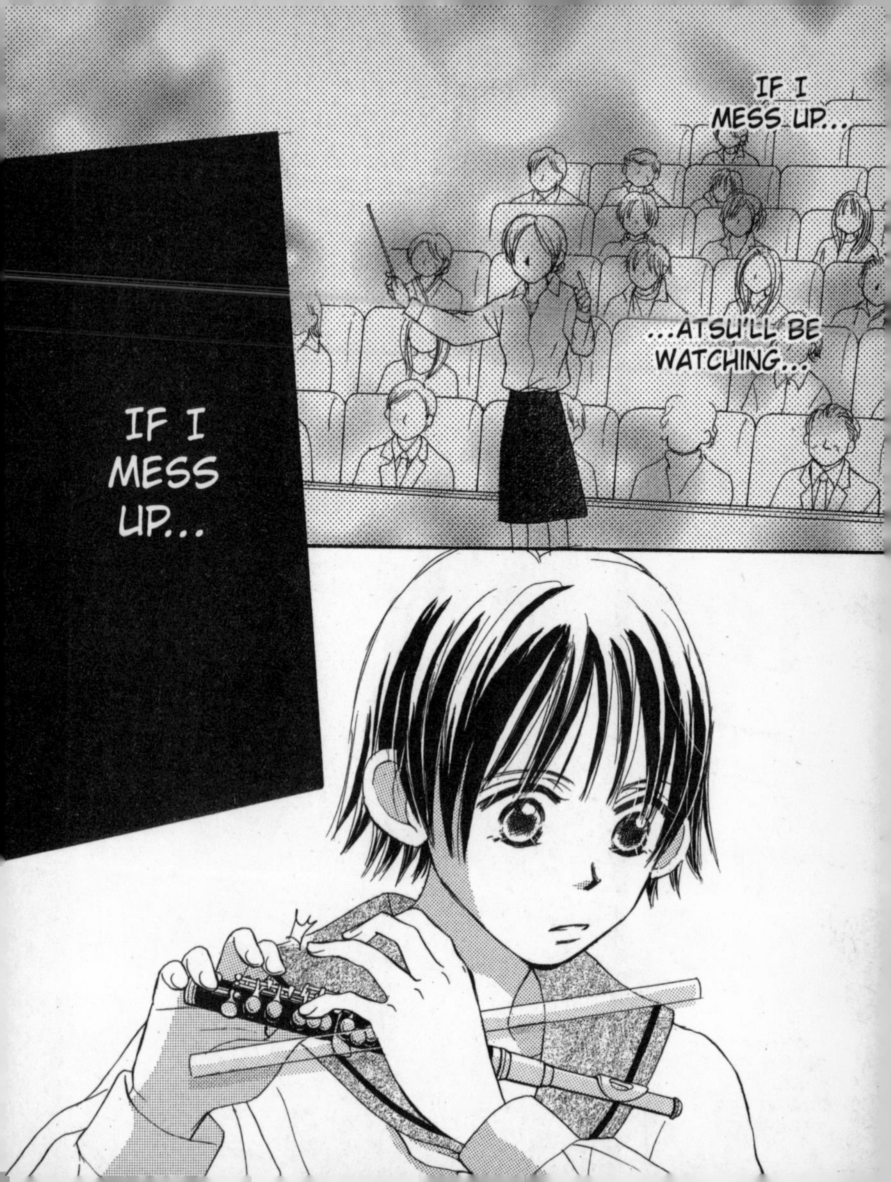
IF I MESS UP...
...ATSU'LL BE WATCHING...
IF I MESS UP...

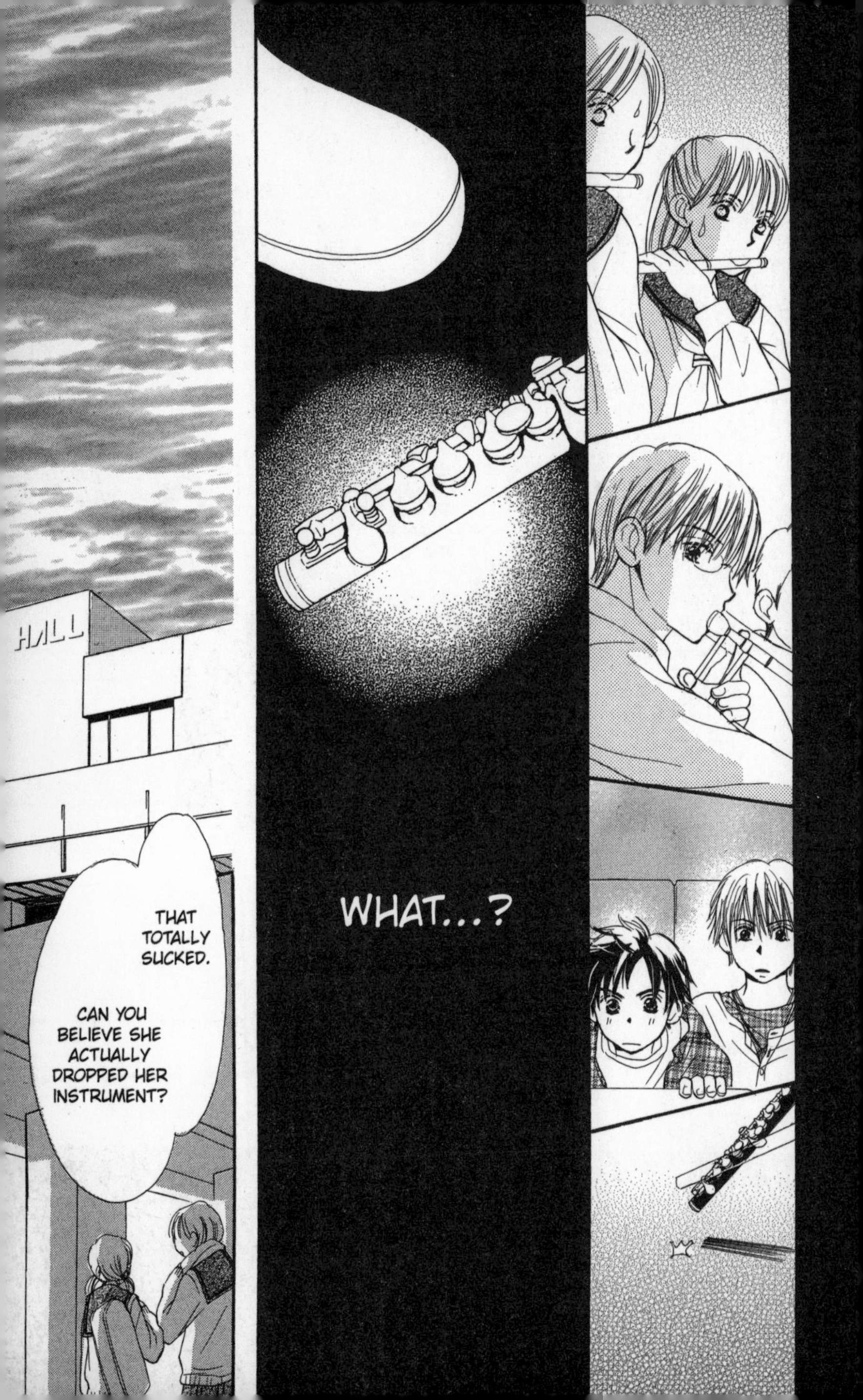
WHAT...?
HALL
THAT TOTALLY SUCKED.
CAN YOU BELIEVE SHE ACTUALLY DROPPED HER INSTRUMENT?

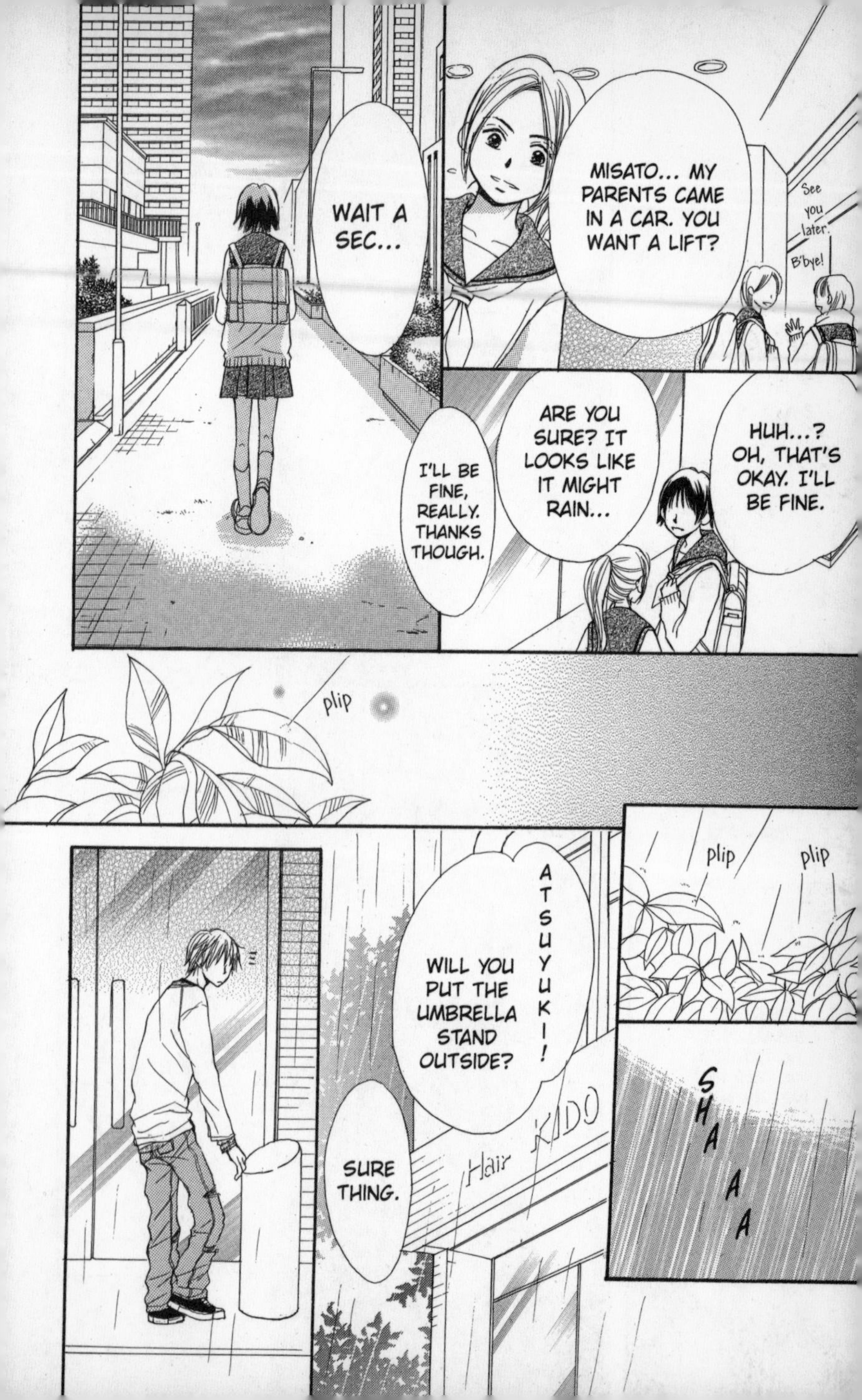

See you later.
B'bye!
MISATO... MY PARENTS CAME IN A CAR. YOU WANT A LIFT?
HUH...? OH, THAT'S OKAY. I'LL BE FINE.
ARE YOU SURE? IT LOOKS LIKE IT MIGHT RAIN...
I'LL BE FINE, REALLY. THANKS THOUGH.
WAIT A SEC...
plip
plip
plip
SHAAAA
ATSUYUKI!
WILL YOU PUT THE UMBRELLA STAND OUTSIDE?
SURE THING.
Hair KIDO

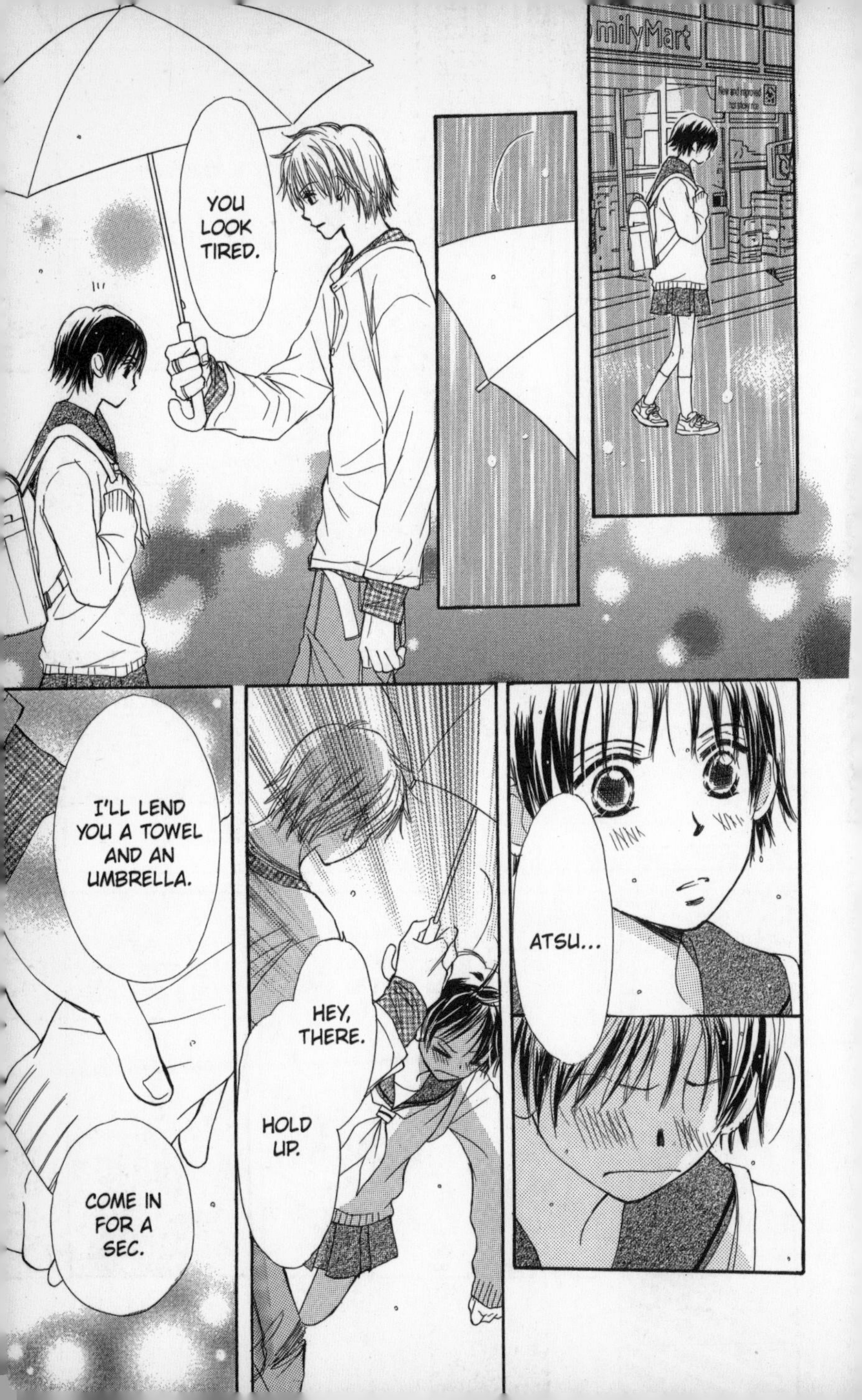
milyMart
YOU LOOK TIRED.
ATSU...
HEY, THERE.
HOLD UP.
I'LL LEND YOU A TOWEL AND AN UMBRELLA.
COME IN FOR A SEC.

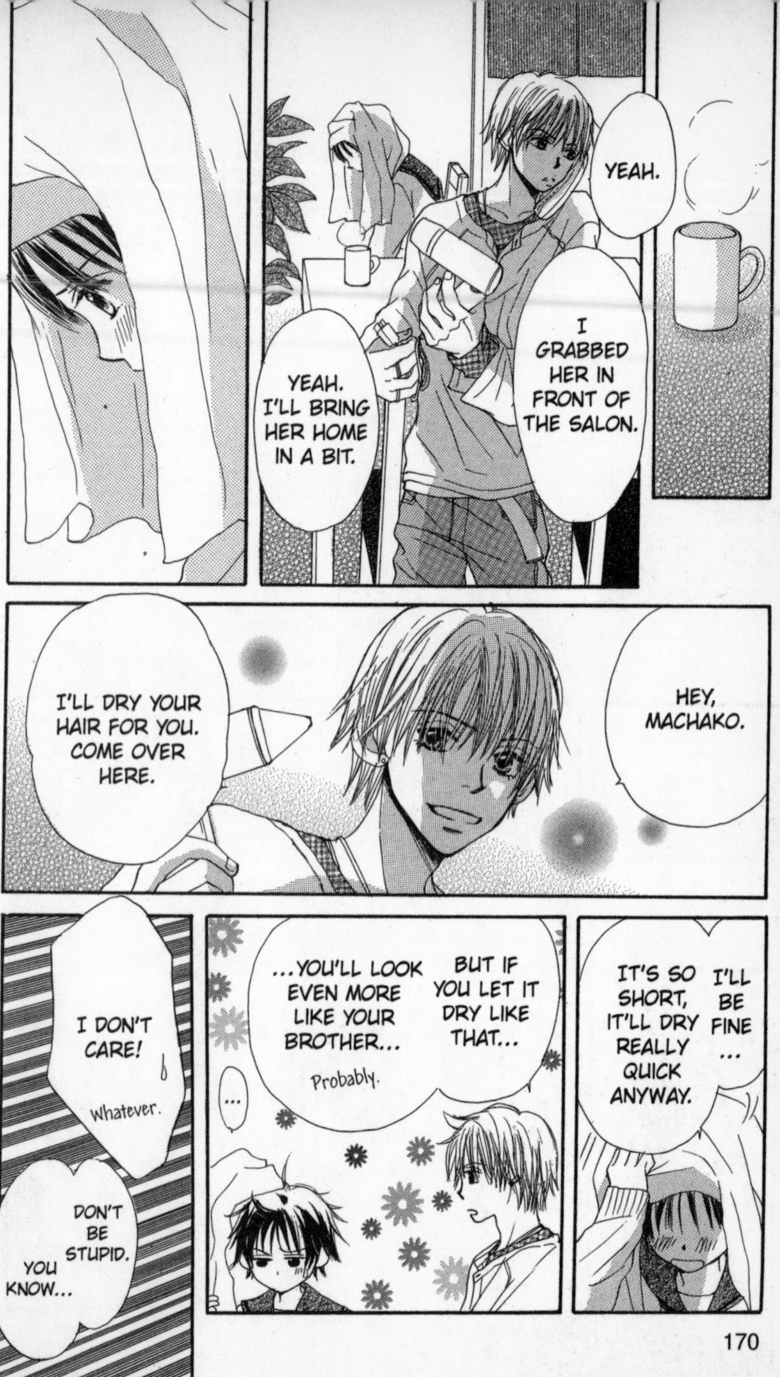
YEAH.
I GRABBED HER IN FRONT OF THE SALON.
YEAH. I'LL BRING HER HOME IN A BIT.
HEY, MACHAKO.
I'LL DRY YOUR HAIR FOR YOU. COME OVER HERE.
I'LL BE FINE...
IT'S SO SHORT, IT'LL DRY REALLY QUICK ANYWAY.
BUT IF YOU LET IT DRY LIKE THAT...
...YOU'LL LOOK EVEN MORE LIKE YOUR BROTHER...
Probably.
...
I DON'T CARE!
Whatever.
DON'T BE STUPID.
YOU KNOW...

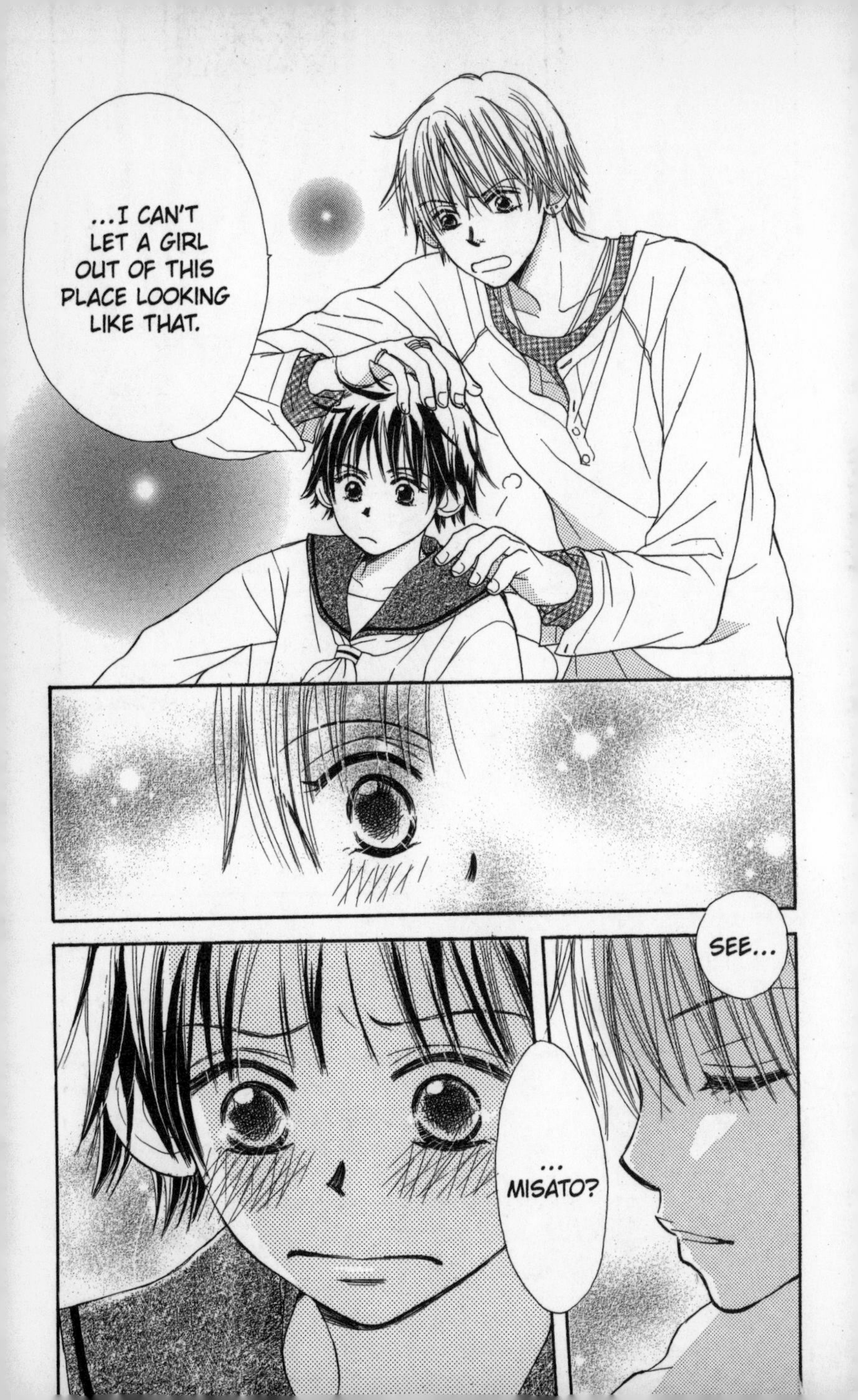
...I CAN'T LET A GIRL OUT OF THIS PLACE LOOKING LIKE THAT.
SEE...
...MISATO?

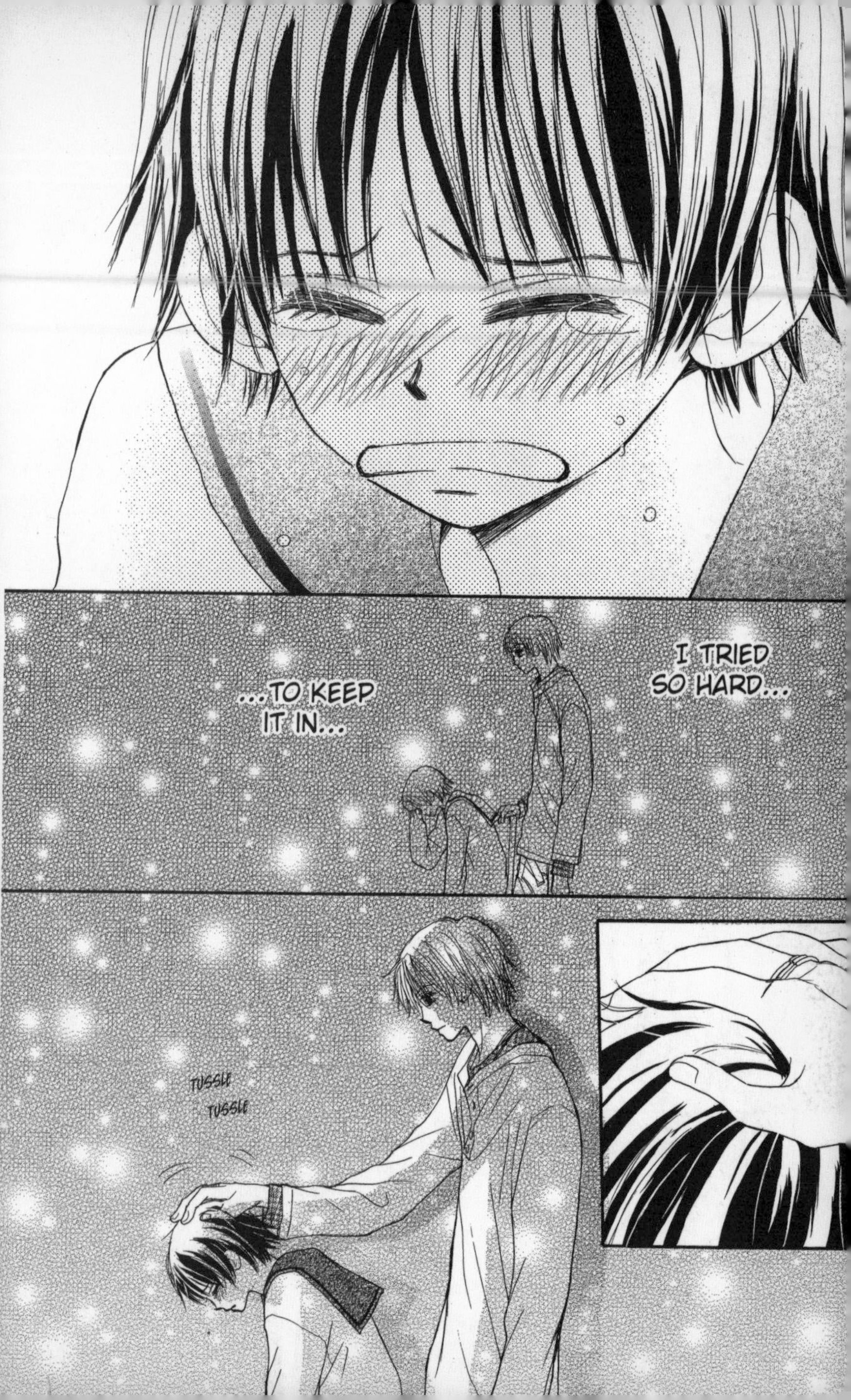
I TRIED SO HARD...
...TO KEEP IT IN...
TUSSLE
TUSSLE

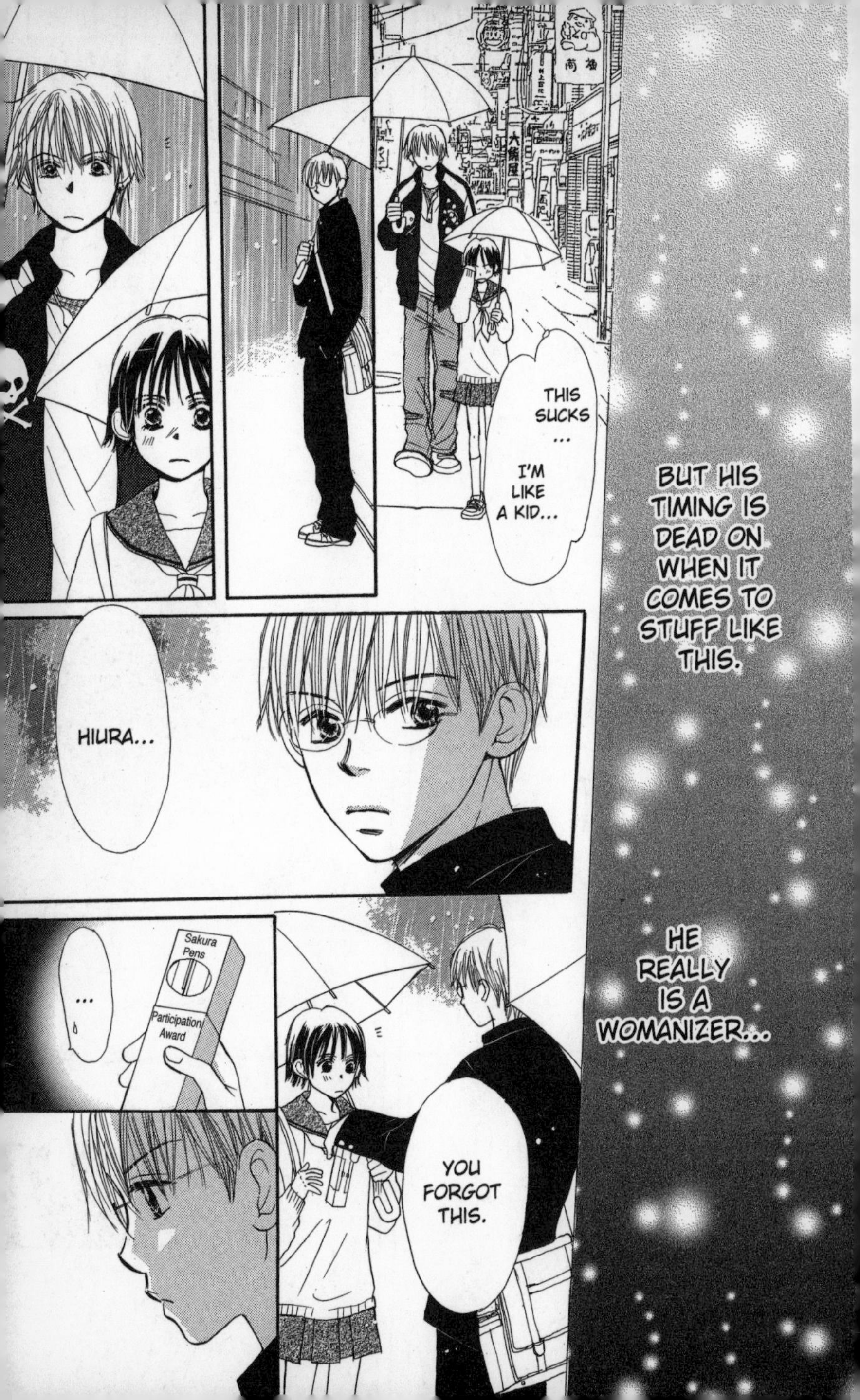
BUT HIS TIMING IS DEAD ON WHEN IT COMES TO STUFF LIKE THIS.
HE REALLY IS A WOMANIZER...
THIS SUCKS...
I'M LIKE A KID...
HIURA...
YOU FORGOT THIS.
Sakura Pens
Participation Award
...

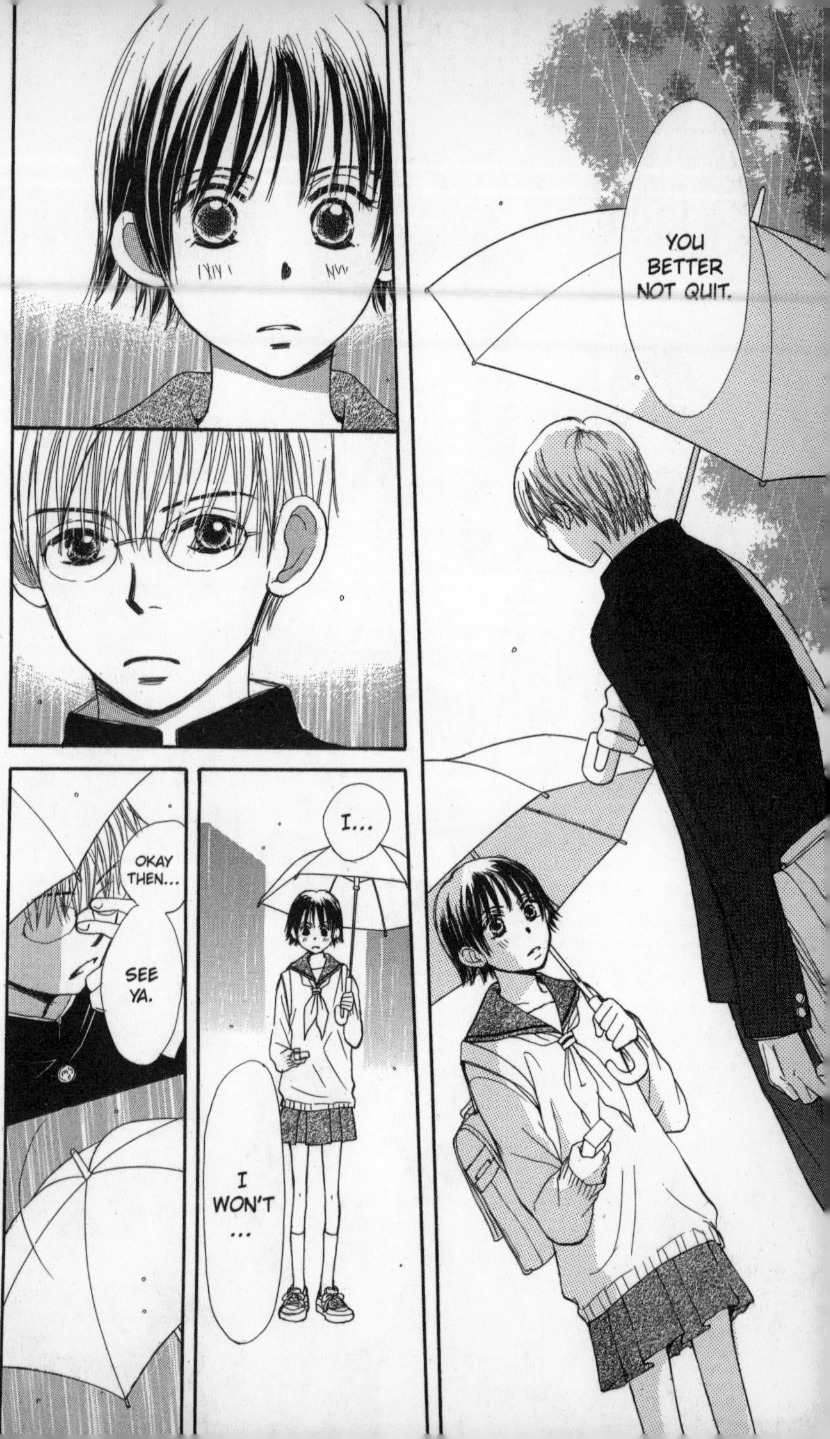
YOU BETTER NOT QUIT.
I...
I WON'T ...
OKAY THEN...
SEE YA.

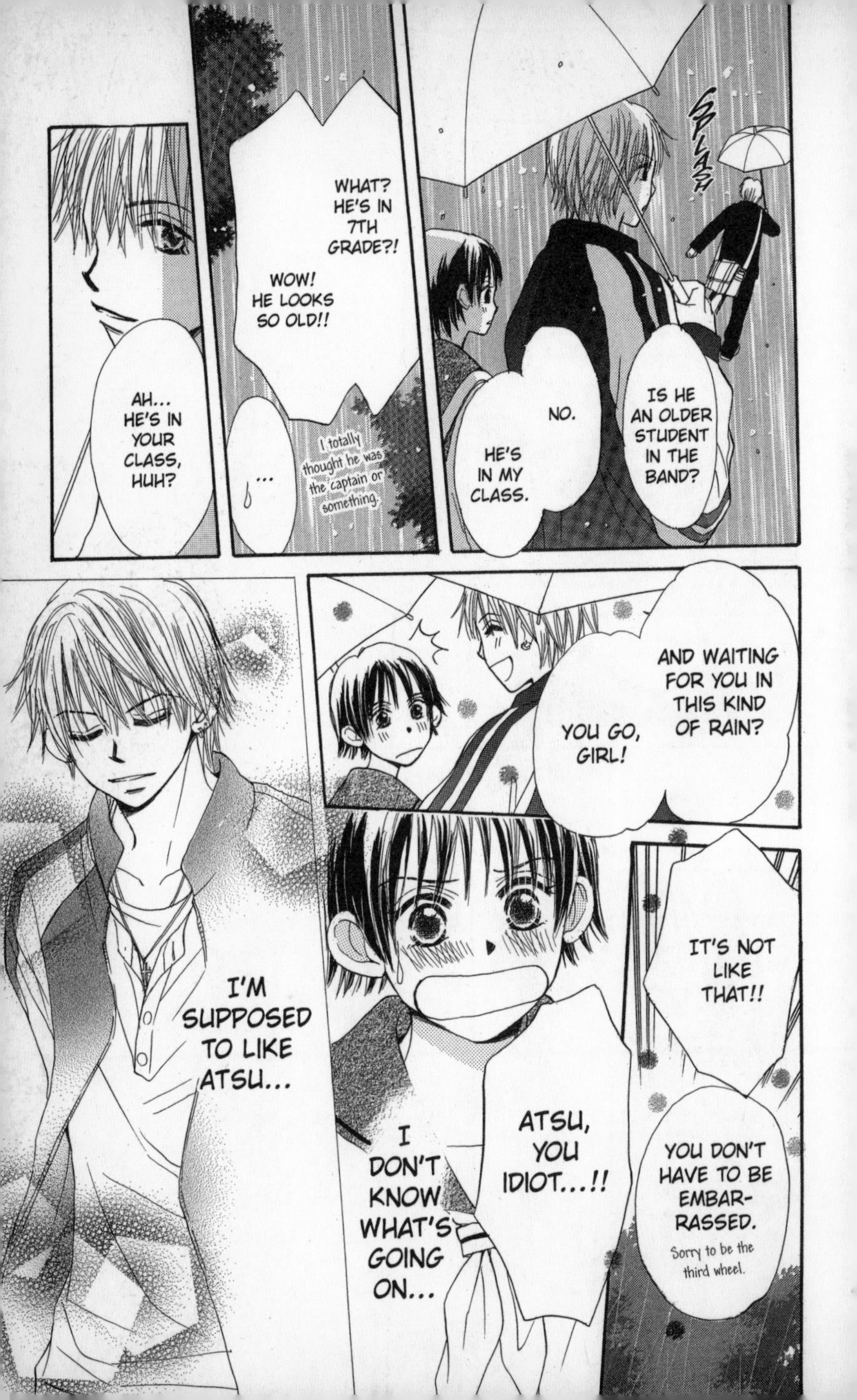
SPLASH
IS HE AN OLDER STUDENT IN THE BAND?
NO.
HE'S IN MY CLASS.
WHAT? HE'S IN 7TH GRADE?!
WOW! HE LOOKS SO OLD!!
I totally thought he was the captain or something.
...
AH... HE'S IN YOUR CLASS, HUH?
AND WAITING FOR YOU IN THIS KIND OF RAIN?
YOU GO, GIRL!
IT'S NOT LIKE THAT!!
YOU DON'T HAVE TO BE EMBAR-RASSED.
Sorry to be the third wheel.
ATSU, YOU IDIOT...!!
I DON'T KNOW WHAT'S GOING ON...
I'M SUPPOSED TO LIKE ATSU...

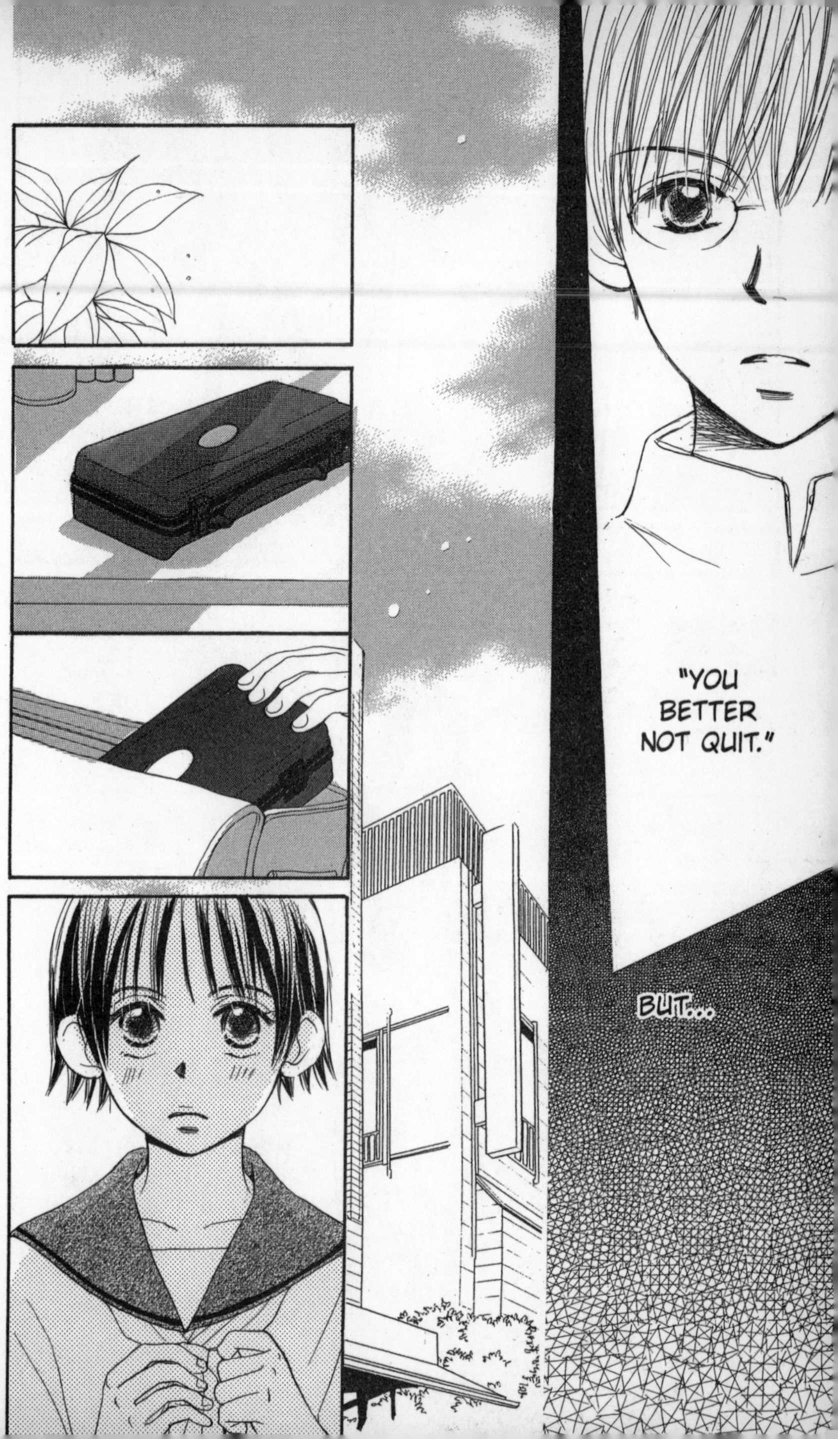
"YOU BETTER NOT QUIT."
BUT...

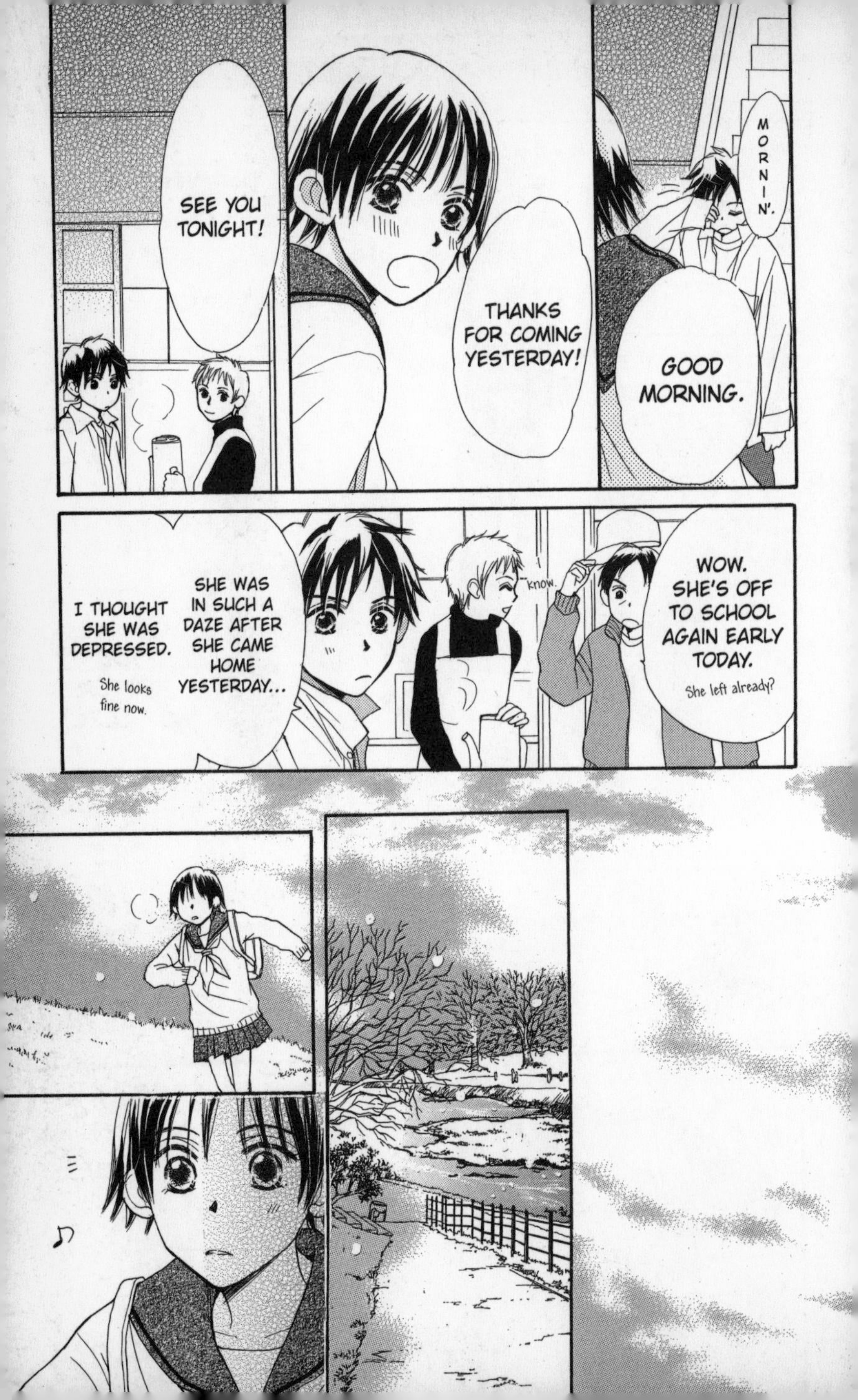
MORNIN'.
GOOD MORNING.
THANKS FOR COMING YESTERDAY!
SEE YOU TONIGHT!
WOW. SHE'S OFF TO SCHOOL AGAIN EARLY TODAY.
She left already?
know.
SHE WAS IN SUCH A DAZE AFTER SHE CAME HOME YESTERDAY...
I THOUGHT SHE WAS DEPRESSED.
She looks fine now.

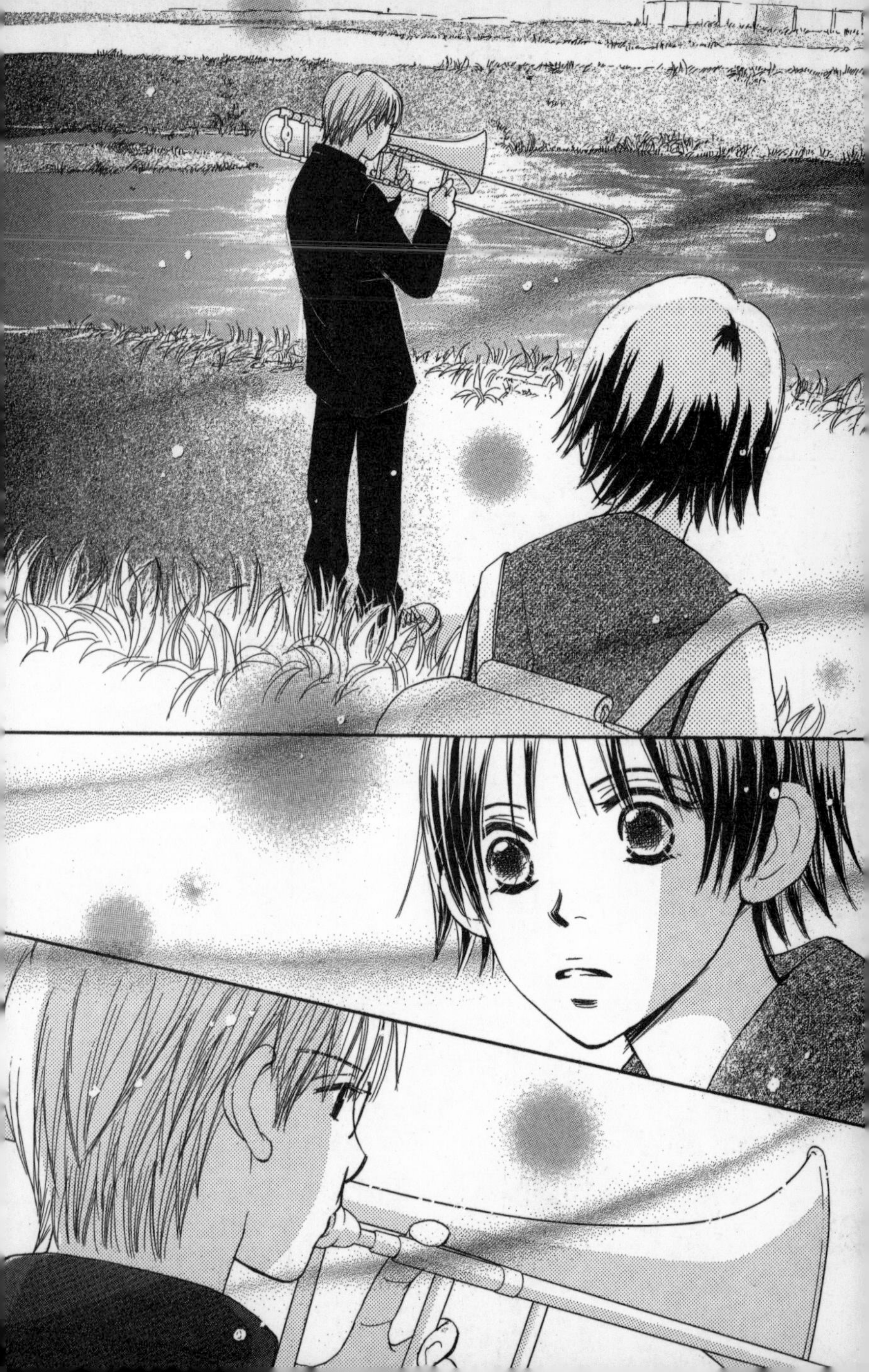

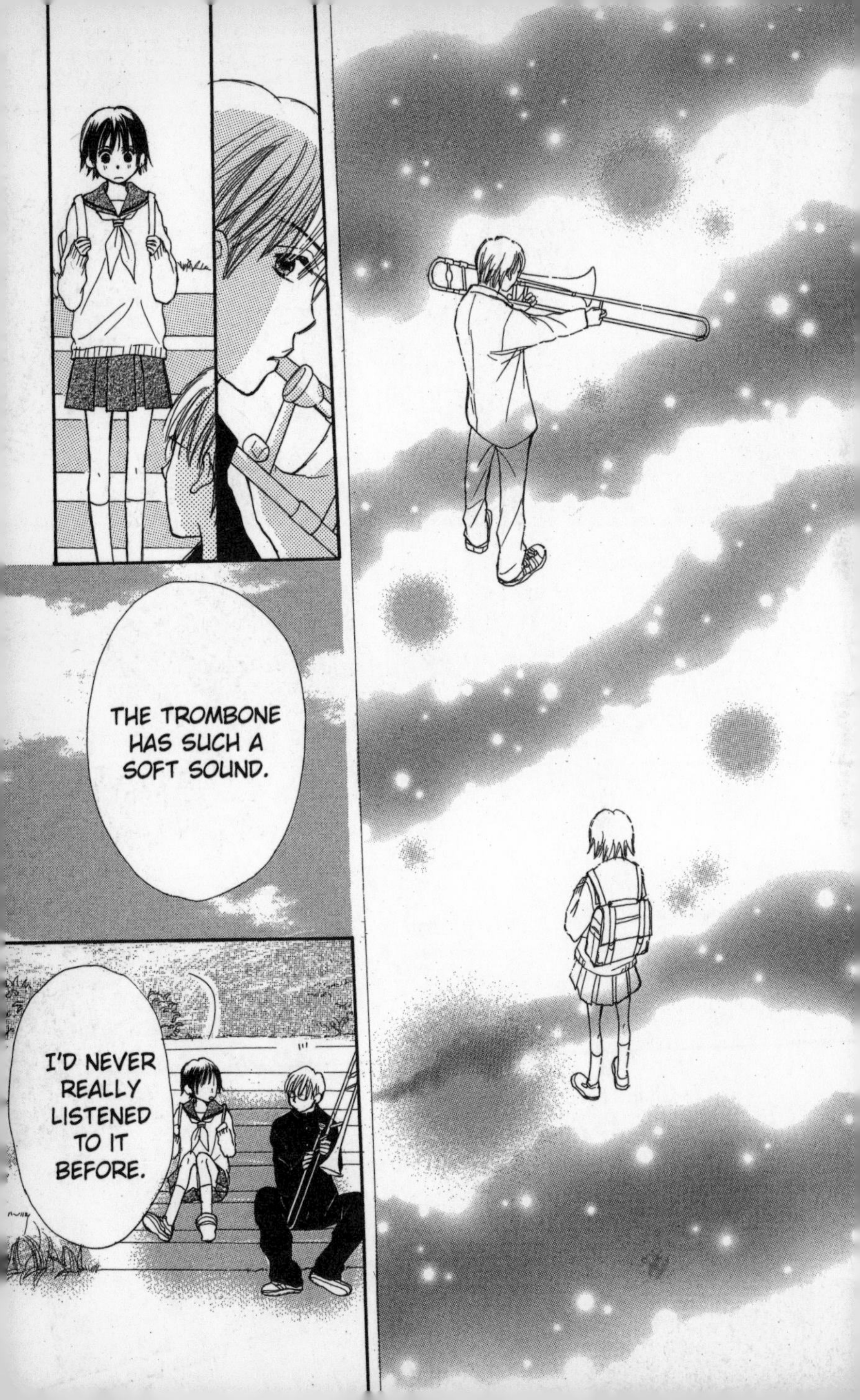
THE TROMBONE HAS SUCH A SOFT SOUND.
I'D NEVER REALLY LISTENED TO IT BEFORE.

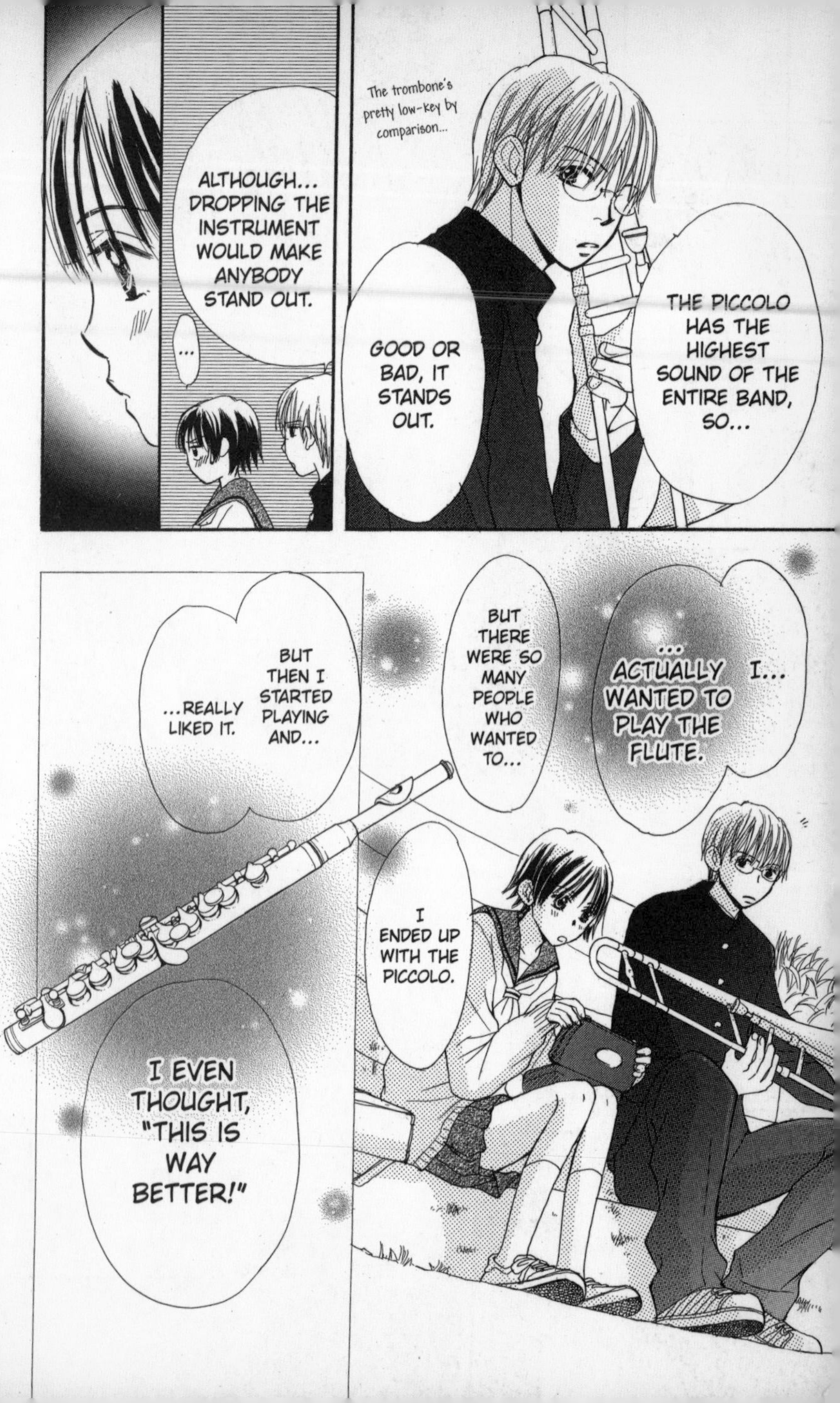
THE PICCOLO HAS THE HIGHEST SOUND OF THE ENTIRE BAND, SO...
GOOD OR BAD, IT STANDS OUT.
The trombone's pretty low-key by comparison...
ALTHOUGH... DROPPING THE INSTRUMENT WOULD MAKE ANYBODY STAND OUT.
...
... ACTUALLY I... WANTED TO PLAY THE FLUTE.
BUT THERE WERE SO MANY PEOPLE WHO WANTED TO...
I ENDED UP WITH THE PICCOLO.
BUT THEN I STARTED PLAYING AND...
...REALLY LIKED IT.
I EVEN THOUGHT, "THIS IS WAY BETTER!"

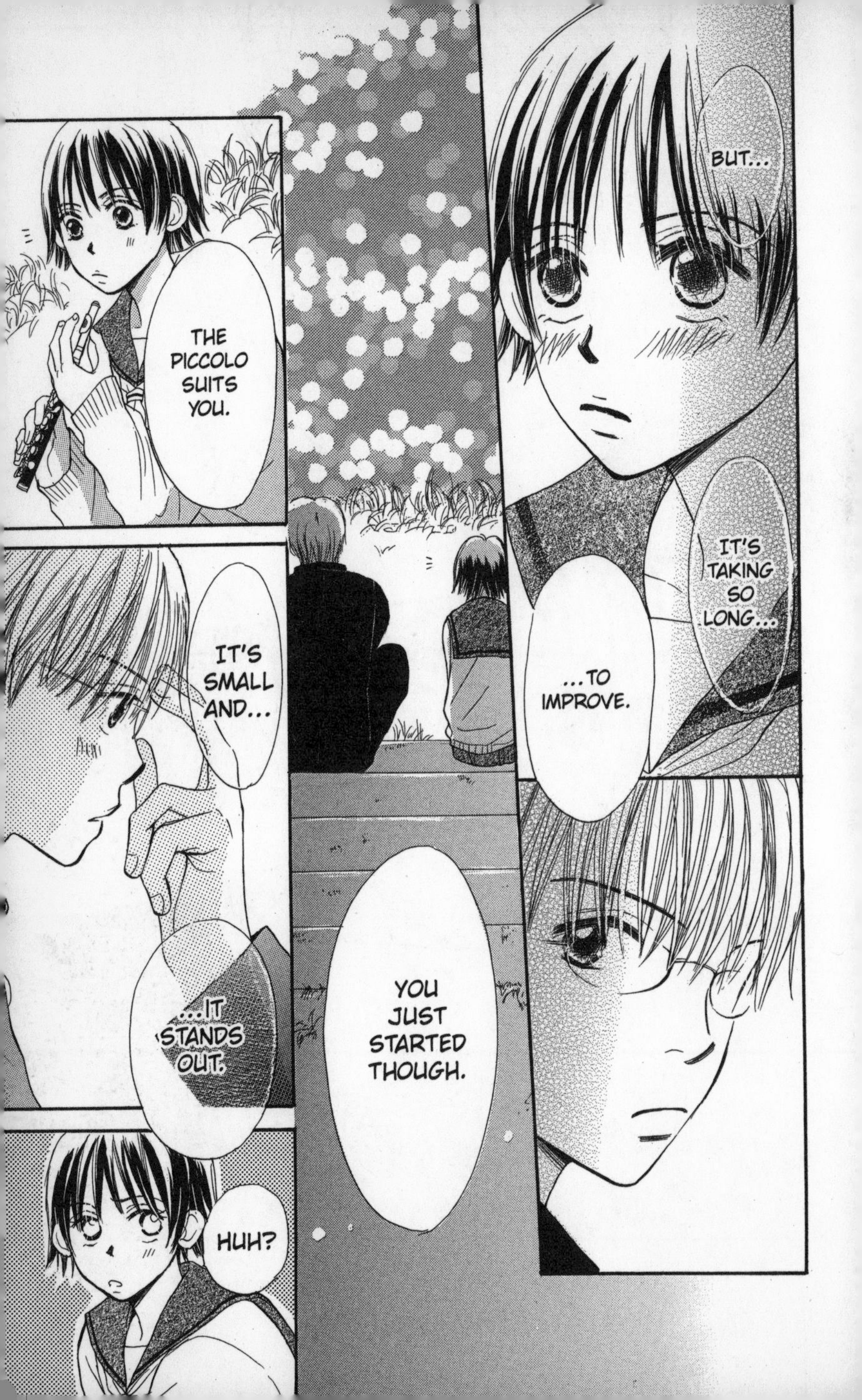
BUT...
IT'S TAKING SO LONG...
...TO IMPROVE.
YOU JUST STARTED THOUGH.
THE PICCOLO SUITS YOU.
IT'S SMALL AND...
...IT STANDS OUT.
HUH?

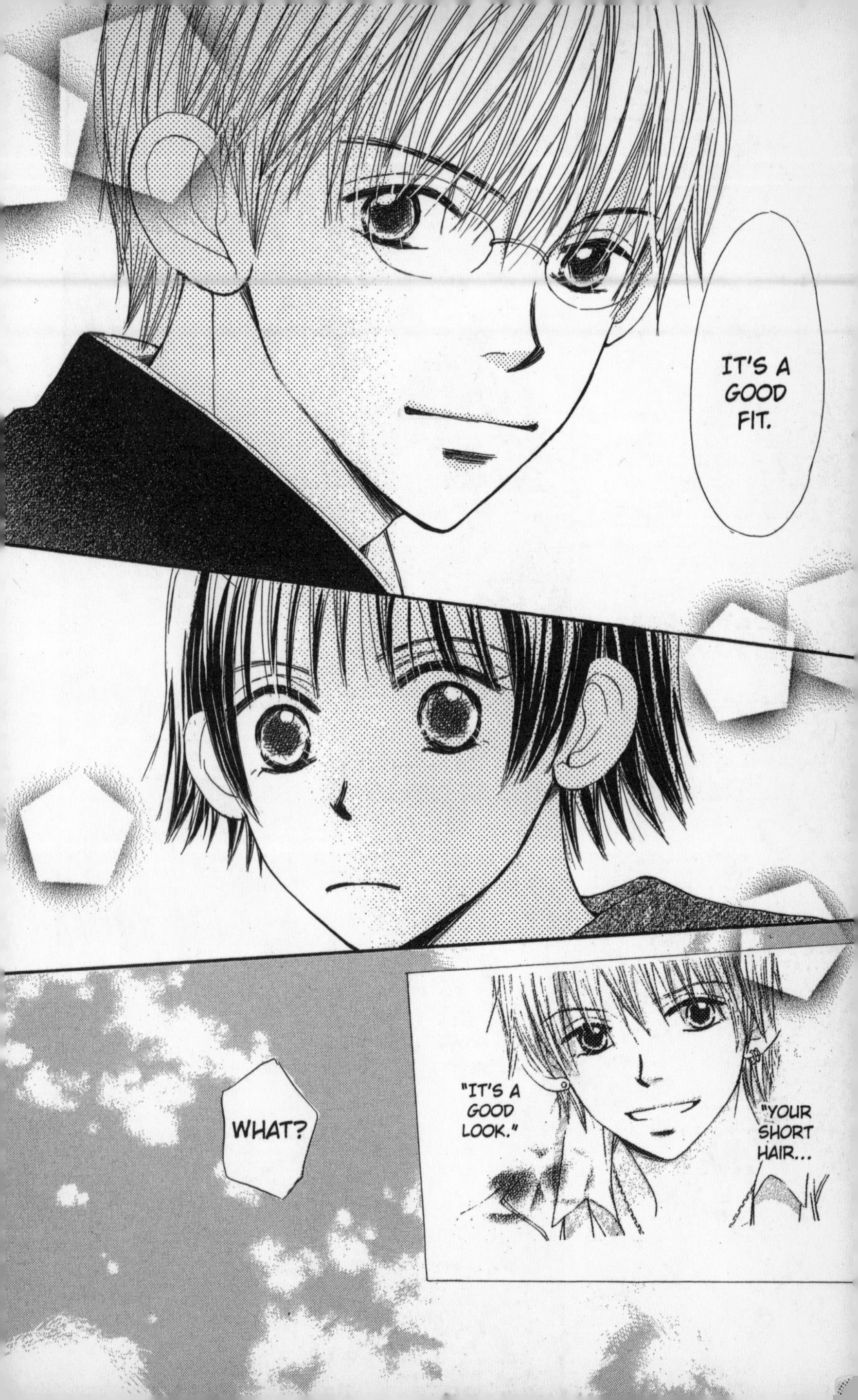
IT'S A GOOD FIT.
"YOUR SHORT HAIR...
"IT'S A GOOD LOOK."
WHAT?

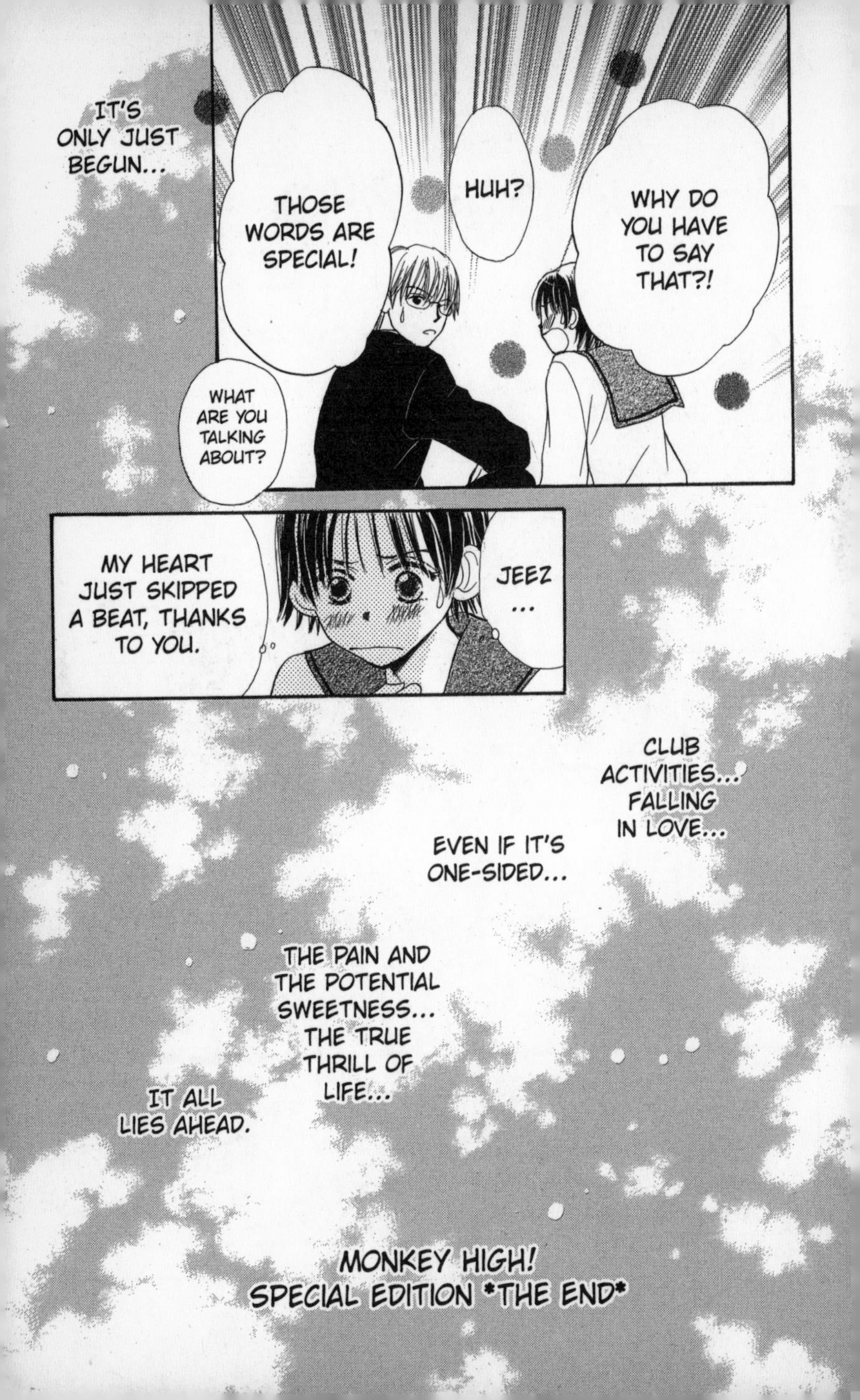
WHY DO YOU HAVE TO SAY THAT?!
HUH?
THOSE WORDS ARE SPECIAL!
WHAT ARE YOU TALKING ABOUT?
IT'S ONLY JUST BEGUN...
JEEZ ...
MY HEART JUST SKIPPED A BEAT, THANKS TO YOU.
CLUB ACTIVITIES... FALLING IN LOVE...
EVEN IF IT'S ONE-SIDED...
THE PAIN AND THE POTENTIAL SWEETNESS... THE TRUE THRILL OF LIFE...
IT ALL LIES AHEAD.
MONKEY HIGH! SPECIAL EDITION *THE END*

★POSTSCRIPT★

THANK YOU FOR READING SHOUKO AKIRA'S MANGA.

I AM SO THANKFUL TO BE ABLE TO PUBLISH THIS SECOND VOLUME.

I'D LIKE TO USE THE REMAINING PAGES TO LOOK BACK ON EACH OF THE STORIES.

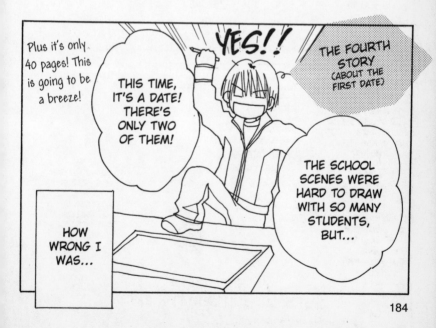

THE FOURTH STORY (ABOUT THE FIRST DATE)
YES!!
THE SCHOOL SCENES WERE HARD TO DRAW WITH SO MANY STUDENTS, BUT...
THIS TIME, IT'S A DATE! THERE'S ONLY TWO OF THEM!
Plus it's only 40 pages! This is going to be a breeze!
HOW WRONG I WAS...

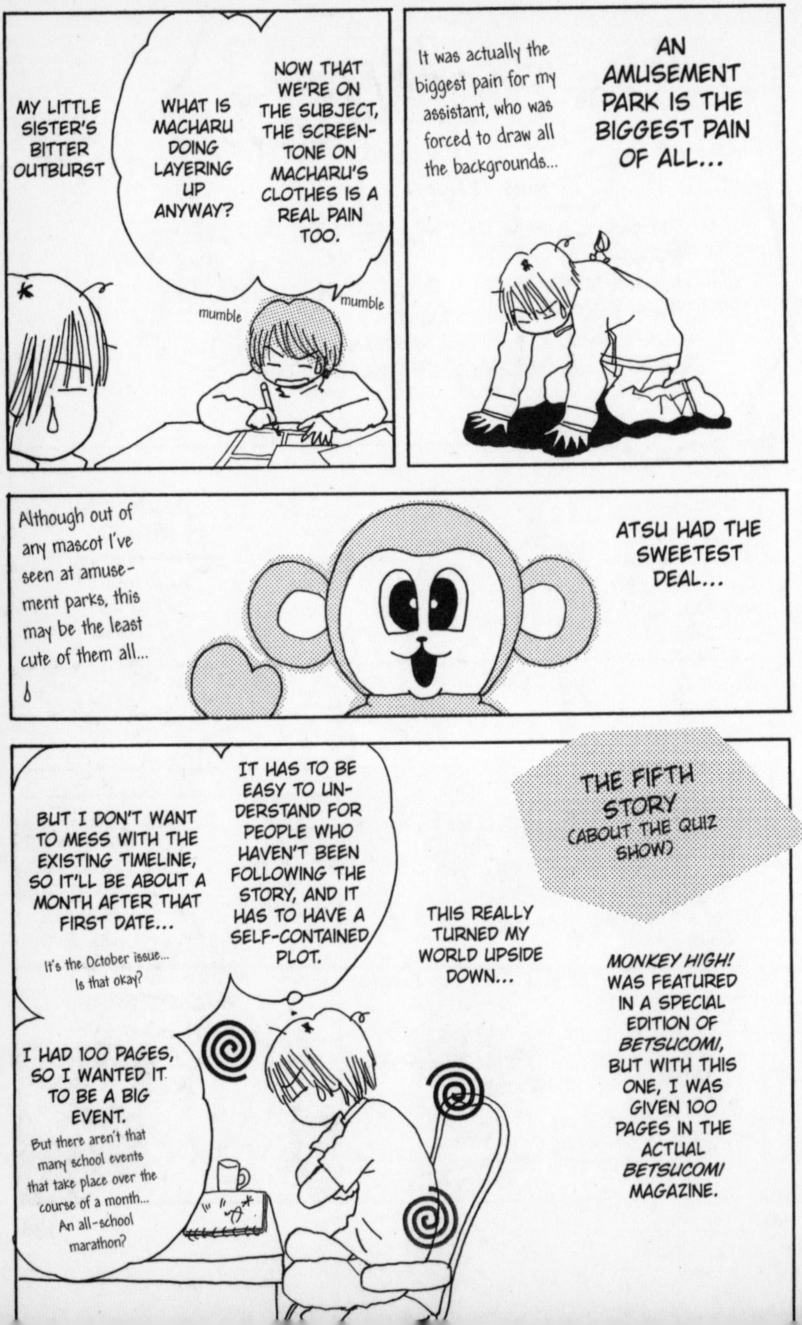
AN AMUSEMENT PARK IS THE BIGGEST PAIN OF ALL...
It was actually the biggest pain for my assistant, who was forced to draw all the backgrounds...
NOW THAT WE'RE ON THE SUBJECT, THE SCREENTONE ON MACHARU'S CLOTHES IS A REAL PAIN TOO.
WHAT IS MACHARU DOING LAYERING UP ANYWAY?
mumble
mumble
MY LITTLE SISTER'S BITTER OUTBURST
ATSU HAD THE SWEETEST DEAL...
Although out of any mascot I've seen at amusement parks, this may be the least cute of them all...
THE FIFTH STORY (ABOUT THE QUIZ SHOW)
MONKEY HIGH! WAS FEATURED IN A SPECIAL EDITION OF *BETSUCOMI*, BUT WITH THIS ONE, I WAS GIVEN 100 PAGES IN THE ACTUAL *BETSUCOMI* MAGAZINE.
THIS REALLY TURNED MY WORLD UPSIDE DOWN...
IT HAS TO BE EASY TO UNDERSTAND FOR PEOPLE WHO HAVEN'T BEEN FOLLOWING THE STORY, AND IT HAS TO HAVE A SELF-CONTAINED PLOT.
BUT I DON'T WANT TO MESS WITH THE EXISTING TIMELINE, SO IT'LL BE ABOUT A MONTH AFTER THAT FIRST DATE...
It's the October issue... Is that okay?
I HAD 100 PAGES, SO I WANTED IT TO BE A BIG EVENT.
But there aren't that many school events that take place over the course of a month... An all-school marathon?

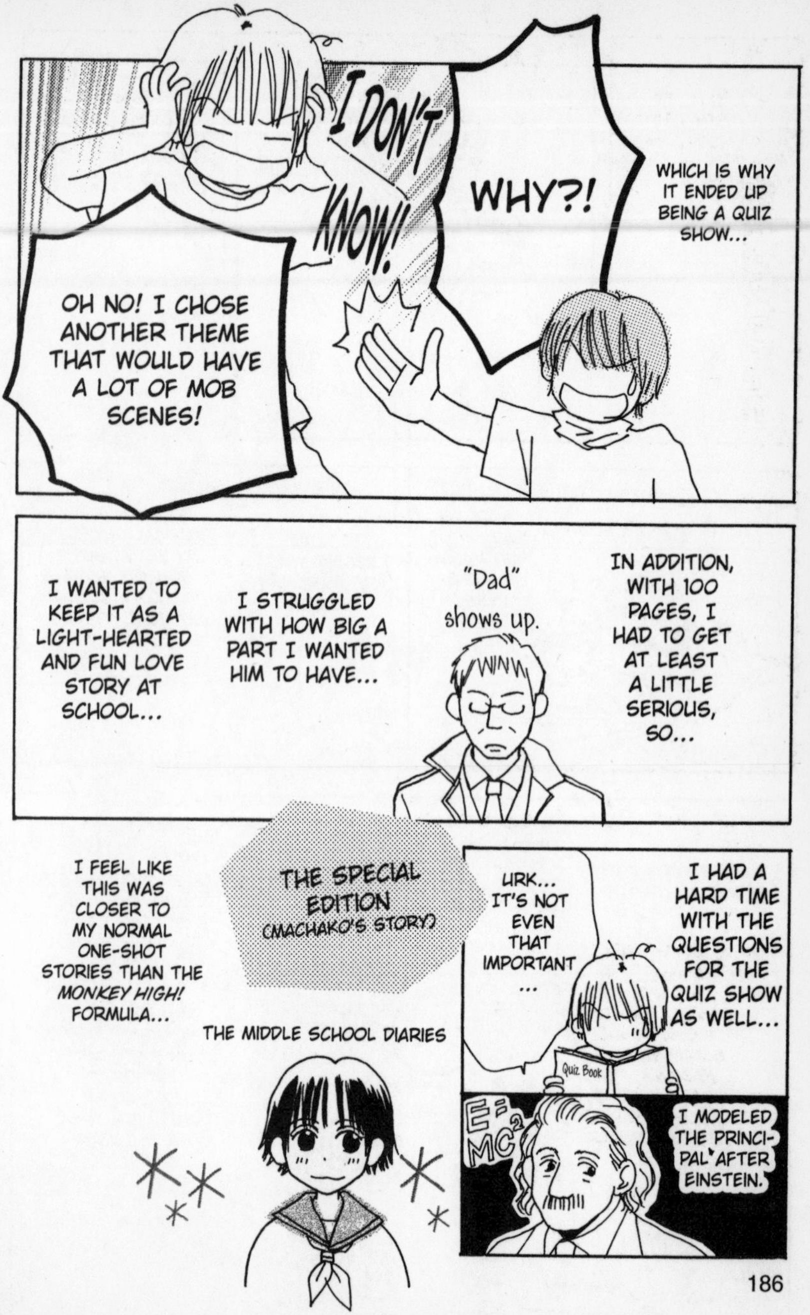
WHICH IS WHY IT ENDED UP BEING A QUIZ SHOW...
WHY?!
I DON'T KNOW!!
OH NO! I CHOSE ANOTHER THEME THAT WOULD HAVE A LOT OF MOB SCENES!
IN ADDITION, WITH 100 PAGES, I HAD TO GET AT LEAST A LITTLE SERIOUS, SO...
"Dad" shows up.
I STRUGGLED WITH HOW BIG A PART I WANTED HIM TO HAVE...
I WANTED TO KEEP IT AS A LIGHT-HEARTED AND FUN LOVE STORY AT SCHOOL...
I HAD A HARD TIME WITH THE QUESTIONS FOR THE QUIZ SHOW AS WELL...
URK... IT'S NOT EVEN THAT IMPORTANT ...
Quiz Book
E=MC²
I MODELED THE PRINCIPAL AFTER EINSTEIN.
THE SPECIAL EDITION (MACHAKO'S STORY)
I FEEL LIKE THIS WAS CLOSER TO MY NORMAL ONE-SHOT STORIES THAN THE *MONKEY HIGH!* FORMULA...
THE MIDDLE SCHOOL DIARIES

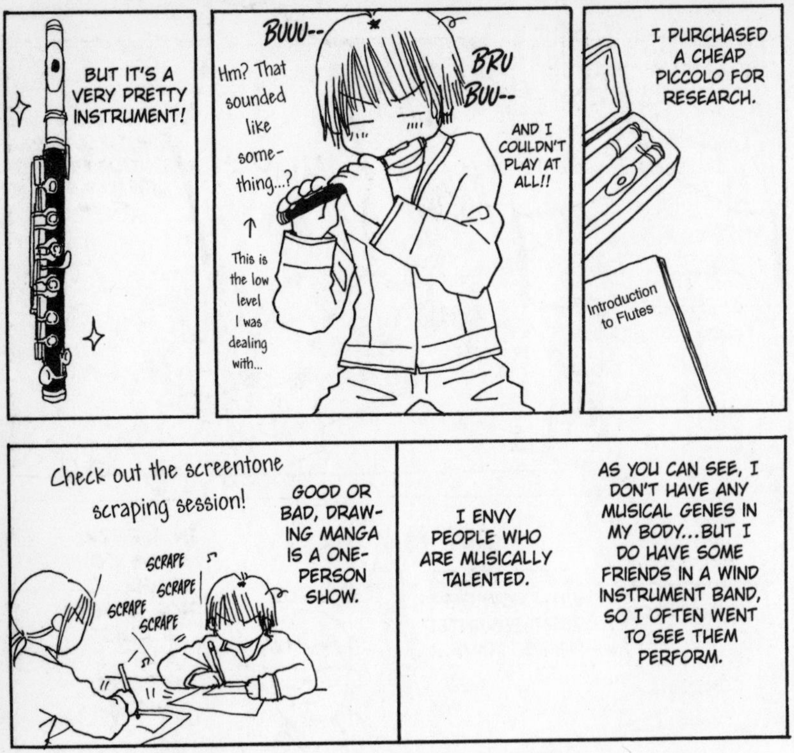
I PURCHASED A CHEAP PICCOLO FOR RESEARCH.
Introduction to Flutes
BRU BUU--
AND I COULDN'T PLAY AT ALL!!
BUUU--
Hm? That sounded like some-thing...?
This is the low level I was dealing with...
BUT IT'S A VERY PRETTY INSTRUMENT!
AS YOU CAN SEE, I DON'T HAVE ANY MUSICAL GENES IN MY BODY...BUT I DO HAVE SOME FRIENDS IN A WIND INSTRUMENT BAND, SO I OFTEN WENT TO SEE THEM PERFORM.
I ENVY PEOPLE WHO ARE MUSICALLY TALENTED.
GOOD OR BAD, DRAWING MANGA IS A ONE-PERSON SHOW.
Check out the screentone scraping session!
SCRAPE
SCRAPE
SCRAPE
SCRAPE

ARE YOU SERIOUS?!

AFTER I PUBLISHED VOLUME ONE, I GOT LETTERS FROM READERS SAYING THEY LIKED MACHARU OR THAT THE PERSON THEY HAVE A CRUSH ON IS A LOT LIKE MACHARU.

I even got letters saying that they thought Macharu was good-looking...

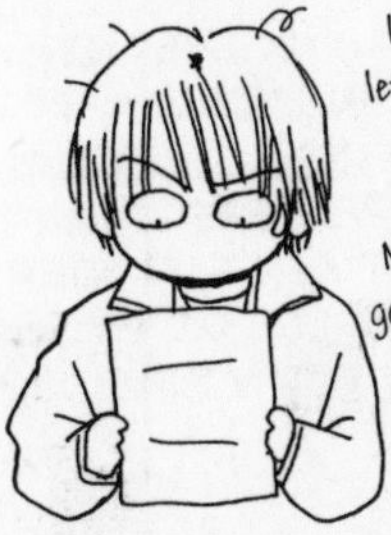

IN ALL HONESTY, I WAS A LITTLE SHOCKED. WHEN I STARTED THIS SERIES, I WONDERED IF IT WAS OKAY TO HAVE THE HERO BE SOMEONE WHO WAS UNPOPULAR WITH GIRLS...

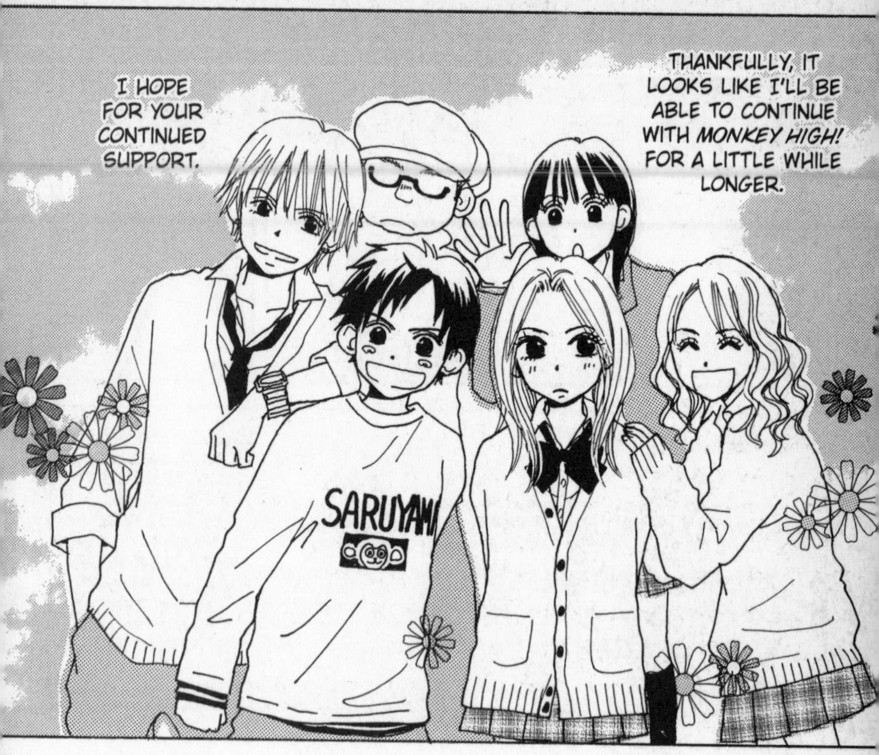
THANKFULLY, IT LOOKS LIKE I'LL BE ABLE TO CONTINUE WITH *MONKEY HIGH!* FOR A LITTLE WHILE LONGER.
I HOPE FOR YOUR CONTINUED SUPPORT.

I'D LIKE TO THANK EVERYONE WHO IS ALWAYS HELPING ME—MY EDITOR, DESIGNERS, FRIENDS, ACQUAINTANCES AND ALL MY READERS! THANK YOU SO VERY MUCH. I ASK FOR YOUR CONTINUED SUPPORT, AND I'LL DO MY BEST TO CREATE A FUN STORY FOR YOUR ENJOYMENT.

DECEMBER 2005
SHOUKO AKIRA

Slightly confused by all the monkeying around?
Here are some notes to help you out!

Page 2: Masaru
Even though everyone refers to him by his nickname, Macharu's real name is "Masaru," which means "superior" in Japanese. Interestingly enough, *saru* by itself means "monkey."

Page 62, panel 2: The Diet
Japan's parliament is called the Diet; it consists of the House of Representatives and the House of Councillors. In addition to passing laws, the Diet is responsible for selecting the Prime Minister.

Page 72, panel 4: Arashi, w-inds, and KAT-TUN
All Japanese boy bands. Arashi has five members, w-inds has three and KAT-TUN has six.

Page 100, panel 4: Nikko
One of the things the Tosho-gu shrine in Nikko is famous for is its carving of the three wise monkeys who embody the principle "see no evil, hear no evil, speak no evil."

Page 160, panel 3: The Great Demon King
A reference to the fictional character Piccolo in the manga series *Dragon Ball Z*.

Page 185, panel 4: *Betsucomi*
A monthly Japanese *shojo* manga (girls' comics) magazine published by Shogakukan.

My jeans have become noticeably tighter... And they're the pair that I wear all the time... I've gotta do something about this...

—Shouko Akira

I'm gonna do a little dance!

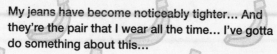

It's volume 2!

Shouko Akira was born on September 10th and grew up in Kyoto. She currently lives in Tokyo and loves soccer, cycling, and Yoshimoto Shin Kigeki (a comedy stage show based out of Osaka). Most of her works revolve around school life and love, including *Times Two*, a collection of five romantic short stories.

MONKEY HIGH!
VOL. 2
The Shojo Beat Manga Edition

STORY AND ART BY
SHOUKO AKIRA

Translation & Adaptation/Mai Ihara
Touch-up Art & Lettering/John Hunt
Design/Hidemi Dunn
Editor/Amy Yu

Editor in Chief, Books/Alvin Lu
Editor in Chief, Magazines/Marc Weidenbaum
VP of Publishing Licensing/Rika Inouye
VP of Sales/Gonzalo Ferreyra
Sr. VP of Marketing/Liza Coppola
Publisher/Hyoe Narita

© 2006 Shouko AKIRA/Shogakukan Inc.
First published by Shogakukan Inc. in Japan as "Saruyama!"
All rights reserved.
The stories, characters and incidents mentioned in this publication
are entirely fictional.

Printed in Canada

Published by VIZ Media, LLC
P.O. Box 77010
San Francisco, CA 94107

Shojo Beat Manga Edition
10 9 8 7 6 5 4 3 2 1
First printing, June 2008

www.viz.com

store.viz.com

PARENTAL ADVISORY
MONKEY HIGH! is rated T for Teen
and is recommended for ages 13 and up.
This volume contains suggestive themes.
ratings.viz.com
RATED T FOR TEEN

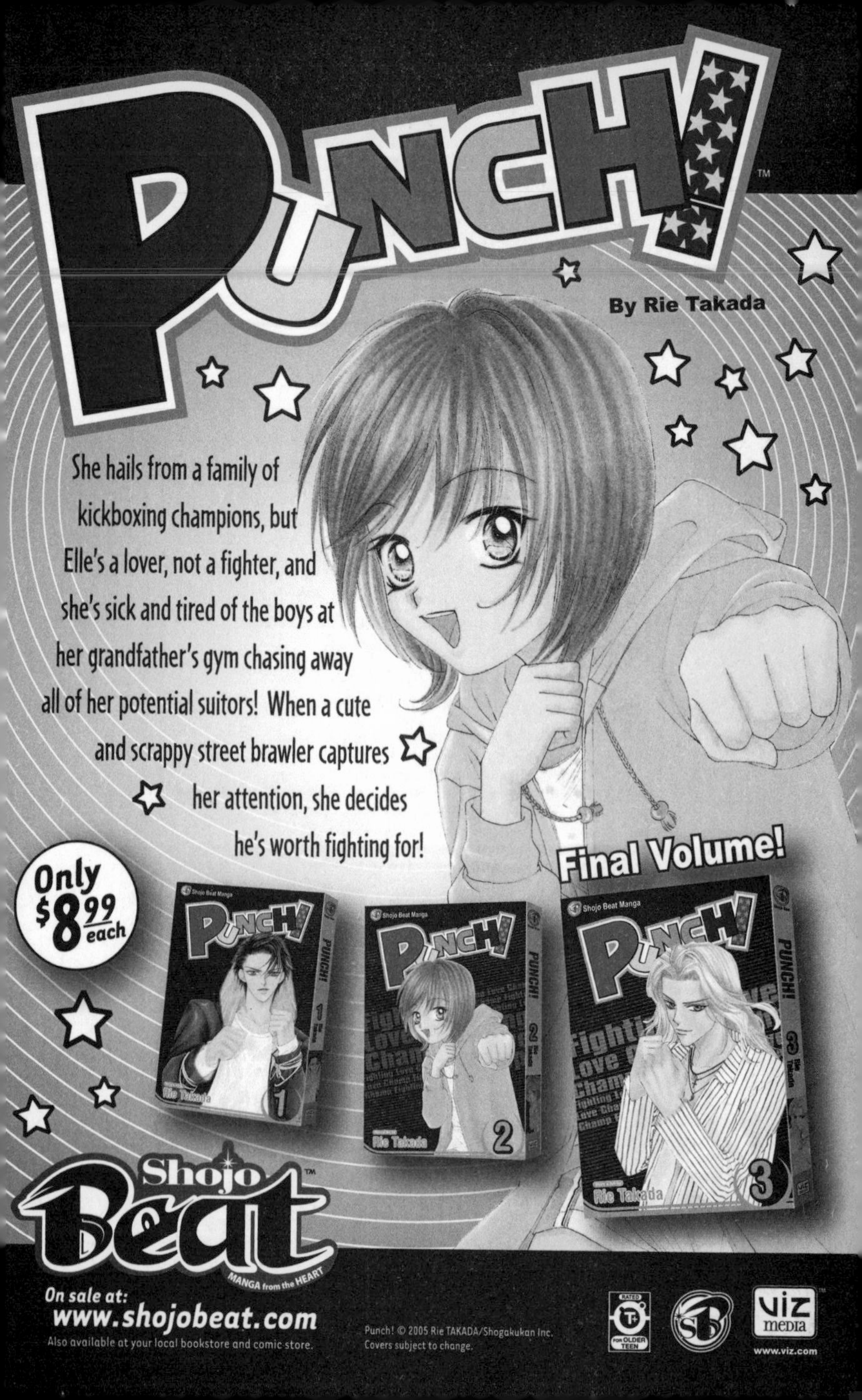
PUNCH!™
By Rie Takada
She hails from a family of kickboxing champions, but Elle's a lover, not a fighter, and she's sick and tired of the boys at her grandfather's gym chasing away all of her potential suitors! When a cute and scrappy street brawler captures her attention, she decides he's worth fighting for!
Final Volume!
Only $8.99 each
Shojo Beat Manga
PUNCH!
Rie Takada
1
2
3
Shojo Beat™
MANGA from the HEART
On sale at:
www.shojobeat.com
Also available at your local bookstore and comic store.
Punch! © 2005 Rie TAKADA/Shogakukan Inc.
Covers subject to change.
RATED T+ FOR OLDER TEEN
VIZ media
www.viz.com

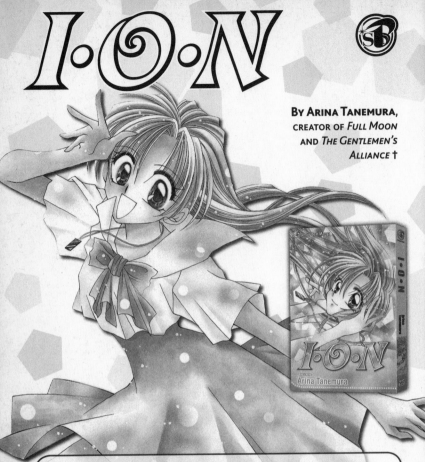

The gripping story — in **manga** format

Get the complete *Be With You* collection—
buy the manga and fiction today!

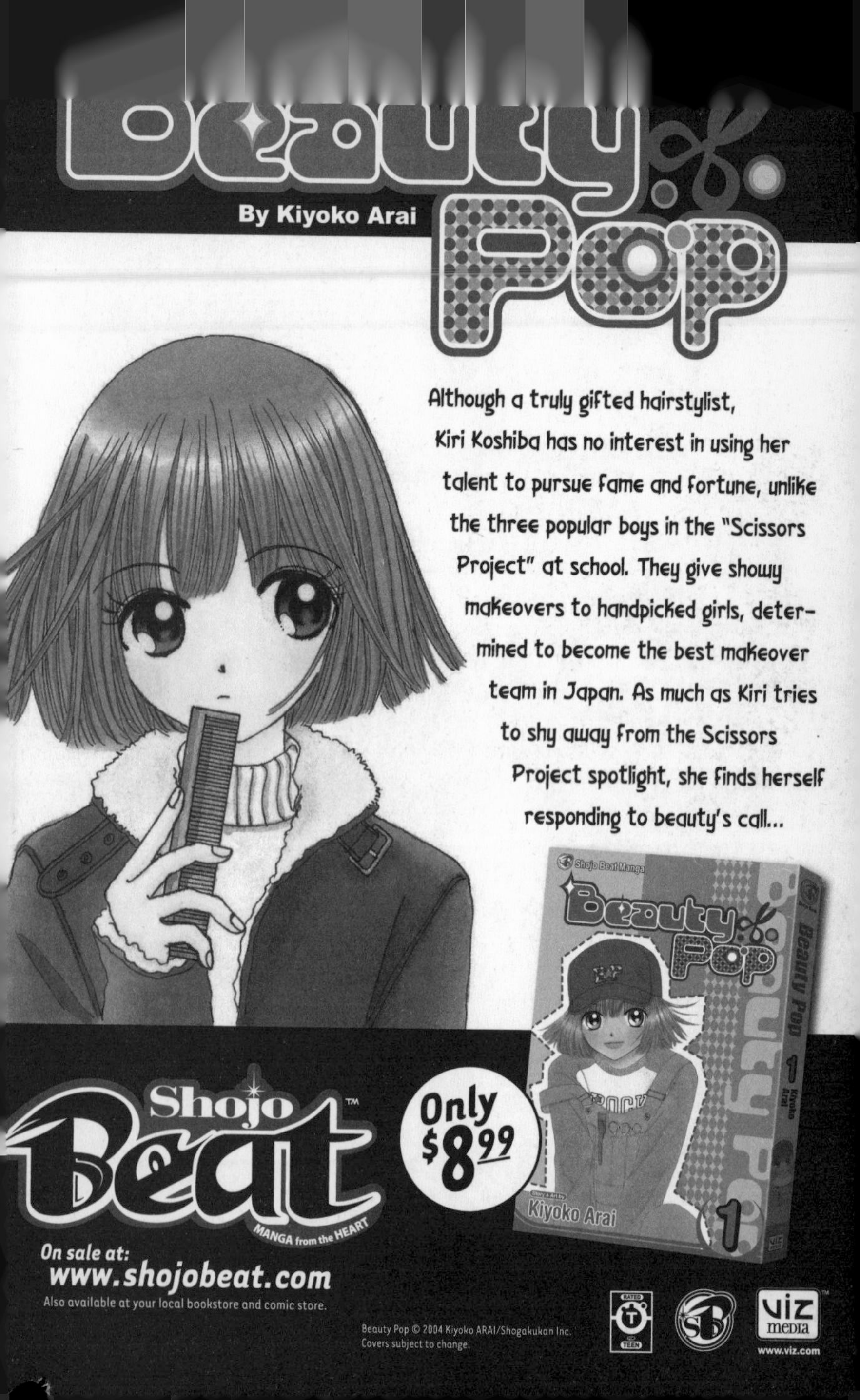
Beauty Pop
By Kiyoko Arai
Although a truly gifted hairstylist, Kiri Koshiba has no interest in using her talent to pursue fame and fortune, unlike the three popular boys in the "Scissors Project" at school. They give showy makeovers to handpicked girls, determined to become the best makeover team in Japan. As much as Kiri tries to shy away from the Scissors Project spotlight, she finds herself responding to beauty's call...
Shojo Beat Manga
Beauty Pop
Story & Art by
Kiyoko Arai
1
Beauty Pop 1 Kiyoko Arai
Shojo Beat™
MANGA from the HEART
Only $8.99
On sale at:
www.shojobeat.com
Also available at your local bookstore and comic store.
Beauty Pop © 2004 Kiyoko ARAI/Shogakukan Inc.
Covers subject to change.
RATED T TEEN
VIZ media
www.viz.com

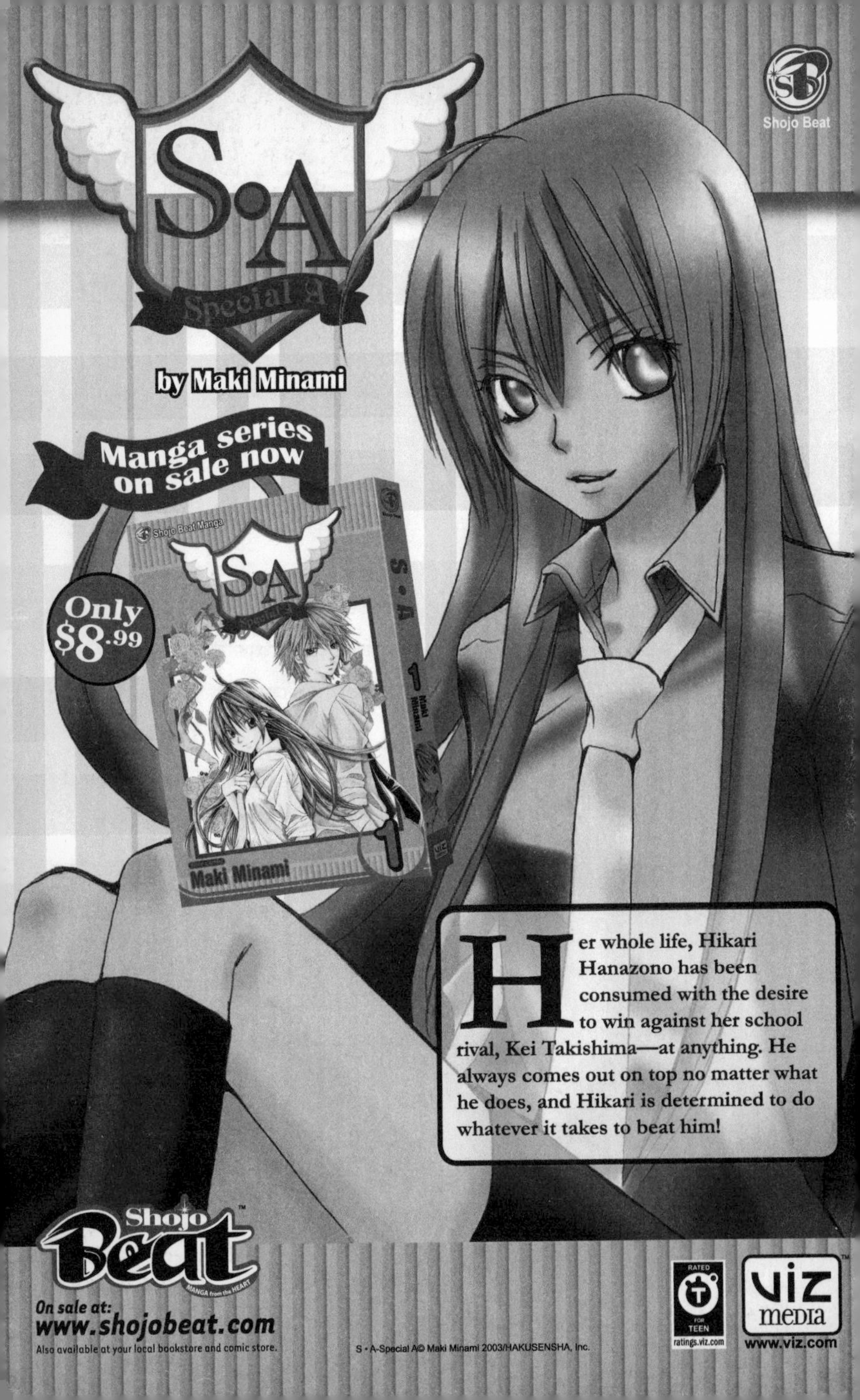

Shojo Beat
S•A
Special A
by Maki Minami
Manga series on sale now
Only $8.99
Shojo Beat Manga
S•A
Special A
1
Maki Minami
Her whole life, Hikari Hanazono has been consumed with the desire to win against her school rival, Kei Takishima—at anything. He always comes out on top no matter what he does, and Hikari is determined to do whatever it takes to beat him!
Shojo Beat
MANGA from the HEART
On sale at:
www.shojobeat.com
Also available at your local bookstore and comic store.
S • A-Special A© Maki Minami 2003/HAKUSENSHA, Inc.
RATED T FOR TEEN
ratings.viz.com
VIZ media
www.viz.com

Tell us what you think about Shojo Beat Manga!

Our survey is now available online. Go to:

shojobeat.com/mangasurvey

Help us make our product offerings better!

Shojo Beat™
MANGA from the HEART

The Shojo Manga Authority

The most **ADDICTIVE** shojo manga stories from Japan **PLUS** unique editorial coverage on the arts, music, culture, fashion, and much more!

12 GIANT issues for ONLY $34.99*

That's 51% OFF the cover price!

Subscribe NOW and become a member of the 🌸 Sub Club!

- **SAVE** 51% OFF the cover price
- **ALWAYS** get every issue
- **ACCESS** exclusive areas of www.shojobeat.com
- **FREE** members-only gifts several times a year

Strictly VIP!

3 EASY WAYS TO SUBSCRIBE!

1) Send in the subscription order form from this book **OR**
2) Log on to: www.shojobeat.com **OR**
3) Call 1-800-541-7876